The Spirit and the Shotgun

New Perspectives on the History of the South

UNIVERSITY PRESS OF FLORIDA

Florida A&M University, Tallahassee
Florida Atlantic University, Boca Raton
Florida Gulf Coast University, Ft. Myers
Florida International University, Miami
Florida State University, Tallahassee
University of Central Florida, Orlando
University of Florida, Gainesville
University of North Florida, Jacksonville
University of South Florida, Tampa
University of West Florida, Pensacola

THE SPIRIT AND THE SHOTGUN

ARMED RESISTANCE AND THE STRUGGLE FOR CIVIL RIGHTS

Simon Wendt

UNIVERSITY PRESS OF FLORIDA

Gainesville/Tallahassee/Tampa/Boca Raton
Pensacola/Orlando/Miami/Jacksonville/Ft. Myers

11   10   09   08   07   06   6   5   4   3   2   1

Library of Congress Cataloging-in-Publication Data
Wendt, Simon.
The spirit and the shotgun: armed resistance and the struggle for civil rights / Simon Wendt.
p. cm. — (New perspectives on the history of the South)
Includes bibliographical references and index.
ISBN–13: 978-0-8130-3018-0 (alk. paper)
1. African Americans—Civil rights—Southern States—History—20th century. 2. Civil
rights movements—Southern States—History—20th century. 3. African American civil
rights workers—Southern States—History—20th century. 4. African American political
activists—Southern States—History—20th century. 5. Government, Resistance to—Southern
States—History—20th century. 6. Political violence—Southern States—History—20th century.
7. Nonviolence—Southern States—History—20th century. 8. African Americans—Southern
States—Politics and government—20th century. 9. Black power—Southern States—History—
20th century. 10. Southern States—Race relations—History—20th century. I. Title.
E185.61.W48   2006
323.1196′07307509046—dc22   2006022835

The University Press of Florida is the scholarly publishing agency for the State University System of
Florida, comprising Florida A&M University, Florida Atlantic University, Florida Gulf Coast University,
Florida International University, Florida State University, University of Central Florida, University of
Florida, University of North Florida, University of South Florida, and University of West Florida.

University Press of Florida
15 Northwest 15th Street
Gainesville, FL 32611-2079
http://www.upf.com

CONTENTS

FIGURES

ACKNOWLEDGMENTS

This book began as a master's thesis in the Department of Afro-American Studies at the University of Wisconsin-Madison, and I would first like to thank those people who inspired and supported me during my days as a graduate student. My greatest obligation is to Timothy Tyson, who became an advisor, a mentor, and a friend. Although a number of chapters, essays, and e-mails I sent him throughout the years fell through the cracks of his life, as he used to say, he never ceased to encourage and help me in any way he could. For this I am eternally grateful. As I embark on my own journey as a teacher, I hope to be able to give back to students the warmth and unflagging support that Tim has given to me.

I am equally indebted to William Van Deburg, who generously shared his insights into black history and culture. Since my early days as a graduate student, he has read and critiqued almost everything I have written, and I am grateful for his thoughtful suggestions and thought-provoking questions. Having remembered some of his advice concerning the publishing business, I am happy to report that I was able to obtain a dust jacket for this book.

I also want to thank Jeannie Comstock, whom Tim rightly calls the "Angel of the Department," and Rhonda Danielson, who helped in my struggles with visa requirements and representatives of the university administration. Other department members who made me feel welcome and always had words of encouragement include Stanlie James, Nellie McKay, Robert Ralston, and Craig Werner.

And there were other Madisonians who helped expand my thinking in immeasurable ways and provided indispensable advice and support. Steve Kantrowitz introduced me to the rigors of historical analysis in his courses on black history and the Populist movement. Michael McManus helped me understand the complexities of the Civil War era and carved out time from his own busy schedule to read parts of my dissertation and drafts of several articles. His fine editing and his probing questions have improved this book tremendously. Cornelius Gilbert became a good friend during our days as graduate students in the Department of Afro-American Studies. Every time I returned to Madison during research trips in the United States, he opened his home to me and cheered me up when things looked bleak. Others who generously provided advice and companionship include Patrick Jones, David LaCroix, Rhea Estelle Lathan, and Gregory Rutledge.

But not only people in the Midwest contributed to the successful completion of this book. On the West Coast, I owe an immense debt to Brian Behnken, who repeatedly shelved his own work at the University of California-Davis to read, critique, and edit both the entire dissertation and the book manuscript. I look forward to repaying this huge debt when Brian starts writing his own book, a fascinating comparative study of the African American and Mexican American civil rights movement in Texas. In Tuscaloosa, Alabama, former civil rights activist Joseph Mallisham kindly shared his recollections and his private archive. And in Nashville, Anthony Blasi made available his extensive research collection on Tuscaloosa, provided a place to stay, and offered sound advice on earlier drafts of the chapter on the Tuscaloosa movement.

On the other side of the Atlantic, I found similarly generous mentors as well as good friends. At the Free University of Berlin, my dissertation advisor, Manfred Berg, not only encouraged me to transform my master's thesis into a dissertation, but he also used every means at his disposal to support my academic ambitions. Most important, he infused my thinking with a healthy dose of skepticism toward my subject and my sources.

I am also indebted to the members of my dissertation committee, Andreas Etges, Thomas Holt, Knud Krakau, and Ursula Lehmkuhl, all of whom provided detailed critiques of my dissertation. Professor Krakau and Professor Holt have been particularly generous with their advice, suggesting important changes for the transition from dissertation to book manuscript. I owe special thanks to Professor Lehmkuhl, who provided me with an opportunity to hone my teaching skills as a lecturer at the John F. Kennedy Institute for North American Studies.

While I was teaching at the John F. Kennedy Institute, Petra Dolata-Kreutzkamp and Rose Beiler provided good company, words of encouragement, and sound advice about teaching and research. The institute's library staff did a marvelous job in digging up numerous important books that had been misplaced by malicious students.

I also want to thank my friends at the Staatsbibliothek zu Berlin, where I joined an army of other doctoral students from various disciplines. Many of us feared that our dissertations might never be finished, hoping (sometimes in vain) that the erudite atmosphere of Berlin's largest library would be conducive to academic productivity and scholarly excellence. The people who provided good company, support, and understanding during those days include Uffa Jensen, Ansgar Pallasky, Wolfram Zeihe, Holger Schrader, and Annette Vowinckel.

First at the University of Bonn and the University of Cologne, and then at the University of Heidelberg, friends and colleagues have done much to ease the difficult transition from graduate school to the "real world." I am grateful for the support and friendship of Danijela Albrecht, Birgit Binder, Eva Bischoff, Heike Bungert, Claus Daufenbach, Edmunda Ferreira, Norbert Finzsch, Philipp Gassert, Michaela Hampf, Christian Jauch, Christian Klöckner, Sophia Komor, Stella Krepp, Gudrun Löhrer, Wilfried Mausbach, Anke Ortlepp, Massimo Perinelli, Sabine Sielke, James Sparks, Olaf Stieglitz, Ingrid Thaler, and Alexander Vazansky.

Research grants and fellowships from several institutions provided crucial financial support for this project at various stages. In particular I want to thank the State of Berlin, the German Academic Exchange Service, the German Historical Institute in Washington, D.C., and the Hamburger Stiftung zur Förderung von Wissenschaft und Kultur.

At the University Press of Florida, I am indebted to John David Smith and Meredith Morris-Babb, who responded to this project with enthusiasm when it was first presented to them. Meredith in particular deserves praise for assisting me in the difficult process of converting my dissertation into a book. I also would like to thank Harvard Sitkoff and the anonymous readers for their very helpful comments on earlier versions of the manuscript.

Finally, I want to thank my family—my sister, Meike; my brother, Hannes; and my parents, Margot and Volker—whose love, encouragement, and support has sustained me throughout the difficult years of researching and writing this book. Without them, it would never have been completed.

The Spirit and the Shotgun

Armed Resistance and the Struggle for Civil Rights

INTRODUCTION

On July 8, 1964, the Ku Klux Klan suffered a humiliating defeat after an armed confrontation with black men in Tuscaloosa, Alabama. That night, a group of African American teenagers had successfully integrated the city's Druid Movie Theater. But when the young activists left the building, they faced a hostile mob of angry whites. While a cordon of police officers struggled to control the crowd, two cars manned with armed blacks arrived downtown, picked up the frightened teenagers, and sped away. Shortly before the men reached the safety of the black neighborhood, several Klansmen shot at the approaching cars from ambush. Unscathed, the black defenders returned the fire, putting the hooded men to flight.[1]

This rescue team was part of a sophisticated self-defense unit that had formed a month earlier in reaction to police brutality and Klan intimidation against Tuscaloosa's indigenous civil rights movement. While black ministers and their followers staged nonviolent demonstrations to protest against racial discrimination, Tuscaloosa's defense squad patrolled the black neighborhood, guarded the homes of movement leaders, and sometimes, as on July 8, saved the lives of student activists. During that night's rescue mission, the group's combat-experienced members demonstrated their resolve to protect the nonviolent freedom movement from racist aggression. The shoot-out marked the end of Klan harassment in Tuscaloosa.[2]

Armed resistance served as a significant auxiliary to nonviolent protest in the southern civil rights struggle of the 1950s and 1960s. Tuscaloosa was only one example of this phenomenon. Confronted with racist terrorism, black activists tended to regard nonviolence as a pragmatic tactic, not as a philosophical imperative, and resorted to armed self-defense on a widespread basis. Such protective efforts helped local freedom movements survive in the face of white violence, bolstered the morale of civil rights activists, instilled pride in black protectors, and sometimes served as an additional means of coercion in the fight against Jim Crow. Of course, nonviolence remained the driving force behind social change in the Deep South, but armed resistance complemented civil rights protest and frequently enhanced its effectiveness at the local level. During the Black Power era, by contrast, armed resistance underwent a process of radical reinterpretation and played a largely symbolic role. Although black nationalists such as the Black Panther Party (BPP) construed self-defense as a revolutionary alternative to nonviolence that would stop police brutality, it served primarily as a gendered symbol of male psychological empowerment.[3]

Previous studies on armed resistance in the civil rights era tend to remain limited in geographical scope and largely ignore the symbiotic relationship between self-defense and tactical nonviolence in the southern freedom movement.[4] To gain a more thorough understanding of how armed resistance operated in the civil rights struggle, *The Spirit and the Shotgun* therefore explores black protection efforts in various southern and northern locales, analyzes the evolution of armed militancy without neglecting the significance of tactical nonviolence, and probes the intricate relationship between self-defense and manhood.

Prior to the advent of Black Power, a number of black activists in Arkansas, North Carolina, Alabama, Louisiana, Mississippi, and other southern locales regarded armed resistance as a practical imperative. Since neither local nor federal authorities provided safeguards for civil rights organizers who worked in the hostile environment of Dixie, black southerners used a wide range of armed actions to protect themselves and their allies. Armed men, and sometimes armed women, guarded black churches, private homes, and meeting places and, on occasion, traded shots with their white attackers. Movement leaders, business owners, and black farmers protected their homes on an individual basis. Others formed highly sophisticated defense groups, which protected civil rights organizers, provided armed escorts, monitored nonviolent demonstrations, and patrolled black communities at night. Many of the working-class men who joined such protective units, especially their leaders, were experienced army veterans. Most of them had seen active combat during World War II or the Korean War. Those who commanded these squads enforced strict membership criteria and rejected anyone who seemed prone to aggressive behavior.

Although black defense efforts in the southern freedom movement were primarily an attempt to save lives, they also reflected a struggle over gender identities. "Violence," sociologist Michael Kimmel has pointed out, "has long been understood as the best way to ensure that others publicly recognize one's manhood."[5] This truism carried special significance for black men, who learned that violence, race, and gender were inextricably linked. The research of Gail Bederman has revealed that middle-class white men at the turn of the twentieth century regarded white supremacy as a reflection of white male power.[6] This racist ideology, which allowed white men to subjugate African Americans and to control white women, primarily targeted black men. "Racist oppression took many forms and damaged Afro-American men and women in numerous ways," historical sociologist Orlando Patterson concluded in his study on the consequences of slavery, "but the single greatest focus of ethnic domination was the relentless effort to emasculate the Afro-American male in every conceivable way and at every turn."[7] Many black men developed a sense of self-worth despite these oppressive conditions, but throughout the nineteenth and twentieth centuries their words and actions reflected a determination to reclaim and affirm the role of patriarchal provider and protector that white men denied them.[8]

Black men's skepticism toward nonviolent protest in the 1950s and 1960s echoed these gendered legacies. In a society that defined masculinity primarily through a man's ability to defend his "honor," Indian activist Mohandas Gandhi's abstract philosophy of nonviolence challenged traditional concepts of gender. In the case of African Americans, Martin Luther King's top aide, Hosea Williams, spoke for many when reminiscing about his attempts to spread the Gandhian gospel: "Nonviolence as a way of life was just as foreign to blacks as flying a space capsule would be to a roach."[9] Similarly, at least among those African Americans who protected the movement with guns, nonviolence was often regarded as degrading to black manhood. While these men understood that nonviolent tactics were essential in the battle against Jim Crow, self-defense nurtured self-esteem among both the protectors and the protected.

Beyond the confines of local civil rights campaigns, however, armed militancy presented the freedom movement with a serious predicament. National black leaders knew all too well that the moral and financial support of white liberals was crucial to the success of their crusade to topple Jim Crow. Public advocacy of armed self-defense was likely to erode such support since it threatened to undermine the legitimacy of black demands. The Deacons for Defense and Justice (DDJ) was a case in point. Founded in 1964 in Jonesboro, Louisiana, the black defense organization gained nationwide notoriety in the summer of 1965, after several shoot-outs with the Ku Klux Klan. Many white observers, including the Federal Bureau of Investigation (FBI), initially believed that the

Deacons foreshadowed the end of the nonviolent era. The Congress of Racial Equality (CORE), whose organizers worked closely with the Deacons, attempted to assuage these fears by reiterating its devotion to Gandhian principles. The Student Nonviolent Coordinating Committee (SNCC) likewise rejected news reports that armed resistance played a role in the organization's Mississippi-based voter registration drives.

Such official assurances reflected the tendency among civil rights leaders to promote a false polarity between nonviolence and armed resistance as a tactical ploy to nurture and sustain white support. Weighing their loyalty to local freedom struggles against the need to convince a national audience of the movement's unwavering nonviolent commitment, black activists, aided by the mass media, jointly elevated Martin Luther King's philosophy to the movement's official creed. As a result, Gandhian ideas of ascetic self-suffering and Christian tenets of brotherly love and forgiveness became major points of reference for journalists and white liberal supporters. Conversely, any deviation from this abstract ideal was branded as illegitimate and dangerous.

The vows of allegiance to King's philosophy that CORE, SNCC, and King's Southern Christian Leadership Conference (SCLC) disseminated in thousands of pamphlets, fund-raising letters, and speeches made it difficult to fully comprehend how nonviolence actually worked. As the Gandhian term "nonviolent *direct action*" implied, the protest strategy did not rely solely on moral suasion—the hope that appeals to the conscience of white Americans would impel them to support the movement's cause. Instead, it was mainly a form of nonviolent coercion, which created crises of local, national, and even international proportions that actively forced white authorities to yield to black demands.

By contrast, as white activist Anne Braden observed in 1967, people who observed the freedom struggle from the sidelines appeared to mistake nonviolence for "inaction, people turning the other cheek, submitting instead of resisting."[10] From this perspective, the movement's tactic was synonymous with pacifism, a philosophy that rejects all forms of violence in human conflict. The fact that the movement's primary spokesman, Martin Luther King, constantly invoked the tenets of Gandhi and Jesus appeared to confirm such an impression and, as veteran pacifist A.J. Muste lamented in 1964, prompted many whites to act "as if" blacks had "a peculiar obligation" to adhere to King's teachings.[11]

Skillfully manipulating the media representations of their activities, King and other civil rights leaders firmly established the mythical nature of a philosophy that legitimized black claims to civil rights but bore only superficial relations to the day-to-day reality of civil rights activism. At the same time, as Jenny Walker has pointed out, the black and white press tended to contribute to these distortions by deliberately neglecting violent aspects of the southern freedom struggle.[12]

Despite the movement's reassurances that black activists adhered strictly to the principles of nonviolent protest, the brutal realities of white supremacy provoked vigorous debates about the legitimacy of armed resistance among civil rights activists. In the case of the National Association for the Advancement of Colored People (NAACP), bitter controversies erupted between the organization's national leaders and their southern working-class constituency, some of whom practiced and occasionally openly advocated self-defense. While the NAACP's executive secretary, Roy Wilkins, was able to mute such internal dissent, organizers of CORE and SNCC were deeply affected by the home-grown militancy of the local people with whom they worked in the Deep South. In these two organizations, activists repeatedly debated whether pistols and shotguns conflicted with their nonviolent mission, although white northerners tended to be more troubled by the use of armed force than their southern black comrades.

Years of beatings, shootings, and bombings, coupled with countless discussions about how to confront such racist attacks, steadily eroded the willingness of CORE and SNCC to uphold the seemingly pacifistic façade. Of course, some continued to regard nonviolence as a way of life, but by 1965, their number had dwindled drastically. A few organizers even followed the example of local people and began to carry guns for protection. During the Meredith March of 1966, the long-simmering debate on armed resistance was finally forced into the open. Ten days into the three-week trek across Mississippi, SNCC leader Stokely Carmichael first voiced the slogan "Black Power," which clearly reflected the movement's radicalization. Calling for political and economic empowerment, black pride, and armed self-defense, this militant program became the guiding principle of CORE and SNCC shortly after the march.

Although this tactical evolution was comprehensible to insiders as a logical outgrowth of civil rights organizing in the Deep South, Black Power terrified white America and, as some civil rights leaders had predicted, cost the movement most of its moral and financial support. Many confounded white observers construed the militant slogan as a harbinger of racial warfare. The fact that the NAACP's Roy Wilkins publicly denounced Black Power as a racist call for violent retribution seemed to confirm their worst fears.

Ironically, by the time that CORE and SNCC officially embraced self-defense, armed protection was becoming increasingly irrelevant to the southern freedom movement. Remnants of violent white opposition persisted, but by 1967 federal and state authorities finally began to protect black demonstrators. Equally important, most white southerners grudgingly acquiesced in the inevitability of social change. With the rationale for their armed actions gone, defense squads that had emerged in Alabama, Louisiana, and Mississippi had outlived their usefulness. Consequently, the end of nonviolent mass protest in the Deep South likewise sealed the end of the region's era of armed black resistance.

By contrast, a number of Black Power militants came to see self-defense as a full-fledged strategy, which they deemed a viable alternative to nonviolence. Compared with southern defense units, however, armed resistance played a fundamentally different role in the Black Power era. A closer look at the Black Panther Party and its black nationalist precursors suggests that self-defense remained largely confined to militant rhetoric and reflected psychological rather than physical imperatives. Black nationalist leaders such as Malcolm X, Ron Karenga, and Huey Newton, among others, would have wholeheartedly agreed with activist James Meredith's statement in October 1966 that "the biggest problem facing" African Americans was "the development of manhood and dignity in the men of the race."[13] For them, armed resistance became a primary way to achieve this goal.

The preoccupation of the BPP and other black nationalists with armed resistance, then, can best be understood as symbols of defiance that served to affirm and nurture militant black manhood. Although defensive efforts in Alabama, Louisiana, and Mississippi instilled a similar sense of pride in African American men, the key rationale behind their militant activities remained the simple necessity to protect black communities. During the Black Power era, on the other hand, gender and identity became one of the central pivots around which self-defense revolved.

Of course, the Black Panthers initially regarded their armed actions as an effective way to curb police brutality, and ensuing confrontations with law enforcement had serious real-life consequences for black militants, including numerous incarcerations, shoot-outs with the police, and the deaths of party members. Yet, while armed resistance during the Black Power era was *intended* to be a revolutionary alternative to nonviolence, it *functioned* primarily as a vehicle of psychological liberation. Despite these beneficial aspects of armed militancy, many black nationalists appropriated and reproduced prevailing notions of manhood, which were grounded in patriarchal privilege and the subordination of women.

The gendered function of armed resistance also affected black nationalist concepts of self-defense, which clearly diverged from the ideas of their southern peers. Southern black guards might have been skeptical of nonviolence but rarely questioned its strategic validity. By contrast, the Black Panthers, at least in their public statements, spurned what its chairman, Huey Newton, considered "bankrupt" tactics.[14] In the analysis of many black nationalists, nonviolence was the antithesis of self-defense. Like Malcolm X, whose attacks on Martin Luther King's philosophy had a tremendous impact on civil rights activists, the BPP and other Black Power militants argued that nonviolence was not only futile but would also emasculate African American males. To their mind, the ability to protect black women and black communities against white violence was a much more effective way to preserve black men's self-respect.[15]

As the Black Power movement gained momentum, Robert F. Williams, Stokely Carmichael, Huey Newton, and other radicals abandoned such ideas of the patriarchal protector and began to view aggressive violence as part of a revolutionary, but essentially defensive, struggle against the white oppressor. The ideas of Karl Marx, Frantz Fanon, Mao Zedong, and other theorists allowed groups such as US (black nationalist organization founded by Ron Karenga) or the Black Panther Party to justify urban riots and even guerrilla warfare as legitimate forms of self-defense. A comparison of southern protective units and black nationalist advocates of self-defense thus suggests that the rise of Black Power, despite its southern roots, represented a break with the civil rights struggle of the first half of the 1960s.[16]

Ultimately, self-defense strategies during the Black Power era proved self-defeating. African American militants' show of armed assertiveness was part of an important process of psychological empowerment, but what many of them considered a tactical innovation obscured the social, cultural, and political core of their programs. In addition, armed militancy provoked a wave of government repression, which seriously undermined the effectiveness of groups such as the Black Panther Party. In many ways, these activists had abandoned the important insight of their southern peers that the movement's ultimate success depended on both the spirit and the shotgun.

1

BLACK SELF-DEFENSE AND THE EMERGENCE OF NONVIOLENT PROTEST

On the cold and dreary afternoon of December 1, 1955, black seamstress Rosa Parks watched the passing traffic through the window of the bus on which she regularly rode through Montgomery, Alabama. She tried to ignore the irate white bus driver who shouted orders that she vacate her seat for a white passenger. Calmly awaiting the police officers that she knew would soon arrive to arrest her for defying Jim Crow, Parks's thoughts drifted back to her grandfather and the shotgun that he had kept to protect his family from the Ku Klux Klan.[1] The black woman's arrest triggered a 381-daylong boycott of Montgomery's bus line, lauded by many as the beginning of the nonviolent civil rights movement.

But initially, local blacks were skeptical of nonviolent protest. Like Parks's grandfather, some of them readied their shotguns when whites launched a wave of terror to stop the boycott. On January 30, 1956, blacks even pondered violent retaliation. That day, a powerful explosion shattered the house of the movement's young leader, Baptist minister Martin Luther King Jr. Fearing for the lives of his wife, Coretta, and their young daughter, Yoki, King hastened home from a mass meeting just as hundreds of angry blacks armed with knives and guns gathered in front of the parsonage. After Coretta assured him that she and Yoki were unharmed, King stepped outside to calm the crowd. He urged them to take their weapons and go home.[2] King reminded them of Jesus's tenet that those who lived by the sword would perish by the sword, declaiming:

"I want you to love our enemies. Be good to them. This is what we must live by. We must meet hate with love." Heeding King's exhortations, the crowd gradually dispersed.[3]

The following day, his invocation of Jesus notwithstanding, King applied for a pistol permit at the county sheriff's office. The rejection of his application together with another bomb attack, this time on the home of local NAACP leader E. D. Nixon, reinforced the resolve of King's followers to protect the young pastor. Members of King's Dexter Avenue Baptist Church brought guns and ammunition to the parsonage, installed bright floodlights around the white wood-frame building, and began guarding the house in shifts.[4] Veteran civil rights activist Bayard Rustin, who arrived in February to assist the nonviolent movement, later recalled that King's home resembled "a virtual garrison."[5] Pistols, rifles, and shotguns lay scattered in the living room, while armed sentries stood guard outside.[6]

Prior to the Montgomery bus boycott, armed defense efforts against white violence constituted a bleak story of pyrrhic victories and numerous defeats. In the South, where white supremacy brooked no black dissent, let alone armed resistance, African Americans who repelled white aggressors with arms had not only been outgunned and outnumbered but also faced swift retaliation. The fact that some black men resorted to self-defense regardless of the consequences reflected more than a general concern for the safety of African American communities. For them, it also became a way to affirm their manhood in the face of white men's disrespect. The power of such traditional gender norms partly explains the limited success of the Congress of Racial Equality's attempts to convert black Americans to Gandhian nonviolence in the aftermath of World War II.

The obstacles that CORE faced in the 1940s foreshadowed the tensions between nonviolence and armed self-defense that confronted Martin Luther King and other civil rights leaders in the 1950s and 1960s. The Montgomery bus boycott marked the beginning of a surge in black activism, which culminated in the nonviolent mass movement that CORE had envisioned. For this movement, Martin Luther King's nonviolent philosophy was an essential strategy to legitimize black demands and to secure support from liberal white America. However, King's widely disseminated message, which stressed reconciliation, forgiveness, and brotherly love, created a precarious dichotomy between nonviolence and armed resistance. This dichotomy was problematic because it falsely implied that nonviolence was based primarily on moral suasion—the idea that appeals to the conscience of white America alone would bring about racial change—while in reality it constituted a pragmatic strategy that frequently depended on tactical coercion.

In addition, these binaries masked African Americans' largely tactical commitment to nonviolence. In the 1950s, black activists in Montgomery; Little Rock, Arkansas; Birmingham, Alabama; and Monroe, North Carolina believed this tactic to be fully compatible with armed protection. The vicious and widely publicized debate that NAACP activist Robert F. Williams's armed militancy triggered in 1959 indicated that civil rights leaders would make concerted efforts to uphold the movement's nonviolent image to sustain white liberal support.

To fully understand the roots of this entangled relationship between racial violence, nonviolence, and gender, we have to probe the brutal history of the American South. In part, the region's violent nature stemmed from its longtime status as a frontier settlement. Battles with Native American tribes coupled with a long tradition of extralegal vigilantism made white men comfortable carrying guns.[7] Violence also reflected an important aspect of southern male identity. Antebellum notions of honor and chivalry created an idea of masculinity that subsequent generations learned, used, and reinforced primarily through violence. White men felt pressured to prove their manhood, and the skillful use of firearms and the willingness to defend one's honor in duels frequently served this end. In antebellum southern society, these violent rituals could promote or devastate a man's reputation.[8]

At the same time, violence became an important means of racial control. Antebellum plantation owners maintained their power over black slaves primarily through the threat of brutal punishment, suppressing any signs of unrest or rebellion. The Civil War marked the end of slavery, but white oppression continued. In the aftermath of the war, white terrorist groups such as the Ku Klux Klan launched a reign of terror that echoed the brutality of antebellum slave patrols. The end of Reconstruction in the 1870s marked both the success of white attempts to crush black political participation with violence and the emergence of lynching as a new form of racial terror.

Although lynching arose within an economic and political context, it became a significant tool to control race and gender relations. White men conceptualized lynching exclusively in terms of "protecting" white women from stereotypical black rapists. This form of ritualized murder allowed white men not only to maintain economic, political, and racial hierarchies; it also allowed them to assert their masculinity by proclaiming themselves guardians of southern white womanhood. While pledging to protect their wives and daughters, white men abused African American women with impunity, continuing a form of sexual exploitation that had been institutionalized during slavery. If one follows anthropologist Claude Lévi-Strauss's idea that men use women as signs to communicate with one another, white southerners clearly challenged black manhood. Masking the sexual exploitation and suppression of black and white women, white men's "rhetoric of protection," as Jacqueline Dowd-Hall has argued, primarily expressed a power struggle between men.[9]

It is difficult to comprehend the black response to white violence in the nineteenth and twentieth centuries without acknowledging this struggle over manhood. Black self-defense became more than an attempt to protect one's life. It also reflected black men's determination to reclaim the respect denied them by whites. Consequently, as historian Jim Cullen has noted, the end of the Civil War marked a "watershed for black manhood."[10] The ability of freedmen to protect themselves and their families from former masters was an important transformation of their perception of themselves as men. The right to bear arms and the ability to defend oneself against white attacks became a powerful symbol of this new freedom.[11]

In the face of an unabated wave of racial terror in the 1880s and 1890s, a new generation of militant black editors began to invoke such gendered symbolism in their condemnations of black men's passivity. While Booker T. Washington, the most visible black leader during this era, publicly advocated accommodation, patience, and economic self-reliance, these intellectuals vociferously denounced white terror and called for manly resistance. In numerous articles and editorials, they countered white southerners' "rhetoric of protection" with their own "discourse of protection."[12]

One of these militant authors was Ida B. Wells, a graduate of Fisk University who became a militant antilynching activist in the 1890s. As historian Patricia A. Schechter has pointed out, Wells clearly understood that lynching was more than terrorist violence against the black population. It also became "a particular assault on black males and black 'manhood.'"[13] Ida B. Wells's blunt critique of black men's cowardice was harsh. In an 1892 pamphlet, she declared that nothing was "to be gained by a further sacrifice of manhood and self-respect." She believed that only the determination of armed blacks to defend themselves would ultimately deter the white mob.[14]

T. Thomas Fortune could not have agreed more. By the end of the nineteenth century, the owner and editor of the *New York Age* was a renowned black spokesman in the North. Bolstering his militant reputation, Fortune vehemently condemned the federal government's failure to protect southern blacks and urged his people to use arms to counter white terrorism. "We do not counsel violence," he wrote in one editorial, "we counsel manly retaliation." Fortune insisted that armed resistance was necessary for blacks "to assert their manhood and citizenship."[15]

In the early twentieth century, W.E.B. Du Bois became another vocal advocate of armed protection. In 1909, the Harvard-educated sociologist and civil rights activist had cofounded the National Association for the Advancement of Colored People. Though the NAACP battled lynching with publicity campaigns and legal action, Du Bois also published scathing condemnations of black timidity in the organization's magazine, the *Crisis*. A particularly uncompromising critique appeared in October 1916. Commenting on a recent lynching in Gainesville, Florida, Du Bois scorned the black community's submissiveness. In Du Bois's eyes, blacks had "acted like cowardly sheep" when they surrendered a man who had injured two white police officers in a nighttime altercation. Noting that blacks had outnumbered the mob two to one, he accused them of allowing whites to harass and attack innocent men and women. Du Bois concluded that lynching was going to stop only "when the cowardly mob is faced by effective guns in the hands of people determined to sell their souls dearly."[16]

No one could accuse the combative editor of failing to practice what he preached. During the Atlanta riot of 1906, Du Bois, then professor of sociology at Atlanta University, rushed back to the city to protect his wife and young daughter. After buying a Winchester double-barreled shotgun and plenty of ammunition, he took position at the front porch of his house. "If a white mob had stepped on the campus where I lived," he later reflected in his memoirs, "I would without hesitation have sprayed their guts over the grass."[17] Numerous black Atlantans were similarly prepared, forcing back white invaders with volleys of buckshot. It is conceivable that many of these men preferred a manly fight—even if fought in vain—to what Wells, Fortune, and Du Bois derided as passive submission.[18]

But prior to the civil rights era, only a minority of blacks was able to put such militant appeals into organized action. During Reconstruction, former black Union soldiers founded paramilitary organizations to defend their community against the Ku Klux Klan and other terrorist groups. These black militias were unable to stop entirely the reign of terror that whites launched in the aftermath of the war, but on several occasions they successfully drove back white vigilantes with force.[19] In 1899, blacks in McIntosh County, Georgia, prevented the lynching of a man whom whites accused of rape. In what came to be known as the "Darien Insurrection," almost one hundred black men armed themselves and stood guard in front of the local jail.[20] In Mississippi, some all-black communities were notorious for their armed resistance, fighting several pitched battles with white invaders. In 1906, in the town of Wiggins, for example, blacks traded more than five hundred shots with a white mob that had vowed to lynch a member of the black community.[21]

The NAACP's Walter White suggested in 1929 that such resolve to repel white attacks had contributed to a decline in mob violence. Yet the available evidence suggests that armed black resistance more frequently *provoked* mob violence. In a society where a white man could murder an African American for brushing up against him on the sidewalk, wounding, let alone killing, a white man in self-defense meant almost certain death.[22] On numerous occasions, black sharecroppers killed their white employers in violent arguments over a perceived lack of racial deference. During the short period that passed until a lynch mob gathered, few black communities were able to come to the victim's rescue. Cases like the one of a black tenant in Wilcox County, Georgia, were common. In 1912, the man's white employer attacked him for his seeming reluctance to go to work. The tenant fought back, killing the planter in self-defense. Shortly thereafter, a group of whites seized him, hanged him to a tree, and emptied their guns into his dead body.[23]

As late as 1944, Swedish sociologist Gunnar Myrdal reached the discouraging conclusion that southern blacks could do little to protect themselves. "They can, of course, strike back," he wrote, "but they know that that means a more violent retaliation, often in an organized form and with danger to other Negroes."[24] Supported by local police or militias and condoned by southern politicians, white mob violence crushed most black attempts to fight back.[25] Tulsa, Oklahoma, where the arrest of an alleged black rapist triggered a white attack on the city's black neighborhood, was a case in point. Black attempts to halt the invasion during the night of May 30, 1921, led to the obliteration of the entire black community.[26]

While such examples of black militancy might have been deemed futile by many, some African Americans nevertheless continued to protect their communities against white aggression. In the aftermath of World War I, especially black soldiers, who had hoped that their courage in the trenches of France would translate into better treatment at home, refused to tolerate the wave of violence that greeted them upon their return. In cities across the country, disillusioned veterans met southern black migrants, whose dream of finding equality and prosperity outside the South had been similarly shattered. The result was a rising spirit of defiance that exploded into racial violence in the aftermath of the war. Sometimes, as in the Houston Riot of 1917, this militant mood turned into aggressive violence. Constantly mistreated by white police, almost one hundred black soldiers mutinied against their white officers, seized rifles and ammunition from an army depot, and provoked a furious gun battle that left dozens dead on both sides. Predictably, the leaders of the revolt suffered swift and violent punishment by white authorities.[27]

But far more often, as during the "Red Summer" of 1919, black Americans simply attempted to protect their communities from white attacks. Among the thirty-seven racial clashes that the *New York Times* counted that year, the one in Chicago was the most brutal.[28] In few places, according to historian William M. Tuttle Jr., was blacks' willingness to fight back "more evident than in Chicago during the city's race riot."[29] During the days of violence, which had been triggered on a hot day in July by an alleged breach of the color line at one of Lake Michigan's segregated beaches, a few black veterans used their army training to organize the defense of black neighborhoods. Guarding strategically located street corners with submachine guns and rifles, these men repelled white invaders with gunfire. When the smoke from burning buildings had cleared, sixteen blacks and fifteen whites lay dead.[30]

Even in the Deep South, where state and local authorities suppressed any signs of resistance with brutal force, some blacks openly challenged white supremacy with arms. According to historian Rupert Lewis, some branches of black nationalist leader Marcus Garvey's Universal Negro Improvement Association (UNIA) organized paramilitary units to protect its members and their meetings from racist aggression. And in July 1923, armed blacks guarded a hospital for black veterans in Tuskegee, Alabama, after whites had threatened to remove the hospital's new black leadership. In most cases, however, such acts of resistance were confined to individual incidents of self-defense in violent confrontations with white employers or police officers.[31]

In the 1920s, NAACP lawyers worked hard to defend this right in the courts. Southern juries rarely exonerated African Americans who defended themselves in an altercation with whites. For that reason, blacks welcomed the NAACP's efforts to take up the cause of those who injured or killed their white attackers. In the aftermath of the 1919 race riot in Elaine, Arkansas, for example, over one hundred blacks who had protected a secret union meeting with arms faced trial. White authorities had charged seventy of them with murder or attempted murder. By 1925, NAACP lawyers had managed to free all defendants.[32]

Two years later, the organization won another important victory in the

North. In 1925, the organization widely publicized the case of Dr. Ossian Sweet, a young black physician who was accused of killing a white man while defending his Detroit home against a hostile crowd that sought to preserve residential segregation.[33] NAACP assistant secretary Walter White had no doubts as to why Sweet had been arrested. "Dr. Sweet and the other defendants are in jail not because they have committed a crime," he wrote in a memorandum, "but because they are Negroes and dared defend their home and their lives against a mob."[34] To White's mind, a conviction of Sweet would deal a major blow to the NAACP's argument that African Americans had the same right as whites to defend themselves against such attacks.[35] At least in a northern court, the legitimacy of such demands could no longer be denied. In 1927, after two trials, all charges against Sweet were dropped.[36]

Despite such legal victories, armed black resistance in the South of the 1930s confronted the same predicaments that had prevented effective protection in previous decades. Across the region, individual self-defense efforts against white sheriffs or white employers continued, but organized resistance remained rare.[37] Still, Socialist labor organizers who attempted to bring about a union movement in Dixie during the Great Depression were astonished to find local sharecroppers and tenants in armed readiness. Harry Haywood, who after defending black neighborhoods during the Chicago riot of 1919 became a field-worker for the Communist Party, recalled in his memoirs that few of the blacks who attended union meetings in Alabama in 1933 came unarmed. "There were guns of all kinds," he wrote, "shotguns, rifles and pistols. Share-croppers were coming to the meetings armed and left their guns with their coats when they came in." A year earlier, black labor activists in the region had engaged in several shoot-outs with police officers who sought to put an end to their organizing efforts.[38]

Members of the interracial Southern Tenant Farmers' Union (STFU) likewise came armed to rallies. White activist Howard Kester recounted in his history of the union that when rumors of an imminent white attack spread, few black members left their homes without guns.[39] But the STFU soon realized that armed protection remained a risky venture. Eventually, the union's members removed the weapons to reduce the potential of provocation.[40] Confronted with white violence and economic hardship, both attempts to organize African American protest and organized protection efforts gradually fizzled.

Although the preconditions for black mass protest seemed less than ideal in the late 1930s, World War II initiated and accelerated structural changes that provided critical groundwork for future activism. The booming war industry provided jobs for thousands of black southerners who swelled African American communities in northern and western cities. Increasing resources in these communities meant larger black churches and colleges, independent newspapers, and powerful political organizations, all of which strengthened the vital social networks of black America. Moreover, blacks outside the Deep South emerged in the 1940s as an important voting block in national politics, frequently providing the winning margin in presidential elections. Finally, America's promise to defeat racist dictatorships in Europe and Japan to establish genuine democracy abroad, while nearly 10 percent of its citizens suffered political, economic, and social discrimination, struck friend and foe alike as rank hypocrisy. In the looming Cold War rivalry with the Soviet Union, race would become a serious liability in American foreign affairs.[41]

The war years also saw important legal decisions that eroded traditions of white supremacy at the same time that black activism was growing to maturity. The NAACP had challenged segregation and disfranchisement in the courts for several decades, but one of the most significant victories came in 1944. That year, in its *Smith v. Allwright* decision, the U.S. Supreme Court outlawed the white primary, a tool designed by southern Democrats to exclude blacks at an early stage of the political process. Now able to vote in states of the Upper South in addition to those in the North, blacks gained additional political weight. Similarly encouraging, civil rights organizations experienced unprecedented growth. By 1946, the NAACP's membership had soared tenfold to five hundred thousand in over one thousand chapters around the country. While the NAACP was busy sending out application forms, the black *Pittsburgh Courier* launched its Double-V campaign, loudly demanding victory over both Adolph Hitler abroad and Jim Crow at home.[42]

But neither realignments in national and international politics nor legal victories would have affected race relations in the least had not African American citizens attempted to challenge white supremacy at the local level. Black soldiers were at the forefront of these efforts. Already during their training at segregated military facilities in the South, some of the over nine hundred thousand black draftees clashed with white officers and local whites over discrimination and segregation. In January 1942, for example, over five hundred black soldiers from Louisiana's Camp Livingston and nearby Camp Claiborne revolted in the town of Alexandria, defending a black private who had been clubbed by a white policeman. The violent melee left dozens of whites and blacks wounded.[43] One and a half years later, black soldiers at Camp Stewart, Georgia, rose up against constant mistreatment, killing a white MP and wounding four others. In 1943 alone, 242 racial clashes erupted in forty-seven cities across the United States. After the bloodiest disorder of that year in Detroit, twenty-five blacks and nine whites lay dead.[44]

Unlike black leaders and editors, who tended to tone down their militant rhetoric toward the end of the war, black veterans were no longer willing to wait for social change.[45] Upon their return, many of them took it upon themselves to challenge the racial status quo in their own communities. Across the South, these men launched voter registration drives and political campaigns. In January 1946, for example, some one hundred uniformed black veterans marched in double-file formation through downtown Birmingham, Alabama, to the Jefferson County Courthouse, demanding that their names be added to the voter rolls.[46] In some southern towns and cities, returning soldiers became the first black registered voters since Reconstruction, organizing new NAACP chapters and voters leagues to enroll others. By 1950, almost twenty thousand southern African Americans had added their names to the registration books. In the words of civil rights historian John Dittmer, black veterans became "the shock troops of the modern civil rights movement," their military service the catalyst of black activism.[47]

One of these men was A. Z. Young from Bogalusa, Louisiana. Before the war, Young had never given much thought to civil rights or to what lay beyond the boundaries of his native state. But his military training in the North and 168 days on the front line in Europe profoundly altered his views and sparked his career as political activist. "I felt to believe a this point as I was returning . . . to America," he confided to an interviewer in the 1960s, "whether it be Bogalusa, or New York, or Los Angeles that the same privileges executed by whites should be executed by me because there is no more that a man can do than to risk his life for his country." For Young, "this is where the turning point actually came in my life, where I was willing to stand up and to fight not only for myself but for my people wherever they be." Back in Bogalusa, Young did just that. Becoming a labor organizer in the local paper plant in the 1950s, he later joined the civil rights movement and helped found the Deacons for Defense and Justice, a black self-defense organization that protected civil rights activists from the Ku Klux Klan.[48]

For David Matthews from Sunflower County, Mississippi, World War II also changed everything. The war "gave us a broader outlook and view of life in that we were traveling in various places across the United States and overseas," he recalled decades later. He and his friends "felt that once we come out of this, we deserved the right to be citizens."[49] Like Young and Mathews, many black soldiers refused to adhere to the traditional racial etiquette when they returned to their hometowns. On southern buses and trains, veterans deliberately defied segregation laws, which they found difficult to bear after defending American democracy on Europe's battlefields. Government reports warned that black ex-soldiers might be willing to use violence to secure their rights, while rumors spread in the South that blacks plotted to massacre the white population.[50] Although black veterans were far from plotting an armed rebellion, it became obvious that they were no longer willing to acquiesce in white aggression.[51]

Amidst a brutal war abroad and racial clashes at home, a small band of pacifists from Chicago talked about launching a nonviolent revolution. Since the fall of 1941, several black and white college students had met regularly to discuss the problem of American racism. They all were members of the Fellowship of Reconciliation (FOR), a pacifist organization that was founded in 1914 and strove to create a colorblind society in a world without war.[52]

In part, these young activists were inspired by the Protestant Social Gospel. This moral reform movement emerged in the late nineteenth century and was a reaction to the catastrophic effects of urbanization and industrialization on the poor. Determined to alleviate their plight, the Social Gospel movement advocated social justice, brotherhood, and Christian love.[53] The teachings of Indian nationalist and anticolonial activist Mohandas Gandhi were another major influence on the students' thinking. Spending hours discussing how Gandhi's philosophy of nonviolence could be adapted to the United States, they believed that the Social Gospel's ideal could be accomplished only through nonviolent protest.[54]

Black theology student James Farmer wanted the group to do more than merely talk about social action. He envisaged an interracial organization that would use nonviolent protest to attack segregation and discrimination across the United States. Farmer had meticulously studied Gandhi during his years at Howard University Divinity School and was deeply committed to racial justice. Rather than serve in a segregated Methodist congregation after his graduation in 1941, he refused ordination to work as a FOR race-relations secretary. In discussions with A. J. Muste, the white president of FOR, he promoted his dream and eventually secured Muste's support. Several months later, in April 1942, a group of fifty young pacifists from the Chicago area gathered to found a group that they named the Committee of Racial Equality (CORE). In May 1942, while the United States still mobilized for war, CORE activists launched what according to James Farmer was the first nonviolent sit-in in American history.[55]

Of course, black Americans had experimented with nonviolent protest before. As early as 1841, blacks in Massachusetts launched boycotts against segregated railroad cars. When southern state legislatures enacted a flood of Jim Crow laws in the late nineteenth century, boycotts against segregated streetcars erupted in over twenty-five cities in every state of the former Confederacy. Some of these boycotts lasted over a year, but they ultimately failed to halt the advent of segregation. What CORE proposed, however, was more than mere noncooperation with the unjust system of racial discrimination. Grounded in Gandhi's teachings, its pacifistic message insisted that only "loving" nonretaliation that directly confronted segregationist injustice would topple white supremacy. Like Richard Gregg and other white pacifists who began to study and promote Gandhi's teachings in the 1920s, CORE believed that the Gandhian protest strategy had the potential to achieve extensive social change in the United States.[56]

News of CORE's successful "sit-down" campaigns in 1942 and 1943 against segregated restaurants in downtown Chicago spread rapidly among pacifist circles. Soon similar groups formed in Detroit, New York, and Syracuse. During CORE's first national conference in 1943, delegates from a handful of local CORE chapters established a loose federation of autonomous affiliates, each of which pledged to fight discrimination in restaurants, movie theaters, amusement parks, and other public places. James Farmer became the organization's first national chairman. One year later, activists adopted Congress of Racial Equality as the permanent name of the organization. By the end of the 1940s, CORE had affiliates in fifteen northern and midwestern cities.[57]

Most of CORE's founding members had thoroughly studied Gandhi's complex philosophy. The Indian activist's concept of *Satyagraha*, or "Truth-Force," was rooted in his struggle against anti-Indian prejudice in South Africa in the second decade of the twentieth century. After his return to India in 1917, Gandhi helped launch a nonviolent mass movement against British colonial rule. *Ahimsa* (the refusal to do harm) was the central idea of his teachings. According to Gandhi, no one could expect to find truth (*Satya*) without applying the principles of *Ahimsa*. Self-sacrifice and voluntary submission to violence would become the "weapon of the weak" against the seemingly omnipotent British enemy. In Gandhi's fusion of Indian spirituality and Western thought, nonviolence became both the end and the means of the struggle.[58]

Satyagraha roughly followed four stages. After thoroughly investigating the injustice, activists attempted to win over their opponent through reason. Following this, *Satyagrahis* appealed to the conscience of the oppressor by dramatizing the injustice through their own suffering. Finally, they used tactics of nonviolent coercion such as noncooperation and civil disobedience. Gandhi insisted that *Satyagraha* was not passivity but an active form of nonviolent resistance that required courage and, ultimately, the willingness to die. Still, goodwill toward those who inflicted violence, along with ascetic self-suffering, was essential to the success of the struggle. In the minds of many, Gandhi's famous 241–mile Salt March to the Indian seacoast in 1930 epitomized his philosophy. The demonstration focused on the injustice of the British salt law as a symbol of the unpopular foreign government that was unrepresentative of the Indian people. Gandhi's example inspired hundreds of thousands to engage in similar acts of civil disobedience to protest British colonial rule.[59]

Although African Americans largely ignored CORE's experiments with Gandhian principles, they were familiar with the Indian freedom struggle and the idea of nonviolent protest. Throughout the 1920s and 1930s, black newspapers and journals had reported extensively about the Indian movement. As a result, several black leaders traveled to India to learn more about the struggle and its famous leader, sharing their experiences with others upon their return. Militant pacifists, such as Richard Gregg, and like-minded organizations, most notably the American Friends Services Committee and the War Resisters League, also publicized Gandhi's ideas in the United States. In addition, Gandhians such as Krishnalal Shridharani, one of Gandhi's disciples who had participated in the Salt March, visited the United States to acquaint black college students and intellectuals with the principles of *Satyagraha*. Pondering the parallels between the Indian freedom movement and the African American struggle for civil rights, some black editors began to call for "a black Gandhi" in the United States.[60]

One possible candidate, longtime labor and civil rights leader A. Philip Randolph, while a commanding figure, was unable to match the Indian activist's ascetic charisma. Yet his all-black March on Washington Movement (MOWM) clearly foreshadowed the potential of nonviolent mass protest. Founding his organization in early 1941, Randolph threatened to bring one hundred thousand African Americans to Washington, D.C., to protest against blatant discrimination in the defense industry. The international implications of the looming march promised utter embarrassment for the U.S. government in its avowed struggle to defend democracy against racist Nazi Germany. Thus pressured, President Franklin D. Roosevelt yielded to Randolph's demands, issuing executive order 8802, which ended discrimination in the defense industry and established the Fair Employment Practices Commission (FEPC). In the following years, despite the weaknesses of the FEPC, thousands of black Americans found lucrative jobs in the roaring war industry.[61]

Randolph's insistence that blacks had to use "extraordinary, dramatic and drastic" methods to win their freedom proved visionary, but prior to the civil rights era black support for the Gandhian's strategy was far from unanimous.[62] In the 1930s, critics stressed that the obvious differences between the two countries would make the success of nonviolent protest highly unlikely. Indians, they argued, vastly outnumbered British troops while African Americans constituted only 10 percent of the population. Similarly, Indians fought against a foreign occupation force, while blacks would oppose fellow citizens. Some of these skeptics were certain that civil disobedience would inevitably lead to racial slaughter.[63] It came as no surprise, therefore, that the *Pittsburgh Courier* attacked Randolph in 1943 for his "irresponsible talk about suicidal civil disobedience and mass marches which never materialize."[64]

When CORE activists attempted to introduce Gandhi to Americans in the 1940s, they ran into similar resistance. To many of those whom CORE sought to recruit, nonviolence seemed at best bizarre; some thought it outright laughable. Writing in 1942, FOR member Bayard Rustin conceded that few blacks were able "to conceive of a solution by reconciliation and non-violence" in the charged atmosphere of the war years.[65] "The idea of non-violence has gotten to be something to be ridiculed everytime it is mentioned," activist Mary Klein similarly concluded four years later about her frustrating efforts to discuss Gandhi's teachings.[66] James Farmer recalled in his memoirs that the idea that "violence could be greeted with love generally evoked only contempt." "You mean that if someone hits you, you're not going to hit back? What are you, some kind of a nut or something?" was a common response by perplexed listeners.[67]

Even within CORE, the support for *Satyagraha* was not undivided. In 1946, pacifist and nonpacifist members of the organization's Chicago branch clashed on the question of whether armed self-defense against white terror was justified. During the war, tensions had intensified in the midwestern city, which had become a magnet for thousands of southern migrants. Some African Americans began to look for affordable homes in traditionally all-white neighborhoods. White people feared an erosion of the traditional color line, and racist groups burned crosses in front of black homes, attacked blacks on the street, and launched a wave of bombings to halt black migration. White police did little to stop the violence.[68] Confronted with this reign of terror, members of the Socialist Workers Party (SWP) who had joined the Chicago CORE chapter discussed and approved a resolution in August 1946 that called for a system of armed black sentries to combat racial violence. In the September issue of the branch's newsletter, CORE and SWP member Berry Bessler declared, "CORE has put itself on the record as being in favor of the formation of defence squads to guard Negroes living in 'tension' areas who are in danger of attack." Prepared to be called upon at short notice, these defense groups would patrol and protect black neighborhoods.[69]

Although Chicago CORE never implemented these plans, the chapter's unexpected stance reflected fundamental disagreements about the interpretation of nonviolence among its members. Pacifist Robert Gemmer reported in December 1946 to CORE's white national executive secretary George Houser: "At each meeting, practically, much time is spent with the violent vs [sic] the nonviolent approach being discussed." Gemmer doubted that CORE's Socialist members would remain passive during peaceful picketing campaigns and insisted that activists "act in a *spirit* of non-violence or they should not remain in CORE."[70] George Houser was similarly disturbed by these reports and briefly pondered expelling the Chicago branch from the national organization if it continued its ambiguous policy.[71]

Such debates were not confined to the Chicago branch. Among the leadership of the national organization, the question of tactical versus philosophical nonviolence aroused controversy as well. Of course, CORE's pacifist founders had adopted Gandhi's teachings as their way of life and believed in the power of moral suasion. "The goal of the early organization," James Farmer explained in 1965, "was to change the hearts of those who discriminated; if the group succeeded in changing practices and not the hearts, they had something less than success."[72] Yet even among these apostles of pacifism, some members questioned their belief in such idealistic principles. CORE's first chairperson, Bernice Fisher, a white theology student whom James Farmer described as a "passionately committed religious pacifist," lay bare her doubts in a letter to George Houser in 1944.[73] "Despite a temperamental trend toward absolutes," she wrote, "I am on constant guard against establishing any." The same was true of her thoughts about nonviolence. "I'd hesitate very much to say that I have a right to decide that taking another[']s life is justified in a cause in which I am interested," Fisher ventured, "but can I make it an absolute rule?" Fisher had no solution for her dilemma.[74]

Houser objected to Fisher's reasoning for both moral and tactical reasons. As an avowed pacifist, CORE's executive secretary abhorred all forms of violence. During the Depression, he first learned about pacifism in Christian youth groups. In 1940, he spent a year in prison for refusing to register for the draft.[75] His personal convictions aside, he argued pragmatically that black violence would only invite retaliation by the white majority. Houser also felt that endorsing any form of violence would confuse the moral dimension of their goals in the public mind. Outlining CORE's future in a memorandum on mass protest, Houser stressed that nonretaliation would be crucial to the success of civil rights activism. When attacked, blacks should "absorb the physical punishment" rather than respond in kind, possibly "changing the hearts of the opposition" through their actions.[76]

James Farmer knew that few blacks would join CORE because of the speculative prospect of changing the heart of a white man. They would join because the nonviolent technique produced tangible results, such as the desegregation of restaurants or movie theaters. "The masses of Negroes will not become pacifists," he conceded in a discussion with FOR president A. J. Muste. "Being Negroes for them is rough enough without being pacifists, too."[77] Rather, he planned to forge an alliance between pacifists and nonpacifists, an alliance that might be transformed into an interracial mass movement against Jim Crow in the years to come. Prior to the 1960s, however, CORE remained a northern elitist organization that consisted of predominantly white middle-class pacifists.[78]

Over two decades after the attempts of CORE and other pacifists to bring Gandhi to America, the Montgomery bus boycott finally catapulted nonviolence into the national spotlight. On November 14, 1956, after almost one year of sacrifice and white intimidation, the U.S. Supreme Court finally affirmed the unconstitutionality of segregation on the city's bus line. That night, thousands of blacks crammed into Holt Street Baptist Church to celebrate their victory. Speaking to his followers about the difficult prospect of returning to the integrated buses, the movement's young leader, Martin Luther King, evoked the symbols of Gandhi and Jesus. "With understanding, goodwill, and Christian love," he said, they should now return to the buses. He was certain that their nonviolent suffering would not only redeem African Americans but could also change the prejudiced hearts of white racists.[79]

King's words reflected both his deep roots in the religious tradition of black America and his impressive rhetorical ability to identify with multiple audiences. While instilling black listeners with hope, pride, and courage, King's references to Christian traditions were equally comprehensible to a majority of white Americans. As Richard Lischer has pointed out, King's goal "was the merger of black aspirations into the American dream," which required him

to "convince black Americans that his methods represented their best interests" and "to convince white Americans that his vision was consistent with
their heritage and in their best interests as well." King's nonviolent philosophy
proved a significant asset in reconciling this need to nurture commitment to
civil rights activism among black audiences with the necessity to enlist white
moral and financial support for the emerging civil rights movement.[80]

But King's journey toward becoming one of the movement's most skillful nonviolent tacticians was neither static nor preordained. Only during the
Montgomery movement did the twenty-six-year-old pastor begin to ponder
the significance of spiritual nonviolence and its strategic implications.[81] Bayard
Rustin, who had come to Alabama to assist the local struggle, was shocked to
find King's house guarded by armed black men. The living room resembled a
minor armory. Rustin's friend, black journalist William Worthy, almost sat on
a pistol that lay on his chair. King assured the two baffled men that the weapons were only defensive precautions against white attacks.[82] When recounting
the early days of the boycott movement to the War Resisters League in March
1956, Rustin lauded its potential for nonviolent protest but noted "considerable
confusion on the question as to whether violence is justified in retaliation to
violence directed against the Negro community."[83]

In response to these shortcomings, Rustin and FOR activist Glenn Smiley, a
white Methodist minister from Texas, began to tutor King in the philosophical
nuances of Gandhi's *Satyagraha*. An enthusiastic Smiley noted in a report to
the FOR that the young Baptist minister seemed to be profoundly influenced
by the Indian's philosophy. He speculated that King might become a future
"Negro Gandhi" if he could "*really* be won to a faith in non-violence."[84] By
Rustin's account, King's ultimate conversion came in March 1956, when a white
telegram delivery boy parked his bike across the street from the parsonage
and, hiding behind a nearby bush, answered an urgent call of nature. As the
relieved teenager suddenly emerged, one of King's armed guards confused him
with an intruder and nearly killed the boy.[85] Only after this incident, as Rustin
later recalled, did King become receptive to the spiritual side of nonviolence,
banning guns from his house and developing an Afro-Christian interpretation
of Gandhi's teachings.[86]

Of course, Montgomery blacks heard familiar lines when King clad Gandhi
in the language of Jesus. His biblical references to redemptive suffering invoked traditional themes within African American religion, which frequently
likened blacks to Christian prophets and martyrs.[87] Despite a general familiar-
ity with such ideas, however, there continued to be those who found nonvio-

lence nonsensical. Even Rosa Parks, etched in public memory as the symbol of the Montgomery boycott, conceded in her memoirs that she and others remained skeptical about the Gandhian technique.[88] As a result, some African Americans complemented the boycott with armed protection. College teacher and local activist Jo Ann Robinson recalled in her autobiographical account of the movement that a number of black men, faced with constant threats and bomb attacks, took their guns and "placed them conveniently near their beds." One of the main organizers of the early boycott, Robinson too acquired a pistol and ammunition. She was afraid to shoot the pistol, since she was unfamiliar with the handling of guns, but, as she remembered, "it was a comfort to have it."[89]

Confronted with such examples of armed precautions, King agreed with Rustin's assessment that the movement's leaders would have to accomplish a "tremendous educational job."[90] King and Glenn Smiley worked hard to convince local people of the tactical merits of nonviolence, explaining its principles at virtually every mass meeting. Using nonviolent workshops, pamphlets, and appeals to Christian traditions, pacifists such as Smiley sought to dissuade local blacks from retaliating against white provocation.[91] According to King, these efforts proved successful. In late September 1956, he enthusiastically reported to Rustin of "a growing commitment to the philosophy of non-violence on the part of the Negro community." "Even those who were willing to get their guns in the beginning," he wrote, "are gradually coming to see the futility of such an approach."[92] While local African Americans may not have adopted nonviolence as a way of life, many of them seemed to have recognized its tactical potential in the fight against Jim Crow.

Despite the victory over bus segregation in Montgomery and similar protests that were springing up across the South in the ensuing years, the NAACP's executive secretary, Roy Wilkins, remained skeptical of the new method. He and fellow NAACP leaders initially feared that the Montgomery model would lead only to a series of unsuccessful boycotts. A staff member since 1931, Wilkins was a staunch supporter of his organization's traditional legal strategy, which sought to expand the protection of black civil rights by securing favorable legislation and court decisions. The Association's widely acclaimed victory in the U.S. Supreme Court's 1954 *Brown v. Board of Education* case, which declared school segregation unconstitutional, undoubtedly confirmed the general belief in the superiority of legal tactics.[93]

Despite the NAACP's jubilations, however, the *Brown* decision not only failed to integrate southern schools but also triggered a wave of massive white resistance. In 1955, Mississippi businessmen founded the White Citizens' Council, which vowed to thwart racial integration by "respectable" means such as economic reprisals against the black community. One year later, the organization boasted almost 250,000 members. Others intimidated the black population with violence. Racist extremism also flourished among southern politicians, who condoned racial terrorism in the name of white supremacy.[94]

In Little Rock, Arkansas, where Governor Orval Faubus led the state's resistance movement against school desegregation, this fanatic atmosphere exploded into violence in the fall of 1957. Soon after word of the impending integration of Little Rock's Central High School had spread, white residents mobilized, attacking the nine black teenagers who had enrolled there. Faubus's refusal to ensure the safety of the new students enraged President Dwight D. Eisenhower, who, while being no champion of racial equality, brooked no insubordination. In an action unprecedented since Reconstruction, Eisenhower dispatched federal troops to Little Rock to quell the disorder and to protect the black youths.[95]

In the minds of many, the federal government seemed to live up to its democratic ideals. But Daisy Bates, the local leader of the integration efforts in Little Rock and president of the Arkansas NAACP, knew better. "The phone rang constantly with threats," she recalled of the dangerous aftermath of the school crisis. "They broke the window with rocks. They burned crosses in the yard all the time. Huge ones. And they set the house on fire."[96] Since neither federal soldiers nor local police officers responded to her requests for protection, friends and neighbors began to guard the Bates residency with shotguns and pistols. Well armed, the volunteers took positions at windows in bedroom, living room, and kitchen. In a similar fashion, the grandmother of Melba Patillo, one of the nine black students who had integrated Central High, on one occasion stood guard with a shotgun to defend Melba and her family against potential racist attacks.[97]

Once Governor Faubus ordered out the National Guard, local police felt even less responsibility to protect Bates. This prompted her guards to redouble their defense efforts, which culminated in the formation of a "volunteer guard committee." Black men also installed bright floodlights at the front of the building to detect white attackers more easily. Later, they added heavy steel screens in front of the windows to shield Bates and her husband from rocks, bricks, and buckshot. By 1958, the building was protected around the clock.[98]

White police officers seemed intent on thwarting such private protection efforts by arresting Bates's friends on concealed weapons charges. In a desperate plea for protection to President Eisenhower in August 1959, Bates recounted the campaign of terror and bitterly complained that police harassment left her allies "defenseless before those who constantly threaten our lives."[99] But such appeals fell on deaf ears. The Eisenhower administration provided no assistance to combat white aggression.

In Monroe, North Carolina, meanwhile, black NAACP activist Robert F. Williams had long given up hope that the federal government would come to the aid of African Americans. Born and raised in Monroe, Williams was a veteran of the U.S. Marines and had reorganized the town's defunct NAACP chapter in 1955. He felt inspired by the Montgomery movement and soon initiated his own nonviolent campaign to desegregate Monroe. Still, Williams was no admirer of King's philosophy. "I had just come out of the Marine Corps," he recalled years later, "and I had been in the Army, and I didn't believe in the pacifist document." Nevertheless, Williams did believe that African Americans "should use or utilize any method that brought results." In his mind, these methods included both nonviolent protest and what he called "armed self-reliance."[100]

In 1957, Williams launched nonviolent stand-ins and picket lines to integrate Monroe's local swimming pool. Soon the revived North Carolina Ku Klux Klan launched a campaign of harassment and intimidation, staging nighttime parades through the black neighborhood. Led by the local police chief, a procession of cars manned with hooded men slowly drove down the neighborhood's main road, throwing rocks and bottles at houses and firing their pistols into the air. The home of local black physician Dr. Albert E. Perry became the night riders' primary target. Shotgun attacks on Perry's house became a common occurrence. Confronted with this unprovoked wave of violence, Williams and several black army veterans formed a defense organization that guarded the black community with pistols, machine guns, and dynamite. When another car convoy of Klansmen approached the home of Dr. Perry in early October 1957, black men, fortified in trenches around the building, put the hooded men to flight with volleys of gunfire. This incident together with a hastily passed local ordinance against motorcades in reaction to the shoot-out marked the end of Klan harassment in Monroe.[101]

A similar defense group emerged in Birmingham, Alabama, where charismatic minister Rev. Fred Shuttlesworth led the city's black freedom movement. Although the black pastor urged his followers to remain nonviolent, he readily accepted their efforts to protect him and his church with arms. In 1957, after Shuttlesworth had miraculously survived a bomb attack that virtually obliterated the parsonage, members of his Bethel Baptist Church established a self-defense group that became known as the "Civil Rights Guards." Led by Colonel Stone "Buck" Johnson, one of Shuttlesworth's most loyal followers, armed sentries guarded the front and rear of the church from a provisional guard station in two nightly shifts.[102] Birmingham's flamboyant civil rights leader later stressed the defensive character of the guards. "We didn't want anybody to get shot," he recalled, "but we did wonder if anyone was going to throw any more dynamite. . . . I said to the men if you got to shoot, shoot a man in the foot[;] don't try to kill anyone."[103] In spite of repeated attempts by Birmingham police officers to disarm them, the guards stood their ground. In the following four years, they prevented further bomb attacks on the church and Shuttlesworth's home.[104]

In the meantime, Martin Luther King had begun to put into action the idea of Bayard Rustin and other activists to build an organization that would promote nonviolent protest across the South. During a meeting in New Orleans in February 1957, some one hundred southern black ministers agreed to establish the Southern Christian Leadership Conference (SCLC), an umbrella organization that would consist of local affiliates in a loose alliance. Stressing Christian principles and Gandhian nonviolence, SCLC's stated goal was to secure full citizenship for African Americans and their integration into American life.[105] The organization's constitution echoed King's emerging Christian-Gandhian philosophy, vowing to refuse "to cooperate with evil," and to appeal "to the conscience of man." Most important, SCLC reiterated its commitment to the "spirit of good will and non-violence" to achieve its ultimate goal: the "beloved community."[106]

In Monroe, however, many blacks felt that goodwill would do precious little to topple Jim Crow's reign of terror. In particular, the lynching of Emmett Till in 1955 and the brutal murder of Mack Charles Parker three years later had disillusioned Robert Williams and his followers. Hopes of securing racial justice were dashed once more in the spring of 1959, when all-white juries acquitted two local white men who had been accused of raping and harassing black women. Williams, who had dissuaded Monroe's black men from retaliating against the white community, was devastated.[107] On May 5, 1959, the day on which the second acquittal was announced, a furious Williams told news reporters who covered the trial that blacks themselves would have to take action. Since they could not rely on the government for justice and protection, he said, African Americans would have to "meet violence with violence" and "be willing to kill if necessary." If it required lynching to stop lynching, Williams burst out, blacks would have no choice but to retaliate in kind.[108]

The following morning, as newspapers across the country published verbatim quotes of Williams's statement, a fuming Roy Wilkins telephoned the North Carolina activist. Wilkins interrogated Williams, first asking whether the statement that he had read in the newspapers was correct. Not only was it correct, a belligerent Williams retorted, but he intended to make the very same statement on national TV that afternoon.[109] Wilkins had heard enough. Only a few hours later, he informed Williams of his suspension as president of Monroe's NAACP chapter. His "meet violence with violence" statement, Wilkins explained in a letter to Williams, was "in direct violation of the national policy of the NAACP" and jeopardized "the position and the effective functioning of the Association."[110] Wilkins simultaneously issued an official repudiation of Williams's utterances. In a press release, the Association's executive secretary conceded that the apparent "double standard of justice" angered many African Americans, but he averred that his organization had "never in its history advocated the use of violence."[111]

A few days later, a much calmer Williams clarified his emotional remarks in the media, explaining that he was far from calling upon African Americans to "go out and attempt to get revenge for mistreatments or injustice." Rather, since blacks could not rely on the Constitution for protection against mob violence, they should "defend themselves on the spot whenever they are attacked by whites."[112] But in the mind of the NAACP's board of directors, these belated attempts to clarify his outburst were not sufficient to spare him from disciplinary measures. During a meeting on May 11, 1959, the board upheld the suspension of Williams.[113]

Contrary to the impression of Williams, neither Wilkins nor the national NAACP opposed the right to armed self-defense. Speaking at a fund-raising dinner in Chicago on June 12, 1959, Wilkins stated: "Of course, we must defend ourselves when attacked. This is our right under all known laws." Wilkins found the assertion that his organization refuted this right preposterous.[114] Indeed, the NAACP's tireless efforts to provide legal council to Ossian Sweet and other African Americans who faced prosecution for protecting themselves from white aggression had established its reputation as a steadfast champion of the right to self-defense.

What Wilkins did object to was what he believed to be the use of violence as a deliberate strategy. Accordingly, he was determined to protect the NAACP from any accusations that it favored such tactics. Journalist Robert Penn Warren would later note the "vein of hard realism in Mr. Wilkins' thinking."[115] The Williams controversy was a reflection of this realism. Rather than stemming from disagreements over a black man's right to protect himself, the prompt suspension of Williams was an example of the Association's hardheaded public relations policy. Already in the early 1950s the NAACP had put its reputation for reasonableness before supporting those activists who questioned the conservative consensus. During a period that was overshadowed by anti-Communist hysteria, the NAACP quickly distanced itself from leftist members such as veteran activist W.E.B. Du Bois and prominent singer Paul Robeson.[116] As historian Manfred Berg has pointed out, these efforts to disprove allegations that Communists had infiltrated the organization were rather opportunistic but helped the Association survive an era that virtually paralyzed civil rights activism well into the mid-1950s.[117]

Robert Williams uttered his militant statement at a time when the NAACP continued to suffer from the fallout of this anti-Communist onslaught. The previous year, moreover, Roy Wilkins had officially pledged that his organization would use every weapon except violence to win the struggle for civil rights.[118] As journalist and Williams supporter Julian Mayfield rightly concluded in 1961, supporting Williams would certainly have cost the Association credibility, political influence, and financial contributions from white sympathizers.[119] Particularly in 1959, when the NAACP prepared for its fiftieth anniversary celebration in New York City amidst continued charges of Communist infiltration from southern segregationists, this support seemed essential.

The Williams controversy also highlighted lingering class differences within the hierarchical organization, which black nationalist Marcus Garvey once mocked as the "National Association for the Advancement of Certain People."[120] Like Garvey, Williams and his followers accused Wilkins and the NAACP of being "just interested in a few Negroes, not the masses of Negroes."[121] Wilkins was aware of such grassroots opposition and grew concerned that NAACP dissidents would use the Williams case to challenge both his leadership and the organization's hierarchy. The specter of losing power only heightened his personal animosity toward the militant North Carolinian. To him, Williams was "a tragic sort of stubbornly resentful David, convinced that the Light and Call have struck him and him only of all the prophets and crusaders on this question down through the decades."[122] As long as he was in command, Wilkins would brook no dissent.

In the realm of public relations, Wilkins's handling of the Monroe story had the desired effect. The white media unanimously praised his decision to reprimand the militant North Carolinian. The *Charlotte Observer* found that the "the N.A.A.C.P. moved wisely in suspending Robert Williams as president of its Union County chapter."[123] The *Winston-Salem Journal Sunday and Sentinel* editorialized that "law-abiding citizens of both races can applaud the prompt action of NAACP leaders in disassociating themselves from Mr. Williams' alarming statements."[124] Northern newspapers similarly approved of Wilkins's actions. For example, the *Newark Evening News* stated that Wilkins had "reinforced his own and his organization's position by his prompt repudiation and suspension of the chapter president."[125] In short, Wilkins's forceful condemnation of Williams had won the NAACP a major public relations victory.

Wilkins skillfully used the NAACP's fiftieth anniversary convention in July to settle both the Williams debate and the looming challenge to his leadership once and for all. Lobbying the delegates to affirm the suspension of Williams, the Association's executive secretary distributed a pamphlet entitled "The Single Issue in the Robert F. Williams Case" among the delegates. In the leaflet, Wilkins reminded readers of "the orderly legal, legislative and educational procedure the NAACP" had "successfully pursued for half a century." The Monroe case, he insisted, was not about self-defense or free speech but only about Williams's "call for aggressive, premeditated violence."[126]

During the tumultuous convention, the "Lancelot of Monroe," as Wilkins once derided Williams, attempted to sway the delegates, reiterating that he had never called for more than self-defense. But Williams faced overwhelming odds. The Association's powerful executive secretary had secured the support of an array of renowned black speakers who unanimously denounced Williams's call to arms.[127] Most prominent among them was Martin Luther King, who joined Wilkins in portraying Williams as a dangerous agitator. According to King, who spoke on the evening of July 17, "to privately or publicly call for retaliatory violence as a strategy during this period would be the gravest tragedy that could befall us." He warned that black violence would not only cost the movement white support but would also invite brutal retaliation by racist southerners, who might use such incidents as an excuse for murdering African Americans.[128] The other speakers voiced similar criticism, accusing Williams of violating King's nonviolent ideal. Even Daisy Bates, who continued to rely on armed guards for her safety, condemned the militant activist.[129] In the end, Wilkins's lobbying efforts paid off. The delegates unanimously affirmed the suspension of Williams, endorsing the board's verdict that his statement implied "violence as a means of redress of wrongs and not in self-defense of rights of person or property."[130]

In many ways, the scathing criticism of Wilkins, King, and other civil rights leaders was a tactical concession to the political realities of civil rights protest. As King had argued, praising or condoning Williams's stance would certainly have alienated many white supporters. Williams might have been aware of such strategic considerations, but he did not feel that they justified the NAACP's harsh disciplinary measures. Feeling misjudged and insulted, Williams responded to his critics in the September issue of the pacifist magazine *Liberation*. In "Can Negroes Afford to Be Pacifists?" Williams argued for "diverse tactics and philosophies" in the civil rights struggle and impugned the merits of Martin Luther King's philosophy. Clearly simplifying Gandhi's teachings, he argued that nonviolence was "a very potent weapon when the opponent" was "civilized." But King's "turn-the-other-cheekism" could be "no match or repellent for a sadist." Since whites would answer philosophical nonviolence only with "brutal attack on cringing, submissive Negroes," African Americans across the South needed to prepare for armed self-defense. Refuting King's argument that resistance would provoke white retaliation, Williams contended that armed actions actually lessened racial tensions by deterring white attackers.[131]

His blistering attacks did not go unanswered. A month later, *Liberation* published a rejoinder by both Roy Wilkins and King. Wilkins's assessment of the issue had changed little. He insisted that Williams's statement "spread the false impression that the NAACP supports lynching and mob violence," which would have endangered "the effectiveness of the NAACP" across the country.[132] By contrast, King's carefully crafted article titled "The Social Organization of Nonviolence" provided a thorough discussion of the debate's divergent positions. He readily admitted that few blacks would follow his abstract philosophy and conceded that self-defense remained a legitimate concept that not even Gandhi would have opposed. But King strongly condemned what he believed to be Williams's "advocacy of violence as a tool of advancement, organized as in warfare, deliberately and consciously." Not only would this fail to rally people to join the movement, King argued, it also implied that there was "no effective and practical alternative." The SCLC's president averred that well-organized nonviolent protest such as boycotts, sit-ins, and mass demonstrations would be much more effective than what Williams had in mind.[133]

Although the Williams controversy was largely confined to movement circles, the dispute was highly significant because it indicated that King's philosophy of nonviolence was well on its way to become the movement's official credo. In part, this was a consequence of King's rising fame in the national media. By 1957, as Peter Ling has pointed out, the young minister "was already a star, more famous for being famous and for his words than for his current actions."[134] Although King had not led any major civil rights campaign in the years after the Montgomery bus boycott, his evolving ideas on nonviolent protest coupled with the founding of SCLC had caught the public's attention. The Williams debate highlighted some of the same themes that King stressed in his speeches and public statements. Thus nonviolence, reconciliation, and love—rather than diverse tactics and armed self-defense—began to emerge as the dominant points of reference for the American media. Consequently, given the ambiguous connotations of armed force against white aggression, movement leaders found it increasingly difficult to endorse black militancy publicly.

CORE's internal debates on the Williams case illustrate the pragmatism that characterized the politics of nonviolence. As a result of the growing popularity of King, CORE's meager finances had experienced a major boost in the aftermath of the Montgomery bus boycott. Unlike the NAACP, whose funds consisted of both membership dues and financial gifts, CORE was largely dependent on individual contributions from sympathetic whites. With King's help, who frequently lent his name to the organization's fund-raising efforts, CORE nearly doubled the number of its contributors between 1954 and 1957.[135]

In a discussion on the use of the "meet violence with violence" controversy for fund-raising purposes, acclaimed southern author Lillian Smith, one of CORE's longtime allies, argued that emphasizing a strong commitment to Gandhian principles might raise additional funds.[136] Smith was dissatisfied with a fund-raising letter that CORE's executive director James Robinson had asked her to sign. Robinson's original draft joined in the public condemnation of the NAACP firebrand's call to arms. "I was alarmed when one Southern Negro leader recently declared that Negroes should meet violence with violence," the letter began. Unless CORE received generous financial support to train blacks in the art of nonviolent protest, Robinson predicted, the "spread of bitterness" among blacks would "almost inevitably" lead "to violence and bloodshed."[137]

Smith disapproved of the way in which Robinson exploited Williams. "To say that a southern Negro leader had advocated violence (for me to say it)," she explained, "would shock many southern Negro leaders." Smith also suspected that Robinson's wording would terrify white supporters and bolster the position of white racists.[138] After revising Robinson's draft, Smith was certain that she had "put the pressure on where it counts: People are afraid of violence." If CORE's appeal could assure readers that "their five dollars or ten or fifty can help keep down violence they are more likely to send it—even those who do not understand what we mean by the philosophy of nonviolence."[139] In the end, CORE mailed fifty thousand copies of Smith's letter to potential contributors.[140] Smith's fund-raising concept, while clearly distorting the realities of the southern freedom struggle, clearly illustrates how movement leaders sought to mute debates on armed militancy while highlighting an unwavering commitment to Gandhi to sustain white support.

The Monroe story had already vanished from newspaper stands when on February 1, 1960, four African American students from the North Carolina Agricultural and Technical College in Greensboro triggered a nonviolent sit-in movement against segregated lunch counters, which spread like wildfire across the South. Within a mere two months, black students had launched protests in fifty-four cities in nine southern states, reviving the stagnating freedom movement and forcing Woolworth and other national companies to integrate their diners and lunch counters in many parts of the region.[141] The method that the students used—occupying all available seats at the counters and accepting white harassment and beatings as well as arrest without retaliation—echoed CORE's campaigns against segregated restaurants in the 1940s. Seeing its pioneering technique practiced across Dixie, CORE was the only organization with enough expertise and manpower to assist the emerging student movement. Immediately after the sit-ins began, CORE workers fanned out to black college campuses, offering workshops in nonviolent resistance and organizing new affiliates. Long considered a "never-never land," the South soon boasted numerous new CORE chapters.[142]

Not only CORE hoped to benefit from the unexpected surge in student activism. Martin Luther King and Roy Wilkins also intended to infuse their organizations with fresh blood and youthful enthusiasm. Veteran activist Ella Baker, however, after experiencing the restrictive hierarchies of both the NAACP and SCLC, encouraged the young activists to remain independent. During a student conference that Baker organized in Raleigh, North Carolina, on April 16, 1960, she exposed some 120 delegates to her vision of conducting "spadework"— developing local leadership in southern black communities.[143]

Besides Baker, Martin Luther King and James Lawson, a thirty-one-year-old black Methodist divinity student at Vanderbilt University in Nashville, were the main speakers. In their remarks, both men stressed the importance of nonviolence as a way of life and encouraged the young activists to adopt Gandhi's teachings. The large student delegation from Nashville dominated the following discussions. Most of them were black ministerial students who, under the guidance of devout pacifist Lawson, had become dedicated *Satyagrahis*.[144] The passionate speeches of King and Lawson generated an enthusiasm for nonviolent activism among all delegates. In the end, the young activists chose to found their own organization: the Student Nonviolent Coordinating Committee (SNCC). Marion Barry, a black chemistry graduate student from Fisk University in Nashville, became its first chairman.[145]

The new group's statement of purpose seemed to reflect a deeply felt commitment to nonviolent principles. "We affirm the philosophical or religious ideal of nonviolence as the foundation of our purpose, the presupposition of our faith, and the manner of our action," it read. SNCC pledged to strive for "a social order of justice permeated by love," which would remain "loving and forgiving even in the midst of hostility." Echoing King's rhetoric, SNCC vowed to appeal to the conscience of men, and thereby create an atmosphere of justice and reconciliation.[146]

But these idealistic words, which had been penned by Lawson, reflected the author's religious pacifism rather than the new organization's unanimous acceptance of King's teachings. Founding member Charles "Chuck" McDew, a student from South Carolina State University who would succeed Barry as chairman in 1961, later recalled that most students "saw nonviolence as a viable sort of method" but were far from embracing it as a philosophical imperative. According to McDew, devout Gandhians remained "a distinct minority." He and his fellow students from South Carolina "took the position that it was totally inconceivable that we would accept nonviolence as way of life."[147] In fact, except for the students from Nashville, the majority of SNCC's founding members viewed nonviolence merely as a tactic.[148] But in the early 1960s, such minor notes of discord could not dampen the students' enthusiasm.

Like the sit-in movement, the Freedom Ride of 1961 became a demonstration of the power of nonviolent direct action. CORE's plan to test the recent *Boynton v. Virginia* Supreme Court decision, which had declared segregated waiting rooms and restaurants in interstate travel unconstitutional, echoed its first national campaign, the Journey of Reconciliation. In 1947, interracial teams of activists had traveled the Upper South to test a Supreme Court ruling that had outlawed segregation on interstate buses and trains. Although black veterans had to rescue the activists from an angry white mob in Chapel Hill, North Carolina, the media virtually ignored the Journey.[149]

By contrast, the Freedom Ride led activists into the Deep South, the very heart of white supremacy. CORE rightly suspected that few reporters would be able to ignore the massive violence that they expected to encounter in Alabama and Mississippi. The campaign, then, was a calculated risk to draw federal and public attention to racial segregation. But this time, the stakes were much higher. When the integrated group of thirteen activists boarded two buses in Washington, D.C., on May 4, 1961, few of them expected to make it back alive. As Gandhi had pointed out, nonviolent direct action required both discipline and courage to the point of accepting death as a witness to the brutal injustice of Jim Crow. Contrary to Robert Williams's claim in *Liberation*, the Freedom Riders could hardly be called submissive cowards.

The violence that greeted the protestors in Anniston, Alabama, on May 14, when an angry mob of white people bloodied the Freedom Riders and bombed one of the buses, made front pages around the world. More racist attacks in the following days promised utter embarrassment for the United States in the eyes of international audiences, which impelled President John F. Kennedy to dispatch troops to protect the activists. On May 24, after a round of negotiations with the Kennedy administration, a cordon of police cars as well as a helicopter accompanied the activists from Montgomery to their next stop, Jackson, Mississippi. Despite their arrest in Jackson, the Freedom Riders had won a major victory. Pressured by the White House, the Interstate Commerce Commission eventually issued official regulations to enforce the desegregation of interstate travel facilities.[150]

As evidenced by the Freedom Ride, nonviolent protest, by deliberately provoking a violent white response, not only drew national and international attention. More important, the crisis that racist attacks against black activists created compelled the federal government to protect the lives of civil rights protestors and to assist in the enforcement of integration in interstate travel. Yet it is doubtful that the movement's white supporters fully grasped the coercive qualities of nonviolent protest. One moderate probably spoke for many when he commended the Freedom Riders for their "practice of nonviolence and love toward those that hated you and brought violence against you."[151] From this perspective, activists from CORE and SNCC assumed the role of passive martyrs who appealed to the conscience of ruthless white racists.

A group of mainly white civil rights activists who traveled to Monroe, North Carolina, to assist Robert Williams in his struggle against racial segregation learned that nonviolent campaigns that drew no national media attention would compel no one to protect the movement against white aggression. Williams, whose suspension as president of the local NAACP chapter had not dashed his spirit, welcomed their help, but he simultaneously viewed their presence as an opportunity to prove "that what King and them were preaching was bullshit."[152] In *Negroes with Guns*, a brief account of the Monroe movement, the former marine stressed that he was far from opposing King's philosophy per se but rather believed that the movement "shouldn't take the attitude that one method alone is the way for liberation."[153]

In August 1961, Williams's young visitors were quickly disabused of the notion that their protest would have an immediate impact on the entrenched traditions of white supremacy. A spontaneous picketing campaign against segregation did not desegregate Monroe but triggered a violent race riot that forced Robert Williams to flee the city after rumors circulated that local police, National Guardsmen, and Ku Klux Klan forces planned to invade the town's black neighborhood. After a perilous odyssey from North Carolina to Canada, while being hunted by the FBI for allegedly kidnapping a white couple who had strayed into the black neighborhood during the riot, Williams eventually managed to reach Cuban exile.[154]

Now branded a gun-toting militant, a Communist, and a kidnapper, Williams became a serious liability in the eyes of black civil rights leaders. In the aftermath of the Monroe debacle, for example, CORE was at pains to avoid the impression that it approved of the militant North Carolinian. When James Farmer received a call for funds from the Committee to Aid the Monroe Defendants (CAMD), an organization that had been formed by white supporters to assist in the legal defense of several activists who, like Williams, had been charged with kidnapping, CORE's National Action Committee refused to support the CAMD's cause.[155]

A year after CORE's successful efforts to stay clear of the potentially damaging effects of supporting Williams, SCLC's protest campaign in Birmingham, Alabama, once more proved the effectiveness of organized nonviolent direct action. One year prior to the Alabama project, King had suffered a humiliating defeat in Albany, Georgia, where local sheriff Laurie Pritchet parried SCLC's demonstrations with a nonviolent strategy of his own. Together with activists' failure to realize that a general attack on all aspects of segregation would soon exhaust the local movement's momentum, Pritchet's policy of restraint earned the police chief praise by whites and frustrated SCLC's efforts to dramatize the injustice of Jim Crow in the media.[156]

In Birmingham, therefore, King's organization focused on the economic aspects of segregation, launching a boycott against the city's discriminatory white merchants. In addition, SCLC's carefully staged nonviolent demonstrations provoked a violent white response that led to the breakdown of public order and focused the world's attention on the injustice of segregation. The tactical advantages of the nonviolent strategy were obvious: the SCLC's carefully staged morality play, in which violence was aimed solely at peaceful protestors, put both southern segregationists and national authorities on the defensive. In the eyes of national and international audiences, it was impossible to deny the legitimacy of black demands. Consequently, it became increasingly difficult for white authorities to justify delays in yielding to these demands. Moreover, neither city administrations nor federal authorities were eager to struggle with a sustained breakdown of public order. Finally, the economic leverage that blacks wielded through sustained boycotts forced white merchants to learn an important lesson: if one followed the logic of capitalism, maintaining racial discrimination was simply unprofitable.

Yet, despite these tactical benefits of nonviolence, maintaining discipline at Birmingham's demonstrations proved difficult. To many local blacks, remaining peaceful in the face of attack seemed simply implausible. SCLC staffer Andrew Young remembered years later: "Everybody looks at the Birmingham demonstration and thinks that there was some sort of miracle performed, but it was a lot of hard work." "Birmingham," he said, "was not a nonviolent city. . . . [it] was probably the most violent city in America, and every black family had an arsenal."[157] A number of African Americans brought their weapons to the demonstrations. As one activist recalled, SCLC organizers "used to have to run people home, because they would bring their guns and that kind of thing."[158] Before some marches, King's aides collected trash cans full of knives, razors, and other weapons, urging people not to hit back when attacked.[159]

Unsurprisingly, the patience of those blacks who were not directly involved in the local movement was wearing thin even more rapidly. In May, armed protection gave way to violent protest. During the night of May 11, 1963, a powerful dynamite blast destroyed the hotel room of Martin Luther King, while another bomb damaged the house of King's brother, A.D. Both men were absent when the bombers struck, but shortly after the two blasts had roused Birmingham's residents from their sleep, thousands of angry blacks surged into the streets. During the turmoil that followed, bricks and bottles rained down on police officers, while a group of black men overturned a car and set it afire. Hastily called in state troopers struggled to quell the upheaval until after dawn. The *New York Times* considered the riot "without a doubt one of the worst racial explosions seen in the South in years."[160]

The fact that the movement's nonviolent image remained intact despite such examples of black rage was a result of both civil rights leaders' rhetorical strategies and the media's tendency to neglect certain incidents of black violence. As Jenny Walker has demonstrated, both conservative and moderate journalists had reason to downplay events that challenged the movement's nonviolent reputation. Some liberal white journalists did so out of concern that such reports might undermine the effectiveness and moral power of the nonviolent movement. Conservative southern pundits frequently opted not to report about black violence because they felt that nonviolent protest already drew enough negative attention to the South's white supremacist traditions. Some black newspapers, on the other hand, remained largely silent on black violence because they frequently faced economic reprisals and violent threats if they published accounts about such incidents.[161]

Probably in part because of the media's multilayered agendas, the efforts of some Birmingham blacks to organize for self-defense in the face of a new wave of racist terrorism in September 1963 went largely unnoticed. On Sunday, September 15, 1963, a women's Sunday school class was discussing the topic "The Love That Forgives" in Sixteenth Street Baptist Church when a powerful explosion shook the building. Between scattered plaster and other debris that covered the floor of the destroyed basement, four little black girls lay dead, while fourteen others crawled out of the ruins injured and shocked. Black residents were outraged at the crime, and thousands of them assembled in the streets, throwing stones and bottles at the police. Throughout the day, sporadic gunfire echoed in the black section of town. At the end of the day, two other black teenagers had fallen victim to racial violence—one shot by a police officer, the other boy slain by a local segregationist. These murders further aggravated the city's volatile atmosphere.[162]

Once the first wave of anger had passed, African American residents organized the protection of their community. In a black upper-class neighborhood that was known as "Dynamite Hill" because it had become one of white bombers' favorite targets, residents set up a guard system with observation posts and communications networks to prevent further attacks. Armed blacks regularly patrolled their neighborhood and searched churches and other buildings for explosives.[163] As in Montgomery, armed protection became a largely invisible means of support for the nonviolent movement.

While Martin Luther King may have been personally troubled by such examples of armed militancy, he clearly understood that most African Americans adopted nonviolence as a tactic, not as a way of life. "I think it is still true that people by and large are using it as a technique and not following it as a philosophy," King conceded in an interview in November 1963. "But I think that most of the students and adults who have engaged in nonviolent demonstrations have felt that nonviolence is the best practical technique for the Negro . . . and they have followed it for that reason." Nonviolence was so powerful, the civil rights leader said, "because it can bring about these meaningful changes, it can rally people, and it works." Like CORE's James Farmer in the 1940s, King did not intend to convert a majority of black Americans to *Satyagraha*. Rather, he planned to convince them of the practical necessity to resort to the nonviolent strategy.[164]

At the same time, King was a skillful politician who was well aware that the movement was dependent on white support. His pledges to inculcate in African Americans a deep commitment to the philosophy of nonviolence reflected these tactical entanglements. Already in his first book, *Stride Toward Freedom*, written shortly after the Montgomery bus boycott, King argued that blacks had to "meet the forces of hate with the power of love" and insisted that nonviolence did "not seek to defeat or humiliate the opponent, but to win his friendship and understanding." Coupled with his exhortations that activists would have to abjure "not only external physical violence but also internal violence of the spirit," such statements reinforced connotations of passiveness and clearly implied that blacks ought to adopt nonviolence as a way of life.[165]

SCLC, too, hammered home the message that means and ends were inseparable. "Only through nonviolence," one pamphlet quoted the organization's constitution, "can reconciliation and the creation of the beloved community be effected."[166] In a manifesto penned during a nonviolent workshop in 1959, SCLC pledged "to adhere to the best of our ability to the practice of Christian love and nonviolence, not simply as a tactical measure, but always moving towards it as an all embracing rule of conduct."[167] In a similar fashion, a brochure on the genesis of nonviolent protest explained that activists would launch direct action only if "actual love" was felt for their adversaries.[168]

If white America was hopeful that an increasing number of blacks would adopt King's teachings, King and SCLC appeared determined to meet such expectations. In his message to SCLC's annual convention in 1963, for example, King warned against the "great temptation to accept nonviolence solely as a strategy." One of SCLC's chief aims therefore was "to broadly disseminate . . . the heart of nonviolence, that our commitment to nonviolence will not only be a technique, but shall become for us a way of life with love and redemption as its center."[169] One year later, delegates supported a resolution that reiterated the need "to inculcate in others the philosophy of nonviolence" as SCLC's "prime responsibility."[170]

King's second book, *Why We Can't Wait*, which was published in 1964, echoed such idealistic pledges. Not only did he claim that African Americans had broken with America's "eye-for-an-eye philosophy." He also averred that the teachings of Gandhi and Jesus enabled the black man to "transmute hatred into constructive energy, to seek not only to free himself but to free his oppressor from his sins."[171] Disseminated and amplified by the mass media, King's message probably reassured white liberal Americans that their financial contributions as well as their moral support were invested in a cause worth fighting for.

While it is difficult to determine how white movement supporters perceived the message of King and other civil rights leaders, there is some evidence to suggest that the movement's pledges had the desired effect. During the Birmingham crisis, for example, hundreds of letters from sympathetic whites inundated SCLC's headquarters in Atlanta, commending King and his followers for their "peaceful" campaign. One white man from Chicago was "especially impressed by the extreme degree of patience and passiveness that you and your fellow workers have shown in light of the dastardly acts of white people without a conscience."[172] Another admirer from Madison, Wisconsin, expressed her hope that King and SCLC would continue their "non-violent and passive resistant [*sic*] technique."[173]

Yet, while King's abstract philosophy was essential to the success of the movement, it circumscribed the ability of national civil rights leaders to talk about nonviolence in tactical terms, let alone to justify black self-defense. As white terrorists continued to bomb churches, burn crosses, and shoot at activists in the Deep South, the movement's predicaments grew in direct proportion to the media's attention to black self-defense efforts. In Tuscaloosa, Alabama, however, where armed resistance became an integral part of the local freedom movement, African American activists managed to keep the media's interest focused on nonviolent protest.

2

GANDHI, GOD, AND GUNS IN TUSCALOOSA

Martin Luther King's Christian-Gandhian philosophy deeply affected the American public, but its impact upon those who closely worked with him was far greater. T. Y. Rogers was one black activist who committed himself to fighting for nonviolent social change after serving as King's assistant minister during the final months of the Montgomery bus boycott. After graduating from Alabama State College in Montgomery in 1955, the gangly Alabama native initially considered a career as a high school teacher. But he quit within a year and chose instead to become a minister.[1]

Although King was only six years his senior, Rogers felt inspired by Montgomery's boycott leader when serving at Dexter Avenue Baptist Church. His admiration went so far that he began to study King's sermons to emulate his preaching style. Immersing himself in the Gospel and Gandhian philosophy, Rogers adopted nonviolence as his way of life. With the help of his teacher, Rogers later entered Crozer Theological Seminary in Pennsylvania, King's alma mater. After graduating in 1960, the young man assumed the pastorship of Galilee Baptist Church in Philadelphia. As one of the numerous ministers who participated in the Rev. Leon Sullivan's highly successful boycott campaign against employment discrimination in the city's white-owned businesses, he honed his skills as civil rights organizer.

When King informed him in 1963 that the First African Baptist Church in Tuscaloosa, Alabama, planned to call a new minister, Rogers was overjoyed.

He longed to return to his native state to become more involved in the southern freedom struggle. He knew that Tuscaloosa would provide an opportunity to do so. With King's recommendation and a style of preaching virtually identical to that of his mentor, Rogers easily secured the prestigious position at the city's oldest and largest church. The arrival of the Baptist minister and his wife, LaPelzia, in Tuscaloosa in January 1964 marked the beginning of a rejuvenated nonviolent freedom movement, which would force white authorities to integrate the city by spring of 1965.

However, although Rogers seemed to follow in his idol's philosophical footsteps, he accepted and benefited from the decision of black Tuscaloosans to arm for protection against white aggression. Similar to the experience of King in the early days of the Montgomery boycott or that of Fred Shuttlesworth in Birmingham, a highly sophisticated defense group that formed in June 1964 made sure that the minister remained unharmed. Like its precursor in Birmingham, the Tuscaloosa squad was secretive, well organized, and followed the orders of a combat-experienced army veteran. The armed group protected black activists and white allies against Ku Klux Klan attacks for several years and on one occasion rescued nonviolent protestors from an angry white mob. Tuscaloosa's indigenous freedom movement, while largely ignored by civil rights scholars, thus provides another example of how nonviolent direct action and armed resistance worked side by side in southern civil rights campaigns.[2]

Located about fifty miles southwest of Birmingham, Tuscaloosa was an industrial and manufacturing city. One-third of the city's sixty-three thousand residents were black. Although African Americans had challenged segregation in numerous Alabamian cities by 1964, the "Druid City" remained a blank spot on the map of the civil rights movement. Rigid racial segregation continued to permeate public life, and whites had traditionally used violence to enforce it.[3] The city's Ku Klux Klan had a long and brutal history. During the Great Depression, the county seat of Tuscaloosa County remained a stronghold of the hooded order. In 1933, Klansmen killed several blacks accused of raping white women. In the aftermath of the lynching, frenzied white mobs destroyed local black homes, churches, and businesses.[4] Although diminished in numbers after World War II, the Klan continued to menace Tuscaloosa County's African American residents with cross burnings and parades through their communities. Police brutality too was common. In particular, when black men appeared to violate the old taboo of interracial dating, white officers' punishment was swift. In the early 1950s, a shy glance at a white girl could still bring arrest and jail, as a local white lawyer who defended such a court case later recalled.[5]

The first challenge to segregation came in 1956 when lawyers from the NAACP successfully argued that Tuscaloosa's prestigious University of Alabama could not deny the enrollment of African Americans. That year, on February 1, after a three-year battle in the courts, a shy and nervous young woman named Autherine Lucy arrived at the all-white campus. Accompanied by Birmingham civil rights leader Fred Shuttlesworth, she was determined to become the university's first black graduate. But white animosity was palpable as soon as Lucy walked to her first classes. Many of the more than seven thousand students enrolled at the university at that time opposed integration. On February 6, some of them joined a crowd of about five hundred angry whites from the Tuscaloosa area, yelling racial epithets and pelting Lucy with eggs and gravel.[6]

Officers of the state highway patrol finally rescued her from the mob and brought the unnerved woman to the safety of the city's black neighborhood. At Howard and Linton's barbershop, beauticians washed Lucy's hair and cleaned her clothes, while the white mob began to regroup in the vicinity of the shop. Its owner, Nathaniel Howard Sr., feared that the crowd of enraged whites might attack Lucy and immediately dispatched telephone calls to his friends, asking for protection. Shortly thereafter, black men armed with rifles and shotguns arrived on the scene. Confronted with this little army, the white crowd weighed its chances and then, discouraged, gradually dispersed. Later that afternoon, the armed men escorted Lucy to nearby Birmingham.[7]

When NAACP lawyer Thurgood Marshall arrived there a few days later to challenge the university's decision to expel the black student, African American residents took no chances. At night, men armed with machine guns guarded the home of Marshall's host, a local NAACP lawyer. When Lucy's trial began at the end of February, armed watchmen positioned themselves along the route to the federal building, where the trial took place. But Marshall's efforts proved fruitless. The court upheld the young woman's expulsion.[8]

The injustice of the Lucy incident stirred black Tuscaloosans. They knew all too well the humiliating feeling of being discriminated against on the basis of skin color. But in the 1950s, few of them seriously considered engaging in political activism to challenge the racial status quo. On occasion, a small group of men met at Nathaniel Howard's barbershop to discuss the community's grievances. In addition, a few businessmen sometimes met with representatives of the city administration to discuss ways in which race relations could be improved, but with little success.[9]

Only a black Baptist minister named W. B. Sheeley seriously attempted to organize for active protest. When Sheeley became the pastor of the city's prestigious First African Baptist Church in the early 1950s, he openly discussed civil rights and began to hold small meetings. Prior to 1956, when Alabama attorney general Lloyd Patterson banned the NAACP from the state, Sheeley also urged the Association's Tuscaloosa chapter to become more active in the local freedom struggle. But his conservative middle-class congregation, which consisted mostly of businesspeople, teachers, and school principals, vehemently opposed his efforts. Comparably well off and respected in their community, few of them were willing to risk their status. Black teachers in particular were likely to lose their jobs if white authorities learned that they officially supported racial integration. By the time that Autherine Lucy arrived in Tuscaloosa, the church had already forced Sheeley to resign.[10] Only the Ministers' Alliance, a small group that six young black preachers had founded in the mid-1950s, remained interested in organizing for social change. The group's semi-public meetings resulted in no overt protest, but the concerned pastors were willing to take a stand against discrimination and injustice.[11]

In spring of 1962, the Ministers' Alliance evolved into Tuscaloosa's first active civil rights organization. The group's involvement grew out of an incident on the city's bus line. On May 5, 1962, a white bus driver ordered three students from Tuscaloosa's black Stillman College and one high school student to vacate the front seats for two white passengers. Since Tuscaloosa had adopted an official policy of nonsegregated seating in 1957, the teenagers angrily refused and started a heated argument with the driver. As the debate went on, a few students left the bus and rushed to find Willie Herzfeld, a black minister who they believed would be willing to support them. Herzfeld was a member of the Ministers' Alliance since he moved to Tuscaloosa in 1960 and had been a counselor to the first sit-in protestors in Greensboro, North Carolina. He immediately agreed to assist the students and hurried to the bus stop to settle the argument, but his efforts were unsuccessful. About an hour after the incident began, police arrested the four students on disorderly conduct charges.[12]

That night, after a local black physician named Woody Robinson had bailed out the four youths, Herzfeld invited several members of the alliance and a handful of black community leaders to attend an emergency meeting. During the gathering at Herzfeld's Christ Lutheran Church, this group decided to form the Tuscaloosa Citizens for Action Committee (TCAC). Herzfeld became the new organization's president and immediately started negotiations with the bus line about their ambiguous stance on segregation. In addition, hundreds of students from Stillman College marched in protest, blocking the buses that approached the campus. In the end, TCAC secured the bus company's assurance that it would ban any future discrimination and harassment. Buoyed by this victory, TCAC affiliated with Martin Luther King's Southern Christian Leadership Conference and held a number of meetings at the churches of Herzfeld and TCAC's vice president, Methodist minister Rev. Norman Stevenson.[13]

But few African Americans supported Herzfeld's ambitious plan to fight for full equality in Tuscaloosa. Neighbors avoided him and his pregnant wife on the street, and his relationship with fellow ministers quickly deteriorated. Worse, he received numerous death threats from white residents, prompting some members of his church to guard the activist's home with guns. "[A]t that point," Herzfeld recalled years later, "I guess I was the loneliest man in the city of Tuscaloosa."[14] Although the activist minister continued to meet with SCLC's Alabama affiliates for another year, he knew that his efforts were leading nowhere. Herzfeld's denomination was a major obstacle to mobilizing the black community. As a Lutheran minister, he faced an overwhelming majority of established Baptist preachers, few of whom were willing to support the dangerous ventures of a relatively unknown newcomer. Since the rest of TCAC's officers were comprised of Methodists, Herzfeld was able to reach only a small fraction of the city's African American population.[15] Even if the Baptist ministers had supported TCAC, however, building a local movement would have proved difficult. Teachers and principals employed with the local board of education still feared losing their jobs and thus opposed civil rights activism, while black businessmen worried about possible economic sanctions by the white community.[16]

More than economic pressure, African Americans feared the United Klans of America (UKA). Its leader, ex-tire salesman Robert Shelton, managed the powerful UKA from a modestly furnished three-room suite in an old office building in downtown Tuscaloosa. The blond and blue-eyed Shelton, whose father and grandfather had already burned crosses in the name of white supremacy, joined the Klan in the early 1950s. While crisscrossing Alabama to promote the products of a Tuscaloosa rubber company, Shelton became a skillful Klan organizer. Within a mere decade, he successfully laid claim to the most powerful position within the hierarchy of the Invisible Empire. During a meeting of several Klan groups in Indiana Springs, Georgia, in July 1961, the then only thirty-two-year-old was instrumental in uniting several splinter groups of the hooded order into the UKA. As the new organization's Imperial Wizard, Shelton managed to transform it into the largest multistate Klan of the 1960s.[17]

By that time, membership of the Ku Klux Klan had soared to over twenty thousand. This enormous increase was primarily a reaction to the failure of the White Citizens' Councils to stop desegregation through economic reprisals against the black community. Alarmed at the continuing prospect of integration in the late 1950s, a growing number of southern working-class whites favored the Klan's terrorist methods to halt the black freedom movement. In the following years, thousands of new members swelled the ranks of the Invisible Empire. Since Reconstruction, no hooded order had been as violent. According to historian Wynn Craig Wade, the Klan of the 1960s represented "a near-perfect replica" of the brutal vigilante group that Confederate veterans had founded in 1866.[18]

The UKA, which had recruited about thirty thousand members and sympathetic supporters in nine states by 1965, did much to establish the Klan's violent reputation. Although its leader, Robert Shelton, repeatedly denied his organization's proclivity to violent terror, the UKA's bloody record proved otherwise. Bomb making was the organization's specialty, and several of Shelton's most extreme Alabama "Klaverns" were responsible for dynamite bombings and racially inspired murders throughout the state.[19] With the headquarters of this violence-prone organization right on their doorstep, black Tuscaloosans undoubtedly feared its wrath.

By the time that two black students in the summer of 1963 made another attempt to break the color line at the University of Alabama, TCAC's efforts to build a local movement had fizzled. Since 1956, when a white mob had forced Autherine Lucy from campus, university trustees had devised a successful strategy to prevent similar incidents. Hiring private detectives to find incriminating material that could be used to disqualify potential black candidates, white officials had managed to throw out most applications. Vivian Malone and James Hood, however, two qualified African Americans who applied for admission in 1963, were outstanding citizens with faultless records. When it became clear that the university could not reject them, recently elected governor George Wallace announced that he would carry out his long-promised "stand in the schoolhouse door" to block school desegregation.[20]

In early June, an army of news reporters descended upon Tuscaloosa to cover the showdown between Wallace and the administration of President Kennedy, who had vowed to enforce integration on campus. On June 11, 1963, Deputy U.S. Attorney General Nicholas Katzenbach, soaked with sweat in the sweltering heat, faced Governor Wallace at the university's entrance. For several minutes, the ambitious segregationist lectured Katzenbach about states' rights and the tyranny of the federal government. Eventually, however, Wallace had to step aside. Later that day, Malone and Hood became the University of Alabama's first two official black students. Still, in the eyes of white southerners, Wallace's defiant gesture elevated him as the region's most prominent defender of white supremacy.[21]

Although the federal administration lauded the enrollment of Malone and Hood as a victory against segregation, their presence on campus had no impact on the situation of Tuscaloosa's black community. Restaurants, theaters, and other public facilities remained racially segregated. African Americans had not even witnessed the spectacle, since only university officials had been allowed on campus. Few of them cared. Rev. T. W. Linton spoke for many when he later explained, "The university was kind of a different world."[22] In fact, except for law professor Jay Murphy and his wife, Alberta, the white campus community rarely interacted with blacks. Unsurprisingly, the battle over the integration of the university did little to rally people, and even Willie Herzfeld balked at using the incident to make another attempt to win black support. Tired and frustrated, the Lutheran minister prayed for someone else to lead and organize the local freedom movement.[23]

In 1964, he got his wish, when the twenty-eight-year-old Baptist minister T. Y. Rogers arrived in Tuscaloosa. In Herzfeld's words, Rogers turned out to be "the catalyst" of the city's civil rights struggle. Herzfeld enthusiastically threw his full support behind the charismatic newcomer. He hoped that Rogers, with his experience in civil rights organizing, and as a Baptist head of one of the city's largest congregations, might be able to rejuvenate TCAC and win new converts to the civil rights cause.[24] "Look," Herzfeld told the new arrival, "I'm tired. I have worked, and they have not accepted me. . . . Maybe you are not tired and you can do something. Whatever you want to do, I'm with you in it."[25] Former members of TCAC also committed themselves to assisting Rogers. In this spirit, at a state meeting of SCLC in Montgomery, Herzfeld, Rogers, and three other ministers decided to revive TCAC with its veteran leadership. Rogers joined as the organization's new executive secretary.[26]

With a reliable organizing network already in place, TCAC immediately went to work. The first problem was how to involve Rogers's middle-class congregation, which had earlier forced W. B. Sheeley to resign. People's initial reaction to their new minister's message was indeed outright opposition.[27] But Rogers's charisma and eloquent oratory smoothed over the congregation's concerns. As Herzfeld reminisced later, shortly after the arrival of Rogers, the First African Baptist Church "was literally turned over to the civil rights movement."[28]

In February, TCAC cautiously began to spread its message among the black population. Its strategy was simple. "No one else was going to move," Rogers recalled of this difficult phase a few months later. "So we had to move, and hoped that . . . the people would join us in our efforts."[29] TCAC's first rallying point was voter registration, "a good catch-all," as Rogers explained. Canvassing the black neighborhoods together with a few SCLC field-workers, TCAC activists promoted the ballot and prepared the ground for their primary goal: nonviolent direct action.[30] "We knew that we would get involved in direct action," Rogers made plain, "but we could not say it to the people at this point. We had to first gain the confidence of a larger group of people before we could move into this area."[31] Although TCAC sought to mobilize the entire black population, college and high school students, who were less vulnerable to economic pressure, provided the bulk of the first mass meetings. By early March, when Martin Luther King visited Tuscaloosa to install Rogers as new pastor, TCAC had already won widespread support among the young.[32]

In April 1964, TCAC finally launched its nonviolent direct action campaign. Tuscaloosa's new county courthouse became the first target. Originally, the $3 million project had been planned without the "white" and "colored" signs, which traditionally segregated bathrooms, jails, and courtrooms. One year prior to the opening of the courthouse, the city administration had emphatically assured African Americans that no discriminatory signs would be erected. But when Governor Wallace came to Tuscaloosa on April 12, 1964, to dedicate the new building, the detested reminders of white supremacy were in place.[33] Tuscaloosa's leading white businessman, George LeMaistre, confided to an interviewer several months later that he too had presumed that the new courthouse would be integrated. He speculated that some of Wallace's overzealous followers, probably heeding his famous line "segregation now . . . segregation tomorrow . . . segregation forever," put up the signs in the belief that they acted in the interest of their racist governor.[34]

The courthouse controversy became an important rallying point for TCAC. "We felt that this was a good time to dramatize our situation," Rogers later commented on their decision to organize a nonviolent protest march to the courthouse. The march was unlikely to bring down the signs, but Rogers believed that TCAC could exploit the feud to recruit more people. In addition, he hoped that police would help dramatize the injustice of segregation by making mass arrests.[35] On April 16, TCAC sent a letter to probate judge David M. Cochrane and representatives of the city administration, demanding an end to the discriminatory practices at the courthouse. The activists hinted that if white authorities ignored their letter, blacks would launch nonviolent demonstrations.[36] In the following days, TCAC printed thousands of flyers calling for a large mass meeting at First African Baptist Church on Monday, April 20, and asked Baptist ministers to announce the meeting in their churches. Rogers also went on the air on the local black radio station, urging people to attend. Despite the growing popularity of TCAC, Rogers still had to calm a group of hostile black ministers, who threatened to denounce the demonstration publicly. Jealous of his prestigious position and superior education, they accused Rogers of assuming the role of the black community's sole spokesman. After assuring them that he made no claims to speak for every minister in the city, Rogers and TCAC went ahead and made final preparations for the protest march.[37]

The surprisingly large turnout of several hundred at the meeting on Monday night raised activists' spirits. TCAC was now prepared to march. Few people were surprised when the County Board of Revenue unanimously voted on Tuesday to deny blacks' demands. In response, the TCAC officially announced the nonviolent march to the courthouse for April 23. In addition, TCAC launched a boycott against downtown merchants in protest against their racist hiring practices. The night before the demonstration, a crowd of several hundred jammed First African Baptist Church. Over thirty people were still waiting outside when the meeting began. In an inspiring speech, Rogers accused the city administration of breaking their promise to integrate the courthouse. For that reason, he said, blacks would march the next day "in a quiet and orderly fashion to the courthouse building" and "stand with dignity." The audience greeted his announcement with enthusiastic cheers.[38]

On the morning of April 23, three hundred protestors gathered at First African Baptist Church. Most of them were students from Stillman College, which was located only a few blocks away. Since Tuscaloosa's chief of police, William Marable, had denied TCAC's request for a parade permit, the demonstrators followed their leader's instructions to walk two abreast on the sidewalk. Rogers started out with the largest of three groups, which walked toward downtown in intervals. Carrying signs that read "Segregation Must Go," the groups of marchers joined shortly before noon at the steps of the courthouse. A large crowd of several thousand whites and dozens of policemen, county deputies, and firemen looked on in the warm sun. For a moment, the protestors stood silent, holding up their signs. When Rogers mounted the steps to read a prepared statement, police officers immediately herded him and his fellow demonstrators down the steps and away from the building. Policemen pushed and beat those teenagers who spilled into the street, but they made only a few arrests. At that point, TCAC's leadership recognized that their plan to fill the jails with nonviolent protestors had failed.[39]

Despite this setback, African Americans had made their point. At a mass meeting that night, Rogers summed up the demonstration's message: "We stated that we would march. We marched today. And all Tuscaloosa knows that our determination shall last until complete integration is achieved."[40] He then announced that TCAC would file a suit in federal court to force city authorities to remove the segregation signs at the courthouse. But activists already pondered new targets, such as the city's lunch counters and public parks. A few days later, Rogers disclosed that the boycott of downtown stores and the voter registration drive would be intensified as well.[41]

Such proclamations were no empty threats. Impressed by Rogers's charisma and his unwavering determination, more and more people attended the rallies on Monday night.[42] Throughout April and May, at least four hundred people regularly crammed into First African Baptist Church to listen to the eloquent oratory of their leader. He preached Martin Luther King's philosophy of Christian love and Gandhian nonviolence, and his frequent biblical allusions expressed TCAC's uncompromising resolve to fight for full equality. "We're gonna march around that wall of segregation," he declaimed one night, "and like another wall a long time ago," referring to the Wall of Jericho, "it's gonna come tumbling down."[43] Such inspiring words instilled in many blacks a confidence that they themselves might be able to topple white supremacy.

Indeed, the nascent movement was gaining momentum. By the end of May, TCAC had set up citizenship schools for voter education in six churches and two local homes. Martin Luther King's SCLC provided some of the funds. King also dispatched numerous civil rights workers and guest speakers to Tuscaloosa, among them his right-hand man, Ralph Abernathy. Sometimes, King himself visited the community, conferring with Rogers about the course of the city's civil rights struggle. SCLC field-workers regularly assisted the TCAC. Their workshops on nonviolent direct action became an integral part of the local movement.[44] On May 18, buoyed by this growing support, TCAC sent another letter to the city administration, now demanding the integration of all public facilities, including schools, hospitals, hotels, and restaurants. Black activists also called for equal job opportunities, which they stressed by picketing the Kwik Chek supermarket in one of Tuscaloosa's shopping centers.[45]

White resistance to racial change grew in direct proportion to the increasing number of protestors. Initially, it remained confined to threatening phone calls to movement leaders. T. Y. Rogers and his wife had to bear the brunt of this nighttime harassment. Interestingly, LaPelzia Rogers appeared to be her husband's exact opposite. If T. Y. evoked the soft-voiced language of Christian love, she silenced the racist callers with vile curses. "To tell you the truth," LaPelzia later said, explaining why she never participated in demonstrations, "I wasn't too nonviolent. I had a temper, and I had a big mouth."[46] While T. Y. might have argued with his Catholic wife's position, he acknowledged that her anger deterred many racist callers. In August 1964, he confided to an interviewer: "I felt sorrier for the people who called than I did for her. If she got a chance to talk to them, she talked to them worse than they talked to her. It stemmed some of the tide, because they finally reached the point, I guess, where they said, 'Well, that lady's crazy, anyway, so there's no point in calling so much.'"[47]

By contrast, Rogers advocated philosophical nonviolence. Unsurprisingly, his manner and rhetoric reflected the tremendous influence of his famous mentor. Evoking King's religious rhetoric on the night before the first demonstration, he declared: "We are coming here tomorrow without hatred in our hearts and without violence. We are not going to strike back, but will go in a spirit of Christian love."[48] Local activist Ruth Bolden remembered that Rogers strictly enforced nonviolence, telling teenage demonstrators to "carry no knife, no gun, no stick, no nothing." TCAC officers similarly exhorted them to stay away from the demonstrations if they could not accept these rules.[49]

Among black adults, however, police brutality against women and children during a demonstration on June 9, 1964, seriously eroded support for nonviolence. TCAC had planned the march to be the culmination of a new wave of direct action, which started on June 2. Until June 8, when Police Chief Marable banned any further protest, small groups of African American teenagers had staged sit-ins and marches in downtown Tuscaloosa.[50] But on the morning of June 9, over five hundred blacks assembled at First African Baptist Church. Rogers and his followers knew that Police Chief Marable had prohibited their long-planned protest march to the county courthouse, but TCAC had already announced that it would defy the ban. The large crowd of college and high school students that crammed in the church this day agreed; parade permit or not, they were ready to march. The teenagers expressed their resolve with the music of the black freedom movement. Singing "Ain't Gonna Let No George Wallace Turn Me Round" and "Keep on Keep on up to Freedom Land" at the top of their lungs, the students mustered the courage to face the impending demonstration.

TCAC leaders expected the local police to stop them, possibly with violence, and their concerns were fully justified. A phalanx of blue-helmeted police officers and deputies, armed with nightsticks and cattle prods, surrounded the historic old brick building. Nearby, firemen readied high-pressure water hoses to disperse potential protestors. Rumors that the police might be in collusion with Robert Shelton's hooded order intensified the activists' apprehension.[51]

When Rogers led the long column of marchers out of the church into the summer heat, they faced the cordon of police officers. Chief Marable immediately confronted the bespectacled minister, reminding him that the demonstration had been banned. He asked bluntly, "Do you intend to march anyway?" "Yes," Rogers said firmly and nodded. Marable was furious. "You're under arrest," he snarled and motioned his deputies to lead the minister to the waiting squad car.[52] Shortly thereafter, police officers arrested TCAC's remaining leadership. Yet the black students were undaunted by the arrests. Singing and clapping, they made another attempt to break through the line of Marable's men but were brutally forced back. Using their cattle prods, sticks, and fists, policemen pushed the demonstrators back into the church, while firemen began to spray them with high-pressure streams of water.

When a few angry teenagers allegedly began to throw rocks and bottles at the police, Marable's men suddenly hurled a tear gas canister into the church. Inside, the gas immediately caused a panic. "Tear gas, tear gas," the protestors screamed and began to break some of the church windows with chairs and other objects to let in fresh air. This prompted the police to shoot another barrage of gas shells into the building. Gasping for air and their eyes welling with tears, the frightened students poured out of the church. Outside, they received a violent welcome. Angry policemen chased fleeing demonstrators and bloodied them with sticks and fists. When the almost one-hour-long siege finally ended, ninety-four demonstrators had been arrested. Thirty-four persons, among them one policeman, needed hospitalization for cuts, bruises, and injuries caused by tear gas.[53]

Tuscaloosa's black community was outraged at the brutal police response. Not only had police officers attacked one of the last sanctuaries of the African American community; worse, they had brutalized peaceful women and children. Shock soon turned into apprehension and anger. Many blacks began to arm themselves. Ruth Bolden, for example, after seeing police brutally beat her young nephew, feared for her life. She telephoned a friend from nearby Northport to ask for protection. Over two decades later, she recalled: "I called my friends . . . to come over here and stay with me that night 'cause I was really scared to death. . . . We had to talk in codes. I said 'come and bring a lot of sandwiches,' and he knew what that meant: it was guns and a lot of bullets." By Bolden's account, she began to carry a pistol hidden in a Bible.[54]

When factory worker David Gordon's wife telephoned her husband to inform him of what had happened at the church, he immediately left the plant and hurried home. Concerned about his wife's safety, Gordon picked her up, took his shotgun, and drove down to First African Baptist Church. "At that time," he recalled later, "I wasn't [a] civil rights man . . . cause if anybody hit me I [was] gonna hit him back."[55] While not explicitly stated by Gordon or other black men in their recollections of the police attack, their forceful reaction indicates that many of them considered this incident a challenge to their manhood. Their inability to protect women and children against white brutality probably evoked traditional concerns among these men of failing to conform to the role of provider and protector of their families.

When police officers ordered Gordon to go home, he complied, but some angry African Americans remained downtown with their rifles and shotguns. They were determined to retaliate with violence against both the police and the white community. The city's atmosphere was explosive. During the night, residents could hear gunshots, and scattered violent incidents left two African Americans wounded.[56] Joseph Mallisham, a Korean War veteran and longtime labor organizer at Tuscaloosa's Zeigler meatpacking plant, later recalled, "I have never in my life seen so many folks walking down the street with shotguns on their shoulders."[57] Mallisham was one among several older activists who sought to convince the angry group of hotheads of the futility of violent disorders. Rather than burn down the city, he argued, blacks ought to organize their own protective agency to prevent violent incidents like the one at the church that day and to protect the movement against the Ku Klux Klan. "If we're going to do this," Mallisham told them, "let's do it right."[58]

One by one, Mallisham and some of his friends persuaded the enraged men to give up their weapons, promising to return them at a meeting later that night. World War II and Korean War veterans dominated that meeting. They all agreed that their community needed safeguards against police brutality and Klan intimidation. At a second gathering the following night, almost three hundred men, including youth gang leaders, workers, teachers, and businessmen, enthusiastically endorsed the plan. That night, a small group of army veterans formed the nucleus of the new defense organization.[59] It came as no surprise that Tuscaloosa's black men entrusted Joseph Mallisham with the leadership of the group. His military training and service during the Korean

War together with his impressive record of labor activism made him an ideal candidate.

Son of a Methodist minister, thirty-six-year-old Mallisham had been born in Tuscaloosa. As a senior at the city's Druid High School, he dreamed of becoming a doctor but soon realized the futility of his plan. Financing a college education was far beyond the family's means, and in any event no medical school in Alabama admitted African Americans. When he graduated in 1948, Mallisham therefore took a job at Zeigler's meatpacking plant in Tuscaloosa. Shortly before the Korean War broke out, the young man joined the U.S. Army. Like A. Z. Young, David Matthews, and thousands of other black men, Mallisham found his military service in Japan and Korea to be a transforming experience that spurred him to political activism. Upon his return in 1951, the combat-hardened veteran became a labor activist at the Zeigler plant, where he served as an officer of that factory's first integrated union. As an AFL-CIO organizer, he traveled extensively, attending leadership seminars at Highlander Folk School in Tennessee, a well-known meeting place for civil rights activists. At other workshops in Chicago and Atlanta, he frequently met A. Philip Randolph, the veteran labor leader and founder of the March on Washington Movement.[60]

Inspired by Randolph and equipped with new leadership skills, Mallisham, in his words, "crammed all this stuff" in his "head and brought it back home."[61] At the Zeigler plant, his aggressive negotiating style won him a reputation as an agitator. Despite the management's attempts to ban his activities, Mallisham continued his unpopular work and braved the consequences. At the same time, he became involved in the first tremors of Tuscaloosa's civil rights struggle. In the mid-1950s, he participated in the short-lived activities of Reverend Sheeley. In 1957, when a white mob threatened Autherine Lucy, Mallisham was one of the armed locals who rushed to her defense. Five years later, he joined TCAC and became chairman of its membership committee, a position that he would hold throughout the 1960s.[62]

The black defense organization clearly reflected its leader's army training. Its structure mirrored that of a military combat unit. Mallisham led a small executive board that determined the group's strategy. A group of lieutenants and the rank and file executed specific operations. The organization established strict criteria for membership, accepting only married war veterans who had served in active combat. In addition, new recruits had to be discreet and were required to conform to a rigid code of morality. If candidates passed the thorough background check, they solemnly pledged to protect fellow blacks at the cost of their lives. Throughout the summer and fall of 1964, about one hundred men took this oath. Though it was a motley crew that varied widely in age and educational background, their common goal to protect the black community bound them together.[63]

Such rituals were part of the great secrecy that characterized the defense squad. Mallisham believed that avoiding general publicity would lessen tensions in the city and increase the group's effectiveness. For this reason, it never acquired a name. Sworn to confidentiality, members never talked about the organization, which explains why whites remained unaware of its existence. Even among blacks, few had full knowledge of the sophisticated protective system. Police officers, who sometimes encountered members of the group on their nightly patrols, appeared to tolerate its existence, since there were no official attempts to outlaw or disarm the group.[64]

The security of T. Y. Rogers and other TCAC officers was the defense unit's major concern. By early June, death threats against the civil rights leader had become routine, and few nights went by without suspicious cars slowly passing by the parsonage. Only one day after the official formation of Mallisham's group, about twenty armed black men began to guard Rogers's home. Concealing themselves in bushes around the one-story building, the sentries were ready to repel potential Klan attacks. No hooded terrorists showed up that night, but the guards continued to protect the house in two shifts almost twenty-four hours a day.[65] Interestingly, while local blacks anticipated racist violence in their neighborhood, Vivian Malone and two other black women had quietly entered summer school classes at the University of Alabama without incident. The civil rights battle had now shifted to the trenches of segregated everyday life.[66]

In the following weeks, Rogers's small house became a fortress. Nathaniel Howard Jr. remembered, "Going by T. Y.'s house [was like] going on a military installation."[67] Armed guards requested identification from those who approached the building, and cars that passed the checkpoint had to blink a prearranged signal to avert being welcomed with a volley of buckshot. According to Ruth Bolden, the guards fired at several cars whose white drivers had ignored their motion to halt. A few teachers and others who hesitated to participate actively in demonstrations secretly assisted the movement by preparing sandwiches and refreshments for Rogers's bodyguards.[68]

Willie Herzfeld received protection as well. He later remembered that several of Mallisham's men "spent a lot of sleepless nights, some of them sleeping on the top of my house . . . trying to protect me from what would have been the ravages of the Klan."[69] Since death threats against Herzfeld—sometimes in the form of burning crosses in his front yard—had become common, the Lutheran minister found the armed sentries an immense relief. Rev. T. W. Linton, a Presbyterian minister who became TCAC's main representative in the tense negotiations with white merchants, similarly recalled that a group of about ten men regularly guarded his home. Throughout 1964, armed bodyguards followed Rogers, Herzfeld, Linton, and other activists wherever they went.[70]

Finally, the defense unit watched over the handful of TCAC's white allies, frequently escorting them to the black section of town and back to their homes. Most prominent among them were Jay and Alberta Murphy. Because of their legal expertise—Jay was a law professor at the University of Alabama while Alberta worked as a lawyer in private practice—African Americans had learned to appreciate their assistance. Particularly Joseph Mallisham was grateful to the Murphys, who defended him in 1955 in a labor arbitration case against the Zeigler Company. In the early 1960s, Alberta founded the Council for Human Relations, a group that consisted of like-minded white liberals who regularly met to discus civil rights. In 1964, the couple joined TCAC and began to attend its mass meetings. In the eyes of white Alabamians, these activities branded Alberta and her husband as dangerous Communist agitators. Like Rogers and other black activists, the Murphys received numerous threats against their lives.[71]

Armed blacks made sure that this menace was not translated into actual harm. When Alberta ventured into the rural areas of Tuscaloosa County to teach voter registration, for example, members of the defense unit inconspicuously followed her. Mallisham explained later, "When we saw the way she went all over the country any time of day or night to instruct voters without any regard of danger, we knew that woman needed some kind of protection."[72] Only later did Alberta find out that black veterans regularly ensured her safety on these dangerous trips.

University of Alabama sociology professor Harold Nelson not only benefited from similar security measures but also gained deep scholarly insight into the defense group. Nelson befriended Mallisham in the aftermath of the June 9 incident and subsequently participated in virtually all activities of TCAC and the self-defense unit. Documenting the activities of the protective agency over the course of several years, he summarized his findings in a sociology article that he published in 1967.[73] Except for the Murphys and Nelson, few other whites openly aided the black movement. Even among Tuscaloosa's white clergy, support was negligible. But those ministers who did come out in favor of integration could count on black protection against racist repercussions.[74]

Some white activists still felt insecure. They too armed themselves. When hostile racists began to threaten Jay Murphy, for example, he informed them that he and his young son carried pistols, and that they would not hesitate to use them.[75] Another was James Jaquith, an assistant professor of anthropology at the university who participated in TCAC's attempts to integrate the city's movie theater. Jaquith had never owned a gun, but as harassment against him and his family increased, he purchased several firearms. In August 1964, Jaquith conceded in an interview that before the threats began, "The thought of shooting someone was just revolting to me." But by the time of the interview, this scruple had vanished. The prospect "of shooting any of those people who come on my property now," he said, "is not revolting to me. I would look forward to it with some anticipation."[76] Given this virtual arms race between Klansmen and civil rights activists in the aftermath of the police attack on First African Baptist Church, it seemed only a matter of time before the two opposing camps would clash.

Yet the following weeks were relatively calm. TCAC had halted further demonstrations, waiting for a federal court to issue an injunction against police interference. The city's white administrators sought to slow down the legal process, flatly denying all allegations of restricting African Americans' civil rights. Although TCAC was unable to continue its direct action campaign, it had at least won the battle over the segregated new courthouse. On June 25, federal judge Seybourn H. Lynne ordered Tuscaloosa County to remove all discriminatory signs from the building's restrooms. Less than a week later, the "white" and "colored" placards were gone.[77]

Still, white supremacy was far from defeated. In particular the UKA stepped up its campaign of intimidation. Two days after Judge Lynne's decision, Klansmen held a huge rally on the outskirts of Tuscaloosa. Almost 1,500 whites cheered the speeches of Imperial Wizard Robert Shelton and other Klan leaders. The eerie scene was bathed in the blazing light of a burning eighty-foot cross. Calvin Craig, the leader of the Georgia Klan, called upon whites to resist the civil rights movement. "Do not start violence," he cautioned, "but if Negroes start it, you have the right of self-defense."[78] It was ironic that Craig would invoke the right that African Americans had relied on for generations to repel the Klan's violent attacks. But for Craig, Shelton, and their followers, this actually was about self-defense: the defense of white supremacy.

Violence was not the only tactic employed by white Tuscaloosans. One group that shared the Klan's goals but rejected its violent methods founded the White Citizens for Action Committee (WCAC), which vowed to use economic pressure to deprive its black adversary of its army of working-class protestors. Suggesting in a leaflet that white businessmen who were subject to the black boycott launch "Operation Ban," the WCAC argued that firing black employees would weaken the local freedom movement. At the group's semi-weekly meetings, president James L. Frazier exhorted his followers to force civil rights "agitators" out of town.[79]

The Civil Rights Act of 1964, signed into law on July 2, brought the city's uneasy peace to an abrupt end. The trouble began when blacks began to test the compliance of the city's movie theater and its restaurants with the new legislation, which prohibited segregation in all public facilities. Predictably, many restaurants and snack bars refused to serve the small groups of young activists. To add insult to injury, angry whites accosted them on the street.[80]

On July 8, white harassment exploded into violence. That night, a group of black teenagers desegregated the city's Druid movie theater. When they left the building, a jeering crowd of two hundred hostile whites greeted them with a barrage of stones and bottles. Fortunately, a cordon of police officers prevented the mob from surging forward. But the deputies had difficulty controlling the belligerent crowd, and the black students waved in vain for cabs to pick them up.[81] Desperate, they telephoned Joseph Mallisham, who immediately led a two-car convoy manned with armed blacks to rescue them. When the two cars arrived, the teenagers jumped in and crouched to the floor. As the drivers sped away, the angry mob continued to hurl bottles and rocks toward the vehicles. Racing toward the black neighborhood, the rescue team joined up with other defense squad members, who escorted them to safety. Suddenly, Klansmen who had hidden behind trees next to the street opened fire on the convoy. Poor marksmen, they missed, and several black men rolled down their windows and returned the gunfire. The stunned white assailants, not expecting armed resistance, quickly fled.[82]

The following night, white mobs again rampaged at the Druid Theater. This time, they attacked famous white actor Jack Palance, who was in town to visit his wife's family. Loitering in front of the movie theater, the mob waited for African Americans seeking to enter the building. When Palance arrived with his family to see a movie, the crowd mistook the dark-tanned actor for a black man boldly trying to integrate the theater with a white woman. The sight of what the mob believed to be an interracial couple threw the crowd into frenzy and triggered a violent riot that police officers had problems quelling. In the end, police resorted to tear gas and water hoses to disperse the raging mob. Meanwhile, Palance and his family, given helmets for protection against rocks and bottles, were escorted out of the building. When the actor finally reached his car, he found a menacing sticker pasted on his bumper. It read: "The Knights of the Ku Klux Klan Is Watching You."[83]

In reaction to the nighttime turmoil, police imposed a curfew on minors and patrolled downtown Tuscaloosa for the following two weeks. The police department's hard line on rioters diminished intimidation and violence against African Americans, but the restraint of Shelton and his UKA appears to have been a direct result of the black defense organization's determined resistance during the nighttime shoot-out on July 8. Indeed, the Klan's organized campaign of harassment ceased almost completely after this incident.[84]

While local African Americans helped thwart Klan violence with arms, SCLC field-workers enforced strict adherence to nonviolence. Their account of small direct action projects in early July read like a report from a nonviolent army platoon: "Sunday July 5, 1964: On Sunday 7:55 one Bat. of the 101st Freedom army proceeded down town to the Bama Theater located on Greensboro ave. & 6th street. The Bat. consisted of 25 men but only 15 reached the rendevousz [sic] point." The author of the report then "decided that four of us would go into the establishment. We proceeded accordingly, with no weapons in our hands. (I checked all of the men)." Despite these careful preparations, police arrested the protestors shortly before they reached the theater.[85] Asked in late June 1964 about SCLC's responsibilities in Tuscaloosa, one fieldworker replied emphatically, "I'm here to see that the struggle remains nonviolent." In his opinion, this was "going to be quite a task."[86] Blacks, SCLC activist Powell A. Middlebrook explained two months later, should at least acquire "an idea and a better concept of what nonviolence is, and the practical approach to nonviolence."[87] Perhaps the field-workers sensed that African American activism stemmed not from their belief in redemptive love but primarily from their anger about the police attack on First African Baptist Church.

Unlike King's aides, those who protected the local movement with rifles and shotguns saw no conflict between their weapons and nonviolent direct action. Their leader had never considered nonviolence a way of life, but he accepted it as a successful tactic. In fact, Mallisham viewed it as the only possible strategy in the black freedom struggle. The black defense agency, he emphasized years later, would have never started a fight. "Our membership," he reminisced, "was a membership of peace." Protection was the group's main responsibility. "Any violence would be the last resort, and that was stressed," he said.[88] In his article on the organization, Harold Nelson also noted that its members sought to defuse rather than aggravate volatile situations, knowing that publicized black violence might impede the Tuscaloosa movement's moral position.[89]

Probably because of the unit's purely defensive character, TCAC leaders fully accepted the armed men into their ranks. T. Y. Rogers, despite his deeply felt commitment to philosophical nonviolence, welcomed the group and frequently consulted with Mallisham and his men about movement tactics. In addition, several members of the defense group became an integral part of TCAC's executive board. Martin Luther King, who seems to have had little knowledge of the magnitude of the city's sophisticated protective system, would certainly have opposed Mallisham's group. But on balance, Tuscaloosa's defense organization not only operated in tandem with TCAC but also successfully complemented its nonviolent campaigns.[90]

Surprisingly, not only African Americans actively opposed the Ku Klux Klan. While the defense squad fought the hooded terrorists with buckshot, Buford Boone, the white editor of the *Tuscaloosa News*, blasted the UKA with a barrage of verbal bullets. By southern standards, Boone was unusually progressive on the race question. Editor of the *News* since 1947, the Georgia native argued for racial equality before the law. In 1956, he supported Autherine Lucy's admission to the University of Alabama and deplored the mob violence on campus. One year later, this courageous stand won him the Pulitzer Prize for editorial writing. Privately, however, he continued to refer to blacks as "niggers."[91]

When TCAC launched its nonviolent campaign against segregation, Boone again called for reason and moderation. He harshly criticized the UKA, in particular its leader Shelton, whom he mocked as "a sickly-looking, pitiable little man."[92] Rather than take the law into their own hands, the white editor argued, Klansmen should let local police preserve law and order. Although he also disapproved of T. Y. Rogers, Boone saved his most caustic remarks for the Imperial Wizard. On July 7, he quipped that Shelton had been "reduced to living as a human jackal on a racket known as the Ku Klux Klan."[93] In Boone's opinion, "decent people" could not condone Klan vigilantism and mob violence.[94]

James Frazier, the president of the racist WCAC, was the first to attack Boone for his stance. Whites, Frazier said at a meeting on July 16, needed to "stick together" in their fight against "outside and local agitators."[95] Boone's editorials undoubtedly undermined this goal. But Frazier's criticism remained confined to angry diatribes. Robert Shelton, on the other hand, sought revenge for the public humiliation he had suffered. On July 24, Shelton filed a $500,000 libel lawsuit against Boone and the *Tuscaloosa News*. Shelton charged that Boone's editorial from July 7 was "false and malicious," intended only to ridicule him publicly. Although Boone had printed Shelton's reply to the editorial, the UKA leader demanded a full retraction.[96] Boone refused, patiently enduring the Klan's campaign of harassment and threats that followed. After a four-year legal battle, a jury awarded Shelton a mere five hundred dollars in punitive damages. Boone chose not to appeal.[97]

The controversy between the combative editor and Shelton indicated that the white community was far from united in the fight against racial integration. The local black freedom movement, on the other hand, was stronger than ever before. By the end of July, a majority of African Americans stood behind TCAC, with students and the unemployed still at the forefront of civil rights insurgency. "It was basically the little people who broke Tuscaloosa wide open," LaPelzia Rogers later said, acknowledging their contribution.[98] Neither jail nor economic reprisals could intimidate them. "The poor people," as TCAC leader T.W. Linton later explained, "had nothing to lose."[99] However, if young and poor people provided the manpower, the black middle class and some white liberals provided the necessary funds. Teachers, principals, doctors, and white university professors still shied away from actively participating but contributed considerable amounts of money to the cause. Without these financial contributions, TCAC would have struggled to continue its voter registration drives and direct action campaigns.[100] Finally, working-class people like Mallisham assisted the movement by spending long and sleepless nights to protect their leaders. Without a doubt, the black movement had reached its peak.

In August 1964, TCAC used this unity to put an end to discrimination on the city's bus lines once and for all. By that time, fifteen of Tuscaloosa's restaurants faced a federal civil rights suit for their segregation policy. But on the buses, racial incidents continued. Although the bus company had agreed two years earlier to enforce integrated seating, black passengers who sat in the front section of the buses still faced discrimination and harassment. Drivers and white customers frequently hurled racial slurs at blacks and sometimes attacked them. In response to these grievances, TCAC announced on August 1 that blacks would boycott the bus line unless the company's integration policy was made public. The management of the Druid City Transit, Inc., refused. Two days later, one white bus driver drew a .38 caliber pistol and fired in the direction of a black man, who allegedly had cursed the driver. This incident only reinforced people's impression that the white drivers had never respected their African American passengers. In the following days, angry black teenagers pelted buses with bricks and bottles. But the bus company remained silent, which prompted TCAC to initiate the boycott on Monday, August 10. Now, activists demanded both an end to discrimination and the hiring of black bus drivers.[101] That night's mass meeting at First African Baptist Church was a demonstration of the community's unity and strength. The large and confident crowd's first song was "If You Miss Me from the Back of the Bus."[102]

The boycott was nearly 100 percent effective within the African American community, cutting off the company's entire business within a few days. Like in Montgomery eight years earlier, TCAC sustained people's morale by organizing a system of "courtesy cars" as a substitute for the bus line. After only three days of empty buses, the management laid off over twenty employees. Although the company's resistance to hiring blacks gradually waned, the Amalgamated Transit Union that represented the interests of the bus line's drivers still refused to cooperate. The union argued that no white driver could be fired without a just reason. Confronted with financial ruin and no prospect of resolving the impasse, the company threw in the towel. On November 10, 1964, the Druid City Transit, Inc., surrendered its franchise to the Tuscaloosa City Commission.[103] The following months were difficult ones for TCAC. Especially the fleet of private cars that had replaced the buses strained the organization's finances. In late December, the situation forced T. Y. Rogers to appeal to SCLC for direct financial assistance. But TCAC's perseverance paid off. On April 12, 1965, the new Tuscaloosa Transit Co. resumed bus services with an integrated workforce and a public policy of nondiscrimination. TCAC had officially ended its boycott the week before.[104]

By that time, the local movement was past its zenith. TCAC had organized one last nonviolent demonstration on March 12, 1965, protesting the brutality against nonviolent demonstrators during SCLC's campaign in nearby Selma. That day, almost 1,200 African Americans marched from First African Baptist Church to downtown Tuscaloosa, singing the songs of the freedom movement. In stark contrast to the brutality against protestors the previous summer, police officers now blocked off the demonstrators' route and permitted them to walk in the center of the street. When the marchers reached downtown, the entire column halted, knelt down and listened to the prayers of Rogers and other ministers.[105]

The tranquil atmosphere that characterized the local movement's last demonstration signaled that white residents grudgingly accepted the advent of integration. By the end of January 1965, most local restaurants and lunch counters had quietly desegregated when groups of black activists tested their compliance with the Civil Rights Act of 1964. While T. Y. Rogers and his followers dined in formerly all-white eating establishments, dozens of white police officers stood guard outside to keep away white spectators.[106] In February 1965, a white member of the biracial Tuscaloosa Committee for Human Rights observed, "People in Tuscaloosa seem ready to accept change at this time and are more open to reasonable negotiation."[107] Indeed, hard-core white resistance had vanished. Even the integration of Tuscaloosa County's schools in September 1965 provoked no visible opposition. About one hundred black students quietly enrolled in four formerly all-white high schools without violent incidents.[108] In retrospect, the pace of racial change in Tuscaloosa was amazing. With the help of federal civil rights legislation, the united determination of local blacks had brought white supremacy to its knees within little more than one year.

Understandably, the movement lost momentum after this series of stunning victories. In 1966, TCAC made efforts to improve the pitiable plight of poor blacks in Tuscaloosa's slum areas. But tackling the complex economic effects of segregation and discrimination proved difficult. In addition, remnants of Jim Crow remained, primarily in the city's white churches. In the 1970s, some white congregations still opposed integrated services.[109] Despite the city's peacefulness, the black defense organization took no chances. Armed men continued to protect the homes of both Rogers and Herzfeld until the two ministers left in 1967 and 1968, respectively. Only toward the end of the decade did the group finally disband. Rogers moved to Atlanta, where he focused on his new position as SCLC's director of affiliates. He remained the pastor of First African Baptist Church, but his departure further diminished local people's flagging enthusiasm for political activism.[110] Only Joseph Mallisham remained interested in politics, running for the post of Tuscaloosa's public safety commissioner in 1968 and again in 1972. Although he lost each time to a white candidate, his ambitions symbolized the new assertiveness of the city's black population. In 1985, Mallisham finally won political office, becoming the first black county commissioner ever elected in Tuscaloosa.[111]

Looking back, one might ask why Tuscaloosa witnessed so little violence during the civil rights era. Compared with the bombings and brutal beatings that civil rights activists endured in Montgomery, Birmingham, and Selma, Tuscaloosa escaped the worst forms of racist terror. In hindsight, some black activists gave credit to Police Chief Marable, who appeared to be more willing to avert mob violence after the police attack on First African Baptist Church.

Others speculated that the UKA's fairly limited campaign of intimidation stemmed from Robert Shelton's hesitancy to launch violence so close to the organization's headquarters.[112]

But the black community's defense organization certainly deserves most of the credit for pacifying Tuscaloosa. While largely invisible, its protective measures ensured the safety of civil rights activists and clearly communicated to Robert Shelton and his hooded followers that blacks were determined to repel white aggression. Joseph Mallisham was certain that his protective unit not only lessened tensions in the community but also thwarted racist aggression.[113] Asked by an interviewer why Klan harassment diminished during 1964, he responded, "Because violence would have met violence, and they knew it."[114]

As in Montgomery, Birmingham, and other Alabama cities, nonviolent direct action was the driving force behind the integration of Tuscaloosa. Yet Mallisham's self-defense squad became an essential means of protection for black activists, serving as a significant auxiliary to the nonviolent movement. Even before the emergence of the Tuscaloosa movement, the Congress of Racial Equality learned that local freedom movements in Louisiana similarly benefited from such fusions of Gandhi, God, and guns.

3

THE DEACONS FOR
DEFENSE AND JUSTICE

In early November 1963, white CORE worker Mike Lesser penned a glowing report about an emerging freedom movement in the rural southwest of Louisiana. "The social and political structure of the parish is being shaken to its roots," the young graduate student from Syracuse University wrote to CORE's southern regional office about events in West Feliciana Parish. "But the really beautiful thing" was "to see and be part of the movement—the spirit, the people, . . . the courage, and the shotguns."[1]

The first tremors of this local movement had begun in the summer. As early as 1962, CORE field staff had scouted the rural areas of central and southwestern Louisiana to set up voter registration drives. But they faced immediate white resistance. The membership of the region's Ku Klux Klan soared, and violent harassment against African Americans ran rampant as hooded white men burned crosses throughout the state to threaten those who dared register to vote. Predictably, few blacks in West Feliciana Parish followed the activists' invitation to make the trip to the registrar's office in St. Francisville.[2]

But in late 1963, "something happened," as one field report described the changing mood among local blacks after the successful attempt of black minister Joseph Carter to add his name to the voter books. Fifty-five-year-old Carter had only a fifth-grade education but had tried to register for almost a decade. In August 1963, police arrested him after yet another confrontation at the registrar's office. Undaunted, Carter accepted CORE's offer to prepare him for the difficult registration exam that white officials traditionally used to disqualify black candidates. Finally, on October 17, 1963, Carter passed the test. He was the parish's first registered black voter since the beginning of the century.[3]

Shotguns were another symbol of the new spirit among parish blacks. Those who joined the local freedom movement—primarily independent landowners, who were less vulnerable to white economic pressure—refused to accept violent harassment passively.[4] "[I]f any hostile white folks should ever try to approach the place without warning," Lesser reported in his letter, "they would find themselves faced by 15–20 high powered . . . shotguns before they got within 50 yards of the building." According to the young CORE organizer, this assertive militancy made a considerable impression on white terrorists. After blacks proclaimed "that they would shoot any strange white face on their property," attacks on the black community stopped.

These protection efforts ran counter to Lesser's commitment to Gandhian nonviolence, but the campaign of terror that confronted the local movement quickly muted any discussion of Gandhi's abstract teachings. Despite his misgivings, the young activist pragmatically accepted the armed guards. "Incidentally, so you don't get the wrong idea," he explained to the CORE office, "we . . . can only *preach* non-violence. We cannot tell someone not to defend his property and the lives of his family, and let me tell you, those 15–20 shotguns guarding our meetings are very reassuring."[5]

Lesser's report exemplified the experience of a majority of CORE's field staff in Louisiana. Unlike the freedom movement in Tuscaloosa, civil rights activism in the rural areas of the Pelican State confronted the hard-core of white violent resistance. Once CORE left the relative safety of New Orleans and Baton Rouge, there was no safeguard against shootings, bombings, and other forms of violent intimidation. In this environment, few of those locals who dared join the freedom movement viewed nonviolence as a way of life. Rather, in virtually all of the civil rights campaigns that CORE helped organize between 1963 and 1965, tactical nonviolence and voter registration worked hand in hand with armed resistance.

The Deacons for Defense and Justice, a self-defense organization that formed in 1964, was the most sophisticated example of this type of southern black militancy. The armed group became an integral part of local movements in Jonesboro and Bogalusa. But the group provided more than mere protection against the Ku Klux Klan. For members and supporters alike, the Deacons also symbolized a new form of assertive manhood that challenged white myths of black powerlessness. The organization's Bogalusa branch gained nationwide notoriety after media reports about their shoot-outs with hooded attackers.

In contrast to Tuscaloosa's defense unit, which generated little controversy and almost no media coverage, the Deacons' publicity provoked intense discussions within CORE. Already in the 1940s, CORE's pacifist founders had pondered whether armed self-defense was compatible with their Gandhian principles. During the era of nonviolent mass protest, civil rights activism in Louisiana provoked similar debates, which neither the organization's national leaders nor its southern field staff were able to settle.

Aside from these internal discussions, the Deacons posed a serious predicament for the public image of national CORE. On the one hand, reports about the gun-toting group blemished the organization's reputation for nonviolence and eroded its legitimacy in the eyes of white America. Dependent upon white liberal financial support, CORE was hard-pressed to justify its close alliance with the Deacons. On the other hand, condemning the Deacons would have meant abandoning activists' commitment to developing local leadership. National director James Farmer thus faced a difficult balancing act between preserving CORE's nonviolent image and demonstrating the organization's loyalty to local African Americans. Eventually, despite the harsh criticism from the white media and other civil rights leaders, CORE came to accept the Deacons and their concept of armed protection as a necessary part of civil rights activism. By the end of 1965, even those field-workers who had once professed philosophical nonviolence advocated armed resistance, a shift that foreshadowed the radicalization of CORE in the ensuing years.

From the outset, the unanticipated wave of terror that greeted CORE activists in Louisiana undermined the nonviolent convictions of the organization's field-workers. In late summer 1963, after barely surviving a manhunt in the little town of Plaquemine, only a short drive north of West Feliciana Parish, even CORE's national director James Farmer began to question his beliefs. On August 19, 1963, local blacks organized the first nonviolent protest march against discrimination and segregation. White police officers were determined to crush any sign of civil rights insurgency and attacked the protestors with massed force and tear gas. They also arrested over two hundred persons, among them James Farmer. Twelve days later, almost nine hundred blacks assembled for another demonstration. The brutality of white authorities' reaction matched the movement's growing number of followers. When the protestors approached Plaquemine's courthouse, mounted state police officers hurled tear gas canisters toward them. They then galloped headlong into the crowd. As screaming demonstrators ran away in panic, mounted police officers bloodied men and women with clubs.[6]

Many fleeing blacks sought refuge in a local church, but state troopers soon surrounded the sanctuary and forced the group out by shooting tear gas into the building. Meanwhile, as clouds of gas descended upon the area, policemen, wearing gas masks, searched the homes of local blacks for James Farmer. "When we catch Farmer," the furious officers yelled, "we're going to lynch him!"[7] Unable to find CORE's national director, they arrested at random almost four hundred black men during their search. By that time, local people had whisked Farmer away to the safety of a black funeral home. But he sensed that it would be just a matter of time before his pursuers would reach the hiding place. CORE's director briefly pondered surrender to avoid unnecessary bloodshed, but his friends warned that such a course would mean certain death. One young man pulled out his pistol and vowed to protect him. "Mr. Farmer," he said, "if a trooper comes through that door, he'll be dead."[8] Farmer wondered how many others were armed, fearing that such defense efforts might trigger a violent clash between local blacks and the police. Finally, shortly before his pursuers reached the funeral home, two heavily armed ex-marines smuggled Farmer out of town in an empty hearse.[9]

The night of terror in Plaquemine shattered Farmer's long-held commitment to pacifism. "For CORE," Farmer later reflected, "nonviolence—never a way of life, but only a strategy—ended on a balmy night, September 1, 1963, in a sleepy town on the Mississippi, when a uniformed mob screamed for my blood." "The casketless hearse in which I escaped," Farmer wrote, "became for CORE a symbol of the burial of the peace."[10] At a regional CORE conference in December of that year, Farmer openly admitted that he no longer considered himself a pacifist. Among blacks in general, he said, nonviolence "had not caught on."[11] Given this persistent skepticism toward Gandhi's teachings, it came as no surprise that what Farmer called "end-oriented militants" gradually gained the upper hand over a decreasing number of those members who had adopted nonviolence as a way of life.[12]

Southern blacks, who had neither Farmer's educational nor his religious background, were even less inclined to view nonviolence in philosophical terms. While white Americans hailed SCLC's nonviolent Birmingham campaign, delegates at CORE's 1963 annual convention in Dayton, Ohio, warned of an "imminent possibility of a violent racial explosion" in the South. Fieldworkers voiced their concern about the increasing tendency among blacks to arm for protection. One staffer reported that it had become common to see

African Americans check their guns and knives on a table outside the meeting place. Some of them, he said, even brought their weapons to demonstrations. Another told of a local man who protected the CORE workers with a loaded shotgun.[13] "It is not easy to tell a man who is being beaten not to reach for his gun or knife," is how one delegate explained the moral dilemma that plagued some organizers.[14]

The convention's tone differed markedly from that of earlier meetings. Delegates to the 1961 conference had vowed to "fight for integration throughout this country . . . with love and without malice." In 1963, many attended a workshop that focused on the question, "Is love really necessary?"[15] For a majority of the 250 participants, it was probably difficult to give an unequivocal answer. Confronted with the mounting determination among blacks to fight back against white aggression, CORE warned of a bloody race war. "CORE recognizes the immediacy of impending retaliation and mass violence on the part of the Negro community," one of the convention's resolutions proclaimed, "as evidenced by the fact that Negroes are increasingly arming themselves for the purpose of self-defense against continued oppression and violence."[16] James Farmer and others stressed that CORE would continue its nonviolent approach, but the idealism that had characterized the organization's early years had undoubtedly vanished.

Some of CORE's members only now seemed to realize that Martin Luther King's invocation of Christian love and moral suasion, while essential for the movement's legitimacy, had little effect on the conscience of white racists. In May 1963, for example, white field-worker Hunter Morey blasted the Fellowship of Reconciliation (FOR) for what he believed to be a flagrant misrepresentation of nonviolent direct action. In an angry letter, the young law student lamented that the pacifist organization's pamphlet on the Gandhian technique offered only philosophical abstractions but no practical programs. Morey was baffled by FOR's suggestion that civil rights campaigns succeeded by removing white hostility. "Why shrink back from the realization," he asked, "that most civil rights campaigns have won by forcing whites against their will to desegregate or to stop discrimination by some means such as economic, legal, or political (and social) force." In his view, doctrinaire pacifists only hampered the movement's success by their unrealistic interpretation of nonviolence. Morey pleaded with FOR "not [to] delude people by telling them that the civil rights movement has succeded [sic] by removing hostility. It is not generally so at all."[17]

CORE's widely distributed pamphlets and brochures, on the other hand, continued to emphasize goodwill and reconciliation. The pamphlet "This Is CORE," for example, insisted, "CORE believes that *nonviolence* in action and attitude is essential to the realization of our aim—interracial brotherhood."[18] But such dedication was the exception and appeared to dwindle rapidly. More important, CORE's insistence on nonviolence was only partially a result of philosophical imperatives. Rather, it reflected the pragmatic necessity to maintain white liberal support. As community relations director Marvin Rich pointed out in a 1963 memorandum, CORE's publicity campaigns had to disseminate "the story of CORE action and philosophy to the widest possible sympathetic audience." Rich stressed that maintaining this sympathy required CORE to convey "the interracial aspect of action, the attempts to secure reconciliation before beginning direct action, and the willingness to persevere until significant change is achieved."[19] In an essay on the state of the movement in 1963, James Farmer explicitly acknowledged this linkage between the movement's nonviolent reputation and white assistance. "Widespread violence by the freedom fighters," he cautioned, "would sever from the struggle all but a few of our allies."[20]

Critical letters from white liberal donors to CORE's national office in New York underscored this point. In March 1962, for example, Culbert Rutenber, a white professor of theology from Massachusetts, complained that CORE chapters appeared to be "run by secularists who are really not committed to nonviolent methods except for the fact that they happen to be working."[21] This was probably an accurate assessment of how most northern and southern chapters approached civil rights organizing. Yet this attitude was not acceptable to Rutenber, who informed Farmer that his future financial contributions would go to the NAACP.[22] Given CORE's dependence on small individual donations, James Farmer could not ignore such critical voices.

Upholding the organization's reputation for philosophical nonviolence, then, was crucial to the survival of CORE, but it also posed a serious predicament. On the one hand, CORE was committed to assisting black southerners in defeating white supremacy, an effort whose success frequently depended on a practical symbiosis between nonviolent protest and armed protection. On the other hand, the organization felt obliged to convince white America of CORE's strict faithfulness to Gandhi's teachings. James Farmer was undoubtedly aware of these complexities and made deliberate attempts to downplay the extent to which blacks relied on armed resistance. On a New York–based TV show in April 1963, Farmer denied the suggestion that blacks might turn to violence. "No," he responded, "I do not think that there will be a growing resort to violence. I think most of the Negroes, especially in the South, realize that violence would be suicidal and that non-violence is the only solution to the problem."[23]

But the southern freedom struggle was far from peaceful. White terror against civil rights activists prevailed, and so did black armed resistance. The Birmingham church bombing in September 1963 was only the most glaring reminder of that reality. Few white Americans knew that blacks in Louisiana faced similar attacks on a daily basis. Fewer still expected southern blacks to confront such racist terrorism with armed force. The Rev. Joseph Carter, for example, after adding his name to the voter rolls in West Feliciana Parish, had no qualms about using a shotgun to protect his neighbors against nighttime attacks. "I value my life even more since I became a registered voter," he said, explaining his vigilantism in late 1963. "If they want a fight," he proclaimed, "we'll fight."[24] Other blacks in the area, after learning of James Farmer's night of terror in Plaquemine, began to bring guns to civil rights meetings to make sure "that nothing was going to happen to Mr. Farmer this time."[25]

Few of CORE's black field staff objected to such protection efforts. According to field organizer Ronnie Moore, only a few white CORE workers remained "hung up" on pacifism. Since the majority of the white activists consisted of college students with a middle-class background, their understanding of non-violence probably closely resembled that of CORE's founders. Virtually all black field-workers, on the other hand, were native southerners whose adherence to nonviolence was generally as pragmatic as that of the local people with whom they worked. Accordingly, Moore had no reservations about discussing with West Feliciana Parish movement leaders their armed response to the Klan's campaign of terror. After the meeting, Moore and his friends informed white residents that they would shoot back if attacked.[26]

In early 1964, a new wave of white terror hit the Pelican State. The newly organized Louisiana Knights of the Ku Klux Klan burned more than 150 crosses near black communities across Louisiana. On the night of January 19, for instance, CORE activists in East Feliciana Parish were shocked to find a blazing cross in front of their headquarters.[27] In West Feliciana Parish, the Klan's campaign of terror also struck fear into many. Some African Americans armed themselves for protection. What united protectors and protected was their skepticism toward nonviolence. One field-worker reported that a "great deal of education" was "needed to cement the relation between CORE and the people of West Feliciana Parish. The idea of non-violence is a new one, and will require much discussion and training, especially for the older people."[28]

To acquaint local blacks with the unfamiliar concept, CORE workers conducted workshops on protest strategies and the philosophy of nonviolence.[29]

CORE intensified its voter registration drive and community organizing during the summer of 1964, but white violence and intimidation incessantly frustrated their efforts. Some CORE workers received as many as one hundred threatening phone calls a day, in addition to numerous bomb threats. Physical attacks against activists and local people became routine. Black economic dependence on whites further impeded civil rights activism. White employers frequently threatened to fire their black workers if they tried to register to vote or intended to become involved in the movement.[30] A few courageous farmers from West Feliciana Parish participated in CORE's voter registration campaigns, but fear persisted. "Violence, bombings, and killings are a very real possibility," white field-worker Miriam Feingold wrote in July 1964, "which explains why so many people have not as yet even tried to learn how to register to vote."[31] Pointe Coupe Parish exemplified the meager result of CORE's efforts. Although slightly more than 50 percent of almost ten thousand blacks whom CORE workers had contacted in their door-to-door canvassing in June later attended voter registration clinics, only about six hundred of that group dared make the trip to the courthouse. In the end, fewer than two hundred people successfully registered.[32]

Despite such setbacks, local people in West Feliciana Parish continued to challenge white supremacy, with guns if necessary. Northern volunteers, whom CORE had recruited to assist in its 1964 Louisiana summer project, were perplexed to find their black host families armed and ready. White college student Peggy Ewan from Iowa wrote home, "Although CORE is a non-violent movement some of the Negroes are armed."[33] Fourteen-year-old Thelma Caulfield, the youngest of the six children in the family that Ewan stayed with, leveled the family's shotgun at a group of hostile white youths on several occasions. After whites had fired into the wooden-frame building one night, the Caulfields taught Ewan how to shoot the gun. Ewan later reflected that the Caulfields and other blacks who lived in Louisiana's rural areas were "totally unprotected." Thelma, she said, "really had to have a gun, you know, just to defend herself."[34] John Holliday Sr., the father of a local activist, was similarly prepared when rumors of an impending Klan attack on his house reached him in mid-July. According to a field report, "Holliday replied that the first white face he saw in his yard would be shot."[35]

The fact that local blacks guarded homes and civil rights meetings with rifles and shotguns provoked serious discussions within CORE. During a staff meeting in February 1964, James Farmer, Bayard Rustin, and the southern field staff discussed CORE's position on the issue. Miriam Feingold's question whether "a violent person" was a "'traitor to our cause'" probably tormented the conscience of many. In the discussion, Farmer made clear that CORE remained committed to nonviolence on civil rights projects, but he offered no definite policy on armed self-defense.[36] In another meeting in July, the summer task force was sworn to CORE's traditional philosophy. "We must at all times advocate nonviolence," their supervisor exhorted and cautioned organizers to be "*very* careful in advocating self-defense in [the] community." "Urge people *not* to carry guns." But this directive was far from dogmatic since it allowed activists to carry weapons "inside [a] home with [a] mob of KKKers outside."[37] National CORE's ambivalent reaction to the problem ultimately left it up to CORE activists themselves to decide whether to accept local people's protection.

Some fieldworkers considered these abstract discussions about CORE's principles useless anyway. "[T]o hell w[ith] CORE, we're w[ith] the people!" the black activists Dave Dennis and Jerome Smith angrily replied to James McCain's comment that their organization could not "afford to advocate retaliation."[38] Dave Dennis, a Louisiana native who coordinated CORE's activities in Mississippi and in his home state, was interested in organizing movements around local people's needs, not around Gandhian principles. Rather than impose complex and alien ideas upon blacks, CORE's policy was to listen to what locals themselves thought would be best for their communities.[39]

Since a majority of the southern staff was committed to these organizing principles, few of them objected when African Americans from Jonesboro formed a sophisticated self-defense group in the summer of 1964 to protect the local movement from the Ku Klux Klan. Jonesboro was located in the northern corner of Louisiana and had a population of nearly four thousand, one-third of which was black. The town's black neighborhood, called the "Quarters," consisted mostly of rows of dilapidated wooden-frame houses with tin roofs, which sat alongside unpaved streets. A few black independent businesses, including a café, a funeral home, and a barbershop, provided some respite from the daily humiliation of segregation. Jonesboro's largest employer, a paper mill that harvested timber in the thick pine forests of northern Louisiana, counted only two hundred blacks among its two thousand workers, a situation that did not change after the passage of the Civil Rights Act of 1964. Jonesboro remained a stronghold of white supremacy.[40]

As in the rest of Louisiana, CORE's ongoing voter registration drive and local people's attempts to desegregate the town's restaurants, libraries, and the public swimming pool were met with racist terror. On the night of July 7, for example, three carloads of whites chased CORE workers Ronnie Moore and Mike Lesser from Jonesboro to Monroe. Boxed in by the cars at high speed, their chances to survive that night seemed slim at best, as Moore later recalled. Only by making a daring U-turn on the highway did the two activists finally escape, racing back to Jonesboro at over ninety miles per hour.[41] In the Quarters, the situation was similarly volatile. Every day, dozens of cars menacingly passed the CORE headquarters on Cedar Street. Meanwhile, white police officers arrested numerous local activists on fabricated charges to intimidate black residents.[42]

In the case of a group of local black men, this type of harassment backfired. In late June, after a group of white teenagers threatened CORE workers in front of their office, dozens of them rushed to the activists' aid, guns in hand. In the following weeks, this informal group shadowed the CORE activists who canvassed the black neighborhoods and continued to guard the office with guns.[43] Allegedly to address the dangerous situation, the local police department deputized five black men to protect the movement—an idea that local black high school teacher Frederick Douglass Kirkpatrick had suggested to the town's sheriff. But CORE questioned the motives behind that surprising concession, suspecting that the chief of police intended to use the new black deputies to enforce segregation. Then, at the end of July, a nighttime Ku Klux Klan parade of over fifty hooded men through the black section of town finally prompted members of the informal guard and some of the black policemen to organize an official self-defense unit. Shortly after the frightening incident, Earnest Thomas, a twenty-nine-year-old Korean War veteran, called for a secret meeting to discuss the formation of the protective group. At the meeting, about fifteen men established what later came to be known as the Deacons for Defense and Justice.[44]

In the following weeks, the group continued to guard the CORE office and began to patrol the Quarters. When whites drove into the black neighborhood, armed Deacons followed them. Few dared to stop after spotting the silhouette of men with rifles in the rear-view mirror. Armed men also guarded civil rights meetings and escorted activists who were canvassing in the dangerous areas of the surrounding Jackson parish. Walkie-talkies facilitated the coordination of guard duties. One member of the new organization, a former army platoon sergeant, became white CORE worker Charles Fenton's personal bodyguard. CORE staffers who visited Jonesboro also received protection from the Deacons, who relied on their own shotguns, .30 caliber and .22 caliber rifles, and pistols.[45]

Fenton, a young college student and member of San Francisco CORE, was both delighted and dismayed by the formation of the Deacons. On the one hand, the group represented the very kind of indigenous leadership that CORE hoped to nurture among local blacks.[46] More important, Fenton readily acknowledged that Jonesboro had become a much safer place with the defense squad around. "[N]o one can tell what would have happened here if the Deacons hadn't formed their own ideas about protection," he told a journalist in February 1965.[47] On the other hand, Fenton was committed to philosophical nonviolence, and his request not to bring weapons into the CORE office perplexed some of the Deacons. Unlike Fenton, they saw no contradiction between their guns and nonviolent protest. Given the unabated wave of violence that confronted the Jonesboro movement, Fenton's hope that the Deacons would eventually abandon their defensive purpose to become a peaceful community organization seemed unrealistic.[48]

The Deacons consisted mostly of working-class war veterans, who established strict criteria for membership. The organization's president, a forty-four-year-old stockroom worker named Percy Lee Bradford, and cofounder Earnest Thomas, a mill worker and handyman, accepted only American citizens who were at least twenty-one years old. The organization preferred married men and registered voters, probably because the founders thought that politically aware heads of families would be less likely to engage in aggressive behavior. Accordingly, applicants who had a reputation for being hot-tempered were quickly rejected. Thus, from the very outset, the Deacons pursued a program of strict self-defense, not aggressive retaliation.[49]

Throughout the fall of 1964 the Deacons patrolled Jonesboro, while the local freedom struggle continued. In October 1964, the police department disbanded the group of black deputies, which left the Deacons as the only protection against white violence.[50] CORE workers and local blacks alike believed that the existence of the Deacons had significantly reduced the danger of racist attacks. In a report on CORE's activities in Jonesboro, white activist Daniel Mitchell concluded that "the group acted as a preventive factor during the period when tension was highest."[51] Another field report acknowledged the armed patrols' effectiveness "in cutting down harassments from the white community."[52] Outside Jonesboro, however, people knew neither of the Deacons' existence nor of their significance for the local freedom movement. Only the FBI, which opened an investigative file on the organization in January 1965, became interested in its activities.[53]

The formation of another Deacon chapter in the mill town of Bogalusa would eventually catapult the organization into the national spotlight. Located sixty miles north of New Orleans at the state's southwestern border with Mississippi, Bogalusa remained a bulwark of segregation when CORE workers first scouted the city and the surrounding Washington Parish in the summer of 1964. The black population, which constituted one-third of Bogalusa's twenty-seven thousand residents, continued to encounter "white" and "colored" signs at restaurants, movie theaters, libraries, and parks. Segregation and discrimination also extended to the city's Crown-Zellerbach paper mill, the largest employer in the region. Only four hundred of almost three thousand employees were black. Organized in segregated unions, these workers had little chance of promotion, regardless of seniority or skill.[54]

Competing with blacks for a decreasing number of jobs, white workers showed little class solidarity. In 1919, there had been a flare of interracial union organizing in Bogalusa. That year, white lumber workers defended a black union leader with guns against the overwhelming might of an armed posse sent by the anti-union Southern Lumber Company. With the insurgency crushed, the region's long tradition of racism again reigned supreme.[55] Almost a half century later, race relations in Bogalusa had changed little. In fact, as the freedom movement of the 1960s gained momentum, the city's violent atmosphere increasingly resembled that of 1919. Journalists speculated in 1965 that what used to be called the "Magic City" had more active members of the Ku Klux Klan than any place else in the South. A civil service commission investigator's estimate that over half of the city's white population actively supported the hooded order may have been an exaggeration, but Bogalusa and the surrounding parish likely had more than eight hundred dues-paying Klansmen.[56]

In early January 1965, Bogalusa's Klan demonstrated its determination to enforce the racial status quo, with violence if necessary. A couple of weeks earlier, six white liberal residents had invited former Arkansas congressman Brooks Hays to discuss the issue of racial integration in southern cities. As soon as word of the meeting spread, the Klan publicly demanded the cancellation of the event, warning that the church where Hays was scheduled to appear would be bombed. The group of white moderates also received threats. Ralph Blumberg, the manager of the city's WBOX radio station, found the windows of his car smashed and its tires slashed, while Lou Major, the young editor and publisher of the *Bogalusa News*, counted three burned crosses on his lawn.[57] The Klan even put out a leaflet warning: "We will know the names of all who are invited to the Brooks Hays meeting and we will know who did and did not attend this meeting. . . . Those who do attend this meeting will be targeted as integrationists and dealt with accordingly by the Knights of the Ku Klux Klan."[58] In the end, frightened and concerned about the safety of their families, the organizers decided to cancel the gathering.[59]

Shortly after the Hays controversy, African American activists from Bogalusa met with CORE field-workers to ask for their assistance in challenging the Klan's brutally enforced customs. Already in the summer of 1964, CORE had recognized the community's potential for civil rights organizing. The black Bogalusa Voters League (BVL) had kept black residents well informed about voter registration and race relations in the city, and the paper mill's black unions were strong community organizations that could serve as a basis for future activism. A CORE scouting report concluded: "In spite of the overpowering stench created by [the] paper mill, we would highly recommend this area for summer work."[60]

But the BVL's leadership remained skeptical of CORE and repeatedly declined its offer to send field-workers to the city. Its president, Andrew Moses, argued that blacks might not need CORE after all, since a recently created biracial commission was working on a plan to improve race relations in the city. Only on January 22, with segregation still firmly in place, did representatives of the BVL, among them Moses and Robert Hicks, a paper mill worker and labor activist, meet with CORE workers in New Orleans. After reporting about the unchanged situation of black Bogalusans, the little delegation asked CORE to assist them in testing the compliance of downtown restaurants with the Civil Rights Act of 1964. The field staff quickly agreed and suggested a four-day testing drive, which they said could begin as early as January 26.[61]

On January 25, two white CORE activists arrived in Bogalusa. Bill Yates, a former English professor at Cornell University, and college student Steve Miller were surprised to hear that black leaders had accepted the biracial commission's request to conduct only one day of testing. Although that night's mass meeting indicated that the BVL's constituency was ready to launch a full-scale assault on segregation, they agreed to supervise the one-day campaign. Three days later, small teams of African Americans sought service at the city's restaurants, movie theaters, and libraries. Eight restaurants and two movie theaters accommodated them, but seven eateries and lunch counters refused their business. Although outright violence was absent, roving bands of white men accosted Yates, Miller, and local activists, while Klansmen photographed the CORE workers and their car.[62]

African Americans celebrated the day of testing as a minor victory, hopeful that more might be accomplished in the future. When Yates and Miller returned to the city for a rally on the evening of February 1, most blacks reaffirmed their determination to wage a campaign against all forms of Jim Crow. But a controversy erupted when the white workers and younger blacks openly criticized BVL's president Moses for the concessions he had made to the white city government. Rumors that Bogalusa's mayor, Jesse Cutrer, had bribed Moses to keep CORE away from the city further damaged his credibility and led to a split between the BVL's conservative leadership and its more militant members. What had been planned as a victory rally ended in disorder.[63]

Meanwhile, after news of the return of Yates and Miller had spread, rumors circulated that angry whites were gathering in downtown Bogalusa. Shortly after midnight, the city's police chief, Claxton Knight, knocked on the door of their host, BVL activist Robert Hicks. Knight informed Hicks that a mob of two hundred had assembled and was threatening to lynch the two men. Despite Knight's offer to escort them out of town, Hicks urged Yates and Miller to stay. If they did so, the angry police chief then plainly stated, he would withdraw his deputies. "We have better things to do than protect people who aren't wanted here," Knight snorted.[64] To make matters worse, local telephone operators refused to place Yates's long-distance calls to the FBI. Hicks then decided to call in help from the black community. Thirty minutes after his daughter telephoned friends for assistance, more than fifteen men, armed with rifles and shotguns, arrived at the home of Hicks.[65]

This demonstration of armed force quickly defused the explosive situation. Hicks later recalled that when his friends "started coming in and they was coming with guns, the police chief saw it so apparently he told people you better not go down there tonight; those people are armed and ready."[66] Indeed, the black men made it clear that they would not hesitate to defend Yates and Miller. In addition, CORE members from across the country bombarded Mayor Cutrer with phone calls to inform him of the volatile situation. Finally, at 4:00 A.M., police officers returned to the Hicks residence. By that time, the danger of a violent clash seemed to have abated, but Hicks's friends continued to guard his house for the rest of the night. After a short and sleepless night, the two CORE workers headed back to Baton Rouge.[67]

As in West Feliciana Parish and Jonesboro, armed black resistance to violent intimidation was no one-time affair. Two days later, when Yates and Miller returned to the city for a new round of civil rights meetings, armed locals again saved their lives. On February 3, the two CORE workers had several meetings with black union workers and local activists. Two police cars shadowed them as they were crisscrossing the black neighborhood. Suddenly, the police officers disappeared and a carload of hostile whites took their place. After a chase at high speeds through Bogalusa, Yates and Miller found their way blocked by several cars. Just before their pursuers reached the vehicle, the two men decided to run for safety to a black-owned café across the street. But before Yates could reach the building, three white toughs caught up with him and brutally beat the activist with their fists. Curled up in the fetuslike position that he had learned in CORE's workshops, Yates took the beating, which left him bloodied and one of his hands broken in two places. When one of his attackers leveled a pistol at him, it seemed doubtful that he would leave Bogalusa alive.[68]

At that moment, a group of armed black men came to Yates's rescue and forced the mob to retreat. As local activist Robert Hicks remembered, "they were about to shoot . . . [Yates] when some Negroes came out of a bar and grabbed one of them, put a knife to his throat and dared him to shoot."[69] According to the *Baltimore Afro-American*, the blacks held the rest of the assailants at gunpoint until the police finally began to disperse the crowd of hostile whites. The armed group then accompanied the injured activists to the safety of Andrey's Café.[70]

Minutes later, though, several carloads of whites arrived back at the café. Continually circling around the block, the whites besieged the people inside for more than six hours. As during the confrontation at the home of Robert Hicks, telephone operators exacerbated the situation by cutting off the phone lines in the entire block. As the trapped activists peered out the window, they could discern local Klan leader Randle "Jelly" Pounds engage in a friendly chat with two deputy sheriffs. Neither of them seemed interested in dispersing the mob that loitered in front of the building. Meanwhile, a little army of black men had slipped into the back door of the building with shotguns and rifles to protect the CORE workers. Several hours later, an armed escort finally moved the two activists to the safety of a private black home. From there, Yates and Miller, escorted by local police, made their way back to Baton Rouge.[71]

While whites and local police continued their campaign of harassment, the Bogalusa Voters League underwent significant changes. Prior to 1965, its president, Andrew Moses, had led an organization that lived in peaceful coexistence with the segregationist city administration. White citizens were willing to grant token concessions to the black community as long as BVL's leadership consented to white supremacy. CORE's offer to come to Bogalusa jeopardized this accommodationist arrangement, leading Moses to oppose it before grudgingly bowing to the BVL membership's desire to bring the organization in. Moses might have hoped that the one-day compromise would satisfy a majority of blacks, but he had underestimated the inspiring effect that the campaign would have in the community. At the tumultuous February 1 meeting, Moses sensed that his days as the BVL's president were numbered. Shortly thereafter, he resigned his position, making way for a new generation of militant activists. A. Z. Young, a forty-two-year-old World War II veteran and experienced labor organizer at the Crown-Zellerbach paper mill, became the BVL's new president. Joined by Robert Hicks as the new vice president and other labor activists, the new leadership quickly transformed Bogalusa's emerging freedom movement.[72]

In February 1965, this assertive new militancy translated into the formation of a chapter of the Deacons for Defense and Justice. William Yates, who had been in close contact with CORE's Charles Fenton in Jonesboro, encouraged local activists to set up another Deacon group in Bogalusa. The men who had informally guarded the home of Robert Hicks since the beginning of February readily endorsed the idea. Invited by Yates, Charles Fenton and several Deacons from Jonesboro made the five-hour trip to Bogalusa. A first informal gathering took place on February 18. Three days later, the Jonesboro delegation met with local activists for an organizational meeting at the black labor hall. Earnest Thomas did most of the talking, providing information about the organization's purpose and membership requirements. The fifteen men from Bogalusa in attendance agreed to pay a ten-dollar initiation fee and monthly two-dollar dues. They also promised to divert 10 percent of those dues to the parent organization in Jonesboro, which would use the funds to buy new walkie-talkies, ammunition, and other equipment.[73]

Thomas then focused on the group's weaponry, urging the men to acquire reliable guns. Many blacks, he said, tended to buy cheap .22 caliber rifles. "That's no weapon," he scoffed. What the Deacons really needed were high-powered .306 caliber rifles, .38 caliber pistols, and shotguns for close-range shooting. Thomas boasted that the Deacons might even be able to acquire machine guns and grenades and suggested that every chapter use the same type of weapon to facilitate less expensive bulk purchases of ammunition. No matter what kind of gun they had, Thomas said, they needed plenty of ammunition. "If you got only three or four bullets," he insisted, "you're out of the fight before it starts. Keep plenty of ammo at your house, in your car, wherever you are." Despite all the talk about guns, Thomas stressed that the Deacons would use their weapons only in self-defense.[74]

The presentation won over the Bogalusa men, most of whom were military veterans. The next day, Hicks officially announced the formation of a new Bogalusa chapter of the Deacons at a BVL rally. Reiterating the points that Thomas had made the previous day, he declared defiantly, "No white person will be allowed in a Negro area at night—salesman or anybody." The mostly teenage audience reacted with cheers and thunderous applause.[75]

Alarmed by such militant proclamations, the FBI, whose interest in the Jonesboro Deacons had dwindled after it became apparent that the group's intent was strictly defensive, resumed scrutinizing its activities. On February 26, FBI director J. Edgar Hoover ordered the agency's New Orleans division "to immediately initiate an intensive investigation of the DDJ because of the potential of violence indicated."[76] One day earlier, two FBI agents had warned Hicks to avoid involvement with the Deacons. Blacks who shot whites in self-defense, the agents said, would be charged with murder. But Hicks was un-impressed, calmly replying that the Constitution protected his right of self-defense. The angry agents, taken aback by Hick's boldness, stomped out of his house without looking back.[77]

Legally, the Deacons were indeed on firm ground. The United States Con-stitution protected the right to bear arms, and Louisiana state law allowed the carrying of weapons as long as they were unconcealed. Consequently, when armed Deacons began to patrol the black section of Bogalusa with rifles and shotguns, there was little that either the FBI or local police could do to stop their activities. Police attempts to impede black protection efforts and civil rights activities remained confined to arrests for carrying ostensibly concealed weapons or other fabricated charges.[78]

On March 5, with the help of a black lawyer from Monroe, the Jonesboro Deacons obtained an official charter from the State of Louisiana. The group's semi-official status convinced many of the Deacons that their armed activi-ties were now legally sanctioned.[79] Of course, the organization's "Articles of Incorporation" made no mention of armed self-defense. Rather, the docu-ment portrayed the Deacons' purpose as educating all Americans, and espe-cially minority groups, in democratic principles. To those who were familiar with the Jonesboro movement, the document's stated intent to safeguard the civil and property rights of all citizens "by any and all honorable and legal means" clearly allowed armed self-defense. But a more specific statement on the group's actual rationale would certainly have prompted white officials to reject the application.[80] In the spirit of the charter, the Bogalusa Deacons, like the Tuscaloosa group, required their members to pledge their lives for the de-fense of fellow African Americans and civil rights workers. Shortly after legally incorporating the Deacons, the Jonesboro group granted an official certificate to the Bogalusa affiliate and issued authorized membership cards.[81]

In the meantime, activists in Bogalusa had learned that the acclaimed integration of a few restaurants in January had been an ephemeral success. When CORE resumed testing for compliance with desegregation on February 21, not a single restaurant or lunch counter served African Americans. Harassment and intimidation by local police officers and the Ku Klux Klan continued as well. In early March, a liberal white minister received an ultimatum to leave town or be killed. Two other moderate white pastors had already been driven out. On the night of March 25, whites fired six shots into the radio transmitter station of white moderate Ralph Blumberg. Boycotted by segregationists for his role in the Hays controversy, he had lost most of his advertisers and faced financial ruin. Four days later, whites hurled a tear gas bomb into the black union's meeting place, where the BVL had just concluded a rally.[82]

But white violence did not frighten local African American activists into submission. It only reinforced their conviction that organized protection was necessary. "What we felt," BVL's president A. Z. Young recalled a year later, was "that the city police did not protect us and give us the type of job we thought we were entitled to."[83] The Deacons for Defense and Justice were the freedom movement's answer to this deliberate neglect.

Although no women participated in the organized activities of the Bogalusa defense squad, they also knew how to handle guns. On one occasion, the wife of Robert Hicks saved William Yates from a group of hostile Klansmen. Early in the morning of April 7, Yates stopped by at the BVL activist's home to pick up forms for a new voter registration campaign that CORE had launched the previous week. Chatting with Mrs. Hicks on the porch, he watched a green pick-up truck slowly approach the house. When Yates walked toward his car, the truck's white driver emerged and menacingly walked toward him wielding a blackjack. Yates immediately recognized local Klan leader Randle Pounds, the man who had broken his hand in front of the black café in early February. Without hesitation, Yates jumped into his car and drove off, the green truck in hot pursuit. Realizing that he was unable to shake off his pursuers, Yates raced back to the Hicks residence. There, Mrs. Hicks, armed with a pistol, waited in the front yard for Pounds and his fellow Klansmen, who drove away, apparently uninterested in a shoot-out with the black woman.[84]

That night, the Hicks residence became the scene of yet another armed clash, this time between Klansmen and a group of Deacons. In the evening, the Klan had held a rally near the BVL's meeting place, which included burning a ten-foot cross and gathering around two makeshift coffins. One of them bore the name of William Yates. A few hours later, armed whites appeared determined to make this macabre ritual a reality. Shortly after midnight, three carloads of whites circled the home of Hicks, where Yates was still a guest. Driving by the house, the attackers fired several shots into the building and threw a brick into the back window of a CORE volunteer's Volkswagen bus that was parked in front of the building. When the Klansmen returned a few minutes later and again fired at the house, they were greeted with disciplined return fire from a dozen armed Deacons, who by then had positioned themselves around the building.[85] "I ran out of the porch," Robert Hicks described the incident to a reporter, "and BLAM—there was a shot from the car. I snatched out my gun and fired twice. Some of the other men fired. But it was dark. I don't think anybody was hit."[86] Trading twenty to thirty shots with their assailants, the Deacons successfully repelled the attack.[87]

The next day, a nonviolent protest march, led by a frightened James Farmer, brought renewed racial clashes. Farmer knew that returning to the city was risky. Forewarned by the FBI that the Ku Klux Klan intended to kill him, he nevertheless led a long column of almost five hundred marchers. The atmosphere was indeed ominous. On their way to city hall, the protestors passed a makeshift coffin that Klansmen had placed on two folding chairs next to the street. Then, after a police car accidentally injured a white bystander, several of the hundreds of white onlookers began to attack a news photographer and then broke through the line of police officers who had been ordered to protect the marchers. At least six whites began to batter black demonstrators. One angry man pounded a black teenager on the head with a picket sign. James Farmer barely escaped an assault from Randle Pounds, who grabbed the CORE leader by his shirt and was about to hit him with a blackjack before a police officer finally arrested the attacker. But the police were unable or unwilling to protect the rest of the marchers, forcing Farmer to call a halt to the demonstration. A few hours later, blacks returned to complete the march.[88]

Numerous Deacons had observed the melee but decided not to intervene. Like the Jonesboro Deacons, they had promised to remain nonviolent during CORE's protest campaigns. In other situations, however, they were armed and ready. The night before, armed Deacons had picked up James Farmer from the airport in New Orleans. Surprisingly, Louisiana state troopers assisted in the defense group's protection efforts. Concerned about the volatile situation in Bogalusa, Louisiana governor John McKeithen had ordered them to guard

Farmer around the clock. In the end, a caravan of two police cars and one car manned with Deacons escorted CORE's national director to Bogalusa, accompanied by a helicopter that hovered overhead. During his stay, Farmer lodged in the house of Charles Sims, the forty-one-year-old president of the Bogalusa Deacons. At night, armed black men and white state troopers forged an unusual alliance, taking turns guarding Farmer against the Ku Klux Klan.[89]

The Jonesboro Deacons were busy protecting civil rights activists as well. On the day of the Bogalusa protest march, Deacon Elmo Jacobs chauffeured a group of white student volunteers to Jonesboro. When a group of whites spotted the integrated group at a gas station, they followed them. After a short chase, the white men opened fire on the activists' station wagon and punctured the car's doors with several volleys of buckshot. In response, Jacobs quickly pulled out his .38 caliber pistol, yelled at the students to keep their heads down, and fired four shots at his assailants. Confronted with this armed resistance, the white toughs fled. Miraculously, despite the fourteen lead pellets that had pierced Jacobs's car, the attack had injured no one.[90]

On April 15, with the crisis in Bogalusa worsening, Mayor Cutrer finally met with the BVL leadership. But A. Z. Young, Robert Hicks, and Charles Sims, who served as the BVL's financial secretary, could do little more than present their long-standing demands: an end to segregation and discrimination, equal economic opportunities, and the inclusion of black leaders in local politics. Although the fact that the mayor finally agreed to the meeting suggested that the increasing pressure that the movement exerted on local authorities was having some impact, it yielded no real concessions and failed to stop racist agression.[91]

A few hours after the meeting broke up, whites firebombed the home of a black man hosting several of CORE's white student volunteers from the University of Kansas and Berkeley, who had arrived in Bogalusa in early April. In a CORE press release, one of these volunteers described the city's atmosphere as "one of terror and violence." None of them dared venture from the homes of their well-armed hosts at night. "To impress you with the sense of fear," the student reported, "most Negro families have guns in their homes and many Negroes carry firearms on their person at all times. There is no communication between white and negro except through violence."[92] Ironically, the only time that black and white citizens mingled without incident was in front of Gibson's general store, where an integrated line of black and white customers patiently waited to buy more rifles and pistols.[93]

The Deacons were well aware of the danger that the students faced and protected them day and night. Jeffrey Dickeman, a Berkeley volunteer who shuttled the students to their black host families with the Volkswagen bus that Klansmen had damaged during the attack on April 7, later recalled that two armed Deacons usually accompanied him on his trips. In addition, men with guns patrolled the area surrounding the ten black homes where the volunteers stayed.[94] In an article for the newsletter of the Berkeley CORE chapter, another student stressed the important role that the Deacons played in Bogalusa: "We never crossed the street without a Deacon. We never drove our car without a Deacon present. Most of our cars were escorted by two carloads of Deacons, one in front and one in back. The homes where we stayed were guarded by Deacons, and our canvassing was protected by Deacons. Our lives were literally in their hands."[95]

While vividly capturing the city's violent atmosphere, these reports also illustrate the high level of organized discipline that the Bogalusa defense organization had attained. At night the black neighborhood resembled a high-security military installation, with Deacon patrols stopping every car that failed to give a prearranged headlight signal.[96] One night, when three white men entered the black neighborhood brandishing rifles and yelling obscenities and threats, a dozen armed Deacons emerged from bushes, driveways, and dark alleys. A. Z. Young recounted: "We ringed 'em around, and then, well we talked to them a little. You know they got mighty polite. They were all smiles. It was 'yes sir' and 'no sir,' and so we let 'em go, and they ain't been back."[97] The armed patrols had the desired effect. By May, attacks on black homes had nearly ceased, and most blacks agreed that simply the knowledge of the Deacons' existence among whites had made the neighborhood a safer place to live.[98]

But the defense unit was about more than protection. The Deacons' armed militancy also reflected southern black men's determination to assert their manhood. To the primarily working-class men who joined the Deacons, Martin Luther King's idea of nonviolence was degrading to their notion of male identity. Robert Hicks explained to an interviewer: "See, we never had adopted CORE's philosophy. . . . We believe in love and brotherhood, but just don't go for the idea that if somebody slaps me on my cheek, I turn the other one. If you slap me on my cheek, then, I have to defend myself."[99] Jonesboro Deacon Earnest Thomas similarly pointed out that members of his group would never let whites brutalize them. "To us," he said, "this does not seem like being a man."[100] On another occasion, Thomas proclaimed: "We don't intend to turn the other cheek. Only a fool does that."[101] Unsurprisingly, the Deacons rarely participated in CORE's nonviolent demonstrations.

Their disdain for philosophical nonviolence echoed freedmen's efforts to assume the role of provider and protector of their families during Reconstruction. For the Deacons, therefore, seeing women and children beaten by white racists provided an additional justification for opposing white attacks with rifles and shotguns. "[W]e had to arm ourselves," Charles Sims explained in late 1965, "because we got tired of the women, the children being harassed by the white night riders."[102] Earnest Thomas, father of five children, similarly pointed out that it was "not natural to let someone destroy your wife, your kids and your property and not prevent it. If this means battle, then that's the way it has to be."[103] Bogalusa Deacon vice president Royan Burris believed that whites only now began to accept members of the defense unit as men. "They finally found out that we really are men," the thirty-six-year-old barber told a journalist, "and that we would do what we said, and that we meant what we said."[104] From this perspective, the Deacons successfully countered traditional stereotypes of black male powerlessness.

On occasion, CORE workers exploited this rhetoric of manly protection as a recruiting tool. Civil rights organizers knew that the majority of local people who participated in demonstrations, attended rallies, or housed white volunteers were women. Men were generally more reluctant to become involved in civil rights activism. Many were afraid of losing their job or of white retaliation. Others refused to participate because of their opposition to nonviolence. According to field-worker Isaac Reynolds, he and other CORE staff managed to recruit some of these men by appealing to their sense of being protectors of black women. "There's nothing wrong with females fighting for their own freedom too," he reflected, "but we felt that man to be a man has to be out there in that forefront putting himself in the position of the dangerous jobs and not . . . putting his woman out front. So we began to talk from that side."[105]

Conversely, the Deacons expected no affection from white southerners. Instead, they demanded respect. "I'm not striving for love. We're striving for respect for one another," Earnest Thomas pointed out in a radio interview.[106] Members of the group argued that only armed resistance, not nonviolence, would ultimately compel whites to give blacks the respect they deserved. The fact that nonviolent CORE appeared to earn only ridicule from whites confirmed their argument. "Most of the guys in the white locals down there just made fun of CORE," a black paper mill worker recalled of his coworkers' reaction. "It was kind of a humorous situation to them. CORE was not mean and tough and belligerent as DDJs and some of those were. . . . Nobody really paid too much attention to CORE." The Deacons, on the other hand, could not be ignored. "I guarantee you," he said, "they were aware of that DDJ bunch."[107]

The Deacons felt that their armed militancy ultimately translated into grudging acceptance among whites. "Well, I think you have the key word here, *respect*," Robert Hicks later said, assessing the organization's impact in Bogalusa. "We got respect from them, [because] one thing that I found the white man honors is his gun. He actually recognizes and will honor a person or respect people that will stand up and speak their mind and will defend themselves."[108] The Deacons, then, considered citizenship to entail more than the desegregation of lunch counters or the right to vote. For them, there was no freedom without dignity, and sometimes, dignity could come only from the barrel of a gun.

In many ways, Charles Sims epitomized the defense unit's ideal of black manhood. Having already lost much of his hair—what was left of it and his mustache were sprinkled with gray—the burly insurance salesman looked older than his forty-one years. A Bogalusa native, Sims had left high school before graduation. When the United States entered World War II, he joined the army and saw action overseas. During his four years in the military, he attained the rank of technical sergeant and became a shooting instructor. Before his career as an activist, Sims had a reputation for being "a loose cannon." He frequently got involved in barroom brawls and accumulated a record of eighteen arrests, mostly for carrying concealed weapons. After taking on the presidency of the Deacons, however, he changed, keeping calm even in the most volatile situations.[109]

His toughness became legendary among many local African Americans. In the big pockets of his denim overall, loose change was frequently mingled with bullets. And if the pistol that he habitually carried was not tucked under his belt, it lay on the nearest table in plain view for everyone to see. Unnerving to some, this menacing habit only enhanced his reputation. White journalist Roy Reed noted in August 1965: "In other times he would have been simply a tough; now he is a hero. Negro teen-agers swarm around him and run his errands. Women look up to him. Even white civil-rights workers lionize him."[110]

A number of black Bogalusans may have had ambivalent feelings about the Deacons, but members of the organization were convinced that they offered important role models for the black community. BVL leader A. Z. Young said in the summer of 1966 that the defense unit had "a psychological effect on a lot of young people," whom he believed to have shed their "inferior [*sic*] complex about the white man."[111] The fact that Roy Reed was "struck repeatedly by the pride" the Deacons inspired among local blacks suggests that Young's analysis was partly correct.[112] Historian George Lipsitz has similarly concluded that the group's "discipline and dedication inspired the community, their very existence made black people in Bogalusa think more of themselves as people who could not be pushed around."[113]

While the Deacons' commitment to self-defense was real, their martial rhetoric was primarily symbolic. Belligerent statements such as A. Z. Young's announcement that the defense squad would let white and black blood "run down" downtown's Columbia Road were an attempt to intimidate the Ku Klux Klan rather than a deliberate plan to initiate racial warfare.[114] Likewise, the Deacons deliberately exaggerated their actual strength. The *New York Times* and the *Wall Street Journal* estimated that its membership had swelled to somewhere between five thousand and fifteen thousand members, spread over fifty chapters throughout the Deep South. Sims and Thomas repeatedly confirmed these numbers and sometimes claimed that the actual number of affiliates was even higher.[115] In reality, as the FBI quickly ascertained, the Deacons had official chapters in only three communities: Jonesboro, Bogalusa, and Homer, a small northern Louisiana town near the Arkansas border. Their membership consisted of several hundred rather than thousands, and the defense group's claims that they had obtained machine guns and grenades to wage a racial war against the Klan were similarly unfounded. Even the FBI conceded that the Deacons and their shotguns posed no major threat, except to white night riders.[116]

The group's confrontational boldness also obscured the fact that the Deacons continued to endorse tactical nonviolence. "I believe nonviolence is the only way," Sims told the *National Guardian* in September 1965. Negotiations, he said, would "be the main point in this fight."[117] The defense group did not believe in nonviolence as a way of life but embraced a pragmatic symbiosis between nonviolent protest and armed protection. The Deacons hoped that by nurturing their martial reputation they would actually be able minimize the prospect of violence. "We will fight only to defend ourselves," Sims said, reiterating the group's credo at the end of July 1965. "But if they think we want an eye for an eye, let them. If they feel that way it should save a lot of bloodshed."[118]

A brutal attack on black Bogalusa police officers in early June was further evidence of this policy of de-escalation. On May 16, Mayor Cutrer had finally yielded some ground to the BVL. A week later, he officially promised to end segregation and improve the conditions of the traditionally neglected black neighborhood. In addition, the city added two black men to the police force.[119] But white segregationists remained determined to block black progress. On the night of June 2, 1965, the new policemen, O'Neal Moore and Creed Rogers, were on patrol near Bogalusa when the driver of an old pick-up truck pulled even with their car and fired several shotgun blasts at them. The first volley shattered the car's rear window. The second one instantly killed Moore and seriously injured Rogers, who managed to radio for help. Later that night, police arrested white mill worker Ernest Ray McElveen in connection with the killing.[120] In the midst of shock and outrage at the brutal murder, the Deacons stepped up their protection efforts but did not retaliate. Before O'Neal's funeral, armed men once more escorted James Farmer from the New Orleans airport to Bogalusa. Since they remained skeptical of the willingness of local police officers to protect Farmer, about fifty members of the defense group mingled with the funeral crowd to thwart the Klan's plan to murder CORE's national director.[121]

At the end of June, the BVL unsuccessfully sued Bogalusa's police chief, Claxton Knight, for his refusal to provide protection. On July 8, when CORE and the BVL resumed nonviolent demonstrations, this lack of protection led to a violent clash between a black activist and his white attacker. Shortly after 3:00 P.M., the column of four hundred demonstrators reached city hall and knelt down for prayer. Hundreds of white bystanders jeered the protestors and threw rocks and bottles. The police officers that walked alongside the protest march did nothing to stop the harassment. On the way back to the black section of town, a rock thrown by a white bystander hit the head of a black girl. Henry Austin and Milton Johnson, two young black men who drove A. Z. Young's Cadillac coupe behind the column, immediately stopped to help the girl. That moment, a white man broke through the line of police officers and began to punch Johnson in the face. Austin, who sat in the driver's seat, tried to help his friend but was unable to separate the two.[122] Then he pulled out a pistol, yelling at the white attacker: "I have a gun, let him go."[123] When the man, a Bogalusa resident named Alton Crowe, still did not react, Austin decided to join the scuffle to subdue the white attacker. But even firing a warning shot did nothing to stop the assault. Confronted with the enraged Crow, Austin finally fired three shots at his attacker. Hit in the chest, the man staggered back before collapsing on the street. After a brief moment of shock, state troopers rushed forward and handcuffed Austin as well as injured Milton. Though seriously wounded, Crowe would survive the shooting.[124]

The violent incident became front-page news across the nation and seemed to prove to many that the Deacons had finally broken with the nonviolent movement. But the defense unit denied responsibility for the shooting. While Austin told journalists that he was a Deacon, Charles Sims stressed that neither of the men was a member. In his opinion, the shooting had been "unnecessary."[125] In fact, Austin's spontaneous and dangerous reaction to Crowe's attack clearly contradicted the Deacons' official policy to accept nonviolence during CORE demonstrations. In the eyes of many local blacks, the gangly Austin was a "meddlesome outsider and a hothead."[126] Dishonorably discharged from the air force in 1964 and shortly imprisoned, the twenty-one-year-old appeared to be exactly the volatile kind of personality that the Deacons—most of them older World War II veterans—tried to keep out of their highly disciplined organization.[127] Although many local blacks undoubtedly admired Austin for his bravado, Sims's attempts to distance the Deacons from the shooting reflected the organization's pragmatic balancing act between practicing armed self-defense and supporting tactical nonviolence.

Eventually, the breakdown of public order that nonviolent protest had caused coupled with the prospect of more racial confrontations compelled the federal government to intervene. A few days after the Crowe shooting, Governor McKeithen attempted to act as a mediator between Mayor Cutrer and the BVL. But his proposition to initiate a thirty-day "cooling-off period" was met with angry disapproval among local activists. The angry reaction of black writer Louis Lomax, who had come to Bogalusa to support the local freedom movement, expressed the sentiment among many. "The Negro has been giving for 500 years," he shouted, "and baby, we ain't got no more to give."[128] Echoing Lomax, the BVL unanimously rejected the proposal. With the negotiations deadlocked, both Jesse Cutrer and A. Z. Young appealed to President Lyndon B. Johnson for federal intervention. Johnson reacted quickly and dispatched Assistant Attorney General John Doar to Louisiana to arbitrate in the conflict. Shocked by the violence that confronted blacks in Bogalusa, Doar decided to make the city a litmus test for the federal government's ability to enforce the Civil Rights Act of 1964. By September 1965, the Justice Department had initiated forceful action against police brutality and prepared lawsuits against restaurants that refused to desegregate. In addition, Doar supported legal action against the Knights of the Ku Klux Klan.[129]

Given the federal government's traditional neglect of the Louisiana freedom struggle, the forcefulness of the Johnson administration's intervention in Bogalusa seems surprising. The Justice Department's decisive action against the Ku

Klux Klan, for example, was without precedent in Louisiana. Historian Adam Fairclough has argued that Bogalusa benefited from the aftermath of SCLC's Selma campaign, where police officers had bloodied nonviolent protestors several months earlier. Fairclough suggests that the violence against black protestors in Alabama as well as the brutal murder of white activist Viola Liuzzo by Klansmen heightened the administration's concern about civil rights.[130]

While this is certainly part of the explanation, it is debatable whether nonviolent demonstrations alone would have put enough pressure on local and national authorities to act. It seems that only the presence of the Deacons and the subsequent prospect of more violent turmoil could create a crisis that was considered severe enough to compel federal officials to intervene on behalf of black activists. At the same time, as historian George Lipsitz has pointed out, CORE's nonviolent demonstrations proved a crucial tactic to win white sympathy.[131] Bogalusa, then, in many ways epitomized the significant role of both nonviolent direct action and armed resistance in the southern black freedom struggle. Not only did the Deacons work in close alliance with peaceful protest but they also ensured the local movement's survival and contributed to its ultimate success.

In this respect, the role of the Deacons was similar to that of defense organizations in Monroe, Birmingham, or Tuscaloosa. What distinguished the Louisiana group from these predecessors was the attempt to export its successful self-defense concept beyond the borders of the Pelican State. On trips to Mississippi and Alabama, Charles Sims, Earnest Thomas, and other Deacon organizers promoted manly self-defense and urged blacks to form new chapters. Speaking at a rally in Jackson, Mississippi, in late August 1965, for example, Earnest Thomas told an enthusiastic crowd of about three hundred men and women, "It is time for you men in Jackson to wake up and be men."[132] Sims and Thomas also traveled to northern cities, primarily to obtain funds. During his trips to San Francisco, Los Angeles, Chicago, Detroit, and New York City, Thomas advocated an expansion to the North. Calling himself regional vice president and northern director of the DDJ, Thomas began to organize the defense group's first northern chapter in Chicago in November 1965. In April 1966, the windy city's newspapers reported the official formation of the Deacons.[133]

But the group's expansive ambitions failed to establish a network of northern affiliates. The defense group's ideas proved of little help in the black ghettos outside the Deep South, where blacks rarely worried about Ku Klux Klan attacks but struggled with poverty, unemployment, and police brutality. In fact, neither the Chicago chapter nor those affiliates that were reportedly organized in Boston, Cleveland, and Newark between 1965 and 1966 had much in common with the original organization. The Deacons' northern supporters, a motley crew of black nationalists and white Socialists, seemed to have only a tenuous grasp on the original purpose of the Deacons. Above all else, they admired the Deacons for their armed toughness but were soon disabused of the hope that the Louisiana defense group might become the vanguard of the coming revolution.[134]

Ultimately, the Deacons' activities remained confined to Louisiana. Deacons from Jonesboro helped organize short-lived chapters in Homer, Minden, Tallulah, and Ferriday, all of which were located in the southern part of the state. Another chapter sprang up in New Orleans, although it was of little value, since Klan terror was most rampant in the rural areas of the state. Except for Homer, none of these chapters ever received a certificate from the parent organization. Neither was there much coordination between the groups. FBI reports about Deacon affiliates in Mississippi and other southern states suggest that what these groups shared with the Louisiana Deacons was little more than their name. Although sometimes inspired by the example of Jonesboro and Bogalusa, they more closely resembled the autonomous and independent groups that had formed in Monroe, Birmingham, or Tuscaloosa.[135]

The Deacons, then, could never assume the southernwide "organizational breadth and political influence" that historian Lance Hill claims the organization had.[136] The Deacons never developed a political program, and except for Earnest Thomas, its members had little interest in sustaining a presence beyond Louisiana.[137] Indeed, expansion proved unnecessary since the gospel that Thomas and others preached was already widely practiced across the region. But neither was the defense organization what Adam Fairclough has called a "gigantic hoax."[138] Deliberately inflated numbers and the failure to establish a national system of affiliates do not diminish the significance of the Deacons. Both the group's ability to thwart the worst forms of white terror and their inspiring effect on local African Americans made the Deacons an integral part of the black freedom movement in Louisiana.

White America's reaction to the self-defense group contrasted sharply with the respect they had won among black and white activists in Jonesboro and Bogalusa. In the minds of many, the Deacons seemed to constitute the twentieth-century equivalent of armed slave revolts, with Charles Sims the heir of slave rebel Nat Turner. As early as March 1965—the *New York Times* had first reported about the Jonesboro Deacons on February 21—LeRoy

Collins, the director of the federal Community Relations Service, sought an appointment with Attorney General Nicholas Katzenbach to express his concern about what he called "the Negro counterpart of the Minute Men."[139] Others considered the group a "Negro KKK" or denounced it as "Mao-inspired terrorist conspirators."[140]

Even comparably liberal national newspapers such as the *Los Angeles Times* criticized the Deacons. Although the editors of the *Times* were mindful of the dangerous circumstances that gave rise to the defense organization, they insisted that "the Deacons—like any other militant, extra-legal group—must still be deplored." The growth of such organizations, the editors warned, would only lead to "wholesale bloodshed and even anarchy."[141] Fred Zimmerman of the conservative *Wall Street Journal* went so far as to suggest that the emergence of the Deacons might mark the end of nonviolence.[142]

The DDJ seemed to cause even more alarm among the champions of white supremacy. In June 1965, one white resident of a town near Bogalusa angrily complained to his congressman: "They are supposed to have Machine guns, and hand grenades. I live seven miles from that arnsnal [*sic*], in the hands of a bunch of idoitic [*sic*] Negros [*sic*], and I want that investigated!"[143] The region's police officers too considered the Deacons dangerous vigilantes. From the perspective of Bogalusa's commissioner of public safety, the group was "a threat to society."[144] Such fears could produce bizarre effects. Months after the media frenzy about the defense unit had waned, Klansmen in Greenville County, Mississippi, seriously claimed that an alliance between black nationalists and Deacons used empty coffins to smuggle thousands of guns into Mississippi. Their goal, the Klan said, was to prepare a bloody uprising. In late November, Greenville County police officers actually agreed to open a grave in a black cemetery, where Klansmen suspected a large cache of guns. Predictably, neither the grave nor the casket contained any weapons, and a visibly embarrassed local sheriff was hard-pressed to justify the grisly operation.[145]

Louisiana governor McKeithen had enough sense to know that the prospect of armed black revolts was pure fantasy, but he too voiced concern about the black defense squad. In the aftermath of the Crowe shooting, McKeithen argued that the Deacons would only provoke more violence. To prevent further clashes, the governor dispatched more police and state troopers to the city. In addition, McKeithen ordered state police to confiscate the Deacons' weapons if they were carried during protest marches. He knew that this measure was illegal, and the governor's assurance that whites would be disarmed as well convinced few blacks to give up their pistols and shotguns. The Deacons argued that heeding McKeithen's request would leave them defenseless in the face of Ku Klux Klan terrorism. In the end, the governor probably sensed that forced disarmament would have provoked even more violence. Although police officers continued to arrest members of the protective unit on concealed weapons charges, both Deacons and Klansmen were allowed to keep their guns.[146]

Black civil rights leaders also condemned the Deacons, albeit for different reasons. "We can't win our struggle with violence," Martin Luther King told reporters in July 1965, "and to cloak it under the name of defensive violence really is no answer."[147] Veteran pacifist Bayard Rustin, who had been a major influence on King since the Montgomery bus boycott, joined in this uncompromising rejection of the Deacons. "I'm against armed defense on either side," he told the *Los Angeles Times*. "I'm against the Klan doing it. I'm against the Minutemen doing it. I'm against the Negroes doing it—for any reason."[148]

An editorial in SCLC's newsletter of fall 1965 voiced similar criticism. "We note with increasing alarm and concern," the editorial read, "that the Deacons for Defense and Justice . . . have begun to spread its preachments to increasing numbers." Citing SCLC's "profound commitment to nonviolence, its philosophy and the proven results of its practical application over the past 10 years," the authors made it clear that King's organization could not "condone in any way the methodology of any organization which advocates violence as a way of providing a solution to social ills."[149]

Such statements were probably a reflection of both King's and Rustin's deeply felt convictions and the pragmatic reasoning that official praise for the Deacons might undermine the moral power of the nonviolent movement. But few of the Deacons pondered the tactical pragmatism that influenced SCLC's critique, suspecting that King's organization sought to impose Gandhian precepts upon their membership. Exhorted by an SCLC activist on a TV show in June 1965 to strive for "reconciliation" instead of armed confrontation, Charles Sims countered that a taste of the violent atmosphere in Washington Parish would certainly change his mind. "After you've been in Bogalusa," Sims responded dryly, "*you* will look for *me*."[150]

By the time of this interview, CORE's southern field-workers and volunteers who worked in Bogalusa had come to accept blacks' protection measures as a matter of course. Even national director James Farmer openly admitted: "I'm glad the Deacons exist."[151] Asked by a journalist whether she approved of the militant organization, a young civil rights volunteer from California responded more bluntly, "Not really, but when you're down there, it's an irrelevant question."[152] Regardless of their philosophical convictions, most activists agreed that Louisiana's violent reality left little room for abstract discussions of Gandhi's teachings. Theory aside, some of CORE's staff even began to emulate the example of the Deacons. In August 1965, *Newsweek* reported that "some CORE workers in Bogalusa," "like practically everybody else in town, . . . are now carrying weapons."[153] As early as April, civil rights volunteers from Berkeley, armed with pistols, had assisted the Deacons in patrolling the black neighborhood. "When their numbers grew short," one of them remembered, "I was deputized as a deacon, carrying a handgun as student volunteers from my college went door to door."[154]

By that time, the philosophy of nonviolence had become a negligible influence within CORE. Meldon Acheson, after working for several weeks in the little town of Ferriday in Concordia Parish, was one of the last to struggle with his conscience. The fact that local blacks began to guard their houses with arms in the aftermath of the Crowe shooting plunged the college student and member of Tucson CORE into serious moral conflict. "Nearly everyone in the community is armed to the teeth," Acheson wrote to his parents on July 10, 1965, lamenting that "all but one are committed to non-violence only as tactic." In Acheson's view, his black fellow workers' arguments for self-defense were "unconvincing, and if they do decide to carry guns I'll have to ask to be removed from the project."[155]

Acheson's attempts to convince blacks through the Ferriday movement newsletter that their passive suffering would prompt the white man "to begin to doubt that what he is doing is right" proved fruitless.[156] Arguing that armed self-defense was "not 'against' CORE rules," local African Americans continued to guard their homes and the new Freedom House. Expectedly, there were armed confrontations. On July 21, when whites shot into the house of a black woman who supported CORE's campaign, she returned fire. Three days later, black CORE worker Archie Hunter met with local men to discuss the formation of a Deacon chapter. Just as in Jonesboro or Bogalusa, armed protection had become a vital part of the Ferriday movement.[157]

The growing acceptance of armed self-defense within CORE was not confined to the southern field staff. The organization's annual convention in Durham, North Carolina, in early June 1965 had already indicated that its traditional commitment to nonviolence was waning among southern and northern activists alike. The Deacons and Robert Williams had considerable influence on CORE's interpretation of the black freedom struggle. In addition, the legacy of black nationalist Malcolm X, a longtime critic of Martin Luther King's philosophy, prompted many to question the organization's traditional principles.[158] It came as no surprise that many of the three hundred delegates who attended the convention enthusiastically applauded Deacon Earnest Thomas's declaration that the era of "total Negro non-violence" was at an end.[159]

As a sign of the strong influence of black nationalists, CORE had invited Muslim minister Lonnie X of the all-black Nation of Islam to speak at the convention. He blasted CORE's two fundamental principles, calling for an end to the organization's policy of integration and nonviolence. Demonstrations, Lonnie X argued, would only degrade black men's dignity. Earning an approving "amen" from some of the delegates, he proclaimed that it was "better to spend 30 seconds in the glory of manhood than 1,000 years on our knees."[160] In this spirit, a number of activists urged CORE to adopt an official policy of self-defense. The Brooklyn chapter introduced a resolution that asked the delegates to "endorse the right and need of people to organize and to defend themselves against terrorist attacks."[161] The convention's Constitution Committee even discussed a proposition that demanded deleting all references to nonviolence from CORE's constitution.

As the debate raged on, black nationalists were probably surprised to hear Earnest Thomas appeal to the delegates to continue CORE's traditional method. Nonviolence, he said, still had tactical validity in southern projects, stressing that he and his fellow Deacons would continue to adhere to this protest strategy in demonstrations.[162] In the end, the lobbying efforts of Thomas and others paid off. On the morning of July 5, an overwhelming majority of delegates opted not to vote on a self-defense resolution. Immediately after the referendum, CORE informed the national media "that the present stand that CORE is a non-violent organization with no exception stands."[163]

But from the perspective of many journalists, the Deacons seemed to contradict this nonviolent image. For that reason, CORE went to great lengths to refute news reports that linked the organization to armed confrontations. As early as April 8, 1965, the *New York Post* had reported in a sensational article about the Deacons' first shoot-out with the Klan that CORE members had been involved in the armed confrontation. "Klansmen and CORE in Louisiana Gun Battle," announced that day's headline.[164] CORE vehemently denied the allegations. The very same day, assistant community relations director Robert Brookins Gore dispatched an angry letter to the editor of the *Post*. "CORE workers were not involved in a gun battle with the Ku Klux Klan," the letter averred. Although Gore conceded that local people might not always adhere to

Gandhian principles, he emphasized that CORE did not "advocate self-defense through the use of violence." Its members, he wrote, still believed "that nonviolence is the most effective approach to social change."[165]

Concerned about such reports, staff members at first believed that downplaying the role of the Deacons might be sufficient to mute media criticism. William Yates advised in a staff meeting on April 12: "The Deacons should definitely be kept in the background as they are not a civil rights organization and they tend to put the concern for protection first and the actual issue second."[166] But the armed confrontations between the Deacons and Klansmen in the following months demonstrated that such a policy of evasion was inadequate in dealing with the probing questions of white journalists. CORE's southern regional director Richard Haley expressed his concern in a memorandum: "[T]he Deacons have taken an increasingly important place in the press and other mass media. Of late the question has been directed to several CORE staff people, 'Do CORE and the Deacons plan together? Do they work jointly? Is CORE still non-violent? Does CORE support the Deacons?' and so forth."[167]

The organization's reputation for Gandhian nonviolence put James Farmer in a difficult position when pressured by reporters to respond to such questions. Since avoidance was no longer an option, he began to use every opportunity to justify CORE's alliance with the Louisiana group. Why, he asked, should African Americans have less of a right to defend themselves than white Americans? At a news conference before the Durham meeting, Farmer countered critical questions about the Deacons by stressing that CORE was "dedicated to the proposition that Negroes have a right to defend their homes."[168] If police officers provided no protection, he said, blacks had no choice but to organize their own protective agencies. To him, likening the Deacons to the Ku Klux Klan was ludicrous. "Some of the bad people like to compare the Deacons with the Klan and that's stupid," he wrote in the *Amsterdam News*. "The Deacons don't lynch, burn, or assault. The Deacons don't ride shotgun in the enemy camp."[169]

Regardless of whether self-defense was deemed justified or not, CORE walked a difficult tightrope in supporting the Deacons without forfeiting public support. Torn between admiration for the group and the need to accommodate white sensibilities, CORE made some statements about the defense group that clearly bent the truth. One of Richard Haley's comments in June 1965 was a case in point. "We live with the Deacons," he told *Ebony*, "even with our nonviolent philosophy, because we are able to accept each other's position. . . . Even in church you have your sinners; we feel we can demonstrate to these people with our philosophy of love and nonviolence that there is another way."[170]

That was an outright lie. Not even Haley, let alone his field staff, adhered to such abstract principles. Asked a few years later whether he believed in King's philosophy, he replied, "No, I think nonviolence is—as a way of life is alien to the human race."[171] In his memorandum on the CORE-Deacon relationship, Haley similarly conceded that any official guideline on the issue would have to be considered "outside the context of pure non-violence."[172] In truth, philosophical nonviolence remained little more than a concession to the organization's dependence on white liberal support. But CORE's experience in Louisiana was far from unique. In neighboring Mississippi, the Student Nonviolent Coordinating Committee struggled with very similar predicaments.

4

ARMED RESISTANCE AND
THE MISSISSIPPI MOVEMENT

At 3:00 A.M. on May 9, 1963, several firebombs exploded inside the home of black farmer Hartman Turnbow. Alarmed by the smell of burning gasoline and the sound of gunshots, he jumped out of bed, grabbed his .22-caliber rifle and ran outside to investigate. On the porch, he was welcomed by another round of gunfire by two white invaders. After repelling his attackers with a volley of shots, the black farmer rushed back inside to help his wife and young daughter extinguish the flames.[1]

The bombing of Hartman Turnbow's farm in Holmes County, Mississippi, was a direct result of local blacks' attempt to register to vote a month prior to the attack. On April 9, 1963, the fifty-nine-year-old farmer and a group of black men from the area had confronted hostile police officers at the county courthouse in nearby Lexington when they attempted to add their names to the voter rolls. The area's white population was inflamed by this unprecedented challenge to white supremacy and blamed "outside agitators" from SNCC for the turmoil. Determined to preserve white rule, segregationists launched a campaign of terror to stop the ongoing voter registration drive. Local police officers frequently covered up the crimes. The day after the attack on Turnbow's farm, for example, deputy sheriff Andrew Smith arrested the black farmer and several SNCC workers for arson, maintaining that Turnbow had firebombed his own house. Like Mississippi's local and state authorities, the federal government offered no protection. Although notified of the incident, the FBI and the Justice Department explained that federal agents could only investigate.[2]

Turnbow concluded that he would have to provide his own protection. Unlike most black Mississippians, Turnbow was a landowner.[3] Fiercely independent, he was not easily intimidated, not even by white police officers. The morning after the bombing, Turnbow, still armed with his rifle, welcomed the local sheriff in the front yard of his home. Told to put away the gun, the black farmer bluntly retorted, "Sheriff, didn't you hear what happened here last night, somebody attempted to burn my house down, and I'm going to keep my gun because I'm on my property and I have to defend it because I can't depend on you."[4] SNCC organizers found Turnbow similarly unresponsive to their pleas to give up his rifle. When black field-worker Charles Cobb queried him about the shoot-out, Turnbow replied: "I wasn't being non-non-violent. I was just protecting my wife and my family."[5]

In many ways, Turnbow's experience encapsulates the Mississippi freedom struggle's complexities. Arguably the most violent stronghold of southern white supremacy, the Magnolia State became the nightmare of many civil rights activists. As early as 1960, when SNCC organizers first ventured into the rural areas of the Mississippi Delta, brutal terror hindered their attempts to register black voters. The federal government's refusal to provide protection against racial murder and violent intimidation compounded SNCC's problems. Only the assistance of an economically independent and heavily armed generation of veteran Mississippi activists, most of whom had battled white supremacy since the end of World War II, enabled the organization to persevere.[6]

Not only these veteran activists relied on armed protection. Between 1963 and 1965, some black-dominated farming communities formed informal defense groups, which protected private homes, churches, community centers, and the offices of SNCC and CORE. Sometimes these guards battled it out with their white attackers. Others, like Hartman Turnbow, protected their families individually or joined with neighbors to organize armed guards in rotating shifts to repel white nightriders. These defensive efforts curtailed at least some of the violence that whites used to terrorize black communities.

Within SNCC, however, the widespread practice of armed self-defense among local blacks provoked serious debates. Organizers who advocated philosophical nonviolence encountered staunch opposition from black farmers. To these men and women, nonviolence as a way of life was difficult to fathom. From the perspective of black men, its connotations of passiveness clearly contradicted traditional notions of manhood. Accepting tactical non-violence in certain situations, few of these local activists saw contradictions between nonviolent demonstrations, voter registration drives, and armed re-sistance. SNCC organizers, on the other hand, repeatedly discussed the legiti-macy of armed self-defense.

In this respect, SNCC's experience in Mississippi paralleled that of CORE in Louisiana but had a more immediate impact on the organization's beliefs. SNCC was little more than a closely knit group of some two hundred field orga-nizers. In contrast to CORE, which consisted of a national office and relatively autonomous chapters and affiliates, SNCC had little interest in organizational expansion. Rather, its members focused on developing local leadership, which would enable blacks to fight their own struggle once the organizers left the state. While CORE workers in Louisiana followed similar principles, SNCC was even less inhibited by any guidelines that a national office might have estab-lished. More important, this approach practically forbade any attempt to im-pose theories of nonviolence on the people with whom they were working.

Conversely, their work with rural blacks deeply affected the beliefs of the small band of activists who determined the organization's program and ide-ology.[7] Philosophical nonviolence had never been a dominant belief within SNCC, and the experience of white terror and black resistance in Mississippi reinforced the conviction of many that nonviolence could never be more than a tactic. Ultimately, SNCC's experience in the Deep South, in particular its work in Mississippi from 1961 to 1964, resulted in a growing acceptance of self-defense among its members by 1965. But like CORE, SNCC depended on fi-nancial contributions from northern white liberals. As such, maintaining the organization's reputation for philosophical nonviolence became essential to continue its civil rights campaigns. While SNCC activists downplayed armed resistance, the NAACP, in a case that echoed the Robert F. Williams controversy of 1959, similarly struggled to mute more militant voices among its Mississippi staff.

SNCC's first voter registration drives in 1961 in the hilly southwest corner of the state were met by a wave of violence. In Amite and Pike Counties, whites routinely assaulted and beat SNCC activists and local black residents, while nighttime shotgun attacks added to their fears. In late September, violence turned to murder when white state representative E. H. Hurst shot and killed Herbert Lee, a black man who had become active in voter registration in the town of Liberty. White authorities refused to charge Hurst with the crime, ac-cepting his assurances and those of several witnesses that Lee had been killed in self-defense. In October, a white police officer escaped prosecution for the unprovoked murder of a black motorist in McComb.[8]

Located in Pike County, McComb exemplified the devastating effect of such violent incidents on civil rights organizing. After the death of Herbert Lee, SNCC's voter registration drive came to a grinding halt. The attempts of local high school students to stage nonviolent protest marches were similarly short-lived. By October 1961, when white authorities sentenced three SNCC workers and several local blacks to long jail terms, the organization's first Mississippi campaign had fizzled.[9]

SNCC's experience in McComb suggested the limits of philosophical non-violence in rural Mississippi and led the student organization's new chairman, Chuck McDew, to embrace armed protection. After most of his fellow activists had already left the county, the former college football player helped a local NAACP activist guard his house with guns. Several years later, McDew recalled: "Everybody pulled out one night [but] . . . Dr. Anderson and I stayed and we armed ourselves. That night when we got everybody out and sent them away, I remember we stayed up all night sitting at the window with guns, watching for anybody to come by." McDew had never felt a strong allegiance to SNCC's founding statement, which pledged philosophical nonviolence as the organization's fundamental principle. A year later, the violent atmosphere of McComb had reinforced his conviction that tactical nonviolence and armed self-defense could work in tandem. "I had no qualms, whatsoever," he said, "about accepting the gun from Dr. Anderson and sitting in the window prepared to shoot anybody who would try and harm us."[10]

Local NAACP activists had already learned this lesson, having armed for protection years before SNCC entered the state. Dr. T.R.M. Howard, for example, a successful black physician and businessman who founded the Regional Council of Negro Leadership (RCNL) in 1951, responded to threats on his life by posting a 24-hour guard at his house in the all-black town of Mound Bayou in the Mississippi Delta. Howard rarely traveled without armed bodyguards. In the violent aftermath of the *Brown* decision, dentist Emmett Stringer, the president of the Mississippi State Conference of NAACP Branches, protected his home with guns and was frequently armed when working at his office.[11] And in 1957, NAACP field secretary Medgar Evers reported protection efforts by blacks in Hattiesburg in the northeastern corner of the state. After a local black minister had testified about the state's racist practices at a congressional hearing, Evers wrote to the Association's national office, "even before he returned, open threats had been made on his family to the extent that the Negroes of the

Hattiesburg community guarded the house nightly to prevent any unnatural occurrence until he had returned."[12]

Evers himself was heavily armed. Like other black World War II veterans, the native Mississippian had attempted to register to vote upon his return to the United States. In 1946, Evers, his brother, Charles, and four other black soldiers had marched to the local courthouse. When they reached the building, a group of white men threatened them with guns and forced them to leave. Armed protection, Evers learned during his ensuing work for the NAACP, would be an essential part of civil rights activism in Mississippi. As his wife, Myrlie, later remembered, the Evers home in the state capital of Jackson was a minor arsenal. The family "had guns in every room of our house. I slept with a rifle next to me on the nightstand. He slept with a rifle next to him. We had one in the hall, we had one in the front room."[13]

For a short while, Evers had considered organizing guerrilla warfare against white segregationists in the Mississippi Delta. Like many African Americans in the 1950s, he admired the Mau Mau rebellion against white colonialism in Kenya and pondered adapting their violent tactics to the Deep South. His Christian faith ultimately prompted Evers to abandon this plan, but his admiration for Mau Mau leader Jomo Kenyatta remained strong. The name of his first son, Darell Kenyatta Evers, reflects a deeply felt respect.[14]

Although Evers realized that guerrilla warfare would be futile in the Deep South, he strongly believed in the right of self-defense. "Medgar," CORE activist Dave Dennis later recalled, "was not a nonviolent person. He did not feel that he should be aggressive, but he felt that he should defend himself."[15] Indeed, bombarded with numerous death threats, he took every possible precaution to protect himself and his family. Activist John Salter, a white sociology professor at Tougaloo College in Jackson, was welcomed with a gun when he and his wife stopped by at Evers's house one night in 1962.[16] While the family's dog continued to bark outside, Salter entered an armed fortress. "Inside the Evers home," he recalled later, "furniture was piled in front of all of the windows. At least a half dozen firearms were in the living room and kitchen."[17] When crisscrossing the state on lonely country roads to promote voter registration and to organize new NAACP chapters, Evers hid a .45 automatic under the pillow of the driver's seat and kept a rifle in the car's trunk. Passenger Salter remembered the tachometer frequently nudging more than ninety miles per hour, another safety measure to elude white pursuers.[18]

Fellow NAACP activists Aaron Henry and Amzie Moore were similarly prepared. They too had been spurred to civil rights activism by their military service during World War II. With the help of the federal GI Bill, Henry was able to attend pharmacy school and later opened a drugstore in Clarksdale, where in 1951 he co-organized the town's first NAACP chapter. By 1960, Henry had become the president of the state conference of NAACP branches. In the ensuing years, threats against him and his family became routine, and in 1963, white terrorists bombed his house and his drugstore. In response, members of the Clarksdale NAACP chapter organized a group of armed sentries to guard both buildings.[19] Moore, after returning from combat duty in Europe, assisted T.R.M. Howard in organizing the RCNL and later became president of the NAACP chapter in Cleveland, located only a short drive from Mound Bayou. Like Evers, Moore carried a gun for protection and frequently slept with a pistol under his pillow. "[W]henever anyone was threatened," SNCC organizer Lawrence Guyot remembered, "Amzie Moore was sort of an individual protection agency."[20]

John Salter soon followed the example of these veteran activists. The son of a Wabanaki Indian and a white mother, Salter and his wife, Eldri, had been inspired by the Freedom Rides and moved south to join the movement. In Jackson, he quickly became involved in civil rights organizing and helped the local NAACP chapter launch a boycott against discrimination in the city's white businesses at the end of 1962.[21] Salter and local black activists also began to stage nonviolent demonstrations and sit-ins to force the desegregation of lunch counters and restaurants. Expectedly, his activism triggered a wave of threats from white segregationists. Shortly before Christmas, white night riders fired into Salter's home on the campus of Tougaloo College, nearly killing his infant daughter, Maria. "For the remainder of the Christmas holidays," the activist wrote later, "several students and myself stood armed guard all night long—and let this be known to the news services."[22]

Despite these protective efforts, the Jackson movement adhered to the principles of nonviolent direct action. During a sit-in in early June 1963, Salter and some of his students were brutally beaten by white toughs, who poured mustard and ketchup on their heads. One of the white men punched Salter in the face with brass knuckles, causing a deep cut that began to bleed profusely. That only increased the mob's fury. Some poured salt into the open wound. Instead of restraining the white attackers, police arrested the injured protestors.[23] Salter was far from accepting these brutal beatings because of a deeply felt commitment to Gandhian precepts. "I'm not a pacifist at all," he stressed in an interview. "I didn't feel that by practicing nonviolence that we were converting the souls of our antagonists." Rather he used nonviolence as a tactic, arguing that aggressive violence on the part of black protestors might have triggered massive white retaliation.[24]

More important, black aggression would have antagonized white northern liberals, whose sympathy and support was crucial to the success of both the Jackson movement and the national freedom struggle. Sometimes Salter had to be reminded of this reality. In a letter to the civil rights organizer in February 1963, Anne Braden, a veteran white activist and editor of the movement publication *Southern Patriot*, elucidated some of the complexities that CORE had already learned in Louisiana. Responding to one of Salter's articles on the Jackson movement, Braden wrote, "One thing I cut out of your story that I should call your special attention to was the sentence on how you armed yourselves and then the attacks stopped." "Frankly," she reasoned, "I was afraid it might lose you sympathy of some people whose support across the country you want and need."[25]

Braden did not attempt to impose any pacifist tenets on Salter. In 1954, while residing in Louisville, Kentucky, with her husband, Carl, Braden herself took to carrying a gun after being threatened by whites for assisting a black family move into an all-white neighborhood. "Don't get me wrong," she assured Salter, "I don't think anybody sitting in a safe comfortable apartment in New York has any right to tell you not to arm yourself . . . but frankly some people react this way."[26] While she considered armed protection perfectly legitimate, she hinted at the need for pragmatism. As the fund director of the liberal Southern Conference Educational Fund (SCEF), Braden had considerable experience in raising contributions from those who sympathized with the cause of African Americans. Like CORE's James Farmer, she undoubtedly knew that reports about armed resistance would do little to win white support.[27]

The death of Medgar Evers, who was killed by a sniper in front of his home on June 11, 1963, prompted a number of black Jacksonians to ignore such considerations. When blacks staged nonviolent demonstrations to protest the murder of Evers, white police brutally dispersed them. In this volatile situation, some African Americans pondered retaliation. One local minister warned: "Some people are ready to shoot, they're going around buying guns. We're trying to keep them under control, but I just don't know."[28] A fellow Jackson activist wrote to Salter on June 14, "I really feel that it is . . . time for violence but don't give that to the press (smile)."[29] Struggling to calm the angry black population, Salter informed Jackson's mayor, Allen Thompson, that blacks were arming themselves. The community, he warned, might soon explode into violence.[30]

Figure 1. An unidentified black soldier during a military training exercise at Fort Belvoir, Virginia, November 1942. Their military service during World War II spurred many African Americans to political activism. World War II and Korean War veterans constituted the core of black defense groups in the southern civil rights struggle. Courtesy of the Library of Congress.

Figure 2. Roy Wilkins, executive secretary of the National Association for the Advancement of Colored People (NAACP), 1963. Wilkins went to great lengths to mute public calls for armed resistance among the Association's officers, most notably in the cases of Robert F. Williams (1959) and Charles Evers (1965). Courtesy of the Library of Congress.

Figure 3. Martin Luther King Jr. at a press conference in March 1964. King proved a brilliant nonviolent tactician who skillfully manipulated the media representations of the movement to nurture white liberal support for the civil rights cause. However, the movement's public focus on King's notion of nonviolence as a way of life created an artificial dichotomy between nonviolent protest and armed self-defense. Courtesy of the Library of Congress.

Figure 4. White police officers arrest a black teenager during the confrontation between the police and the Tuscaloosa Citizens for Action Committee (TCAC) at First African Baptist Church on June 9, 1964. The attack on the church and nonviolent protestors prompted black activists to form Tuscaloosa's defense organization. Courtesy of the *Tuscaloosa News*.

Figure 5. TCAC president T. Y. Rogers, who accepted and welcomed the protection efforts of Tuscaloosa's defense unit, negotiates with white police officers on June 11, 1964. Courtesy of the *Tuscaloosa News*.

Figure 6. Joseph Mallisham, the founder and leader of Tuscaloosa's protective squad, speaking at a roundtable discussion on the legacy of the civil rights movement in Tuscaloosa, Alabama, in January 2004. Reproduced by permission of the *Tuscaloosa News*.

Figure 7. James Farmer, national director of the Congress of Racial Equality (CORE), at a meeting of the American Society of Newspaper Editors in April 1964. Confronted with the militant actions of the Deacons for Defense and Justice, Farmer was hard-pressed to justify the close relationship between CORE and the Louisiana-based defense organization in the national media. Courtesy of the Library of Congress.

Figure 8. Robert Hicks, member of the Bogalusa Voters League (BVL), after a shootout between members of the Deacons for Defense and Justice and the Ku Klux Klan in Bogalusa, Louisiana, during the night of April 7, 1965. Reproduced by permission of AP/Wide World Photos.

Figure 9. Charles Sims, the president of the Bogalusa chapter of the Deacons for Defense and Justice, during a demonstration in Bogalusa on January 28, 1966. © Bettman/CORBIS.

Figure 10. Two black teenagers guarding the Freedom House in Harmony, Mississippi, during the summer of 1964. Reproduced from Nicholas von Hoffman, *Mississippi Notebook* (New York: David White Company, 1964). Photographer: Henry Herr Gill.

Figure 11. A view of the inside of Harmony's Freedom House, which was one among many buildings that black Mississippians protected against Ku Klux Klan attacks during the 1964 Freedom Summer project. Reproduced from Nicholas von Hoffman, *Mississippi Notebook* (New York: David White Company, 1964). Photographer: Henry Herr Gill.

Figure 12. Joe Greer, a black farmer in Harmony, Mississippi, posing with his guns during the summer of 1964. Like Greer, many of the state's black landowners faced racist reprisals because of their civil rights activism and protected their property on an individual basis or joined with others to organize informal defense groups. Reproduced from Nicholas von Hoffman, *Mississippi Notebook* (New York: David White Company, 1964). Photographer: Henry Herr Gill.

Figure 13. Edwin Newman, Lawrence Spivak, Roy Wilkins, Whitney Young (*front row, left to right*), Floyd McKissick, Stokely Carmichael, and James Meredith (*back row*) discuss Black Power and its implications for blacks' right to self-defense on *Meet the Press* on August 21, 1966. © 2005 NBC Universal, Inc. All rights reserved.

Figure 14. Black nationalist leader Malcolm X, the most outspoken critic of Martin Luther King's philosophy in the early 1960s, at a press conference on March 26, 1964. Courtesy of the Library of Congress.

Figure 15. Bobby Seale and Huey P. Newton, the founders of the Black Panther Party, advocated a concept of armed self-defense that differed considerably from the armed actions of southern protective squads. Utilizing the theories of Malcolm X, Karl Marx, Frantz Fanon, and Mao Zedong, Seale and Newton argued that revolutionary violence constituted a legitimate form of self-defense against the white oppressor. Courtesy of the Library of Congress.

Figure 16. The writings and public statements of Eldridge Cleaver, the Black Panther Party's minister of information, reflected an almost obsessive concern with regaining black manhood through armed resistance. Courtesy of the Library of Congress.

As white segregationists stepped up their campaign of terror against the emerging freedom movement, some observers speculated that race war was imminent. In the aftermath of the assassination of Evers, Hodding Carter, Pulitzer Prize–winning editor of the *Delta Democrat*, wrote gloomily in the *New York Times Magazine*: "There is an almost fatalistic acceptance of the belief, openly expressed by members of both races, that a state which a year ago was relatively serene is headed now for a violent showdown."[31] Many local African Americans expected the same and questioned the idea that nonviolent protest could stop segregationist brutality, let alone topple white supremacy. "At that time," activist Dave Dennis recalled, "it wasn't about people being . . . that difficult to get involved in the movement as it was for them to accept the philosophy of nonviolence."[32]

Holmes County illustrates both the difficulties to which Dennis alluded and the significant role of armed resistance in Mississippi's predominantly black-owned areas. In the 1930s, the federal government had distributed plots of land to hundreds of African American families in the county, which is located on the eastern edge of the Mississippi Delta. The goal of this New Deal program was to transform white and black sharecroppers and tenants into independent landowners. In Holmes County, the government's low-interest loans and technical assistance enabled African Americans to build several all-black communities. Landownership and economic self-reliance translated into determined and confident local leadership in the freedom movement of the 1960s. In Holmes County, for example, far more landowners than tenants participated in civil rights meetings, and nearly half of them joined civil rights organizations. By 1965, almost 60 percent had attempted to register to vote.[33]

For some of the county's black men, landownership became an important aspect of their manhood and influenced the African American response to white violence. "It has made me feel like a man," one farmer said, recalling his feelings after receiving a plot of land.[34] Protecting their property and their families with guns became a way to defend this new sense of self. World War II veteran Robert Cooper, resident of the all-black Milestone community, later commented on his shoot-out with Klansmen in 1965: "I felt that you're in your house, ain't botherin nobody, the only thang you hunting is equal justice. An' they gonna sneak by at night, burn your house, or shoot in there. And you gonna sit there and take all of it? You got to be a very li'l man with no guts at all."[35] Hartman Turnbow had similar things to say about his motivation to repel white attackers: "I had a wife, and I had a daughter, and I loved my wife just like a white man loves his'n, and a white man will die for his'n, and I say I'll die for mine."[36] Like the Deacons for Defense and Justice, these independent farmers felt obliged to assume the role of patriarchal protector of their families.

It is likely that many white Americans shared these ideas, but they carried special significance for blacks. The wife of slain NAACP leader Medgar Evers explained in her memoirs: "The willingness—the ability—of a man to protect his family is probably the basic element in our concept of manhood. The willingness to protect one's woman from the sexual advances and assaults of other men is central to it."[37] Women like Anne Moody, a Mississippi native and civil rights activist who was all too familiar with the violent traditions of the state, believed that black men had an obligation to protect their community. If they failed to do so, as in the case of the brutal murder of black teenager Emmett Till in 1955, Moody questioned their manhood. "[I]t was at this stage in my life," she recalled of her feelings after the Till lynching, "that I began to look upon Negro men as cowards."[38] In assuming the protection of women and children, Evers, Turnbow, and other black Mississippians regained part of the manhood that whites had long denied them.

Acknowledging this struggle over the meanings of manhood helps us to understand the ambivalent feelings that some black activists had about the philosophy of nonviolence. "Well, yeah," Holmes County leader Jodie Scaffold remembered in an interview, "Dr. King wanted to see nonviolent; if they slap you on the jaw, turn the other cheek. But if they hit, I was gon' hit 'em back."[39] When Medgar Evers urged Hattiesburg activist J. C. Fairly to become the president of the city's NAACP chapter, he received a similar response. "If you want me to end up being in the NAACP you can count me out being nonviolent," Fairly told Evers. "I ain't going to let nobody do something to me that I ain't going to try to do back to them."[40] Upon meeting Martin Luther King, Hartman Turnbow warned the SCLC's president bluntly: "This nonviolent stuff ain't no good. It'll get ya killed."[41]

In the eyes of these men, armed resistance to white violence was nothing unusual. Recalling a shoot-out with a group of Klansmen, Robert Cooper insisted: "I don't figure that I was violent. All I was doin' was protectin' myself."[42] Turnbow's response to SNCC workers that he "wasn't being non-non-violent" but was simply protecting his family similarly echoed these homegrown traditions of what Robert Williams called "armed self-reliance." Even Robert Moses, a soft-spoken black New Yorker who was probably one of SNCC's most deeply committed pacifists, had to concede that few black Mississippians would accept nonviolence as a way of life. "I could never talk about it to people we were working with," he reflected. "To the farmers in Mississippi, carrying a gun, protecting your home, was a way of life."[43]

As Moses discovered, gun ownership was widespread among black and white southerners. "Almost everybody with whom we stayed in Mississippi had guns, as a matter of course, hunting guns," black activist Julian Bond remembered. "But, you know," he added, "they were there for other purposes too."[44] The veteran activists that assisted in SNCC's voter registration campaigns were no exception. One of the local leaders that Moses and others were working with was E. W. Steptoe, an older independent dairy farmer and chairman of the Amite County NAACP. Steptoe demonstrated his belief in the importance of armed protection on a daily basis. "He never went out of the door unarmed," SNCC staffer Charlie Cobb recalled. Steptoe was also an expert in concealing guns. Although his wife regularly patted him down for weapons, for example, she never found the little derringer pistol that Steptoe kept in one of his socks.[45] The black farmer's house bristled with rifles and pistols. Charles McDew remembered in an interview: "Steptoe was always so wonderfully well armed. . . . It was just marvelous. . . . You'd go to Steptoe's and as you went to bed he would open up the night table [and] there would be a large .45 automatic sitting next to you. Just guns all over the house, under pillows, under chairs." Pacifist Moses felt troubled by this arsenal, but McDew and others heartily welcomed Steptoe's precautions.[46]

Across the state, SNCC as well as CORE, whose activities in Mississippi were confined to the fourth congressional district, relied on local people like Steptoe for advice, shelter, and protection. In Canton, a majority-black town located in the southwest of the state, CORE's voter registration drive would have fizzled quickly had local blacks not supported them. Women like Annie Devine helped the organizers reach the black community, informing blacks about mass meetings and registration clinics.[47] Another crucial figure that sustained CORE and galvanized the local movement was C. O. Chinn. He and his wife owned a restaurant and some property, which afforded them a relatively comfortable standard of living. When CORE arrived in Canton in the fall of 1963, Chinn provided office space next to his café, and Mrs. Chinn fed the organizers fried chicken, black-eyed peas, and other typical southern fare. This unflagging support, however, spelled disaster for Chinn's business, which immediately became a target for white economic reprisals.[48]

Like Turnbow, Chinn was unlikely to become a follower of Gandhi. At forty-two, Chinn had a well-established reputation as "bad-ass C. O. Chinn."[49] Respected and admired by most local African Americans, his irascible personality put fear into many whites. "Every white in that town had an understanding," activist Matthew Suarez remembered, "that you did not fuck with C. O. Chinn 'cause he would kick your natural ass."[50] Predictably, he staunchly opposed nonviolence. "If they wanted to come violent," Chinn recalled, "they got violent. . . . If you hit me, I'm going to hit back."[51] Openly carrying a .45 revolver, Chinn also made sure that the CORE workers were protected against white harassment. When civil rights rallies were scheduled, Chinn frequently guarded the meeting place, sitting in his truck with a gun beside him. Similar to the Louisiana Deacons, Chinn and some of his sons and cousins often chauffeured the CORE organizers and volunteers to towns in the surrounding Madison County. According to Suarez, "all of his family would take and drive us anyplace we had to go. . . . It was like having your own bodyguards."[52]

Faced with an unabated wave of intimidation, some CORE activists in Canton began to carry guns themselves. In early October 1963, rumors spread that white police might raid the local CORE office, but policemen kept the organizers guessing. For several nights, they roused the three female CORE workers who stayed at the Freedom House from their sleep by flashing lights at the building. A few days later, field-worker Anne Moody was stunned to find her friends sitting in the office, cleaning a rifle and a pistol. "[W]e just kinda figured we needed protection around the house," one of her fellow activists told a perplexed Moody. "After all," she said, "three young women just don't live in Mississippi alone without protection."[53] For the following months, Moody and her friends, jumping up in panic at the slightest sound, slept with the rifle standing in the corner next to the bed. The pistol lay within easy reach on the nightstand.[54]

By the end of 1963, such episodes could no longer shock SNCC field-workers. While local people like Turnbow seemed to believe that the organization remained committed to King's philosophy, only a minority was. Like Charles McDew, many activists viewed nonviolence merely as a tactic. Black field-organizer Hollis Watkins later explained, "Well, from my understanding, trying to be realistic in the whole process, SNCC accepted nonviolence as a tactic." According to Watkins, only a minority of members was ready to die for their convictions.[55] Charles Jones, another black field-worker, said in an interview, "I never went so far in my own pilgrimage into nonviolence as to feel that to allow a nut to kill you was healthy. As a matter of fact, that seems to me to be an expression of something less than mental health."[56] African American organizer Don Harris later estimated that as early as 1962 more than 50 percent of SNCC's staff rejected a philosophical interpretation of nonviolence.[57]

As in the case of CORE, however, SNCC's fund-raising literature suggested that the organization's membership held a deeply felt commitment to non-violence as a way of life. One leaflet that SNCC used to appeal for financial contributions clearly gave readers the impression that the students' thinking was dominated by love and reconciliation. The reprinted article from the *Chicago Daily News* prominently noted the organization's statement of purpose. SNCC's aim, "like King's," the author explained, "is to appeal to the white man's conscience—thus setting the stage for equal rights and peaceful co-existence of the races."[58] In another pamphlet that called attention to the campaign of terror against blacks in Mississippi, SNCC's used a reprinted article from the *Saturday Evening Post*. Potential supporters learned that the student group had "revolutionized" the black freedom struggle "with the sophisticated technique of nonviolent protest, adopted from their patron saint, the Indian Mahatma Gandhi."[59] SNCC's sophisticated public relations work cultivated the organization's reputation for Gandhian nonviolence. "The SNCC worker," in the words of historian Taylor Branch, "came to be heralded as a figure of relentless sacrifice, against all conventional ambitions."[60]

In actuality, devoted Gandhians had already become a minority within SNCC, reflecting a process similar to the one that CORE workers underwent in Louisiana. Bob Moses, the bespectacled New Yorker with a master's degree in philosophy from Harvard University, was one among very few who remained committed to nonviolence as a way of life. An avid reader of existentialist philosophy, Moses found the Gandhian technique to be an ideal tool to organize one's life. He hoped that his nonviolent example would convince others to follow.[61] The organization's new chairman, John Lewis, shared Moses's strong commitment to these principles. As a former member of black minister James Lawson's student group in Nashville and a veteran of the Freedom Ride, Lewis adhered to an uncompromising notion of nonviolence. "Being deeply religious," white SNCC member Sue Thrasher later wrote about Lewis, "John, more than any other person I knew during this period, believed in the philosophy of nonviolence. While others were willing to employ it as a strategy, for John it was a deeply held belief."[62] Not surprisingly, Lewis scorned what he regarded as a lack of commitment among those who had joined SNCC after the Freedom Ride. In his autobiography, he lamented that these new activists "were at best merely tolerant of the notion of nonviolence." Their secular pragmatism deeply troubled Lewis.[63]

By contrast, James Forman, a black activist who had joined SNCC in 1961, was surprised that the students from Nashville continued to discuss nonviolence in philosophical terms. About ten years older than the average SNCC member, the former high school teacher interpreted the Gandhian technique in rather practical terms. For him, as he explained in his memoirs, "nonviolence did not commit you not to strike back ever. My nonviolence has always been the most tactical of all possible tactical nonviolence."[64]

SNCC workers' frustration with the federal government's adamant refusal to provide protection for activists and local people in Mississippi left them rather cynical about movement tactics. Plans for the organization's 1964 Freedom Summer Project reflected this cynicism. In the spring of that year, Robert Moses announced that SNCC would bring hundreds of white northern volunteers to the state to conduct voter registration drives. This, the activists hoped, would finally focus national attention on Mississippi and force the federal government to stop white threats. Some activists speculated that the death of a white person might finally bring the attention that a string of racial murders had not.[65]

Shortly before the beginning of Freedom Summer, SNCC organizers engaged in a heated debate about the issue of armed self-defense. At a staff meeting on June 10 in Atlanta, several staffers reported about the violent atmosphere in Greenwood, a city on the eastern rim of the Mississippi Delta. There, armed guards had protected the SNCC office since January. Field-workers James Jones and Charlie Cobb justified these actions with the fact that Klansmen had burned crosses near the office. "The feeling is," Cobb said, "that violence this summer will be directed at black staff members and leaders and not at white summer volunteers. Staff members felt they would be killed." Cobb argued that the armed guards not only prevented burglars from breaking into the office for food and clothes but were also necessary to defend the office in case of racist attacks.[66]

The fact that black Mississippians continued to arm themselves raised difficult questions for SNCC. When Willie Peacock, a young student activist from the Mississippi Delta, reported of a "self-defense structure" that Greenwood blacks had organized to repel white attackers, Don Harris asked his comrades whether SNCC organizers had a right to "stop people from doing what they want to do."[67] They did not, Bob Moses replied. "Self-defense is so deeply ingrained in rural Southern America," he said, "that we as a small group can't affect it. It's not contradictory for a farmer to say he's nonviolent and also pledge to shoot a marauder's head off." Still, he insisted, no staff members should be allowed to carry weapons.[68]

Several months earlier, Moses had requested that field-workers keep no guns in the Freedom House in Greenwood. Concerned that police might use the weapons as a pretext to raid the office, he sent student activist Stokely Carmichael to remove them. During the June 10 meeting, those in attendance

agreed that SNCC ought to follow this directive. Yet, according to James Forman, "many SNCC people did arm themselves" when white attacks continued
in the following weeks. Forman himself positioned "a nightly armed guard
around the Greenwood office which became SNCC's national headquarters for
the summer."[69] John Lewis strongly disagreed with that decision but was unable to reverse it.[70]

Another problem that the staff discussed that day was how SNCC members ought to react if caught in a situation that required armed self-defense.
Charles Cobb gave an example of SNCC's predicament. "We will be living on
a farm with a man who has guns," he hypothesized. "What would happen if
someone attacked his house and he shot back[?] If Charlie were there would
SNCC stand by him, even though SNCC advocates nonviolence[?]" Activist Willie Blue threw in that it was "a personal thing." Prathia Hall said that although
she was far from having "a martyr complex," she would never be able to "take
a life knowingly." In her view, killing a white man in self-defense would only
invite white retaliation. Mike Sayer disagreed. He insisted that defending one's
home was about "dignity." Moreover, he said, the example of Robert Williams
had demonstrated that organized self-defense could be successful. In the end,
the exhausted staffers agreed on two things: first, SNCC would "defend anyone
caught in [a] home of another person who is armed."[71] Second, despite the
request of some activists to officially endorse armed resistance, SNCC would
"take no public position on self-defense."[72]

Although field-workers left the meeting with some vague guidelines, the
discussion had resolved little. In many ways, they had dodged some of the
most fundamental questions. What role should armed self-defense play in the
black freedom movement? Was armed resistance a legitimate, perhaps even
essential, part of SNCC's struggle for civil rights in Mississippi? For many, the
Freedom Summer project would ultimately answer these questions.

Two days after the debate in Atlanta, the first contingent of Freedom Summer volunteers arrived at the Western College for Women in Oxford, Ohio,
for a week of orientation and intensive training. SNCC had managed to recruit
some nine hundred college students, most of whom were from northern upper
middle-class families. Almost 90 percent of the recruits were white. Working
under the auspices of the Council of Federated Organizations (COFO), an umbrella organization that coordinated the efforts of SNCC, CORE, SCLC, and the
NAACP in Mississippi, the volunteers had committed themselves to working in
voter registration and to teaching African American children in independent
Freedom Schools.[73]

In lectures and workshops, veteran SNCC workers and outside speakers prepared the students for the dangerous venture. During one of the first sessions,
COFO volunteers peppered Justice Department representative John Doar with
questions. "What will be the role of the federal government in protecting our
lives?" one student asked, bringing up a subject that was on the minds of many.
"There is no federal police force," Doar informed the student audience, draw-
ing angry shouts and boos.[74] Veteran civil rights activists understood the angry
reaction, but they were not surprised. SNCC and CORE had inundated the federal government with requests for protection for years, but to no avail.[75]

Less than a week after Doar's speech, events in Mississippi became a grim
reminder that the Justice Department's policy was a brutal reality. On June
21, Bob Moses relayed the news that three COFO workers were missing in
Neshoba County, located in the heart of Mississippi. A local black activist,
James Chaney, and two white CORE workers, Andrew Goodman and Michael
Schwerner, had not reported back after investigating one of the latest church
bombings near the town of Philadelphia. SNCC workers had little hope of finding the three men alive. The calmness with which Moses talked about the possibility of death impressed the frightened students. Barry Clemson, a white
volunteer from Pennsylvania State University, recalled later, "you had the feeling that Moses would remain centered and calm no matter what happened and
that was comforting because everybody was scared shitless."[76]

Overshadowed by the ominous news from Neshoba County, the orientation's workshops and lectures put special emphasis on the question of nonviolence. Prior to the beginning of Freedom Summer, some northern commentators had voiced their concern that SNCC might provoke violent turmoil
in Mississippi. In a letter to the concerned parents of the summer volunteers,
Moses attempted to dispel these fears. "All workers, staff and summer volunteers alike," he declared, "are pledged to nonviolence in all situations."[77] During
the Oxford orientation, however, Bob Moses and other SNCC veterans were
less doctrinaire, stressing that every volunteer would at least have to adhere to
tactical nonviolence.[78] "We were taught the 'nonviolent position,' a fetal-like
position one falls into when being attacked," Steven Bingham from Berkeley,
California, later noted, "and were told we *must* accept non-violence as a tactic
if we wished to go to Mississippi."[79] Moses also exhorted the students not to
bring knives or guns. "We will not allow any staff member or volunteer to carry
a weapon," he said. From his perspective, that was "absolutely bedrock."[80]

The discussions that followed made it clear that Mississippi's brutal reality
would make things far more complicated than Moses had suggested in his

letter to the volunteers' parents. For example, while one rule of conduct forbade students to carry weapons, another basic principle exhorted them not to "preach to local people that they shouldn't defend themselves if they decide to."[81] Similarly, SNCC offered no policy to those who would find themselves under attack from white racists. Asked the very same questions that Charles Cobb had raised during the staff debate in Atlanta, Moses responded in a workshop on June 24, "If you were in a house which was under attack, and the owner was shot, and there were kids there, and you would take his gun to protect them—should you? I can't answer that."[82]

While the students pondered these issues, it became obvious that many of them remained skeptical of the philosophical side of nonviolence. According to one participant, pacifist minister James Lawson's talk on this topic on June 24 "was greeted with a great chill."[83] Nonviolence, Lawson exhorted his audience, was not a tactic but a way of life.[84] As "Christians," white volunteer Richard Gould summarized the minister's argument, students were "called upon to pray for the oppressor, even as he kicks us in the stomach and knocks our teeth out." Lawson prophesied that such examples of "loving sacrifice" would "transform Mississippi." Those who felt that they were unable to adopt nonviolence as their "own personal way of life" during Freedom Summer ought to return home.[85]

The black pastor's remarks about the need for "self-bearing goodwill" together with his rather narrow interpretation of nonviolence puzzled a considerable number of students. "[T]hey were irritated," one observer later noted, "and it showed itself in the sharp negative shakes of the head, in the angry rebuttal whispered to a neighbor."[86] A baffled veteran SNCC field-worker asked Lawson how love would help him survive when being shot at by white racists. The minister's abstract response was unconvincing to him.[87] One volunteer, in a letter to his parents, voiced his suspicion that few activists adhered to Lawson's philosophy. "I feel very strongly," he averred, "that he does NOT represent the Movement." From this student's perspective, nonviolence was "a perverted way of life, but a necessary tactic and technique."[88] It is not clear how many activists concurred with this assertion, but according to historian Mary Aickin Rothschild, a "majority of the COFO staff and volunteers . . . seemed to accept nonviolence as a tactic only."[89]

Despite the general consensus that nonviolence had to be adopted for tactical reasons while in Mississippi, a few voices denounced the technique as unmanly. Black writer Louie Lomax argued in his speech to the summer volunteers that one of the reasons why whites refused to respect African Americans as citizens was black men's inability to protect themselves and their families. Describing the growing anger among blacks across America, he predicted that the movement was "almost at the end of non-violence."[90] In this spirit, one frustrated SNCC activist mused that blacks ought to abandon nonviolence and fight back. Only then, regardless of the futility of their resistance, would they be able to feel like men and "go down in history."[91] Tactical necessity or not, the concept of nonviolence continued to evoke negative connotations of passiveness and powerlessness.

The campaign of terror that white racists had launched in anticipation of the Freedom Summer campaign probably reinforced such skepticism. In February 1964, the new White Knights of the Ku Klux Klan had formed in Mississippi. Led by a forty-year-old businessman named Samuel Holloway Bowers, the new organization burned crosses, bombed churches, and attacked black homes across the state.[92] The unabated wave of racial murders was a glaring reminder of the Klan's determination to destroy the Mississippi freedom movement. The same month that the White Knights were founded, Louis Allen, a black logger from McComb who had testified in the 1961 Herbert Lee murder case, was killed from ambush. In 1962, Allen had signed an affidavit in which he confessed that white men had forced him to lie in court. Contrary to his court testimony, the affidavit stated that state representative E. H. Hurst had killed Lee "without provocation," not in self-defense. Since that time, Allen had been a marked man.[93]

In the ensuing months, white supremacists seemed to prepare for more attacks. In May, the Mississippi State Sovereignty Commission, a state agency that spied on the activities of SNCC and other civil rights activists, reported "increased activity in weapon shipments" in Mississippi and Louisiana.[94] Rather than being the herald of freedom, Freedom Summer promised to become what historian Kenneth O'Reilly has termed "the summer of the Ku Klux Klan."[95]

Despite the disappearance of the three civil rights workers in Neshoba County and the violent attacks on black homes and churches, the federal government continued to claim that it could provide no protection. While Attorney General Robert Kennedy was deeply disturbed by the lawlessness in the state, he publicly stated that the Mississippi situation was "a local matter for local law enforcement." Since federal authority in the state was "very, very limited," the administration could take no preventive police action against white terror.[96] Neither the repeated calls for federal intervention by civil rights activists nor the official statement by a group of well-known law professors that existing law actually gave the administration the power to dispatch troops to Mississippi could jolt President Lyndon B. Johnson into action.[97]

As legal historian Michael Belknap has pointed out, the administration's strong commitment to a traditional legal interpretation of federalism, which granted considerable autonomy and power to state and local institutions, precluded any major shift in federal policies.[98] Of course, the disappearance of the three COFO activists had prompted President Johnson to order a large-scale FBI investigation, but the little army of agents that descended upon Neshoba County in June did not make the region safer. Neither did state and local authorities feel any obligation to assist the FBI in finding the three activists. Instead, defiant Mississippi senator James Eastland mocked the incident as "a hoax," which he believed to be orchestrated by Communist conspirators.[99]

Confronted with federal indecisiveness and segregationist ridicule, SNCC organized its own search for Chaney, Goodman, and Schwerner. In the meantime, on June 23, the FBI had fished the missing men's burned-out station wagon out of a swamp near Philadelphia. The news confirmed activists in the belief that their three comrades were already dead. When the first of SNCC's search teams arrived in Philadelphia, Neshoba County appeared more dangerous than ever. Heavily armed Klansmen and local police jointly patrolled the area. Frightened but undeterred, SNCC activists began to investigate, assisted by local people who provided refuge and protection. The old farmer that housed the Howard University students Cleveland Sellers and Stokely Carmichael joined with another black man to guard his farm with shotguns. At night, Sellers and Carmichael searched the swampy woods. Blacks, armed with rifles and shotguns, fanned out during the day, pretending to be on a hunting trip. Their assistance was crucial to the work of SNCC. "Had it not been for the aid of" local people, Sellers reflected, "we could not have survived for more than a few hours."[100] Despite these joint efforts, however, Chaney, Goodman, and Schwerner remained missing.

The search for the three men and the eventual discovery of their bodies in an earthen dam near Philadelphia in early August shattered the nonviolent convictions of many. "Although SNCC and CORE were nonviolent organizations," Sellers wrote in his autobiography, "we did not intend to remain nonviolent if apprehended. . . . I was prepared to kill if that was what it would take to keep me alive."[101] When the dead men were finally discovered, CORE's Dave Dennis renounced philosophical nonviolence as well. The brutal murder of James Chaney—white racists had savagely beaten him before executing him and his two friends—deeply shocked him. At Chaney's funeral, an angry and crying Dennis suggested that nonviolence alone was not enough to win full equality. "At that point," he recalled, "I felt the whole nonviolence bit and everything else was just a mistake. And I didn't believe in it anymore."[102] Dennis had become convinced that the southern movement had to rely on armed self-defense and became a strong supporter of the Deacons for Defense and Justice. After leaving CORE in late 1964, he worked closely with the defense group in his native Louisiana.[103]

Unlike Dennis, black Mississippians needed no reminder that armed resistance was a simple necessity. During the Freedom Summer, African Americans across the state met white supremacist terror with bullets and buckshot. In Holmes County, Hartman Turnbow and other independent farmers had already demonstrated their willingness to defend themselves. Turnbow's defiance and his repeated shoot-outs with white racists had made him a "folk hero" among local blacks.[104] As bombings and harassment against the county's freedom movement increased, so did armed protection efforts in the area. "The Movement may be non-violent," white summer volunteer Eugene Nelson wrote to his parents in early July, "but the people here are by no means so when it comes to protecting their families and property."[105] Virtually all families in the all-black community of Milestone guarded their houses with guns. Volunteers who failed to honk a prearranged signal when approaching the buildings risked being welcomed with a volley of buckshot.[106] In the town of Tchula, by Eugene Nelson's account, a group of white men who had attempted to bomb a private black home "escaped only by the same grace of God that put their bomb out: the owner of the house had them in his sights, but his wife had hidden the shells."[107]

In addition, groups of black men protected local churches and meeting places. After a bomb attack on a church in Milestone in August, African Americans guarded the building with rifles and shotguns.[108] The town's community center, which had been built by a group of sympathetic carpenters from California, became the hub of movement activity and was similarly protected.[109] Positioning themselves on both sides of the wooden building during mass meetings, armed men controlled the country road next to the building. "An attacker might get in," Nelson explained the defense group's tactic, "but he'd have little chance of getting out."[110] The strategy was highly successful. In 1965, a car manned with Klansmen was caught in the crossfire of the defense group during an attempt to attack the community center. "[F]rom that day on," local civil rights leader Walter Bruce recalled, "we never had no more problems."[111]

In Leake County, located next to the notorious Neshoba County, blacks started similar defense efforts. This county also had a long tradition of independent black landownership. When visiting the area around the all-black community of Harmony, journalist Nicholas von Hoffman found many farmers ready to repel white invaders with rifles and shotguns. According to von Hoffman, the practice was so common that it was "dangerous to drive off the paved highway into the Harmony area after sundown if your car is unfamiliar there."[112] Some of the town's residents organized a defense unit to protect the local community center. Built by African Americans and summer volunteers, the 30′ x 60′ frame building housed an office, a library, and one of COFO's freedom schools.[113] After Klansmen had fired into private homes and burned several crosses in the vicinity, one volunteer noted in a letter that the black community did "not intend to have all their hard work go up in flames right away." Several armed men therefore began to guard the community center around the clock.[114] Local activist Winson Hudson recalled in her memoirs that in 1965, after white terrorists had managed to bomb the center twice, the armed guards repelled a third attack by firing at the carload of whites that approached the building.[115]

Similar to the Deacons for Defense and Justice, the Leake County defense group was highly organized. CORE staffer Jerome Smith remembered being stopped by armed sentries on the city line every time he approached the community. Only after identifying himself would the guards let him pass.[116] Similarly, drivers who approached the community center were required to honk a prearranged signal. "If anyone does attempt to bomb or burn the center," said a volunteer assessing the efficacy of the guard system, "they haven't got a chance."[117] For many SNCC and CORE staffers, all-black communities like Milestone and Harmony became what historian Akinyele Umoja has called "haven communities," which provided shelter and security in a dangerous and hostile environment.[118]

Organized protection was not confined to all-black communities. In Meridian, a city of about fifty thousand located at the Mississippi's eastern border to Alabama, African Americans, who constituted one-third of the city's residents, also formed a "mutual protection society" to guard black churches against Klan attacks. The defense group served its purpose well. Unlike thirty-eight other black churches that went up in flames in the state in 1964, the First Union Baptist Church of local civil rights leader Rev. R. S. Porter was still intact when the summer project ended.[119] The Meridian defense group also guarded the homes of NAACP leader Claude Bryant, white attorney and movement-ally William Ready, and other local activists. "All of my neighbors, when we passed the word that I would be a target for that night," one of them later recalled, "would be sitting up in their windows with their shotguns."[120] In late July, Claude Bryant's guards exchanged gunfire with a group of white attackers. Meridian was no exception. In the Delta towns of Greenwood and McComb, blacks launched similar security measures. In McComb, where bombings had destroyed dozens of homes since the beginning of 1964, black residents guarded private homes, businesses, and churches with guns. By September, the town had become what historian John Dittmer has described as "an armed camp."[121]

In addition to these collective defense activities, there were numerous attempts by individual blacks to protect themselves and the COFO activists that lived in their modest homes. Those blacks who were known to house white summer volunteers became prime targets for Ku Klux Klan attacks. The mother of a white volunteer who visited two Freedom School teachers on a farm near Canton was relieved to know that the young women's host and his sons were prepared to repel white intruders with gunfire. In August 1964, the concerned woman wrote to Assistant Attorney General Burke Marshall: "Cars have stopped there last night; prowlers have been seen. Luckily, no trouble has ensued, because at least one of the homes has four rifles ready, and its owner, a Negro farmer, was quite determined to use them in defense of his home."[122] One of the young women had told her mother that the house looked like "an armory," with "rifles in every room."[123]

In Tallahatchie, a local black man was equally prepared to defend himself and the summer volunteers who stayed in his house. "He has become rather nervous these days," law student William Holdes wrote north, "and hurries us into the house as soon as we get home. He has 4 pistols in the house, & certainly has enough fight to use them on an intruder."[124] In the town of Helena, black men likewise protected SNCC's Freedom House with rifles and shotguns after carloads of armed whites had circled the building the night before. "Local people are getting fed up with this sort of harrassment [sic]," a SNCC field report stated in late July, "and they are planning on continuing to guard the house."[125]

Although men were at the forefront of these protection activities, African American women were also prepared to repel white invaders with armed force. There is no evidence of female participation in the state's numerous informal defense groups, but it was not uncommon for women to protect their homes on an individual basis. One COFO volunteer was perplexed to find her host,

Mrs. Fairly, heavily armed. In late July 1964, the young student wrote in a letter: "I met Mrs. Fairly coming down the hall from the front porch carrying a rifle in one hand [and] a pistol in the other. I do not know what is going on. . . . [All she said was] 'You go to sleep; let me fight for you.'"[126] Working near Canton, SNCC worker Jo Ann Ooiman Robinson was similarly puzzled to hear that her host slept with an ax hidden under her bed. In the past, Robinson learned, she had slept with a gun under her pillow but removed it after nearly shooting a neighbor's son.[127] Sometimes women fired their weapons at white attackers. In McComb, for example, the wife of local civil rights leader Charles Bryant shot at a car manned with Klansmen who had hurled a bomb toward the couple's home.[128]

The fact that women actively participated in the Mississippi freedom struggle is hardly surprising. As Charles Payne has pointed out, women were the backbone of the movement in the early 1960s. Not only did they host and feed civil rights workers and volunteers, they also participated in civil rights meetings, voter registration drives, and demonstrations far more often than did men.[129] What is surprising is that women practiced what most men viewed as a male prerogative. One explanation could be that white supremacy had traditionally impeded the ability of black men to defend themselves and their community. Since self-defense often resulted in brutal retaliation against the black community, many black women might have been forced to rely on their own protection against white attacks, in particular against the sexual advances of white men. Cotton picker Lou Ella Townsend, for example, growing up in the early twentieth century, had been raped numerous times by white men. When working in the fields of the Mississippi Delta, the strong and outspoken woman habitually carried a pistol hidden in a bucket. Unlike many of her peers, Townsend was unafraid to openly challenge white people.[130]

Women like Townsend probably imparted to their children a unique tradition of black female militancy that reemerged during Freedom Summer. Lou Ella Townsend's daughter Fannie Lou Hamer had certainly inherited her mother's defiant personality. Hamer had been a timekeeper on a plantation in the Mississippi Delta but was fired from her job in 1962 after trying to register to vote. Rather than return to the life of sharecropping, she became a full-time field secretary for SNCC. As such, she had to endure savage beatings and numerous attempts on her life. But like her mother, Hamer refused to be intimidated. Asked why she had survived so many years of white aggression, she responded: "I'll tell you why. I keep a shotgun in every corner of my bedroom and the first cracker even look like he wants to throw some dynamite on my porch won't write his mama again." From her perspective, whites might "act like they's crazy" but were sensible enough to stop violent harassment if confronted with the possibility of their own death.[131]

Regardless of whether guns were used by men or women, such militant practice continued to trouble some COFO activists. One volunteer recounted in a letter: "We had a problem with a man, and some of his friends, who took it upon themselves to protect us. . . . He came over at night with his friends and brought along a machine gun and ammunition. And told us not to worry. But he finally got ticked off at us, because we got ticked off at him. That machine-gun made us edgy."[132] White SNCC staffer Mary King was similarly hesitant to accept armed guards. Recalling in her memoirs how two teenagers protected her and some fellow activists—one of the youths perching on the roof with a loaded shotgun, the other one hiding under the front armed with a rifle—she noted that the incident plunged her into painful moral conflict. "I did not want this kind of protection, and it created great tension for me," she remembered.[133] Another white volunteer who spent a night at activist Amzie Moore's house in Cleveland was just as startled when Moore placed a pistol on the night table and suggested that he and his friends use it to repel white intruders. The indignant young man argued that weapons might endanger the entire Freedom Summer project and told Moore that he could not accept the gun.[134]

Conversely, local blacks were frequently bewildered by such examples of nonviolent dedication. In a debate on nonviolence in a Freedom School in Hattiesburg, for example, black teenagers concluded that "violence" was "necessary to obtain civil rights." African Americans, the children said, had to demonstrate to white people that they were "not afraid."[135] Recalling that Medgar Evers once pondered organizing guerrilla warfare in the Mississippi Delta, another volunteer teacher noted in a letter from Bolivar County that some teenagers had "come close to advocating" the same strategy.[136] In a debate between white SNCC staffer Bob Zellner and a local activist before a teenage Freedom School audience in Greenwood, nonviolence was greeted with similar skepticism. Zellner's opponent, a six-foot-six paratrooper named Clarence Robinson, argued for armed self-defense. "I've never been the one to start a fight," he said. "But if someone is pushing me, I have to defend myself."[137] Several months later, when local activist Silas McGhee was shot in the face by a local white man, other black residents of Greenwood demonstrated that they agreed with Robinson. Shortly after the shooting, dozens of angry black men, most of them army veterans, arrived at the SNCC office with rifles and shotguns. One of them shouted at the perplexed field-workers: "They keep killin' our people! *When* are we goin' to stop them? *When*?"[138]

Many SNCC workers were as disillusioned as these veterans, and some of them became strong advocates of armed resistance. As early as June 1964, one activist told *Jet*, after being chased by three carloads of whites in the little town of Valleyview, "I had a shotgun and I'll tell you if they had come in to get me, I would have used it." While adhering to nonviolence on demonstrations, he had no scruples about using the gun for protection in face of white vigilante attacks.[139] According to one of the Mississippi Sovereignty Commission spies, SNCC staff in Jackson began to advocate a "doctrine of self-defense" among local activists in July 1964. "We are told that if we find ourselves under physical attack," the informer reported, "we may take steps to defend ourselves until we are out of danger."[140] Journalist Nicholas von Hoffman, during his trips across the state, also observed that some SNCC and CORE activists had "stopped preaching" nonviolence and were "urging the contrary."[141]

In large part, this shift in SNCC's thinking was a direct result of their experience in Mississippi. In his memoirs, James Forman reflected that the Freedom Summer campaign "confirmed the absolute necessity for armed self-defense— a necessity that existed before the project but which became overwhelmingly clear to SNCC people during and after it."[142] In their view, the fact that some communities in Mississippi experienced less white terror than others was not the result of the presence of FBI agents but of black armed resistance.[143]

As in the case of CORE, some of SNCC's field-workers even began to carry guns themselves. Charles McDew recalled in an interview that on a trip to the Klan stronghold of Natchez in the southwest corner of Mississippi, he and several of his fellow activists helped guard the house of local NAACP leader George Metcalf. "We hired people to help us guard the house," he said. "Plus," he added, "we were all armed."[144] Historian Godfrey Hodgson claims that even before the end of the summer, "virtually every SNCC worker in the field was carrying a gun."[145]

Officially, however, SNCC continued to make deliberate attempts to preserve the organization's nonviolent media image. In late June 1964, for example, SNCC's communications director Julian Bond strongly reprimanded Joseph Alsop of the *Washington Post* for an article that had mentioned COFO's armed protection efforts in Mississippi. In his column "Matter of Fact," Alsop had reported about the COFO office in Jackson: "Negro armed guards are posted to guard the offices every night. Other cases of this sort could also be cited."[146] In his letter to the columnist, Bond averred that nothing could be farther from the truth. He insisted that there were "no armed guards outside, inside or around the COFO office in Jackson, or any civil rights office anywhere in the state of Mississippi."[147]

In early July 1964, SNCC's chairman John Lewis made a similar effort to assure the media of both his personal commitment to nonviolence and that of his organization. On July 1, 1964, the *New York Journal-American* had reported on its front page that Lewis was among the supporters of the new black nationalist Organization of Afro-American Unity (OAAU). Founded by black nationalist Malcolm X after his break with the Nation of Islam, the OAAU called for black political and economic power and advocated armed self-defense against white violence.[148] The very same day, Lewis released a statement in which he denied any connection with the OAAU and denounced its call for armed resistance. "I would like to reaffirm my philosophical adherence to nonvilence [*sic*]," he wrote in the press release, "both as a meansofprotest [*sic*] and as a way of life." SNCC too, he insisted, "believes today, as it has since its formation in 1960, in achieving an interracial democracy through peaceful protest." In his view, attempts to link SNCC to black radicals and their gospel of self-defense were part of a deliberate effort to discredit SNCC and other civil rights organizations.[149]

Several months later, Julian Bond, in a letter to the pacifist magazine *Fellowship*, continued his efforts to convince black and white skeptics of SNCC's unwavering loyalty to nonviolent principles. In July 1964, black veteran activist Bayard Rustin had reported on the pages of *Fellowship* that an increasing number of "young people who formerly were preaching nonviolence in the Student Nonviolent Coordinating Committee, are now advocating quite openly limited forms of violence."[150] Like Alsop of the *Washington Post*, Rustin simply recounted his personal observations, but Bond strongly objected. Referring to SNCC's statement of purpose, he insisted that his organization did not advocate violence, limited or otherwise.[151] In light of the emerging consensus within SNCC on self-defense, Bond's letters to the media appeared to be a deliberate attempt to mask the organization's ongoing radicalization.

The national NAACP, meanwhile, was similarly hard-pressed to mute militant voices among its Mississippi staff. To the dismay of executive secretary Roy Wilkins, NAACP state secretary Charles Evers—the brother of slain civil rights leader Medgar Evers—repeatedly warned in 1964 and 1965 that black Mississippians would defend themselves against white attacks. Evers, who had moved north in the 1950s, returned to his native state only after the death of his brother and vowed to follow in Medgar's footsteps. Prior to his return, Charles held numerous odd jobs, working in Philadelphia as a disc jockey, operating a hotel and a cabstand, before moving to Chicago, where he made a living as a pimp. Using the money that he earned in his illegal activities, Charles bought several nightclubs in the city. In an environment that was dominated by gangster rivalries, he commonly carried two pistols.[152] Confronted with constant white terror after his return to Mississippi, he continued the habit. Evers kept two rifles in his Natchez apartment and slept with a .38 caliber pistol under his pillow.[153]

Natchez, a city with a population of twenty-four thousand, was the hub of the state's white supremacist resistance. "The town," one civil rights volunteer wrote in the summer of 1964, "is practically run by the KKK and our informants tell us that everyone is armed to the teeth—submachine guns, hand grenades."[154] In addition, Natchez served as the Klan's weapons distribution center. One activist noted that the town struck "fear in even the veteran civil rights workers."[155] Evers doubted that federal agencies would protect him against this arsenal on his doorsteps. "I never relied on the FBI for anything," he recalled in his memoirs. Instead, he "trusted to God, to other Negroes, and to my .45 pistol. Not always in that order."[156]

Like the Deacons, however, Charles Evers was a staunch supporter of nonviolent direct action. "The only way we have is through nonviolence," he told a journalist in 1964, "there's no other way."[157] Although heavily armed himself, he urged people to give up their guns at demonstrations. Prior to a demonstration in Canton in February 1964, for example, he collected knives, razors, and several pistols from black protestors.[158]

But unlike his brother, Charles Evers had a volatile personality and made no secret of his belief in armed resistance. Occasionally, he publicly warned the white population that blacks would fight back. At a fund-raising event of the NAACP's Nashville, Tennessee, chapter on February 15, 1964, he proclaimed: "I have great respect for Mr. Martin Luther King, but non-violence won't work in Mississippi. You get on your knees down there praying for justice and those white hoodlums will stomp your brains out." Blacks had made up their "minds that if a white man shoots a Negro in Mississippi, we will shoot back. If they bomb a Negro church and kill our children, we are going to bomb a white church and kill some of their children."[159] The provocative statement shocked the white South and immediately alarmed the NAACP's national office. A week after the *Nashville Banner* had ominously headlined "Evers Rejects Non-Violent Technique," the NAACP sought to perform damage control. A press release denied the accusations and explained that Evers had been misquoted. Far from advocating violence, he had only warned that some black extremists might resort to retaliation, a thing that he hoped would never occur. In early March, the *New York Times* reported Evers's retraction, which marked the end of the affair.[160]

Both the national office in New York and local COFO organizers had been critical of Evers in the past. Many considered him an opportunist who took advantage of his slain brother's reputation to further his personal gain.[161] The fact that Evers had opened several grocery stores in the Natchez area while African Americans were boycotting the city's white merchants, for example, irritated many. NAACP officials also questioned his administrative abilities.[162] Proclamations that blacks would fight back against white terror were unlikely to improve Evers's relations with the Association's national office.

In 1965, another of Evers's outbursts provoked a major conflict with the NAACP's executive secretary Roy Wilkins. The case echoed the storm of indignation that had been triggered by Robert Williams in 1959. Like Williams and his followers in Monroe, black residents of Natchez knew all too well that self-defense was necessary. By 1965, armed protection had become routine for the black community. Since the summer of 1964, bodyguards protected Evers, and in the summer of 1965, a group of local men formed a self-defense organization to guard the town's NAACP leader, George Metcalf.[163] Despite these safety measures, Metcalf was seriously injured by a car bomb on August 27, 1965. One day after the attack, hundreds of outraged blacks, armed with guns, roamed the streets of the town's black neighborhood and threatened retaliation.[164] In a militant speech, Evers captured the angry mood of his followers. "We are going to arm ourselves and protect ourselves," he thundered. "We're just not going to take any more beatings, bombings, shootings and killings."[165]

Evers was undoubtedly aware of the explosive effect that his militant rhetoric would have on the NAACP's national office. Yet he reiterated his views in a telephone interview with Drew Pearson of the *New York Post*. Interviewed shortly after the bomb attack, Evers said, "We're not going to take it any longer. We're not going to start any riots, but we've got guns and we're going to fight back. I may be fired for saying this, but that's what we're going to do."[166] In this spirit, Evers dispatched a telegram to President Johnson, urging him to use federal power to bring peace to the tense city. "The starving, desperate and hopeless segments of the Negro population in Natchez have armed themselves with rifles and pistols," the *Memphis Commercial Appeal* quoted the message. "Even small children," the cable continued, could be "seen with homemade bombs."[167] One day later, when Mississippi governor Paul Johnson ordered 650

National Guardsmen into Natchez to bring the explosive situation under control, Evers was much calmer, exhorting blacks that violence and destruction would accomplish little.[168]

But this belated attempt at conciliation was small consolation to Roy Wilkins, who believed that the NAACP's public image had already been blemished. On September 3, a fuming Wilkins sent Evers a chilling letter in which Wilkins first demanded to know whether Pearson had quoted Evers correctly. He then turned to the telegram that Evers had sent to President Johnson. Wilkins could hardly hide his anger at the militant language that Evers had used. "I ask you directly," he wrote, "not whether you said this because it is recorded in a telegram to the President, but on what occasion or occasions you have seen 'small children' in Natchez 'with homemade bombs.'" Why, Wilkins asked, had Evers not consulted with the national office before sending the telegram? From the executive secretary's perspective, these statements implied that the Natchez movement's course of action "has been the result of a consensus of NAACP staff work and is being taken within the framework of NAACP policy." Wilkins stressed that this was "not the case. We have never authorized you, as our representative, to state either privately or publicly, 'We are armed, we have taken all we will take, we will fight . . .' or any sentiments approximating that language." Wilkins pointed out that the national NAACP could not "afford these damaging statements in a nationally syndicated newspaper column" and ordered Evers to clarify his statements by September 10.[169]

In what seemed to echo the ouster of Robert Williams in 1959, rumors spread that Evers would be fired as a field director. Both the *New York Times* and the *Baltimore Afro-American* reported that the NAACP's board of directors might soon dismiss Evers for his militant statements. Toward the end of September, citing several "reliable sources," the Mississippi Sovereignty Commission's director Erle Johnston was convinced that Evers had been ousted.[170] Indeed, Roy Wilkins had already drafted a letter that requested Evers to resign. In this draft, Wilkins called the Mississippi activist's attempt to clarify his radical statements "unsatisfactory" and asserted that the remarks in the *New York Post* remained a "call to armed action." Two other accusations that Wilkins brought against the combative civil rights leader—the unauthorized calls for SCLC's assistance in Natchez and his announcement that the NAACP would hire local voter registration workers—appeared to be simply a pretext to justify a long predetermined decision. The militant utterances in the Drew Pearson column were Evers's real offense. "Although this was a serious matter," the letter read, "involving the long-standing national policy of the NAACP and of other civil rights groups against the advocacy of violence, you did not consult with this office." Accusing Evers of "open and deliberate insubordination," Wilkins requested him to resign by September 15.[171]

Yet Wilkins never mailed the letter, and Evers remained on the NAACP's payroll. Two years after this feud, Wilkins even granted Evers a salary increase and later praised Evers as a "capable and dedicated" activist.[172] The reasons for this surprising retreat probably had to do with Wilkins's waning power within the NAACP hierarchy. During the Williams controversy of 1959, despite increasing criticism of his leadership among the rank and file, Wilkins easily secured the support of the board of directors and of the annual convention's delegates. Six years later, this seemed to be far more difficult. According to a Sovereignty Commission informer, Evers's supporters in Mississippi were able to put considerable pressure on Wilkins and the national office. They demanded that their nationally renowned leader be allowed to keep his post.[173] More important, Wilkins struggled with an internal revolt against him. Since 1962, a group of NAACP members who called themselves the "Young Turks" had repeatedly criticized the organization's centralized and undemocratic leadership. Sovereignty Commission director Johnston recalled in his autobiography that Wilkins confided to him in a secret meeting in late summer of 1965 that he "could not touch" Evers since members of the Young Turks only waited for an opportunity to challenge his power.[174] It is likely that Wilkins hesitated to risk his job over a dispute that might have proved too difficult to win.

While Wilkins struggled to preserve his organization's reputation for reason and moderation, blacks in Mississippi continued to meet white terror with rifles and shotguns. In Natchez, the bomb attack on NAACP leader Metcalf prompted some of his bodyguards to form an organization that was modeled on the Louisiana Deacons. Like the protective agencies in Jonesboro and Bogalusa, the Natchez group patrolled black neighborhoods, guarded local activists, and provided protection at protest marches and demonstrations. Although never affiliated with the Jonesboro organization, it became known as the Natchez Deacons for Defense and Justice among local activists.[175]

In Hattiesburg, a similar group emerged in early 1966. According to its founder, Vietnam War veteran James Nix, the organization guarded civil rights meetings and the homes of local black leaders Dr. C. E. Smith and J. C. Fairly. Called "Da Spirit," the group also helped enforce boycotts against discriminatory white merchants by harassing those who violated the selective buying campaign.[176] Like other defense squads in the Deep South, the program of "Da

Spirit" focused strictly on self-defense. "[W]e weren't naïve enough to know that we could just get violent and win," Nix recalled later; "we knew better than that because they had all the weapons. We had some weapons just for protection, but we didn't want anybody getting killed, anybody actually getting hurt."[177] Like Birmingham's Civil Rights Guards, the Tuscaloosa unit, or the Deacons, the defense groups that emerged in Mississippi during the 1960s had little interest in initiating racial warfare. Instead, they focused on the safety of the black community.

COFO volunteers who returned to the state in the spring and summer of 1965 reported that black protection efforts against white attacks continued not only in Hattiesburg. A college student who worked with the Delta Ministry noted in his diary in July 1965 that blacks in Summit and McComb continued to post armed guards at local churches. On one occasion, two sentries prevented a bomb attack on a Methodist church in Summit by firing at the white attackers before they could detonate the bomb.[178] In August, blacks in the little town of Pheba in Clay County began similar protection efforts after white night riders had shot into the COFO office. During the night of August 14, black guards shot back when another group of white terrorists attacked the building.[179]

The resolve of local people to defend themselves coupled with the tendency among SNCC workers to carry guns inflamed new internal discussions on the issue. In early April 1965, news reached SNCC workers in Mississippi that one of their comrades had been arrested in Georgia for carrying three pistols in his car. They learned that he could face a large fine and up to one year on a chain gang if convicted. During the debate among the members of SNCC's executive committee in Holly Springs, Mississippi, on April 12, 1965, Marion Barry suggested that the incident could negatively affect the public image of SNCC. "I fe[e]l," he said, "this is very serious and that if staff is carrying guns, this could be very bad for the organization." Despite these misgivings, a majority of those in attendance supported the right to self-defense. One activist said, "I would never be in an organization that would tell me not to protect myself." Stokely Carmichael hinted that their work in the dangerous areas of the Deep South simply required more flexibility on the question of nonviolence. "We are not King or SCLC," he explained. "They don't do the kind of work we do nor do they live in the areas we live in. They don't ride the highways at night."[180] Ruby Doris Smith agreed. She went even further, proposing that SNCC ought to train its staff "in judo and karate and gun-firing." In the end, everyone agreed to hire a lawyer for the defense of the Georgia activist.[181] It is likely that this consensus was helped by the fact that those in attendance were in danger of finding themselves in the same situation. A majority of them had come to the discussion armed.[182]

As evidenced by this discussion, a growing number of SNCC workers advocated and, on occasion, practiced armed resistance by 1965. In their view, defensive protection, coupled with tactical nonviolence, had become an integral part of the southern black freedom movement. Consequently, statements such as Julian Bond's declaration on February 21, 1965, that not even the assassination of Malcolm X "could influence our deep-seated belief in nonviolence" hardly reflected SNCC workers' reality.[183] Historian Emily Stoper has convincingly argued that the organization maintained its nonviolent image primarily for financial reasons. In fact, like CORE, SNCC was dependent on moral and financial support from northern white liberals. The group's reputation for Gandhian nonviolence was essential if the young activists wanted to continue their civil rights projects. As Stoper has pointed out, "SNCC was simply not strong enough or rich enough to be able to abandon openly its initial moralistic stance."[184] But as SNCC's radicalization evolved, black activists eventually concluded that such concessions to white America's sensitivities only hampered the progress of the black freedom struggle. In their mind, the time was ripe for Black Power.

5

BLACK POWER
AND WHITE FEAR

On a hot and sultry night on June 16, 1966, SNCC's new chairman, Stokely Carmichael, climbed a wooden makeshift podium in Greenwood, Mississippi. Ten days earlier, SNCC, CORE, and SCLC had begun a two-hundred-mile trek to the state capital of Jackson to protest a brutal shotgun attack on civil rights activist James Meredith. A few hours before the marchers arrived in Greenwood, white state troopers arrested Carmichael for putting up a tent on the grounds of a black high school. Like the twenty-five-year-old activist, the tired demonstrators were outraged at the injustice that continued to confront them in the Deep South. When Carmichael rose to speak, the crowd of about six hundred people welcomed him with an approving roar. Once the noise died down, he thundered: "This is the 27th time I have been arrested—I ain't going to jail no more, I ain't going to jail no more."[1] Again, the audience cheered approvingly.

Carmichael then introduced a slogan that would change the course of the black freedom struggle forever. "The only way we gonna stop them white men from whuppin' us is to take over," he shouted. "We been saying freedom for six years and we ain't got nothin'," he continued. "What we gonna start saying now is Black Power!" The crowd immediately exploded, roaring back in unison: "BLACK POWER!" SNCC worker Willie Ricks joined Carmichael on the platform, yelling, "What do you want?" "BLACK POWER!" the audience hollered, and, spurred by Ricks, it kept chanting: "BLACK POWER!! BLACK POWER!!! BLACK POWER!!!!"[2]

The new slogan deeply disturbed white America. What did it mean? Was Black Power "a call for retaliatory combat and riot," as journalist Paul Good mused in the *Nation*?[3] Carmichael's cry for political control, black pride, and the right to armed self-defense coupled with news reports that the Deacons for Defense and Justice protected the Meredith March with guns, led many whites to answer Good's question with an uneasy yes. The *Commercial Appeal* likewise suspected that the presence of the Louisiana defense unit "marked a significant, and to many frightening, shift in tactics of Negroes who for 10 years had been lulled and led by the nonviolent oratory of Dr. Martin Luther King Jr."[4]

In reality, however, the Meredith March denoted no abrupt shift but represented the culmination of the long-simmering debate over the legitimacy of self-defense within the southern freedom movement. By the time of Meredith's venture, local activists in the Deep South had protected the movement with guns for almost a decade. Many civil rights organizers, moreover, had come to accept the movement's symbiosis between tactical nonviolence and armed resistance as a simple necessity. After years of heated discussions about their response to racist terror, many had grown weary of professing love for their enemy. No longer willing to preserve the movement's reputation for philosophical nonviolence, both SNCC and CORE officially endorsed armed self-defense shortly after the Meredith March.

The unprecedented fervor with which SNCC and CORE began to voice their support for armed resistance in the national media terrified white America. Coupled with the growing opposition to racial integration within the movement, such assertive rhetoric triggered precisely the type of castigating disapproval that some black leaders had predicted if the movement abandoned the principles of interracial nonviolence. White liberals in particular were deeply disturbed by what they perceived as a betrayal of Martin Luther King's teachings. Thousands of sympathetic whites deserted the two organizations once it became clear that Black Power was more than a transient catchphrase. By the end of 1966, financial contributions to SNCC and CORE had dwindled to almost nothing. By contrast, the popularity of the NAACP, whose unrelenting criticism of Black Power exacerbated white America's anxieties, soared in direct proportion to the downfall of the new militants.

The arguments during the vicious Black Power controversy that followed the Meredith March echoed the internal self-defense debates that had raged within movement circles for years. This time, however, the discussions were scrutinized by the national media and revolved around tactical principles rather than physical necessities. Indeed, while the movement's various factions passionately discussed the pros and cons of armed self-defense, this form of resistance was becoming increasingly irrelevant to the southern movement. A few pockets of segregationist aggression persisted, but by 1967 federal and state authorities finally began to live up to their promise of protection, and a majority of white southerners seemed to have acquiesced to the inevitability of social change. Consequently, armed organizations such as the Deacons were no longer necessary. By the end of 1967, most black guards had put their shotguns back on the rack.

Like the support for self-defense, the militant ideas that were first formulated during the Meredith March resulted largely from activists' experience in the Deep South. The failure of the indigenous and interracial Mississippi Freedom Democratic Party to unseat the state's segregationist Democratic delegation at the party's 1964 national convention in Atlantic City had shattered SNCC's trust in America's political system. "After Atlantic City," activist Cleveland Sellers recalled in his memoirs, "our struggle was not for civil rights, but for liberation."[5] Freedom Summer, on the other hand, had convinced many of the black members that white participation hampered rather than benefited the freedom movement. Too often, white northern student volunteers had assumed leadership positions in local civil rights projects, failing to realize that their behavior prevented local blacks from developing their own potential for leadership.

But SNCC had also been influenced by events and people outside the South. Urban unrest in the black ghettos of Harlem and Watts in 1964 and 1965 had called their attention to the growing frustrations among northern blacks over poverty, unemployment, discrimination, and police brutality. The Civil Rights Act of 1964 and the Voting Rights Act of 1965 had done little to change these dismal conditions. The ideas of black nationalist Malcolm X on black pride, self-defense, and Pan-Africanism, coupled with the militant calls for armed rebellion from exiled activist Robert Williams, further radicalized the organization. Finally, the escalating military involvement of the United States in Vietnam, along with the militancy of African Independence movement and the significant role of race in the Cold War, led the young civil rights organizers to consider the international implications of the black freedom movement.[6]

A staff meeting in Kingston Springs, Tennessee, in May 1966, illustrated the impact of these various factors on SNCC's thinking. Staffers not only discussed the implications of black nationalism but also thoroughly reassessed their original expectations and assumptions. With hindsight, the activists admitted to themselves that they had clearly underestimated the scope of the brutality that their challenge to white supremacy would provoke. Hopes that the federal government would assist and protect the freedom struggle had been similarly shattered. The white media, moreover, had proved to be an ambiguous friend. In the past, activists noted on May 11, "we projected our image to them more than to the black community." The band of organizers agreed that this was no longer tenable.[7]

The issue of armed resistance was a case in point. SNCC had repeatedly downplayed self-defense incidents to preserve its Gandhian image. By 1966, the organization's members were no longer willing to mask the protective measures that the southern movement required. One staffer even suggested that the organization drop "the name nonviolent . . . from the organization."[8] While only a minority would have supported such a proposition in 1966, it foreshadowed the radical transformation that SNCC would undergo in the ensuing years. In his memoirs, James Forman regarded the Kingston Springs meeting as "a prelude to changing the nature and direction of SNCC's work." According to Forman, SNCC was "shedding the mantle of nonviolence as a tactic."[9] The replacement of the organization's deeply religious chairman, John Lewis, with movement veteran Stokely Carmichael during the meeting was another symbol of this ongoing radicalization.

The Meredith March finally forced these festering debates into the open. On June 5, 1966, James Meredith, a black army veteran who had braved thousands of hostile whites when integrating the University of Mississippi in 1962, started a 220–mile March Against Fear from Memphis, Tennessee, to Jackson, Mississippi. He hoped that this one-man demonstration would inspire blacks to register to vote and help them overcome their fear of white supremacy.[10] But on the second day of his trek, Meredith learned that the violent spirit of southern racism was far from defeated. Walking along a highway near Hernando, Mississippi, he noticed an armed white man standing conspicuously in the roadside foliage. Leveling a 16–gauge shotgun, the unemployed forty-year-old Aubrey James Norvell yelled toward the companions of the black activist: "I only want James Meredith. All the rest of you stand aside."[11] Seconds later, Meredith, who had thrown himself on the ground, was hit in the back by a volley of buckshot.

A few hours after the severely injured Meredith had been rushed to a Memphis hospital, CORE's newly elected black chairman, Floyd McKissick, announced that his organization would take up the march and asked other civil rights organizations to join.[12] From the perspective of McKissick, a forty-four-year-old black lawyer who had led the civil rights struggle in Durham, North Carolina, before joining CORE's staff, the attack on Meredith was "further savage proof that brutality is still the white American way of life in Mississippi."[13] Indeed, despite federal civil rights legislation and the Justice Department's concerted efforts to end the brutal reign of the Ku Klux Klan, black communities in the state continued to suffer from racist terror. In January 1966, for example, civil rights leader Vernon Dahmer died of severe burns after white extremists firebombed his house in Hattiesburg. Dahmer had encouraged blacks to vote in the upcoming Mississippi primary, in which thousands of African Americans would cast their first ballots since Reconstruction. Less than a month later, white night riders shot into the office of voter registration activists in Kosciusko, wounding two white volunteers. Although some voter registration workers returned the fire and pursued their assailants in a night-time car chase, no one was punished for the crime.[14] The white liberal Southern Regional Council informed the press shortly after the attack on Meredith that the number of black registered voters in Mississippi remained "the lowest in the South," primarily because of such violent reprisals.[15]

James Meredith had hoped that local authorities would protect him against white attacks. In March 1966, he had sent an official letter to the sheriff of Holmes County, inquiring whether local police officers would be able guard his one-man demonstration.[16] Three months later, recovering in the hospital after physicians had removed over sixty lead pellets from his body, Meredith had come to the conclusion that he would have to rely on his own protection. "He shot me like I was a goddam rabbit," he angrily said to reporters. "If I'd had a gun I could have got that guy. I'm not going to get caught in that situation again."[17] One civil rights worker at his bedside jokingly asked how he would reconcile this statement with his nonviolent philosophy, but Meredith was not in a laughing mood. "Who the hell ever said I was nonviolent?" he snapped in response. "I spent eight years in the military and the rest of my life in Mississippi."[18]

Meredith's emotional outburst verbalized an issue that had long been festering within movement circles. Black activists had realized that many white Americans were neither able to comprehend the violent complexities of the southern struggle nor willing to concede that blacks had the right to fight back. White liberals in particular seemed to expect the entire movement to adhere to King's nonviolent philosophy. As black writer John Oliver Killens sarcastically noted in the *Saturday Evening Post* in July 1966, "The one thing most friends and all enemies of the Afro-American have agreed upon is that we are ordained by nature and by God to be nonviolent."[19]

As movement leaders had done on previous occasions, A. W. Willis, Tennessee's only black state assemblyman at the time, was at pains to perform damage control after Meredith's militant utterances. Rather awkwardly, he assured *Jet* that his friend "did not mean what it seemed he meant."[20] This was an obvious attempt to salvage the nonviolent movement's reputation, but Meredith no longer cared about white sensitivities. In subsequent interviews, he insisted that he would return to the march armed.[21] In an article for the *Saturday Evening Post*, Meredith later expressed how the attack had crushed his belief in the power of nonviolent protest. "The Negro has tried nonviolence," he wrote in August 1966, "he has turned the other cheek, he has said 'love' when the white man said 'hate,' and it has made no difference." Meredith suspected that a large number of African Americans felt that Martin Luther King's philosophy was "no longer tenable."[22]

SNCC and CORE agreed, provoking a major clash with the NAACP over whether to use the Meredith March to criticize the federal government's failure to protect activists and its reluctance to push for a more forceful civil rights agenda. At a meeting with King, Carmichael, McKissick, and Charles Evers in Memphis on June 7, Roy Wilkins and Whitney Young of the National Urban League contended that a nationwide appeal to bring sympathetic whites to Mississippi would rally support for new civil rights legislation. Carmichael countered that the two leaders ignored the changing mood among African Americans. From SNCC's perspective, the demonstration ought to remain a local, and thus black, affair. The Deacons for Defense and Justice, who had offered to protect the march, became another contentious issue. Carmichael, McKissick, and Evers insisted that they be allowed to stay, while Wilkins, Young, and King vehemently opposed their presence and demanded that the march be pledged to nonviolence.[23] During the heated debate that followed, "some hard and stupid things were said," as Carmichael remembered in his autobiography. Both sides insisted on their demands.[24]

When the young SNCC leader asked his fellow leaders to sign a provocative manifesto that summarized the march's goals, the fragile coalition finally split apart. The hastily drafted document demanded federal voting registrars across the Deep South, the enforcement of existing laws to protect civil rights activists, amendments to the pending new civil rights bill, and a federal multibillion-dollar budget to support poor blacks in northern ghettos and rural southern communities. The strongly worded manifesto introduced the march as "a massive public indictment and protest of the failure of American society, the government of the United States and the State of Mississippi" to make civil rights a reality.[25]

In Wilkins's view, the document simply represented a personal attack on President Johnson and would do little to garner support for new legislation. In an angry exchange of words with Carmichael, both Wilkins and Young made it clear that they would not sign the statement.[26] When King surprisingly sided with SNCC's chairman and McKissick, Wilkins recognized that further discussion would lead nowhere. "Finally, in disgust," Wilkins recalled in his memoirs, he left the meeting with Whitney Young in tow. On June 8, the organizers of the march released the statement to the press.[27]

When the remaining civil rights leaders took up Meredith's march, the militant influence of SNCC and CORE was clearly visible. About a dozen members of the Deacons for Defense and Justice, equipped with walkie-talkies and pistols, accompanied the protestors and guarded their encampments at night. In addition, they fanned out into the wooded areas along the route, checked suspicious cars, and questioned whites who loitered near the column of marchers. No one had invited the Louisiana defense organization, and although the media critically noted their presence, most activists heartily welcomed them.[28] "We did not permit the news media's criticism of the Deacons to upset us," Cleveland Sellers recalled. "Everyone realized that without them, our lives would have been much less secure."[29]

The handful of white marchers that trudged along with the group of black protestors railed against the guns the Deacons carried. After seeing a .45 caliber pistol on the front seat of one of the defense squad's cars, a white pastor from New Jersey exclaimed, "The movement is no place for guns." Earnest Thomas disagreed, explaining to the minister that he had no right to deny African Americans the right to self-defense in a dangerous environment such as the Deep South. Thomas assured the minister as well as concerned journalists that the march was nonviolent but stressed that guarding the campsite and escorting marchers to the airport in Memphis were necessary precautions to ensure demonstrators' safety.[30] Those who attempted to impose Gandhian principles on the marchers were quickly silenced. Irate at a woman's suggestion "that those who didn't believe in nonviolence were discrediting the civil rights movement and should go home," several marchers shouted, "We're already home, baby, and we are the civil rights movement."[31] While incomprehensible to this white supporter, such statements reflected the growing consensus among black activists that the movement had tailored its message to white audiences far too long.

The Black Power slogan further radicalized the marchers and provoked heated debates between black activists and Martin Luther King. The SCLC's president considered the two words "unfortunate," warning that they implied support for black nationalism and violence. "I'm sick and tired of violence," he said, venting his frustration and pleading with SNCC and CORE to abandon the slogan and to send the Deacons home.[32] According to a Sovereignty Commission informer, "a heated argument" erupted after King's critical remarks.[33] Especially Earnest Thomas resented King's attacks on the defense unit. Another secret report from a closed meeting of the demonstration's organizers stated that Thomas "got mad at King for preaching nonviolence and called him an SOB."[34] Most marchers agreed that the pragmatic marriage between tactical nonviolence and armed protection was far more effective than the image of philosophical nonviolence that movement leaders promoted.

A nighttime rally in Yazoo City on June 21 signaled that the protestors had become increasingly receptive to the more militant rhetoric of SNCC and the Deacons. At the meeting, Willie Ricks led another defiant chant, shouting, "White man attack us," to which the audience enthusiastically responded, "We attack him back!" Earnest Thomas joined in the militant language. "We plan to practice non-violence," he said, "but we do not intend for any redneck to abuse any black people any more . . . if they do, there'll be a blood-red Mississippi."[35] Such belligerent statements were an obvious response to the brutal attack that had occurred in Philadelphia several hours earlier. During a memorial service for the three activists who had been murdered near the town in 1964, a hostile white mob surrounded the protestors. One CORE worker considered the subsequent march to the Neshoba County Jail "by for [sic] the roughest and most dangerous demonstration any of us had ever been in." White hoodlums sprayed the column with water hoses, drove their cars into the crowd, and pelted the protestors with eggs, bottles, and rocks. When it became apparent that white police officers refused to intervene, some of the marchers began to fight back.[36]

While the bruised marchers pitched their tents in Yazoo City, white night riders attacked the headquarters of Philadelphia's Mississippi Freedom Democratic Party chapter. This time, however, the activists were prepared. Armed with shotguns, several guards were perched on the rooftop of the small wood-frame building. They spotted the first night rider, and, when the white driver began to shoot, they immediately returned fire. Their shotgun blasts shattered the car's windows and injured the attacker, who quickly drove away. Shortly thereafter, the guards had to repel a second attack. As in the past, it took hours before FBI agents finally arrived on the scene to investigate.[37] While one of the agents questioned the SNCC workers, another carload of white men approached the Freedom House and opened fire. Mrs. Johnnie Mae Walker, a local MFDP leader, recounted: "The FBI didn't really believe we were being shot at, but when those cats came back up the street with high powered stuff, the agent said, 'I'll be god-damned! They're shooting at me! I'm going to get that son of a bitch!'" But as one-legged white activist Jim Leatherer painfully learned when trying to hobble away from the line of fire, the agent never fired a shot. White minister Rims Barber recalled: "He couldn't even get his gun out of the holster. There he was hiding behind the car and there was poor Jim in the street chanting, 'I pay my taxes! Protect me! Protect me!'" The agent's inglorious performance became the subject of scathing ridicule among the organizers and did little to bolster their confidence in the effectiveness of federal protection.[38]

Canton civil rights leader "bad-ass" C. O. Chinn had long abandoned the hope that the FBI would prevent white attacks. On June 23, he took it upon himself to pursue a group of white attackers who had hurled a smoke bomb at the town's Freedom House and braved the consequences of his armed actions. After reportedly shooting at one of the white men during an ensuing car chase, police arrested Chinn and charged him with attempted murder.[39] When the Meredith March reached Canton a few hours later, the explosive atmosphere became even more volatile. Exhausted from another long day in the blistering sun, the demonstrators attempted to pitch a large tent on the property of a public school. But Mississippi highway patrolmen had prohibited the encampment and began to disperse the large crowd with a fog of tear gas. Coughing and with their eyes welling with tears, the protestors who held the center pole of the large tent fled in panic. Those who remained were bloodied by club-wielding police officers.[40]

The police attack outraged the demonstrators and further eroded their faith in the efficacy of nonviolent protest. Once more, President Johnson had ignored their appeals to dispatch federal marshals to provide protection. Without the threat of federal intervention, local authorities still appeared to feel little responsibility to enforce the new civil rights statutes.[41] In a meeting after the incident, Martin Luther King argued that the tear gas attack would focus national publicity on Mississippi and might generate additional financial contributions. To the SNCC organizers, these considerations no longer mattered. According to a Sovereignty Commission report, Stokely Carmichael angrily declared that he intended "to shoot the patrolmen from ambush if they used tear gas again."[42]

Carmichael's plan reflected anger and shock rather than an actual plan to attack the police, but a growing number of marchers publicly voiced their support for armed self-defense. Neil Maxwell of the *Wall Street Journal*, for instance, was shocked to hear Charles Evers proclaim: "Don't let anybody tell you I'm nonviolent. If I'd been James Meredith and that white man cut loose on me with a shotgun, I'd have been shooting back, and I'd have something to shoot with, too." Recounting his frightening experience in Bogalusa, one of CORE's field-workers had reached the same conclusion. "Man," he told Maxwell, "non-violence got me nothing but an ulcer," a stress symptom that he said ceased only after he had purchased a gun for protection.[43]

In the aftermath of the Meredith March, which concluded on June 26 with a large rally in Jackson, it became obvious that this CORE member was no longer an exception. During the organization's annual convention in Baltimore in early July, CORE officially embraced Black Power and the right to self-defense. In his speech to the delegates, Floyd McKissick spoke for many when he angrily denounced his organization's traditional protest strategy. "Negroes are not geared to nonviolence," he said on July 3 and insisted that blacks needed self-defense organizations like the Deacons for Defense and Justice to confront white terrorists. The white journalists who attended the conference listened attentively when CORE's chairman declared: "The black man's cup is run over. I think the philosophy of nonviolence is a dying philosophy. I think nonviolence in the future will only be a technique and a strategy."[44]

In the eyes of the media, McKissick's irate proclamations were a radical departure from the attempts of his predecessor, James Farmer, to preserve at least a semblance of commitment to the philosophy of nonviolence. But as Stokely Carmichael told the Baltimore conference, black activists could no longer afford to conform to white expectations when the ultimate goal was to build an independent freedom movement. "What we have to do," he said, "is build a movement not run by LBJ, nor the press, nor the white liberal establishment."[45] In their struggle for jobs, decent housing, and resources, African Americans would have to define their own tactics, whether whites liked it or not. In this spirit, McKissick pointed out that the movement had to challenge the traditional double standards that whites forced upon blacks. Why, he asked, were African Americans required to remain nonviolent while whites attacked the black community with impunity? From his perspective, the right to self-defense was "a constitutional right" that blacks would not surrender as long as white racists continued to attack African Americans.[46]

This interpretation received almost unanimous support from the delegates. As early as February 1966, CORE's southern field staff had discussed alternatives to philosophical nonviolence. In a report on their meeting, Richard Haley noted: "A committee also got together to draw up a statement on nonviolence. The paper stated that non-violence has been unsuccessful in solving any of the problems which confront the Negro population; that the CORE policy on non-violence should be either m[o]dified or removed in keeping with the current situation."[47] The additional thrust of northeastern and western chapters at the 1966 conference tipped the balance toward the decision to revise CORE's founding principles. The organization's chapters outside the South had been strongly influenced by black nationalist Malcolm X and exiled radical Robert Williams. Some of its members had abandoned nonviolence as early 1962.[48] That year two field secretaries told an interviewer, "In meetings with northern CORE groups we don't talk about nonviolence anymore."[49] Gory news reports about racist murders in the Deep South coupled with a growing number of urban riots further fanned the flames of northern radicalism.

Not surprisingly, many CORE chapters outside the South deeply admired the Deacons for Defense and welcomed them as the herald of the end of nonviolence. Shortly after James Meredith was shot in Mississippi, for example, Harlem CORE announced, "In any future action wherein we want to behave in a nonviolent manner we will seek the protection of our brothers to guarantee this right."[50] At the 1966 convention, one resolution reflected the tremendous impact of the protection squad on chapters in the urban Northeast. "CORE accepts the concept of self-defense by the Deacons," their jointly approved document stated, "and believes that the use of guns by CORE workers on a Southern project is a personal decision, with the approval of that project's and the Regional directors."[51] When Harlem CORE's black chairman, Roy Innis, recommended that the organization's requirement that members "adopt the technique of non-violence in direct action" be deleted, the proposal easily passed. Although the delegates stopped short of abandoning nonviolent protest altogether, the right of armed self-defense had now become an integral part of CORE's official policy.[52]

Like the opposition to nonviolence, the growing animosity toward white participation in CORE stemmed largely from activists' day-to-day experience in the South. Like SNCC, CORE had learned that white field-workers could frequently become an obstacle to black empowerment. Jonesboro, Louisiana, where white student Charles Fenton had helped organize the Deacons in 1964, was a typical example. San Francisco CORE member Bill Bradley explained in an assessment of CORE's southern projects: "In Jonesboro, Louisiana Charles Fenton is regarded by many local Negroes as a God. He can get local Negroes to march where no one else can. His safety, judgement [*sic*] etc., in the mind of the community is beyond value." From Bradley's perspective, the Jonesboro movement demonstrated that "the very independence we are trying to encourage is discouraged by the presence and activity of whites." Of course, the Deacons for Defense were an obvious symbol of black empowerment, but their role was mostly confined to protection duties. According to Bradley, their presence did not translate into the kind of independent local movement that CORE had originally envisioned.[53]

The support of white liberals had proved similarly problematic. As Floyd McKissick explained to journalists during the Meredith March, their financial contributions were important, but certain expectations that went along with their checks clearly circumscribed the autonomy of the movement. "[T]he situation is sort of like when you are sick and your neighbor comes in to help you," McKissick explained. "You need his assistance, but you don't want him to run your house or take your wife."[54] Their experience since the early 1960s had taught CORE's staff that white sympathy could be a double-edged blessing.

For many of those who attended the organization's 1966 convention, then, Black Power was a logical outgrowth of the movement's dangerous campaigns in the Deep South. Yet few of CORE's white liberal supporters seemed to grasp these complexities. To their mind, Black Power contradicted everything the traditionally nonviolent and integrationist organization had once stood for. When black delegates to the CORE conference began to chant the new slogan, a shocked white Catholic nun frantically exclaimed that the organization had become "the Congress of Racial Superiority."[55]

Lillian Smith, a longtime CORE member and fund-raiser since the 1940s, was similarly alarmed by the organization's new direction. Smith was a deeply committed pacifist and believed that nonviolent protest could change the hearts and minds of white racists.[56] In a telegram to Floyd McKissick, the famous writer therefore condemned "the dangerous and unwise position CORE has taken on the use of violence in effecting racial change." Announcing her resignation from CORE's advisory committee, she vented her frustration: "CORE has been infiltrated by adventurers and nihilists, black nationalists and plain old-fashioned haters who have finally taken over."[57] By that time, most white activists had already left the organization.

Like Smith, the vast majority of white Americans considered Black Power the antithesis of nonviolence and integration. *Time* magazine spoke of "the new racism," while *Newsweek* denounced the slogan as a "road to disaster."[58] Journalist Paul Good speculated that this extreme reaction stemmed from the fact that white liberals "interpreted [Black Power] as both threat and insult, seeming to undo past efforts at understanding and raising the spectre of violent nights under bloody southern moons."[59] White people, black writer and SNCC member Julius Lester later noted, seemed to be interested only in one question: "Does it mean y'all gon' kill white folks?"[60]

CORE and SNCC claimed that this was exactly what Black Power did not mean. Floyd McKissick, for his part, knew full well why the two words so utterly terrified white America. "I think it scared people because they didn't understand," he reflected in an interview. "They could not subtract violence from power. They could only see power as having a violent instrument accompanying it."[61] Carmichael too was familiar with the sensitivities of SNCC's liberal sympathizers. "Negroes understand me," he told journalist Paul Good during the Meredith March. "But whites get nervous when we don't keep talking about brotherly love. They need reassurance."[62]

The fact that the NAACP viciously denounced Black Power did little to ease white apprehensions. The most scathing attacks came from Roy Wilkins, who remembered being "disgusted" by the new slogan.[63] At the NAACP's annual convention in Los Angeles on July 5, 1966, he condemned Black Power as "a reverse Mississippi, a reverse Hitler, a reverse Ku Klux Klan." Wilkins explained that CORE's militant vow to fight back against white attacks was far from new, since the NAACP had always supported that right. In his view, the organization's new policy suggested that its members were called upon "to retaliate instantly and in kind whenever attacked." He assured his audience that the NAACP would neither support this form of violent retaliation nor any type of "anti-white power."[64] These attacks on CORE echoed Wilkins's uncompromising reaction to the militant statements of Robert Williams and Charles Evers. Once more, Wilkins construed the plea for the right to self-defense as a call for aggressive violence.

Martin Luther King's reaction to the slogan was much more nuanced. Unlike Wilkins, King was at pains to point out to the media that Black Power was a manifestation of black frustration and despair. The slogan was "a cry of disappointment," he explained in *Where Do We Go from Here?* stressing that it was "a call to black people to amass the political and economic strength to achieve legitimate goals." King argued that Carmichael's plea to focus on black unity and black pride was a viable strategy to counter centuries of "the psychological indoctrination that led to the creation of the perfect slave." In many ways, King's efforts to dispel white misgivings about the slogan seemed a pragmatic attempt to maintain the movement's momentum in the face of growing fragmentation.[65]

At the same time, King vociferously criticized what he considered Black Power militants' "unconscious and often conscious call for retaliatory violence" and black separatism. What Carmichael and others had to understand, he explained, was the fact that "the black man needs the white man and the white man needs the black man."[66] For that reason, King cautiously continued to defend Black Power while disassociating SCLC from the new militants. King's refusal to attend CORE's 1966 convention in protest against the organization's radicalization signaled serious reservations, which he voiced openly at SCLC's annual meeting in Jackson, Mississippi, a month later.[67] "If 'Black Power' means aggressive violence, black supremacy and black separatism," King said, "nonviolent direct action opposes it. Through these doctrines, Negroes will never be able to assemble power." The SCLC president insisted that African Americans needed to rely on "the moral power of nonviolence," which would help them reach their goals much faster "than through bewitching slogans which yield emotional satisfaction without concrete achievement."[68]

King's ambivalent stance on Black Power could also be seen in a one-page advertisement that SCLC placed in the *New York Times* on July 26, 1966. Signed and approved by King, the advertisement conceded that the militant slogan reflected real and urgent problems in black communities across the nation. But SCLC also condemned SNCC and CORE for approving "the use of violence to force social change" and "Negro separatism." "Black supremacy or aggressive black violence," King wrote, was "as invested with evil as white supremacy or white violence." Assuring readers that African Americans could "still march down the path of nonviolence and interracial amity," SCLC suggested in a concluding plea for funds that an increase in financial contributions would help the organization achieve this goal.[69]

The national office of the NAACP, by contrast, had few positive things to say about Black Power and appeared to make deliberate efforts to cash in on the panic that the slogan had created. As historian Manfred Berg has pointed out, the militancy of CORE and SNCC provided the NAACP with a much-longed-for opportunity "to regain profile as the voice of reason and modera-tion."[70] A widely distributed fund-raising letter from October 1966 clearly ex-emplified these aspirations. Signed by Wilkins, the letter denounced the new militants' alleged intention "to stand in armed readiness to retaliate and deal out punishment on their own." Wilkins pledged that his organization would neither abandon nonviolent methods nor would it veer away from its original goal of integration. Wilkins urged NAACP members and white sympathizers to contribute "generously" to his organization, promising that their financial support would be "a vote against all forms of racism" and "an affirmation of the principles for which NAACP stands."[71] Reprinted in the *New York Times* as a letter to the editor, this call for funds probably reached hundreds of thousands of white readers.[72]

In his memoirs, Roy Wilkins dismissed accusations that the NAACP deliber-ately used the Black Power controversy to fill its coffers, arguing that the dues from the NAACP's primarily black membership made white funds unneces-sary.[73] However, it is highly suspicious that Wilkins chose to link his position paper on Black Power with a call for funds that was directed toward a primar-ily white readership.[74] It is questionable whether the enormous increase in the organization's funds in the ensuing years could have been generated by black contributions alone. Almost quadrupling its income between 1966 and 1968, the NAACP undoubtedly benefited from its adamant opposition to the new slogan.[75]

But this public feud was about more than financial contributions. It also reflected a long-simmering conflict between the NAACP and the rest of the movement over prestige and influence. Wilkins had frequently lamented that the NAACP, despite being the oldest American civil rights organization, stood in the shadow of nonviolent direct-action groups such as SCLC, SNCC, and CORE. Although the NAACP's Legal Defense Fund provided thousands of dollars to bail out nonviolent protestors, many of whom were members of local NAACP chapters, few people acknowledged this crucial contribution to the success of the movement. Annoyed at this lack of appreciation, Wilkins once snapped, "The other organizations furnish the noise and get the public-ity while the NAACP furnishes the manpower and pays the bill."[76] The fact that some younger activists accused the Association of not doing enough probably rankled Wilkins, who skillfully used the Black Power controversy to lead his organization back toward the prestigious position he thought it deserved. To judge from an editorial in the *Rocky Mountain News*, which lauded Wilkins's attack on Black Power at its annual convention as "well-said statements of a man" who had not given in to "short-sighted hotheadism," this plan was highly successful.[77]

Wilkins might have beamed with pride at his achievement, but the vicious debate practically precluded any opportunity to heal the deep cleavages that had emerged within the splintering movement. One white supporter was right on target when criticizing King and Wilkins for attempting to "preserve their own 'moderate' image" rather than interpreting the freedom struggle's new direction to the American public.[78] Another white critic believed that SCLC deserved blame as well, since it had "betrayed the black people of the country by its position on Black Power and . . . has taken this position because it will appeal to white people who will ease their guilt feelings by contributing to SCLC."[79] Regardless of whether the decision of King and Wilkins to condemn Black Power was influenced by genuine convictions or pragmatic civil rights politics, especially the NAACP's reluctance to mediate between the new militants and the American public certainly impeded the ability of SNCC and CORE to clarify their political message.

Yet even if SCLC and the NAACP had embraced Black Power, it would have been difficult to break the powerful binaries that the movement's nonviolent rhetoric had created. A roundtable that brought together the slogan's supporters and opponents on NBC's nationally broadcast television show *Meet the Press* on August 21, 1966, clearly illustrated these obstacles. Asked by the show's host, Lawrence Spivak, whether CORE's members still adhered to nonviolence, Floyd McKissick replied that they did so in demonstrations. "But if somebody hits us," he added, "then you better have an ambulance on the side to pick up whoever hits somebody." Spivak's comment that there was "a difference between self-defense and nonviolence" pointed toward the heart of the debate. According to McKissick, the two were "not incompatible," an interpretation that was shared by a majority of southern civil rights organizers. But to the mind of Spivak and many other white Americans, nonviolence and self-defense represented polar opposites.[80]

A letter from a white Texan to Martin Luther King shortly after the attack on Meredith illustrates the racial fault lines that characterized the discussion on self-defense. Bewildered by Meredith's announcement that he would return to Mississippi armed, the man wrote indignantly: "What *legal* right does he have to carry a gun on his *particular* mission or future assignments from NAACP." He doubted that the Association's members had "the legal right to carry a gun."[81] Like Floyd McKissick at CORE's annual convention, James Meredith angrily condemned such double standards during the discussion on *Meet the Press.* "Nonviolence is not the opposite of violence," he explained, "and this is where this country has been trying to lead the Negro down a wrong road." From Meredith's perspective, whites "have been trying to say to him, 'If you are not nonviolent—if you don't turn the other check, you are violent.'"[82] This idea seemed to be deeply etched in the white mind, which made it virtually impossible for Black Power advocates to gain acceptance for armed resistance.

The new militants shared some responsibility for America's growing paranoia since their martial rhetoric frequently blurred the distinction between legitimate self-defense and aggressive violence. During the *Meet the Press* interview, for example, Meredith angrily declared: "White killers who kill blacks have to be removed from this society." Asked by Lawrence Spivak whether he suggested that African Americans ought to organize violent vigilante groups that would "take the law into their own hand," Meredith told the puzzled reporter that that was exactly what he had in mind. Stokely Carmichael, who had been silent throughout Meredith's monologue, took the Mississippian's side, asking provocatively: "If you don't want us to do it, who is going to do it?"[83] Such statements obviously went far beyond traditional interpretations of self-defense and undoubtedly added force to the argument of some white commentators that Black Power stood for violent retribution. A white New Yorker who wrote to Lawrence Spivak a day after the broadcast expressed the fears of many. "We are not safe in our homes in the streets no where," the woman wrote ominously. In her mind, whites should "fear the 'black power.'"[84]

White activist Anne Braden was one among very few who defended Black Power against the media's attacks. In the *Southern Patriot*, she argued that SNCC's call for self-defense was not only legitimate but also common practice in the southern freedom movement. Pacifists, she explained in January 1967, had always been "a minority in SNCC" as well as in other civil rights groups. She went on to explain: "Some of the most effective leaders of NVDA [nonviolent direct action] maintained armed guards at their homes. They did not see this as a contradiction. . . . In other words, the civil rights movement in the South was never a pacifist movement."[85]

But Braden was a lone voice in the wilderness. The vast majority of the movement's white liberal supporters felt betrayed by the new militancy and began to keep its proponents at arm's length. James Farmer had prophesied repeatedly that any connotations of violence in the movement's rhetoric would cost the movement legitimacy and financial support. The public's emotional reaction to Black Power proved him right. As a former head of a Friends of SNCC group noted in the *Village Voice* in December 1966, CORE's and SNCC's future looked bleak. "The new financing of SNCC should be interesting to watch," he wrote. "Personally I could accept SNCC's new direction if they showed that their concept of black power was going to be paid for by black money, but I don't think this will happen."[86] The vehemence of the wave of animosity that broke over SNCC took many of its members by surprise. "We'd anticipated a 'backlash,'" Stokely Carmichael reflected in his memoirs, "but perhaps not the extent or the suddenness of the liberals' alienation."[87]

Indeed, within merely a few months SNCC and CORE had practically lost their entire base of financial support. While SNCC's opposition to the Vietnam War also incensed the public, their call for armed resistance appeared to be the most important reason for white resentment. The letter of one white supporter to the organization spoke for many. "Primarily," the man wrote, explaining his refusal to heed SNCC's appeal for funds, "I am going to wait until you decide whether you will remain true to your name and continue to be non-violent. Violence will win you some battles, but never the war."[88] Dozens of irate supporters scribbled angry notes on the appeals for funds that they had received and returned them to SNCC. One note read: "I cannot support your programs with their incitement to violence." Another man wrote tersely: "Dissent OK. Violence—Black Power—No."[89] As a result of this increasing animosity among white liberals, SNCC was on the verge of bankruptcy by 1967. CORE confronted the same problem. Over $200,000 in debt by winter of 1966, its new rhetoric had caused white contributions to wane rapidly. In an appeal to its supporters, CORE acknowledged that Black Power had created "a crisis of confidence among our former supporters and friends," but Floyd McKissick could do little to regain their trust. Between 1966 and 1968, CORE's income declined by more than 50 percent.[90]

Despite this deluge of criticism, the radicalization of CORE and SNCC was irreversible. White funds or not, the new militants were determined to pursue their new course without compromise and hinted that even the support for tactical nonviolence might soon come to an end. Unsurprisingly, King's desperate admonition in October 1966 that nonviolence remained the "only road to freedom" had little effect on Black Power advocates.[91] To the mind of many, the nonviolent movement was dead.

Amidst this national debate on Black Power, local freedom movements in the Deep South continued. Between 1966 and 1967, a few black defense groups remained part of the struggle. In the summer of 1966, for example, African Americans in Port Gibson, Mississippi, reacted to continued police harassment and racist intimidation with the formation of a highly sophisticated protection agency. Organized by NAACP activist Rudy Shields, the group came to be known as Deacons for Defense and Justice, although it was never affiliated with the original Louisiana defense unit. Others simply called them "Black Hats," alluding to the black cowboy hats that many of its members wore in a uniformlike fashion. Like its Louisiana counterpart, the unit protected nonviolent demonstrations and mass rallies. In addition, it assisted in enforcing a local economic boycott against white merchants who refused to hire African Americans. Until the end of the selective buying campaign in 1967, the Black Hats harassed those who had violated the boycott.[92] As Akinyele Umoja has demonstrated, the Port Gibson Deacons were only one among many "enforcer squads" that assisted local Mississippi boycott campaigns in the 1960s.[93]

Like the Deacons, the Black Hats were experienced in the art of psychological warfare, deliberately exaggerating their strength and firepower. In the summer of 1967, the group passed on a forged minute book to the local sheriff, who was shocked to read about nonexistent heavy weaponry and never-to-be-executed strategies.[94] Probably in part because of this bold assertiveness, white racists never attacked the Black Hats. But the town's tranquility also stemmed from the fact that many white southerners finally seemed to accept the inevitability of social change. Disillusioned Sovereignty Commission investigator A. L. Hopkins concluded in early 1967: "From observation and investigation, it appears that many white people have given up."[95] Concerted efforts by the FBI and the Justice Department to weaken and disrupt the Ku Klux Klan further eroded the base of white support for violent terror. By 1967, violent white resistance to the Mississippi freedom movement was crumbling.

Their protection duties might have seemed unnecessary, but the Black Hats also played an important role in nourishing a positive black identity. Historian Emilye Crosby has pointed out in her study of the civil rights movement in Claiborne Parish that the Port Gibson squad became "a source of pride for the black community and through their boldness encouraged assertiveness in others."[96] The speeches of civil rights leader Charles Evers during that period reflected this new spirit among Mississippi blacks. Undaunted by rumors that the Klan planned to reorganize, Evers assured his followers at a rally in Fayette in October 1967 that blacks would meet the Klansmen "with an eye for an eye and a tooth for a tooth."[97] Only a few weeks earlier, whites had learned that these militant statements were far from empty threats. In Centerville, Mississippi, a white man who had leveled a rifle at a nonviolent protestor found himself surrounded by twenty-five armed blacks who had all drawn their guns to protect their fellow activist. Most of these men were members of another defense squad that had formed in nearby Woodville.[98]

Like these Mississippi groups, the Bogalusa Deacons for Defense and Justice remained active throughout 1967. Despite the Justice Department's attempts to crush the power of the area's Knights of the Ku Klux Klan, the spirit of white supremacist terror was alive and well. In March 1966, a white racist fired four shots at a black army captain named Donald R. Sims for talking too long on a public pay phone. The attack was a grim reminder that the Klan was far from dead. In September 1966, a journalist observed that the racial climate in Bogalusa continued to be "close to the boiling point." Discrimination persisted in many of the city's restaurants, and black students who attended the parish's newly integrated schools complained of harassment and heated confrontations with white parents.[99]

In this volatile atmosphere, the Deacons continued to patrol the black neighborhood, escorted CORE organizers and white volunteers in and out of town, and protected those who tested white compliance with the Civil Rights Act of 1964. Peter Jan Honigsberg, a white volunteer who worked in Bogalusa for the Lawyers Constitutional Defense Committee, recalled in his memoirs that members of the defense unit usually positioned themselves in front of segregated cafes to protect him and fellow activists against white aggression.[100] The Bogalusa Deacons also maintained an impressive arsenal of weapons. According to Honigsberg, the trunk of Charles Sims's old yellow 1958 Chevy usually contained "a semiautomatic carbine that looked like a submachine gun, two shotguns, several boxes of shells, and a handful of grenades."[101] Since the shoot-outs in 1965, no Klansman had attempted to attack the black section of town, but the Deacons were certainly prepared for another confrontation.

Despite their menacing arsenal, the Deacons continued to support the non-violent Bogalusa movement, which staged demonstrations as late as 1967. On July 23 of that year, 125 African Americans set out from Bogalusa for a night march to the Washington Parish courthouse in Franklinton. More than fifty police officers guarded the protest march, which BVL activists had organized to call attention to the continued need for equal justice and protection.[102] When the marchers arrived in Franklinton the next morning, the speech of CORE's black associate national director, Lincoln Lynch, to the small crowd clearly reflected the ongoing radicalization of his organization. "The days of black people clapping their hands and singing are over," he shouted, "and many of you are going to be asked to kill for freedom—and you'd better be ready to kill."[103]

While Black Power activists like Lynch conjured up images of imminent race war, the Bogalusa movement remained immune to this type of radicalism and continued its nonviolent protest campaign. On August 10, 1967, about one hundred African Americans started a ninety-four-mile trek from Bogalusa to the state capital of Baton Rouge, where the BVL planned to present Governor McKeithen with a list of grievances. From the outset, the demonstration was overshadowed by violence along the route. On August 14, a violent confrontation between black and white men near Hammond, a little town forty-five miles east of Baton Rouge, left five white men wounded. In the face of this brutal confrontation, Governor McKeithen probably feared racial clashes similar to the ones that had occurred two years earlier in Bogalusa. Three days later, he ordered an additional 650 National Guardsmen to join the 175 state troopers who already escorted the marchers out of Livingston Parish, where whites had repeatedly attacked the protestors.[104] Unbeknownst to the soldiers, armed Deacons had positioned themselves along the march route as well. According to Jan Honigsberg, the armed group had stockpiled rifles, shotguns, and grenades under cases of soda in a truck that provided refreshments for the marchers. "The Deacons never needed to unearth that arsenal," he remembered, "but we all felt safer for it."[105]

The white reaction to the march in Livingston Parish probably convinced many demonstrators that the Deacons might be forced to use their weapons. As the column of about seventy-five blacks and five whites trudged along the highway in the summer heat, white onlookers pelted the group with eggs and bottles and shouted racial epithets and slurs. In stark contrast to the demonstrations in the past, however, almost seven hundred police officers and Guardsmen, some of them armed with submachine guns, the rest of them carrying rifles with bayonets, made sure that no hostile white racists could break through the lines. "It was almost impossible to see much of the Negroes," the *New York Times* reported. "They were preceded by four policemen on horseback, surrounded by four or five ranks of men, and followed by four more mounted officers." In addition, several helicopters constantly hovered above the heads of the marchers. At the concluding rally in Baton Rouge on August 20, more than 2,200 National Guardsmen protected the small group of demonstrators against potential attacks from the Ku Klux Klan.[106]

The Baton Rouge march marked the end of both the nonviolent protest era in Louisiana and the Deacons for Defense and Justice. While African Americans in Bogalusa and other southern communities continued to have grievances, the movement's original goals had been achieved. By the end of 1967, desegregation of public accommodations had become a reality in many southern communities, and hundreds of thousands of African Americans had added their names to the voter rolls. Equally important, state and local authorities finally appeared to take seriously their responsibility to provide protection for black demonstrators. With the original justification for their formation gone, the Deacons had outlived their usefulness. In November 1967, FBI agents reported that the Bogalusa Deacons no longer held official meetings. By March 1968, the FBI believed the Deacons to be "of little or no significance."[107]

The same was true for Mississippi defense organizations like the Port Gibson Deacons, who had disbanded completely by the end of the decade.[108] By the time the Deacons put their shotguns back on the rack, protective agencies in Alabama and North Carolina also were no longer active. Bogalusa activist Robert Hicks believed that the Deacons could quickly reorganize if necessary. In 1969, he told an interviewer: "The Deacons are still in existence today, not in the sense that they were when we were doing door to door and marching and demonstrating, but they are still on call if anything would happen to a black person in the community."[109] Yet, given the symbiotic relationship between protest and protection in the southern civil rights struggle, the demise of nonviolent demonstrations also led to the end of the region's era of armed black resistance.

6

BLACK MANHOOD AND
THE END OF NONVIOLENCE

When Black Power militants vowed to defend themselves against white attacks, brandishing guns to demonstrate their resolve, the president of the Bogalusa Deacons was not overly impressed. "Naw," Charles Sims recalled of his reaction to the ambiguous slogan, "that wasn't down my alley at all, 'cause the cats that was hollerin' Black Power, I was protectin' and guardin' they damn ass. I don't see nothin' they was doin' to even talkin' 'bout no Black Power." Sims later concluded, in a rather unflattering assessment of their accomplishments, that the new radicals "didn't have a damn thing but face and ass. . . . Face for showin', and ass for sittin' on."[1] NAACP leader Charles Evers too had his doubts whether black nationalists such as the Black Panther Party would be able to protect themselves, let alone other blacks. "All this talk about guns," Evers scoffed in his memoirs. "They back you all over the place with their words. But their shotguns wouldn't kill an old sick dog running down the road."[2]

Such scathing ridicule hints at fundamental differences between southern black defense groups and black nationalist advocates of armed resistance that emerged in the second half of the 1960s. Since the late 1950s, Malcolm X and like-minded radicals had called upon African Americans to abandon nonviolence. Deeply influenced by Malcolm's calls to fight back against white violence, black activists in Cleveland, Ohio, formed a defense unit as early as 1964. One year later, Ron Karenga's US organization urged black Californians to repel white attacks with gunfire. In the following years, as militant groups such as the Black Panther Party for Self-Defense (BPP) or the Republic of New Africa (RNA) leaped to national attention, armed militancy became an integral part of the Black Power movement.

At first glance, these organizations seemed to be natural allies of southern defense groups, but the role of armed resistance in the Black Power movement differed considerably from the one it played in cities like Birmingham or Bogalusa. As the dismissive comments of Sims and Evers indicate, none of those black nationalists who brandished pistols, rifles, and machine guns ever repulsed attacks by the Ku Klux Klan. The Black Panthers considered their armed actions precautions against police brutality, which they likened to the racist terrorism that confronted African Americans in the Deep South. But shoot-outs between black militants and white policemen remained rare and resulted primarily from black militants' armed assertiveness, not from deliberate police attacks on African American communities. Probably because it proved so difficult to define and to combat the enemy in the Black Power era, self-defense remained mostly confined to militant rhetoric and represented a psychological rather than a practical necessity. Of course, in the case of the Black Panthers, militant self-defense did have real-life consequences for the organization, including numerous incarcerations, shoot-outs with white policemen, and the deaths of party members. In general, however, armed resistance became mainly a symbol of defiance that served to affirm and nurture militant black manhood.

The gendered function of armed resistance in the Black Power movement also produced radically altered concepts of self-defense. Unlike their southern counterparts, Black Power militants viewed self-defense as the antithesis of nonviolence and scorned mass demonstrations as perpetuating passiveness and powerlessness. Martin Luther King's philosophy, they charged, would only emasculate black men. Although southern defenders voiced similar skepticism, they accepted the civil rights struggle's pragmatic symbiosis between armed protection and tactical nonviolence. By contrast, Malcolm X and some of his heirs reinforced existing binaries by presenting African Americans with a bipolar alternative: picking up guns or being mocked as unmanly cowards. From this perspective, self-defense was transformed into a full-fledged strategy that became the only alternative to nonviolent protest.

The most noticeable difference between black nationalists and southern defense groups was the tendency among certain Black Power groups to redefine aggressive violence as a legitimate form of armed resistance. US and the Black Panthers in particular fused traditional notions of self-defense with the ideas of Malcolm X, Marxist class analysis, Frantz Fanon's anticolonial theories, and the tenets of revolutionaries Mao Zedong and Che Guevara. This ideological hodgepodge allowed them to argue that aggressive violence and even guerrilla warfare, while being revolutionary, constituted an essentially defensive struggle against racist oppression. Unsurprisingly, such interpretations alarmed federal authorities. The ensuing efforts by the FBI to suppress the activities of those radicals that advocated self-defense and amassed weapons hampered the social and political programs with which northern militants had hoped to improve the lives of African Americans.

Black nationalists traditionally rejected nonviolence, a tactic that they deemed incompatible with their interpretation of what it meant to be a man. Long before the emergence of Black Power, the Nation of Islam (NOI) and other black radicals derided Martin Luther King's philosophy as futile and unmanly. As early as 1957, journalist P. L. Prattis of the *Pittsburgh Courier* claimed that nonviolence would "not solve" the problems that confronted African American citizens.[3] In a series of articles, he acknowledged the tactical advantage of nonviolent protest but insisted that black men had to be willing to put their "fist in somebody's face" to "win respect."[4] Reserving for himself the right of self-defense, Prattis vowed "to kick" any white attacker "in his teeth, regardless of what Dr. King exhorts."[5] By adhering to what Prattis dismissed as "passive" resistance, black men would only forfeit dignity and honor.

In the following years, like-minded detractors closely watched the bloody path of the southern freedom struggle and found their skepticism toward nonviolent protest repeatedly confirmed. In 1959, black Muslim Charles X lauded the militancy of Robert Williams in the *Baltimore Afro-American*. To this man's mind, the North Carolinian's stance proved that the African American man had finally reached a point "when he no longer begs for what he wants. From now on if the law can't settle things, buckshot will."[6] Two years later, when white segregationists orchestrated bloody assaults against Freedom Riders in Anniston and Birmingham, the editors of the New York–based black nationalist journal *Liberator* hailed their "heroic sacrifices" but strongly opposed their tactics. "Unlike them," the editors wrote, "we can feel no love or compassion for either the white hoodlums who attacked them or the white officials who failed to protect them." From the perspective of the *Liberator*, the Freedom Ride did not exemplify the power of nonviolent direct action but only proved the futility of King's teachings.[7]

Even one of the Freedom Riders once struggled to rid himself of such dominant notions of masculinity before embarking on the dangerous journey. In an anecdote from his early days in the movement, black CORE activist Jimmy McDonald hinted at the tensions between Gandhian tenets and the urge to defend one's honor. "I was passing out leaflets in Times Square in front of Woolworth's," the singer-turned-activist recalled, "when two white cats came up and . . . said suppose I take that flyer and slap you in the face with it, will you turn the other cheek? I said yes, and his friend said, what would you do if I slapped you on that cheek? And I said I'll put all my tens and a half right up your ass. Now I thought that was the way that I had to react as a man, you know, not realizing that this did not sit well with CORE downtown."[8] While McDonald later managed to face such challenges to his manhood nonviolently, this story illustrates the sentiment of many black nationalists at the time.

Some African American men voiced their resentment in letters to the *Baltimore Afro-American*. One reader from Washington, D.C., insisted in June 1963: "To those who offer the line that 'nothing is accomplished through violence,' they are simply misguided hypocrites attempting to justify cowardice."[9] A black New Yorker similarly concluded in a letter to the black newspaper: "Moses' law was an eye for an eye and a tooth for a tooth. That is the only kind of law real men can respect. Only cowards will hide behind a 'love everybody' teaching."[10] Disputing King and other civil rights activists, these skeptics reiterated the argument that nonviolence would only compound the social and political impotence of black men.

The violent terror that activists faced in Birmingham, Alabama, in 1963 further convinced such critics that armed resistance was necessary. At a memorial service for the victims of the bomb attack on Birmingham's Sixteenth Street Baptist Church, black novelist John Oliver Killens admitted that the incident had shattered his belief in the effectiveness of Martin Luther King's philosophy. Speaking in New York City, Killens said that he could no longer love those who continued to murder African Americans.[11] One black CORE supporter from Santa Rosa, California, argued in a letter to the national office that the Birmingham tragedy left blacks with no alternative but to arm for protection: "I think that every Negro should be armed with machine guns and automatic shotguns if possible, and patrolling the streets and standing guard wherever necessary."[12]

By the time of the Birmingham bombing, Malcolm X had become the most notorious detractor of nonviolence. He had started a career as a pimp and burglar in Boston and New York City before converting to the Islamic teachings of religious leader Elijah Muhammad in prison in the late 1940s. Condemning whites as "devils" and calling for a separate African American state, Muhammad led the Nation of Islam and preached black pride, moral uplift, and economic self-reliance. Malcolm adopted the sect's strict rules of moral conduct and began to read ravenously, devouring philosophy, history, and many other subjects. By the time he was paroled in 1952, Malcolm had become a fervent and highly articulate follower of Muhammad and was determined to spread his pro-black gospel among African Americans.[13]

In July 1959, a TV documentary catapulted the obscure organization into the spotlight of national attention. Entitled "The Hate That Hate Produced," the film horrified white Americans and triggered a deluge of news stories about Elijah Muhammad's organization. *Life*, *Look*, *Newsweek*, and *Time* reported extensively about both the NOI and Malcolm X, its most articulate spokesman. Droves of reporters besieged the young minister, asking him to participate in radio and television panels to discuss the black Muslims' controversial message. While the nonviolent sit-in movement ushered in the turbulent 1960s, Malcolm X plunged into a marathon of press, radio, and television interviews, talking to *Playboy* journalists as well as to academic audiences at Harvard and Yale. By 1961, chiefly because of Malcolm X's tireless recruiting efforts, the Nation of Islam's membership had soared from a few hundred to tens of thousands. More than fifty temples—or mosques, as they came to be called after 1961—had been established across the country. Malcolm X assumed more and more responsibility within the Nation and became the organization's first national minister in 1963.

Spreading Muhammad's teachings, Malcolm X lambasted Martin Luther King. "Any Negro who teaches other Negroes to turn the other cheek in the face of attack," he said in a 1963 television interview, "is disarming the Negro of his God-given right, of his moral right, of his natural right, of his intelligent right to defend himself."[14] King's followers, he charged, "will cut each other from head to foot, but they will not do anything to defend themselves against the attacks of the white man."[15] From the Muslim minister's perspective, there was no "turn-the-other-cheek revolution." Revolutions, he insisted in his famous "Message to the Grass Roots," could not be based on loving one's enemy. True revolutions involved bloodshed, and "modern Uncle Toms" like King were little more than pawns in the white man's scheme to perpetuate black powerlessness. "Be peaceful, be courteous, obey the law, respect everyone," he told his followers, "but if someone puts his hands on you, send him to the cemetery."[16]

This confrontational rhetoric reflected common beliefs among the black Muslims. While Elijah Muhammad called his followers "peace-loving people" and forbade ordinary members to carry weapons, he and his adherents strongly believed in the right of self-defense. In this spirit, the Fruit of Islam, a group of bodyguards who were trained in karate and judo, ensured the security of their leader and maintained order at the sect's large meetings. It came as no surprise that the NOI's official newspaper, *Muhammad Speaks*, praised Robert Williams and his Monroe rifle club.[17]

The increasing popularity and influence of Malcolm X generated increasing conflict between him and Muhammad, which culminated in a split between the two men in March 1964. Freed from the shackles of the NOI's restrictive doctrines, which had forbidden any political or social activism, Malcolm intended to use his popularity among poor African Americans and international audiences to assume a leadership position in the black freedom struggle. A pilgrimage to Mecca in April 1964 softened his views on white people, but Malcolm's political program continued to be inextricably linked to armed self-defense. Through his Organization of Afro-American Unity (OAAU), whose secular program encouraged blacks to control their own educational, cultural, economic, and political institutions, he sought to convert black Americans to active armed resistance against white violence.[18] Even before founding the OAAU, Malcolm reiterated his appeal to abandon nonviolence and predicted that the masses of African Americans would soon pick up the gun. The time was ripe, he said, "for the American Negro to fight back in self-defense whenever and wherever he is being unjustly and unlawfully attacked."[19] Particularly "in areas where the Government seems unable or unwilling to protect our people," blacks ought to organize rifle clubs to defend their communities.[20]

Despite his differences with King, Malcolm was even willing to mobilize OAAU members for the protection of the SCLC president and other nonviolent activists in the Deep South. In early July 1964, when SCLC confronted daily attacks from the Ku Klux Klan in St. Augustine, Florida, Malcolm X sent a telegram to the embattled city, in which he offered armed protection. "If the federal government will not send troops to your aid," he wrote to SCLC's president, "just say the word and we will immediately dispatch some of our brothers there to organize self-defense units among our people and the Ku Klux Klan will then receive the taste of their own medicine. The day of turning the other cheek to those brutal beasts is over."[21] King, whom Malcolm X had met only once in late March 1964, did not respond to the proposition.

In Malcolm's view, self-defense was more than a practical imperative; it also represented a crucial affirmation of black manhood. Rather than follow King's emasculating philosophy, he argued, black men needed to regain their role as protectors of "their" women and their families. Condemning SCLC's 1963 Birmingham campaign, where activists had asked little children to provoke violent attacks from police commissioner Bull Connor, Malcolm X said, "Real men don't put their children on the firing line."[22] The tactical advantage of doing so meant little to Malcolm, who, after learning from Fannie Lou Hamer about the violent abuse that she had suffered in Mississippi, told a Harlem audience that black men deserved no respect if they failed to protect their women. "When I listen to Mrs. Hamer," he told a Harlem audience in late 1964, "a black woman—could be my mother, my sister, my daughter—describe what they had done to her in Mississippi, I ask myself how in the world can we ever expect to be respected as *men* when we will allow something like that to be done to our women, and we do nothing about it?"[23]

Malcolm explained that "passive" resistance stood for powerlessness and effeminacy, while armed self-defense would help black men to be respected and to respect themselves. "Anybody can sit," he once dismissed sit-in demonstrations. "An old woman can sit. A coward can sit. . . . It takes a man to stand."[24] The Muslim minister was convinced that the OAAU, which emphasized the right of self-defense, would regain "our self-respect, our manhood, our dignity and freedom."[25] Although the OAAU also envisioned political activism and social programs to improve the black community, Malcolm X appeared to regard the affirmation of black masculinity through armed force as the first step toward black liberation.

The Muslim leader's biographer Bruce Perry has attributed Malcolm's fixation on manhood to the brutality of his tyrannical father and a trying childhood, but the militant Muslim's socialization in the NOI was probably just as important in shaping his ideas about gender.[26] Elijah Muhammad enforced a traditional separation of gender roles and offered his male followers a vision of racial uplift that was largely based on African Americans' ability to disprove and defy racist stereotypes. Black manhood was deemed crucial to accomplish this goal. For example, early issues of the NOI's newspaper, *Muhammad Speaks*, as well as large banners at the sect's meetings repeatedly urged male members to become guardians of black women. One banner exhorted: "We Must Protect Our Most Valuable Property: Our Women."[27]

Calling on the NOI's female members to be good, chaste, and pious, the black Muslims also created their own ideal of black womanhood. The floor-length white gowns and white headscarves that female members were required to wear reinforced this romanticized imagery of purity. Although this ideal followed widely accepted models of white middle-class womanhood, it also represented a powerful counterimage that challenged white ideals of beauty and the idea that only white women deserved protection from sexual abuse. Black women too were beautiful, the black Muslims conveyed, stressing that black men were determined to protect their purity from white men's attacks.[28] Of course, such pledges certainly reflected genuine concerns about women's safety. But as Farah Jasmine Griffin has suggested, the NOI's rhetoric must also be considered the continuation of a power struggle between white and black men, a struggle in which African American women were confined to the role of passive objects.[29]

If one accepts fear as a benchmark, this symbolism of masculine defiance was highly successful. The militant rhetoric of Malcolm X alarmed white Americans, many of whom considered his call to arms a reckless incitement to open race war. Not surprisingly, white editors generally condemned his militant statements. From the perspective of the *New York Times*, Malcolm X was an "irresponsible demagogue" whose advocacy of self-defense was an open invitation to break the law.[30] "In a cry to arms that borders on sedition," the *Christian Century* similarly warned in April 1964, "Malcolm X lures abused and discontented Negroes into a type of warfare they cannot win."[31] *U.S. News & World Report* was convinced that Malcolm's rhetoric would soon bear violent fruit in the racially charged atmosphere of American cities.[32]

Since Malcolm X had long been the minister of the NOI's Harlem Mosque and had stayed in New York City after his split with Elijah Muhammad, the Big Apple's authorities in particular were concerned about his verbal threats. Police commissioner Michael J. Murphy promised in March 1964 that he would not let Malcolm X "turn New York City into a battleground" and vowed to protect its residents against what he considered advocacy of "bloodshed and armed revolt."[33] Queens district attorney Frank D. O'Connor went so far as to accuse Malcolm of being indirectly responsible for the murder of a white female merchant in Harlem. O'Connor argued that her death could only be the result of Malcolm's incendiary speeches.[34]

More than a year before Louisiana governor McKeithen mulled over plans to disarm the Deacons for Defense and Justice, New York police officers raided the premises of the Harlem-based Tripod Rifle Club. City authorities justified their actions with the argument that the thirty Tripod members colluded with the NOI and other "hate groups."[35] The club's president, Cecil Chisholm, had no doubt as to why only his club, which was one among hundreds in New York City, had been targeted. "They . . . won't say it out loud," he explained to *Jet*, "but they seem to think that Negroes are buying up guns to shoot white people. The whole thing is ridiculous."[36] Irrespective of geography, then, mere talk about armed black resistance continued to conjure up powerful images of armed revolt in the mind of white America.

While New York's police officers seemed to consider him a dangerous prophet of destruction, Malcolm X insisted that he merely called for the time-honored right of self-defense. "This does not mean that we should go out and initiate acts of aggression indiscriminately in the white community," he explained in a television interview. "But it does mean that, if we are going to be respected as human beings, we should reserve the right to defend ourselves by whatever means necessary."[37] The problem was that ominous lines like "by any means necessary," his praise for the violent Mau Mau rebellion against colonial rule in Kenya, and his scathing criticism of Martin Luther King did little to dispel white concerns. At times, moreover, Malcolm X clearly blurred the distinction between defensive and aggressive violence. Still, despite his defiant militancy, Malcolm's violence never went beyond mere rhetoric. Throughout his career as Muslim minister and activist, Malcolm X himself never carried a gun. Only after members of the NOI began to threaten him and his family did he arm himself with a rifle and apply for an official pistol permit to protect himself and his family. Unsurprisingly, white officials denied his application. At the time of his assassination on February 21, 1965, the only weapon he carried was a tear-gas pen.[38]

But the militant ideas of Malcolm X had a tremendous impact on African Americans. Cleveland, Ohio, illustrates how the Muslim leader's gospel of black pride and self-defense contributed to the radicalization of the civil rights struggle outside the South. Civil rights scholars have only recently begun to pay closer attention to the northern movement. *Freedom North*, a recent collection of essays on this subject, has demonstrated that black protest did not stop at the Mason-Dixon Line. Rather, faced with de facto segregation and discrimination, northern activists were just as determined as their southern peers to attain true equality.[39] The midwestern city of Cleveland was no exception. By the early 1960s, African Americans constituted more than 30 percent of the city's eight hundred thousand residents, and, as in many other urban areas outside the South, had to endure segregated schools, job discrimination, inferior housing, and police brutality.[40]

Black housing inspector Lewis G. Robinson was one of the first activists who considered nonviolent direct action to protest these conditions. Born in Alabama, the thirty-three-year-old army veteran attended college on the GI Bill and completed four semesters at Cleveland Marshal Law School before securing a job as housing inspector with Cleveland's city administration in 1959. Three years later, he organized the Freedom Fighters, a small, primarily black, working-class group that intended to stage public protest campaigns to put pressure on the white city administration.[41] Together with the local CORE chapter, which formed in March 1963, the Freedom Fighters first focused on job discrimination at the city's Central Cadillac franchise before tackling the city's segregated schools. Black "ghetto schools," Robinson pointed out in a leaflet, were "hopelessly inferior," and the only way to ensure that African American children received a good education was "to have . . . [them] sit right beside a white child."[42] By September 1963, CORE and Robinson's organization had allied themselves with other groups in the United Freedom Movement (UFM) to negotiate school integration with the local board of education.

A month later, the board finally yielded to the UFM's demands and initiated the busing of black children to white schools. Once there, however, African American students suffered from abuse and harassment. Worse, the school board reneged on its promise to launch a gradual program of desegregation in the entire school system. This resolved the UFM and CORE to stage non-violent protests, beginning at Brett Elementary School on January 29, 1964. One day later, the UFM targeted the formerly all-white Murray Hill Elementary School.[43] But when the demonstrators approached the building that morning, they faced a hostile crowd of several hundred whites. Determined to prevent any picketing or similar forms of protest, the crowd bloodied black fathers who had accompanied their sons to the school, roughed up reporters who covered the event, and threw bottles, eggs, and other missiles at the small group of protestors.[44] The following day, members of CORE and the UFM staged a sit-in at the city's school board office in downtown Cleveland to express their outrage at the violence. Again, board officials backed down, promising to work out a plan that would lead toward full integration. But their proposition to construct three more schools to alleviate the overcrowded conditions in the city's ghetto schools was a deliberate ploy. Activists understood that the location of the new schools in the black neighborhood of Glennville would only perpetuate segregated second-class education.[45]

By that time, weekly news about racial murders in the South had seriously undermined the local movement's enthusiasm for nonviolence. Robinson remembered in his memoirs: "Many people discussed the violence in the South, black people being beaten, the FBI standing by doing nothing, state troopers standing by doing nothing. And they felt that it was time for the black man to defend himself like everybody else."[46] By the end of 1963, Cleveland CORE had become similarly disenchanted with nonviolence. At the Northern Grass Roots Leadership Conference in Detroit in November, the local CORE chapter and the Freedom Fighters applauded the militant speeches by black nationalist minister Albert B. Cleage and Malcolm X. Along with other delegates, they voted for a resolution that expressed the conference's unanimous support for "the principle of self-defense."[47]

The violence at the Murray Hill School had a similarly corrosive effect on black faith in the Gandhian technique and generated heated discussions within Cleveland CORE. "People in the chapter debated the question of nonviolence versus violence at great length," chairman Arthur Evans later recalled. By his account, "There were a number of people who wanted to scrap the nonviolence stance."[48] The members of the Freedom Fighters, who were outraged at the harassment of children and the attacks on black parents, also pondered alternatives to the movement's primary protest strategy. At a party two weeks after the Murray Hill incident, Lewis Robinson and several other black army veterans discussed organizing a "black man's peace patrol" to protect those students who attended white schools.[49]

But Malcolm X was by far the greatest influence on the Cleveland movement's increasing opposition to nonviolence. "Malcolm X's influence was very important," CORE member Ruth Turner later remembered.[50] "Brother Malcolm," Robinson similarly reflected in an interview, "was the only one to tell the white man to his face in public what was wrong with him, and that he didn't give a damn about him. . . . being practical, it's impossible for a black man with his eyes open in America, not to think like Brother Malcolm."[51] His call for armed resistance, in particular his famous "the ballot or the bullet" speech, had a tremendous impact on the Freedom Fighters' decision to form a black self-defense group. In February and March 1964, Robinson and fellow activists repeatedly discussed the Muslim's teachings.[52]

When Cleveland CORE invited the Muslim leader in early April to give the very same speech in the city's Cory Methodist Church, the event confirmed Robinson in his plan to organize for armed protection. Speaking in the crowded church on April 3, 1964, Malcolm stressed the importance of political activism but cautioned his audience that this struggle for power might require armed resistance if politics failed. Cheered and applauded by the primarily black audience, he declared: "[I]t's time now for you and me to become more politically mature and realize what the ballot is for; what we're supposed to get when we cast a ballot; and that if we don't cast a ballot, it's going to end up in a situation where we're going to have to cast a bullet. It's either a ballot or a bullet."[53] At the conclusion of the rally, Robinson provided newsmen who attended the event with a press release that announced his intention to form the Medgar Evers Rifle Club, whose name was a tribute to the slain Mississippi civil rights leader.[54]

Two days later, Robinson's plan had become front-page news in every Cleveland newspaper. In an interview with the *Cleveland Press* on April 6, Robinson conceded that he expected his group to provoke "massive reaction among the whites" but explained that the ensuing confrontation would "awaken the people to the situation and eradicate the entire problem."[55] Most whites in Cleveland disagreed, condemning his idea as reckless and dangerous. The editors of the *Press* predicted that the formation of the defense group would inevitably lead to "bloodshed." They insisted that the civil rights movement's success "has been given stature . . . by its determined nonviolence, as outlined by the Rev. Martin Luther King," not by guns and violence.[56]

But the tragic events that took place the following day led many black activists to believe that nonviolent strategies were ineffective. During a demonstration at the construction site of the new schools, several protestors tried to interrupt construction by throwing themselves on the ground to stop the bulldozer that prepared the location. When the driver backed up, he accidentally killed Bruce Klunder, a young white minister and CORE member who had dropped to the ground behind the machine. That night, bands of angry African Americans roamed the streets of Cleveland's black section, looting stores and battling the police. Malcolm X was still in town when the violence began. Giving an interview to a local radio station at the height of the riot, he fanned the flames by calling upon the rioters to fight back against white attacks.[57] Later that night about forty black men crammed in the small apartment of Louis Robinson and his white wife, Beth, to establish the Medgar Evers Rifle Club.[58]

The official formation of the defense unit generated reactions that clearly split along racial lines. Cleveland's white authorities were deeply disturbed. Only a few days after the city had learned of the new militant group, the city administration suspended Robinson as housing inspector.[59] In the U.S. Senate, Ohio senator Frank J. Lausche condemned the club as "criminal in spirit and purpose." Liberty, he insisted, could "only be preserved through obedience to law and order."[60] Most of Cleveland's white residents agreed, inundating Robinson and his wife with threatening phone calls. African American residents, on the other hand, generally supported Robinson, as did Cleveland CORE, although it had publicly criticized the gun club. Chairman Evans later explained that he and his fellow members felt obligated to CORE's national office, which still professed Gandhian nonviolence. Privately, however, the local chapter wholeheartedly agreed with Robinson. "By 1964," black CORE member Bernard Mandel recalled, "we realized that we would have to abandon nonviolence."[61]

Like Malcolm X, Lewis Robinson viewed armed resistance and black manhood as inextricably linked. In discussions with fellow activists about the atrocities against civil rights workers in the Deep South, he argued that for the black man, self-defense "was the only way of obtaining respect for his manhood and protection of his woman."[62] The Medgar Evers Rifle Club clearly served this purpose and through this affirmation of masculinity evolved into an important community organization. Weekly target practice on a farm east of Cleveland became cheerful family events and instilled the club's members with a new sense of pride in their role as patriarchal guardians of the "weaker sex." Robinson recalled that women who accompanied their husbands on these weekend trips to witness the military training "showed a new respect for their men and the men, in turn, felt like men, masters of their destinies, protectors of their women and families."[63]

Empowered and inspired by the ideas of Malcolm X, those who spent part of their summer on the target range decided to organize a black nationalist cultural center that would promote civic, political, and economic responsibility among black ghetto youth. In mid-November 1964, Robinson obtained an official charter for what came to be known as the "Jomo Freedom Kenyatta" (JFK) House, which was located in the heart of Cleveland's black section. Open six days a week, the JFK House became an important community center and helped reduce juvenile delinquency by offering recreation and cultural events for black teenagers.[64] Thus, two years before Black Power activists began to call for political power, self-defense, black pride, and economic self-help, these elements were already part of Cleveland's black freedom movement.

The city's freedom struggle provides more than insights into the roots of Black Power or the radicalizing influence of Malcolm X; it also illustrates the different role of self-defense in areas where Ku Klux Klan terrorism was absent. In Alabama, Louisiana, or Mississippi, armed resistance was primarily a physical necessity that supported the nonviolent civil rights struggle. Faced with daily intimidations and attacks, black southerners sought to ensure the survival of the movement and their communities. Although armed protection instilled pride and self-respect in these men, it remained a by-product of their pragmatic reaction to the region's brutal reality. In Ohio, on the other hand, organized armed protection against racist aggression was superfluous since Ku

Klux Klan attacks rarely occurred outside the Deep South. The mobilization of black activists and the affirmation of their manhood, therefore, became the primary purpose of Cleveland's Medgar Evers Rifle Club.

Lewis Robinson readily conceded in an interview that his organization had been primarily "a psychological way of our educating the blacks and conditioning them that we're going to have to fight for ourselves."[65] Regardless of whether the club's members were ready to repel actual attacks, moreover, few of them would have been able to do so. Even Robinson "had never owned any kind of firearms" prior to the formation of the defense squad. Only in May 1964 did Robinson begin to buy rifles for himself and his comrades, many of whom had never fired a gun.[66]

Ironically, it was the news accounts of their armed actions that eventually forced them to prepare for self-defense. By Robinson's account, he "later . . . found out that I did have to *really* organize a gun club for self-defense then for my own protection because the police were not interested in protecting me. I was getting 30 and 40 phone calls a day of threats, and I had to organize my own organization to protect myself and the black community did rally toward me."[67] Thus, the Medgar Evers Rifle Club foreshadowed both the Black Power movement's attempts to create a new type of militant black masculinity and the hostile white reactions that these efforts would provoke.

The Cleveland movement's defense group was probably the most visible result of the radicalizing impact of Malcolm X, but his message resounded throughout black nationalist circles. In April 1964, the *Liberator* praised Malcolm for "saying out loud what many Americans of African descent have been thinking for years."[68] Echoing this militant gospel a few months later, black nationalist Richard Henry of the Detroit-based Group on Advanced Leadership (GOAL) called for "a quick and widespread formation of rifle clubs by Negroes all across the North" to assist southern blacks in an imminent guerrilla war against white terrorists. According to Henry, Martin Luther King's "doctrine of non-violence" was dead.[69] A reader of *Ebony* agreed, echoing Malcolm X in his argument in November 1964 that it was "time we stopped turning the other cheek."[70] The assassination of the militant nationalist only reinforced the power of his message, which became the founding document of the Black Power movement. As William Van Deburg has pointed out, Malcolm X "became a Black Power paradigm—the archetype, reference point, and spiritual adviser in absentia for a generation of Afro-American activists."[71]

However, while Malcolm X eventually came to see the tactical merits of nonviolence, his political heirs could see no common ground between nonviolent protest and armed militancy. In early 1965, when visiting Selma, Alabama, during SCLC's famous campaign for voting rights legislation, the Muslim leader explained to Martin Luther King's wife, Coretta, that his militant ideas might actually help the nonviolent movement accomplish its goals. Malcolm X clearly understood that white America was far more likely to support King's demands when confronted with his seemingly violent alternative.[72] The new generation of black nationalists that would become the backbone of the Black Power movement, on the other hand, disputed the benefits of nonviolent direct action. In an article for the *Negro Digest*, black cultural nationalist and poet LeRoi Jones, who later changed his name to Amiri Baraka, spoke for many. "Not only does Non-Violence usually mean no action at all," he wrote in October 1964, "but it's not, nor is it likely to be, a useful moral concept in the impossible social environment of America."[73] From this perspective, the Gandhian strategy stood for complete passiveness, an interpretation that ignored both the coercive elements of nonviolent direct action and Malcolm's insight that armed militancy could contribute to the success of nonviolent tactics.

Such bipolar views were unfortunate, since they precluded any constructive dialogue between black nationalists and those who believed in the power of nonviolence. As early as spring 1963, SNCC's Julian Bond lamented in *Freedomways*: "One of the biggest tragedies of nonviolence is that the biggest critics are those who understand it least."[74] At the same time, Bond and his fellow activists from SNCC, CORE, and SCLC bore part of the responsibility for people's misconceptions. Considering the thousands of pamphlets, speeches, and letters that these organizations produced and disseminated to preserve the freedom movement's seemingly pacifistic image, opposition to Gandhian teachings in black nationalist circles was hardly surprising.

Since black nationalists generally believed in this universally accepted dichotomy between self-defense and nonviolence, many of them welcomed the formation of the Deacons for Defense and Justice as a portent of the end of the nonviolent era. The Deacons, black activist Ossie Sykes concluded in the September 1965 issue of the *Liberator*, "are through taking the crap, whether it is the horse manure flowing from the mouths of Washington officials, or bullets spitting from the guns of well armed Klansmen."[75] Echoing the widespread critique that nonviolence degraded black men, one reader of *Ebony* observed in late 1965 about the Deacons: "This organization in effect explodes the myth of moral weakness and petticoat and pulpit subordination of the Negro male."[76] What these critics failed to understand was that the Deacons, despite all their gun-toting, worked not against but in tandem with the nonviolent movement.

By contrast, in the mind of Malcolm's followers, self-defense became incompatible with nonviolent tactics. This tendency to view armed self-defense as the antithesis of nonviolence was another major element that differentiated southern advocates of armed resistance from their black nationalist counterparts.

Some black militants went even further, reinterpreting aggressive violence as a legitimate form of self-defense against white America. Militant exile Robert Williams was among the first activists who voiced such a radical view. This might seem surprising since Williams had repeated again and again during the feud with Roy Wilkins that his call to "meet violence with violence" was merely an appeal to resort to self-defense in the face of white terrorism. But his debate with Martin Luther King in *Liberation* had already indicated that there were conspicuous parallels between Williams's interpretation of nonviolent protest and that of black nationalists. Like Malcolm X, Williams condemned nonviolence for encouraging white violence and accused Martin Luther King of teaching passiveness and submissiveness. This perspective, white activist Anne Braden noted in a 1963 review of Williams's book *Negroes with Guns*, demonstrated "a total lack of comprehension of what nonviolence means in the current Southern struggle."[77]

Cuban exile further distorted the North Carolinian's perception of the freedom movement. Two years after he had been forced to flee, Williams conjured up fantastic visions of guerrilla warfare against white America and spread his ideas through his radio broadcast *Radio Free Dixie* and the newsletter *Crusader*. In the May-June 1964 issue of this publication, Williams urged African Americans to "prepare to wage an urban guerilla war of self-defense" against the white oppressor. In this battle, southern defenders' traditional weapon of choice—the shotgun—would be no longer useful. Instead, Williams advised to build "a poor man's arsenal," which consisted of Molotov cocktails, acid bombs, machine guns, hand grenades, bazookas, light mortars, and rocket launchers.[78] African Americans, Williams further demanded on *Radio Free Dixie*, ought to turn to "kill-ins" rather than sit-ins and adopt the battle cry "Freedom or Death."[79]

Williams viewed his call for armed insurrection as a natural evolution of the defense efforts that he began in Monroe in the 1950s. "[Y]our first step, if you're abused, is to ask people not to abuse you," he explained to the *National Guardian* in September 1964. "Then you defend yourself against that abuse: and then, if necessary, you must be prepared to destroy in order to defend."[80] From this perspective, self-defense and aggressive violence became practically indistinguishable.

Many whites probably believed that the violent disorders that erupted in the Watts district of Los Angeles in August 1965 heralded the beginning of the struggle that Williams had predicted. As in other cities, the arrest of a black man by white police officers triggered the disturbances. Confronted with yet another case of police brutality on the night of August 11, the crowd that witnessed the incident vented their anger and frustration at this injustice on white property in the area. After looting pawnshops and hardware stores, African Americans torched dozens of buildings. Their chant "Burn, baby, burn" rang ominously in the ears of white observers.[81] By the end of the riot's second night, the area resembled the inferno of a World War II battlefield, with blacks barricading the streets and snipers firing at approaching police officers and firemen. By the time that two thousand National Guardsmen and nine hundred police officers finally managed to repress the turmoil on August 18, thirty-four persons lay dead, one thousand others had been wounded, and four thousand suspects had been arrested. Conservative estimates put the property damage at $200 million.[82]

One black nationalist later praised the disorders as an affirmation of "self-respect, self-determination and self-defense," but the riots of the 1960s had little to do with armed protection.[83] In stark contrast to the urban confrontations between white mobs and black defenders in the aftermath of World War I, there was no racist enemy that blacks were forced to repulse. Rather, the violence was initiated solely by African Americans and consisted of looting and arson that deliberately targeted white property. In many ways, the riots were a spontaneous form of violent protest against economic inequality and racist oppression.[84]

But white Americans seemed to care little about whether the disorders were a response to legitimate grievances. To them the violence that engulfed American cities in 1965 and 1966 coupled with reports about the emergence of black militants in the North seemed to be part of a nationwide black conspiracy. In June 1966, *Life* warned: "In secret recesses of any ghetto in the U.S. there are dozens and hundreds of black men working resolutely toward an Armageddon in which Whitey is to be either destroyed or forced to his knees."[85] Small underground groups like the Revolutionary Action Movement (RAM), which according to the FBI advocated organized guerrilla warfare across the nation and planned selective assassinations of white and black leaders, or the Black Liberation Front (BLF), which had reportedly plotted to blow up the head of the Statue of Liberty, convinced many that black vengeance was near.[86] Confronted with such frightening reports, some white conservatives believed that the riots were far from spontaneous. They suspected that the violence was organized and directed by a dangerous coalition of Malcolm X rifle clubs, the Deacons for Defense and Justice, followers of Robert Williams, RAM, and Communist agitators.[87]

Another nationalist organization that gained increasing notoriety in 1966 was the US organization of 24-year-old black nationalist Ron (Maulena) Karenga. Deeply influenced by Malcolm X and the Watts riot, US—whose members used the name as a pronoun to differentiate themselves from "them," the white oppressor—had formed in the fall of 1965. In contrast to revolutionary nationalists like RAM or the BLF, who advocated immediate attacks against the white oppressor, college-educated Karenga argued that a reaffirmation of the uniqueness and beauty of black culture had to predate any revolutionary action. This cultural nationalism called upon blacks to accept and reaffirm their African roots by adopting African customs and the African language Swahili.[88]

Yet, although US considered black culture the most important aspect of black liberation, armed self-defense became a central aspect of the organization's efforts to nurture pride and self-respect. Karenga shared Malcolm X's aversion to nonviolence and similarly called upon blacks to fight back. Speaking before an enthusiastic teenage audience at a small church in Watts in May 1966, the US leader insisted that a show of force would discourage racist attacks on the black community. In this spirit, US formed a paramilitary wing, called Simba Wachanga (Swahili for "Young Lions"), which was trained in martial arts and the use of weapons.[89]

Like Robert Williams, the US organization argued that aggressive violence was a legitimate means to attain black liberation. The ideas of Frantz Fanon—a black psychiatrist from Martinique who had studied the role of resistance in anticolonial freedom movements—became the basis for this reevaluation of violence. In his analysis of the Algerian struggle against French colonial rule in the 1950s, Fanon argued that violence could serve as a "cleansing force," through which a colonized people would free themselves from their inferiority complex and restore their self-respect.[90] Following this line of reasoning, Ron Karenga considered the Watts disorders an affirmation of self-respect and manhood rather than a senseless act of frustration. Karenga predicted that violent upheavals like the one in Watts were only the herald of things to come. In 1971, according to a Seven Year Calendar that Karenga had created, US guerrilla fighters would initiate an "apocalyptic" struggle to overthrow the white federal government.[91]

The emerging Black Power movement verbalized what Karenga attempted to put into action: a redefinition of black identity. In 1967, sncc's Stokely Carmichael and black political scientist Charles Hamilton attempted to explain the ambiguous slogan and its meaning for black identity to a broader audience. In *Black Power: The Politics of Liberation in America*, the two authors explained that any political activism would have to be preceded by a reevaluation of white attitudes toward African Americans. What blacks needed to do was "to create our own terms through which to define ourselves and our relationship to the society, and to have these terms recognized." Blacks, Carmichael argued, had accepted white definitions and white stereotypes for too long and now needed to reclaim the "power of definition" as a prerequisite to obtaining political power. Carmichael called upon Negroes to view themselves "as African Americans and as black people who are in fact energetic, determined, intelligent, beautiful and peace-loving." At the same time, white people had to be forced to understand that blacks would not remain nonviolent in the face of white attacks.[92] For Black Power advocates, then, claiming the right to self-defense and building a positive black identity were inextricably linked.

The Black Panther Party for Self-Defense epitomized this interrelation between resistance and identity. It came as no surprise that the bpp's two founders were deeply influenced by Malcolm X. While attending Merritt College in Oakland, California, in the early 1960s, Huey P. Newton and Bobby Seale had been fascinated with the Muslim minister. The two friends frequently attended services at Oakland's noi Mosque to hear him speak and devoured his printed speeches and statements. At meetings of the Afro-American Association (aaa), a small, black nationalist discussion group that had formed on the campus of Merritt College, the two students debated the ideas of their idol and other black leaders. But Newton believed that neither the aaa nor other groups were really determined to translate this nationalist message into a realistic program for change in urban black America. This resolved Newton and Seale to organize the bpp in October 1966. The organization's ten-point program, which called for self-determination, full employment, decent housing, quality education, and an end to police brutality and white exploitation, sought to address the problems that confronted blacks in cities across America.[93]

Although Seale and Newton viewed themselves as the spiritual heirs of Malcolm X, they were also deeply influenced by Frantz Fanon's analysis of the Algerian freedom struggle. Incorporating his ideas in their analysis of urban America, chairman Seale and minister of defense Newton likened the situation of African Americans to that of a colonized people. From their perspective, white police officers constituted a foreign occupying army, which served as the military arm of a thoroughly racist system of oppression.[94] Armed self-defense against police brutality in black enclaves, they argued in the organization's official newspaper, *Black Panther*, was a justified means to oppose this occupation. Newton and Seale hoped that their patrols in California's Bay Area would help them recruit new members and might ultimately change policemen's brutal behavior.[95]

The example of Robert Williams and the Deacons for Defense and Justice inspired the organization's paramilitary character. Equipped with rifles, pistols, and law books, Newton and Seale followed police cars and informed African Americans of their rights in case of arrest. Several armed standoffs with police in late 1966 and early 1967 bolstered the BPP's reputation in Oakland's black community. By contrast, white police officers, whom the Panthers mocked as "pigs," became increasingly nervous at the BPP's defiance. However, since Newton, who had thoroughly studied California's penal code, went to great lengths not to violate any laws, city authorities could do little to stop the highly successful patrols. A bill proposed by Republican California state assemblyman Donald Mulford, who sought to prohibit the carrying of loaded firearms in public, was a direct response to the Panther patrols.

The BPP's decision to stage an armed demonstration against the Mulford Bill at the California State Legislature in Sacramento marked the beginning of the organization's rise to national fame and notoriety. On the sunny day of May 2, 1967, a caravan of cars manned with Black Panthers halted in front of the Capitol building. Twenty out of thirty young black men and women who emerged from the vehicles were armed with .357 Magnum pistols, M-1 carbine army rifles, and 12–gauge pump shotguns. The entire group was clad in black leather jackets, black boots, and black felt berets, and several men wore bullet-packed bandoliers across their chests. In what seemed a relaxed stroll, almost like a sightseeing tour, the little army nonchalantly walked toward the steps that led to the Capitol's main entrance. As the armed men and women passed the Capitol's west lawn, white journalists and a group of schoolchildren gaped at them in shocked disbelief.[96]

The Panthers had deliberately scheduled their armed demonstration to coincide with the debate on Mulford's legislative proposal. It came as no surprise, therefore, that throngs of reporters and cameramen surrounded the black militants long before they entered the building. Inside, shocked tourists, security guards, and secretaries quickly moved aside when the small army headed down the long entrance hall. "We're looking for the Assembly," BPP chairman

Bobby Seale said loudly. Directed to the building's second floor, Seale and his companions accidentally entered the assembly floor while trying to find the visitor's section. At that moment, security guards arrested the Panthers and confiscated their weapons.[97]

But since it was legal to carry loaded weapons inside the state Capitol, the officers could hold the group only briefly. After their release, the activists left the building and assembled behind their chairman on the upper steps in front of the Capitol. There, observed by dozens of cameramen and reporters, Seale reiterated a prepared statement that he had read to reporters inside the Capitol. The Black Panther Party for Self-Defense, he declared, called upon white and black Americans "to take careful note of the racist California Legislature now considering legislation aimed at keeping Black people disarmed and powerless while racist police agencies throughout the country intensify the terror, brutality, murder, and repression of Black people." Seale accused the American government of ignoring the oppression of African Americans. Rather than react to black protest against these conditions, hypocritical politicians had only intensified the subjugation of black people. For that reason, "the time" had "come for Black people to arm themselves against this terror before it is too late," Seale declared. "We believe that the Black communities of America must rise up as one man to halt the progression of a trend that leads inevitably to their total destruction."[98]

Neither Newton nor Seale had expected their demonstration to prevent the passage of the Mulford Bill. In fact, it served to convince many legislators that the new law was indispensable to stop the Panthers. It easily passed in July 1967.[99] Rather, they considered their armed protest part of a long-term strategy to establish the BPP as the "vanguard group" of the black revolution. Following a fusion of independent Marxism and black nationalism, Newton intended his organization to raise the consciousness of the black masses to prepare them for the ensuing revolutionary struggle against the racist system of capitalism. Through highly visible, but legal, activities like the protest at the California Capitol, coupled with educational programs, the BPP planned to acquaint blacks with strategies and methods that would enable them to resist the seemingly omnipotent white authorities.[100] "As long as we kept everything legal," Newton later explained their rationale, "the police could do nothing, and the people would see that armed defense was a legitimate, constitutional right. In this way, they would lose their doubts and fears and be able to move against their oppressor."[101]

In this respect, the Sacramento demonstration was a resounding success.

Practically overnight, the Panthers were thrust into the national spotlight. While the *New York Times* condemned the BPP as dangerous anarchists, African Americans from across the nation inundated the organization's Oakland office with requests for permission to start a BPP chapter in their community.[102]

Unlike the BPP's admirers, many white observers were concerned about the party's militant rhetoric, which frequently blurred the boundaries between self-defense and armed aggression. While Seale insisted in his memoirs that the Panthers "had never used" their "guns to go into the white community to shoot up white people," their martial rhetoric suggested the exact opposite to white observers.[103] Citing Chinese revolutionary Mao Zedong, the Panthers repeatedly proclaimed that political power grew "out of the barrel of a gun." Given the colonized situation of the black community, moreover, the killing of white police officers seemed a justifiable part of the black revolution. "We have reached the point in history," the BPP told the *National Guardian* in January 1968, "where we must claim that a black man, confronted by a bloodthirsty cop who is out to take his life out of hatred for the black race, has a right to defend himself—even if this means picking up a gun and blowing that cop away."[104] The fact that the BPP officially threatened its new members with expulsion if they failed to acquire their own gun and enough ammunition or refused to defend their homes did much to reinforce their reputation for being interested primarily in armed struggle.[105]

Like Karenga's US organization, the BPP argued that aggressive violence constituted a legitimate form of self-defense. The teachings of Fanon, Mao Zedong, and Che Guevara provided the theoretical base for this militant stance. For Algerian, Chinese, or Cuban revolutionaries, Newton later explained in his autobiography, "the only way to win freedom was to meet force with force," which, according to the BPP's minister of defense, was "a form of self-defense although that defense might at times take on characteristics of aggression." Newton concluded that oppressed people never initiated violence but simply responded to the violence that the oppressor inflicted upon them.[106] For the colonized people of African descent who resided in the United States, therefore, seemingly aggressive attacks on white racists became justifiable acts of armed resistance. In this spirit, the BPP's ultimate goal was to lead an interracial coalition of revolutionaries in an anticapitalist and anti-imperialist struggle against common enemies.[107]

Such novel interpretations of armed resistance stood in sharp contrast to the concept of self-defense that was espoused by southern defense groups. Neither Charles Sims nor Joseph Mallisham would have contemplated attacks on white police officers or revolutionary warfare against the forces of white supremacy, and the ideas of Marx, Fanon, or Mao had little impact on their activism in the Deep South. The skepticism of southern defenders toward Black Power militancy did not mean that black nationalist radicalism was unheard of in the Deep South. In 1964, for example, organizers of the Revolutionary Action Movement and members of the nationalist Afro-American Student Movement (ASM) met in Nashville, Tennessee, to discuss how to introduce self-defense and black nationalist ideas into the southern freedom struggle. In a report on the conference, white activist Anne Braden asserted that she found considerable "unspoken support" for black nationalism among black southerners.[108] But older activists like Sims and Mallisham remained adamant in their opposition to the revolutionary rhetoric that was uttered in many nationalist programs.[109]

A notion that southern protectors and their black nationalist counterparts did share was the conviction that armed self-defense was a major prerequisite for attaining true manhood. Indeed, as evidenced by Cleveland's Medgar Evers Rifle Club and the US organization, the preoccupation of some activists with guns and armed resistance can be best understood as powerful symbols of black male defiance, which countered the perceived debasement of African American men. Martin Luther King's assertion in June 1967 that there was "masculinity and strength in nonviolence" was ludicrous to Black Power groups like the BPP.[110] "We do not believe in passive and nonviolent tactics," Huey Newton told the *New York Times* in May 1967. From his perspective, nonviolence was "absurd, erroneous and deceitful."[111]

Defining their identities in direct opposition to what they perceived as feminine characteristics—weakness, passiveness, and powerlessness—the Black Panthers believed that they embodied the real traits of black masculinity. Even before forming the Panthers, Bobby Seale dreamed of joining "a group of mighty black warriors" who would engage in guerrilla warfare against racist violence.[112] Fifteen-year-old Bobby Hutton, one of the BPP's first recruits, seems to have joined the organization for similar reasons. According to Seale, Hutton once "said that he didn't think he could stand being pushed around by the cops anymore. That he didn't want to lose his manhood."[113] The Panthers, as Huey Newton pointed out in an interview, provided a model of masculinity that relieved these anxieties. "The black woman found it difficult to respect the black man because he didn't even define himself as a man!" Newton explained. By contrast, the Black Panthers, "along with all revolutionary black groups," had "regained" African Americans' minds and manhood.[114] Of course, the organization's militancy cannot be reduced to mere symbolism. Armed confrontations with white police and federal agencies' concerted efforts to stop the BPP's activities testify to the destructive impact of their militancy on the daily lives of party members. Still, while *intended* as a revolutionary alternative to nonviolence, armed self-defense *functioned* largely as a way to assert militant black manhood.

Some members, especially BPP minister of information Eldridge Cleaver, seemed to be obsessed with this struggle over gender identities. Repeatedly imprisoned on drug and rape charges between 1954 and 1966, Cleaver had become a follower of the NOI in prison but broke with Elijah Muhammad after the assassination of Malcolm X. Shortly after his release in late 1966, the prolific writer joined the Panthers. Cleaver's book *Soul on Ice*, a collection of letters and essays that he had penned in prison, reflects his preoccupation with black masculinity. Echoing the idea that men use women as signs to communicate with each other, he explained his assaults on white women as an insurrectionary act against white men.[115]

Cleaver's scathing criticism of black homosexuality further illustrates his fear of being considered effeminate and unmanly. To Cleaver, as he explained in an essay on gay black novelist James Baldwin, homosexuality was "a sickness" that prompted black men to adopt white principles and white behavior.[116] Philip Brian Harper has pointed out that this perceived lack of racial identification among black homosexuals became a symbol of failed manhood in black nationalist circles. Black poet LeRoi Jones (Amiri Baraka), for example, used homosexuality's connotations of effeminacy to criticize the moderate wing of the civil rights movement. In one poem, he insulted the NAACP's Roy Wilkins as "an eternal faggot" whose spirit, too, was "a faggot."[117] In Cleaver's case, the fact that rape and homosexual encounters were common occurrences in American prisons probably exacerbated his excessive homophobia.[118]

The party's minister of information deemed it crucial for himself and his peers to win back black women's respect. Black men's inability to protect "their" women weighed heavily on his conscience. "I want you to know," he wrote in a fictional letter to all black women, "that I feared to look into your eyes because I knew I would find reflected there a merciless indictment of my impotence and a compelling challenge to redeem my conquered manhood."[119] The Black Panther Party and its repeated vows to protect the black community became the vehicle that Cleaver sought to accomplish this goal. As he explained in an interview with *Playboy* in December 1968, the BPP was "a natural organization" for the young, since it was organized by their peers and supplied "very badly needed standards of masculinity."[120] From Cleaver's perspective, this standard appeared to be defined primarily by guns and the willingness to use them.[121]

The BPP's visual self-representation reflected the type of masculine militancy to which Cleaver alluded. The Panther uniform, which consisted of black beret, black leather jacket, black gloves, and dark sunglasses, generated fear among whites and instilled pride and self-respect in those who wore it. Photographs similarly communicated these characteristics. One famous image that Cleaver arranged depicts Huey Newton sitting in a large wicker chair that is flanked by African shields and animal pelts. Clad in the BPP's uniform and armed with a pump shotgun in one hand and an African spear in the other, Newton posed as the masculine warrior that Cleaver regarded as the epitome of authentic black manhood.[122] Although Newton later severely criticized this fixation on male identity, he agreed with him about the importance of self-respect and pride. In his memoirs, Newton insisted that the BPP was not searching "for badges of masculinity" since the party "acted as it did because we *were* men."[123] Regardless of whether some members were attempting to affirm their manhood while others already felt like real men, the BPP's powerful image of masculinity countered traditional stereotypes of male powerlessness, communicated defiance to white America, and instilled in male members a positive black identity.

Despite these beneficial aspects of the BPP's machismo, it contained serious problems. The Panthers countered white stereotypes and regained self-respect, but they simultaneously appropriated and reproduced dominant notions of masculinity, which were grounded in patriarchal privilege and the subordination of women. Although female Panthers received weapons instruction and were allowed to teach these skills to others, the predominance of male leaders coupled with their masculine rhetoric clearly circumscribed the agency of female members. Some of them remembered being treated like children on numerous occasions. Of course, as O. G. Ogbar has pointed out, "the Panthers were not ideologically static or monolithic chauvinists," and gender relations within the party were constantly contested, negotiated, and reshaped. Still, at least until the late 1960s, the machismo that permeated the party created a largely male-centered organization, whose members regarded women as readily available sexual objects, not as equals.[124] Ron Karenga's US organization was even more explicit in its adamant opposition to gender equality. Like the Nation of Islam, US required its female members to submit to male leadership and male authority without question.[125] In the mind of many Black Power militants, black male liberation seemed possible only in opposition to, rather than in tandem with, women.

Unlike US or the Nation of Islam, the BPP had begun to formulate a program of gender equality by the early 1970s, becoming one the first black organizations to advocate alliances with the women's and gay liberation movements. Moreover, as government repression stripped the party of much of its male leadership in the early 1970s, female participation and the number of women in leadership positions increased considerably, culminating in Elaine Brown's tenure as chairperson of the organization between 1974 and 1977.[126]

But more critical reappraisals of gender inequalities within the Black Power movement could be heard only years later. At the time, many women simply endured the movement's sexism and discrimination for the sake of unity. In the eyes of others, the positive aspects of the Black Power movement's machismo outweighed its shortcomings. Malcolm X, for example, became a symbol of admirable black manhood in the eyes of some female activists. Malcolm, New York CORE activist Sonia Sanchez later recalled, "became the man that most African-American women have wanted their men to be: strong. . . . He made us feel loved. And he made us feel that we were worth something finally on this planet Earth."[127] Black feminist Michele Wallace, despite her criticism of the movement's sexism, similarly concluded: "Malcolm was the supreme patriarch. He would provide for his women and children and protect them. One felt certain of that."[128] Gloria Richardson, the former leader of the black freedom movement in Cambridge, Maryland, also praised the militant heirs of the Muslim leader. Richardson confided to an interviewer in October 1967 that, as a black woman, she admired "the black men who have been coming up in the last two years and some of the changes in them . . . because they are quite willing to give their lives for whatever they happen to believe in, and to take any amount of chance to get it done." For the first time, Richardson said, she could admire these men.[129] Although black nationalists helped perpetuate traditions of gender inequality, then, their promise to reassert men's role as guardians of black womanhood contributed to a new sense of self-esteem among some black women as well.

Yet, as the Black Power movement gained momentum, this image of the patriarchal protector was increasingly superseded by visions of vengeance and destruction. Especially the leadership of SNCC, which developed close links to the BPP in 1967 and briefly pondered a merger with the Oakland-based organization, no longer alluded to the need to protect one's family but began to advocate vengeful guerrilla warfare against white America. Speaking to a crowd of students at Mississippi's Tougaloo College in April 1967, Carmichael insisted that "the real problem with violence is that we have never been violent, we have been too nonviolent." Acknowledged by cheers and thundering applause from black teenagers, SNCC's chairman suggested that the burning of black churches in the South ought to be answered by black counterattacks on white churches.[130] From Carmichael's perspective, even violent destruction was a legitimate means to achieve black liberation. "If you have to burn cities to the ground to get equality," he said at a New York rally a month later, "then they must be burned."[131]

To the mind of many whites, the wave of violent disorders that hit American cities in the ensuing months seemed to stem directly from this type of martial rhetoric. In the summer of 1967, the media reported almost daily about new outbreaks of looting and arson in cities across the nation. A riot in Newark in mid-July killed 26 people and injured 1,500 others. Less than a week later, rioting erupted in Detroit, where authorities counted almost 1,500 separate fires during the seven-day turmoil. Once the smoke had cleared, 33 African Americans and 7 whites lay dead. During what Detroit mayor Jerome P. Cavanagh likened to the embattled German city of Berlin at the end of World War II, 4,700 soldiers and National Guardsmen were mobilized to quell the disturbances. At some street corners, the soldiers engaged in vicious gun battles with black snipers. In 1967, similarly violent riots exploded in fifty-eight communities.[132]

Although these disorders were a manifestation of black frustration over unemployment, poverty, and persistent discrimination rather than evidence of any rebellious sentiment, Stokely Carmichael welcomed them as the herald of the coming revolution. By the time the violence began, the BPP had appointed Carmichael as the organization's field marshal to "establish revolutionary law, order, and justice" in the United States.[133] According to Carmichael, who later became the BPP's honorary prime minister, African Americans were on the right track. Speaking at the meeting of the Organization of Latin American Solidarity in Cuba in early August 1967, he averred that blacks were ready for violent revolution. "We are moving into open guerrilla warfare in the United States," he told the delegates and insisted that blacks had "no alternative but to use aggressive violence" to gain economic and political control of their communities.[134]

H. Rap Brown, a native of Louisiana who had replaced Carmichael as SNCC's chairman three months earlier, viewed the state of the black freedom struggle in similar terms. In an official statement made on the occasion of his arrest for illegally transporting weapons across state lines on July 26, 1967, the twenty-four-year-old Brown said: "We stand on the eve of a black revolution. Masses of our people are on the move, fighting the enemy tit-for-tat, responding to counter-revolutionary violence with revolutionary violence. . . . These rebellions are but a dress rehearsal for real revolution."[135] A day earlier, he had been shot in Cambridge, Maryland, after calling upon local blacks in a fiery speech to burn down the city if white authorities refused to yield to their demands. "Don't love him [the white man] to death," he shouted at the rally. "Shoot him to death."[136] Not surprisingly, many white observers believed him to be responsible for the riot that allegedly erupted shortly after his departure.[137]

The violent rhetoric of Brown, Carmichael, and the Panthers, coupled with the wave of urban disorders, clearly indicated that black support for nonviolent protest had dwindled. To many, Martin Luther King's assertion on *Meet the Press* in August 1967 that "the vast majority of Negroes feel that nonviolence is the best strategy, the best tactic to use in this moment of social transition," probably represented a statement of hope rather than a description of reality.[138] The new generation of black militants, as veteran activist Fred Shuttlesworth learned when visiting riot-torn Cincinnati, Ohio, deemed nonviolence and its adherents a thing of the past. "They still respected me," he said of their reaction to his exhortations, "but they weren't interested in nonviolence. They would tell me, 'You go along home and pray, Reverend, and let us take care of it now.'"[139] Such statements were symptomatic of people's frustration with the nonviolent movement, which had had little impact on the dismal plight of African Americans in urban communities such as Cincinnati, Newark, or Detroit.

Despite the changing mood among black activists, Martin Luther King felt impelled to prove them wrong. Determined to tackle the socioeconomic problems that underlay the problems of all poor Americans, King suggested in late 1967 that a major nonviolent protest campaign in Washington, D.C., would be sufficient to force the federal administration to yield to their demands for economic justice. Dubbing his project the Poor People's Campaign, King envisioned an interracial coalition of thousands of poor descending upon Washington. Camping in the vicinity of the White House, these men and women would engage in disruptive nonviolent demonstrations while organizing major boycotts against selected industries and urban shopping centers in cities across the nation. King was confident that the campaign's pressure would compel the nation's business leaders to lobby Congress for antipoverty legislation.[140]

But the vast majority of Black Power militants considered King's efforts a waste of time. Many believed that violence was the only effective tool to achieve black, in particular black male, liberation. Already in May 1967, Ernest Chambers, a twenty-nine-year-old militant from Omaha, Nebraska, proclaimed at the National Conference on Community Values and Conflict in New York: "Violence is the only way left to the black man to achieve his manhood in America."[141] SNCC's chairman H. Rap Brown also concluded that "the world didn't run on love." "The only thing that was gon' keep white muthafuckas off you was you!" he wrote in his memoirs. Indeed, according to Brown, black men would lose "a bit of manhood with every stale compromise to the authority in which one does not believe." Resistance would not suffice; aggression was now "the order of the day."[142]

The assassination of Martin Luther King on April 4, 1968, convinced many that Brown's conclusion was correct. After the slain leader's funeral, a visibly shaken Floyd McKissick stated at a news conference in Cleveland: "Nonviolence is a dead philosophy and it was not the black people who killed it."[143] Even the Black Catholic Clergy Caucus deemed King's philosophy no longer tenable and publicly called for "a re-evaluation of present attitudes towards violence" in case of white attacks against the black community.[144] It came as no surprise that neither McKissick nor this group of Catholic ministers condemned the new wave of urban violence that swept over the nation in the days and weeks following King's murder. African Americans rioted in at least 125 cities in 28 states, and the human toll paralleled that of 1967. After thousands of soldiers and National Guardsmen had suppressed the last riots, forty-six African Americans and five whites had been killed. Those injured numbered 2,600.[145] King's death marked the definitive end of the nonviolent era.

By that time, CORE had completely abandoned the principles upon which it had been founded a quarter century earlier. In 1967, its membership had voted to delete the term "multi-racial" from the organization's constitution. Defining Black Power as the power of black capitalism, which would help build black-owned and black-led businesses, the financially troubled organization continued to welcome white support but confined white activists to the role of passive "resource persons." Their active participation, McKissick and others argued, would only reinforce traditional stereotypes of black dependence. By late 1967, CORE had become an all-black organization.[146]

In addition to deleting any references to its original goal of interracial activism and integration, CORE renounced all forms of nonviolent protest. By late 1968, even McKissick, a participant in the 1947 Journey of Reconciliation who had helped organize sit-ins in his hometown of Durham, North Carolina, was convinced that "non-violence was a false philosophy, which could never last, and was never intended to really be."[147] In a 1969 pamphlet on its history, CORE condemned Gandhian protest as "damaging to the psyche of Black people" and "contrary to human nature and human psychology." From the perspective of its new chairman, Roy Innis, who had succeeded McKissick in September 1968, nonviolence only promoted "racism and acts of violence against" African Americans.[148] By the end of the decade, the Christian-Gandhian spirit that had once infused CORE's founding members had vanished.

In the eyes of CORE, King's death simply illustrated the ineffectiveness of nonviolence in tackling the intricate set of problems that plagued black America. By contrast, SNCC's Stokely Carmichael viewed his assassination as a declaration of war. In his mind, African American men needed to stand up and fight, even if this meant their complete annihilation. Speaking at a news conference in Washington, D.C., on April 5, 1968, Carmichael thundered: "[W]e're going to stand up on our feet and die like men. If that's our only act of manhood, then Godammit we're going to die."[149]

Like the young SNCC activist, a number of black militants believed that America was finally ripe for revolution. Most prominent among them was exile Robert Williams, who had moved to China in 1965 after his relationship with the Cuban government had soured. In Asia, he further developed his plans for a final apocalyptic struggle with the white oppressor. In an interview with his first biographer, Robert Carl Cohen, Williams prophesied that the black revolutionary juggernaut would obliterate America. Black guerrillas would strike at the heart of the capitalist system such as oil fields and pipelines. Using arson and sabotage, the black underground army would then destroy the nation's cities, and, eventually, the United States itself. Williams was convinced that these revolutionary actions would prompt white authorities to exterminate the black population in large concentration camps but predicted that blacks would not give up their freedom without a fight. "Before we let them herd us behind barbed wire like cattle," he told Cohen, "we will take them down with us into Hell!"[150] In the *Crusader*, which continued to reach America until the U.S. Post Office Department banned its distribution in the summer of 1967, Williams had provided specific advice about how to conduct clandestine guerrilla warfare.[151]

Such doomsday visions propelled Williams to the ideological forefront of the Black Power movement. Together with Malcolm X, he became the idol and major reference point for numerous black militants. As early as 1964, the

founders of RAM had claimed Williams as president of their underground organization. Four years later, he was chosen as the president in absentia of the
nationalist Republic of New Africa (RNA). In their first pamphlet, the founding
members of the RNA praised the "true revolutionary guidance and insight" that
Williams and Malcolm X had provided for them. Like these two leaders, the
RNA was ready to gain black independence "by arms if necessary."[152]

At its founding meeting in March 1968, the RNA called for a separate and
independent black nation, whose territory would consist of five Deep South
states and some black enclaves in northern cities. The RNA's leader, black
lawyer Milton Henry, or Gaidia Obadele, as he began to call himself, warned
that if the federal government refused to yield to the new nation's demands,
it would initiate a "people's war" against the white enemy. The Republic's New
African Security Force was intent on battling federal invaders while the black
nation's population would impede the enemy's advance through sabotage
and harassment. According to Obadele, black guerrillas in ghettos across the
United States would be likely to join the ranks of the Republic's army. The RNA
predicted that this united and armed power would eventually force the U.S.
government to the bargaining table.[153]

The fact that Williams readily accepted the presidency of these two nationalist organizations—he acknowledged the RNA's offer with a note of gratitude—
reflected his utter disappointment with the U.S. government.[154] Prior to his
forced escape to Cuba in 1962, Williams had been an ardent supporter of nonviolent integration through legal means. Six years later, he had turned into a
fiery advocate of black separatism and revolutionary guerrilla warfare. Talking
to Robert Cohen in July 1968, Williams explained that since true integration
was impossible to attain, he now favored "complete separation."[155] Williams
had concluded that it was illusory to expect support from the White House.
"[W]e had the illusion," he reflected, "that the federal government would actually be sympathetic towards us because we were only fighting the clan [sic]
and the racists."[156] The fact that Washington took little interest in the Monroe
movement eventually convinced Williams that African Americans would have
to prepare for a protracted underground struggle against the racist oppressor.

Given this process of radicalization that Williams underwent between 1957
and 1968, the assessment of Malcolm X that the North Carolinian "was just a
couple of years ahead of his time" but "laid a good ground work" for others
was fairly accurate.[157] Williams and southern defense units had emerged out
of the same tradition of homegrown black militancy. But in exile the NAACP
maverick became one of the first activists to redefine these traditions as a jus-

tification for aggressive guerrilla warfare. Had Williams been able to stay in Monroe, black intellectual Harold Cruse argued as early as 1967, "his original tactic of self-defense would probably have led him no further than the current position of the Deacons." According to Cruse's compelling analysis, Williams was forced to change his views because traditional notions of self-defense were simply not "revolutionary enough."[158] This process of radicalization and the subsequent impact of his ideas on the BPP and other militants make Williams a unique bridge figure between the civil rights struggle and the Black Power movement.

Although there were occasional confrontations between black militants and white police officers during the Black Power era, the protracted battle that Williams and others predicted never materialized. By and large, the Black Power movement's violence remained confined to verbal bullets, and most confrontations between police and black militants erupted only when white authorities attempted to stop their activities. In the case of the Black Panther Party, the organization's martial rhetoric coupled with its daring publicity campaigns earned the BPP a reputation for being a menace to society. To confront this alleged threat, the FBI in 1967 launched COINTELPRO, a highly sophisticated domestic counterintelligence program that sought to disrupt and destroy the Black Panthers and other black nationalist groups. FBI agents infiltrated the organization's chapters, attempted to fan animosities between the Panthers and the US organization, and aided authorities in imprisoning its leadership on fabricated charges. By the early 1970s, twenty-eight members of the organization had been killed in confrontations with police or deadly turf fights with US, while most of its original leadership was either in prison or in exile.[159] The organization lingered on until 1982, but the government's repressive tactics had weakened the Panthers considerably by 1972.

Formerly "legitimate" civil rights organizations such as SNCC and CORE were scrutinized as well. Concerned about the influence of CORE's black nationalist leadership in black ghettos, the FBI closely monitored its activities. SNCC, which the *New York Times* now dubbed "Nonstudent Violent Coordinating Committee," similarly alarmed FBI director J. Edgar Hoover.[160] At a congressional hearing in May 1968, Hoover claimed that SNCC, together with the black Muslims and RAM, represented "a distinct threat to the internal security of the nation."[161] By that time, however, internal disputes, lack of funding, and governmental harassment had already reduced the group to a mere shadow of its former self. Like SNCC, other militant groups such as RAM, RNA, or the US organization could put up little resistance to the government's large-scale onslaught. A few militants such as the Black Liberation Army continued a clandestine guerrilla struggle against police and other representatives of the white oppressor until 1981, but by the mid-1970s the COINTELPRO program had crushed the majority of groups that advocated revolutionary violence.[162]

Although government repression had evidently increased in direct correlation to the rhetorical threats of black militants, few activists were willing to admit that their preoccupation with guns might have gone too far. Huey Newton was probably the only one who frankly admitted that the BPP's public self-defense posture had ultimately become counterproductive. As Newton remembered in his memoirs, the police had not started any concerted efforts to disarm the BPP until the Sacramento demonstration. The news media, moreover, distorted the revolutionary message of the Panthers, focusing solely on the group's paramilitary character rather than on the dismal conditions that Newton intended to improve.[163] The resulting one-sided press coverage of their activities obscured the BPP's significance as a local community organization, whose ten-point platform listed the call for self-defense after the demand for self-determination, full employment, decent housing, and education for the black community. As Newton later explained, the platform was a clear reflection of the party's priorities. Indeed, the white media virtually ignored the important social services that BPP chapters provided, such as free-breakfast programs for schoolchildren, legal assistance, or medical care for African Americans across the nation.[164]

Even within the black community, the focus on self-defense blurred the message that Newton and Seale intended to convey. Newton later assessed the years 1966 and 1967 as "a necessary phase" that provided "a positive image of strong and unafraid Black men in the community" and raised the consciousness of African Americans. Yet he admitted that this focus had ultimately worked to their disadvantage. Newton recalled that many blacks viewed the BPP as "an ad hoc military group, acting outside the community fabric and too radical to be part of it."[165] Many militants seemed to believe that Mao Zedong's tenet "Political power grows out of the barrel of a gun" meant that political power *was* the gun. Instead, as the party's head told his followers in 1971, "The culmination of political power is the ownership and control of land and the institutions thereon so that we can get rid of the gun." From this perspective, the gun was merely a strategic tool, not an end in itself.[166] As early as 1968, the BPP had dropped the term "self-defense" from its name to preclude such misinterpretations. By the end of the decade, the party also began to make concerted efforts to tone down its violent rhetoric, erroneously hoping that less provocative language would both prompt the government to end its repressive tactics and improve the public perception of the party.[167]

In this respect, the gradual decline of radical Black Power groups such as the Black Panthers in the 1970s was tragic. As many black militants repeatedly stressed, Black Power was about much more than guns. Rather, the movement attempted to address a plethora of social problems that the civil rights movement had left unsolved. Theoretically, it was difficult to argue that affirming one's identity, seeking more political representation, or attempting to escape from the vicious cycle of poverty were illegitimate demands. But the violent rhetoric of groups such as the BPP, the RNA, or US precluded sympathy for their message among many. As the Black Panthers painfully learned, ensuing government repression seriously undermined the effectiveness of their political activism. What was left once the last cries for revolution died away were ambivalent affirmations of a positive black identity. This was to become the lasting legacy of Black Power.

7

CONCLUSION

The Deacons for Defense and Justice, CORE activist Isaac Reynolds said a few years after their demise, could hardly be considered an aberration in the southern civil rights struggle. Rather, as Reynolds explained, "black men in communities across the South . . . formed into [armed] groups." According to the CORE veteran, these men "had just reached the point to say well, you're not going to ride through my community any longer and shoot up, pet my women on their butt and snatch the woman off my arm and take her somewhere and screw her and grin."[1] Armed resistance efforts in local freedom movements in Alabama, Arkansas, North Carolina, Louisiana, and Mississippi testified to both the determination of black activists to confront such forms of white aggression and the gendered subtext of their militant countermeasures.

There is ample evidence that these states were not the only places where armed black resistance became a significant auxiliary to nonviolent demonstrations and voter registration drives. In July 1963, for example, NAACP activist and Korean War veteran Robert Hayling organized a black defense squad in St. Augustine, Florida. A few weeks earlier, black protestors had launched a picketing campaign against the city's traditional segregation policy in restaurants, movie theaters, and other public places. Within days, the home of movement leader Hayling became a target for shotgun attacks by the Ku Klux Klan. In response, the black dentist purchased a cache of rifles and shotguns, taught a group of black teenagers how to use them, and stationed these guards around his house and other strategic locations in St. Augustine's black neighborhood. On July 1, 1963, the military veteran's house became the stage for several shoot-outs between his bodyguards and white attackers, which left men injured on both sides. In the following months, tensions remained high and led to more racial clashes. In October 1963, when a carload of Klansmen sought to intimidate local NAACP activist Goldie Eubanks, the defensive squad repelled the attack and killed one white man.[2]

After these events, the movement's momentum temporarily waned, but the arrival of SCLC in March 1964 revitalized civil rights activism. It also triggered a new wave of racist terror. By that time, Hayling had quit the NAACP. As in the case of Robert Williams and Charles Evers, his public warning to Klansmen that his guards would "shoot first and ask questions later" triggered a heated debate with Roy Wilkins, who once more felt obliged to assure concerned journalists of the NAACP's allegiance to nonviolence.[3] Freed from the restraints of the NAACP's public relations policies, he kept his guns, joined SCLC, and asked Martin Luther King to assist the St. Augustine movement. As in Birmingham, carefully staged nonviolent protest marches, which took place in May and June 1964, triggered a violent white response and pressured federal authorities to intervene in the crisis. In the midst of a torrent of death threats and shotgun attacks, King grudgingly consented to the deployment of armed guards to protect his life. When SCLC finally departed, the city's mood remained one of bitterness and racial animosity. Still, St. Augustine was another example of the power of nonviolent direct action and the important, yet largely unnoticed, role of armed resistance in protecting the nonviolent movement.[4]

In Cambridge, Maryland, by contrast, black self-defense was far from invisible, which produced predicaments that echoed the dilemma faced by activists in Louisiana or Mississippi. Although African Americans had never been disenfranchised in Cambridge, the city's custom of segregation closely resembled the racist traditions of the Deep South. In addition, many blacks suffered from employment and housing discrimination. Assisted by young SNCC organizers, local blacks first took to the streets in late 1961, staging peaceful marches to call attention to their grievances. The following year, the formation of the Cambridge Nonviolent Action Committee (CNAC), a grassroots group that coordinated the protest movement, marked the beginning of a concerted effort to press on for racial change.[5]

In June 1963, a wave of demonstrations sparked an ugly riot, which had to be quelled by a contingent of several hundred National Guardsmen. In the midst of the violent turmoil, roving mobs of angry white people attacked black homes in the Second Ward, the city's black neighborhood. As in the Deep South, black residents repelled white invaders with gunfire. During the night of June 11, two white men were struck by a shotgun blast after chasing black demonstrators.[6] Concerned about such attacks and the death threats against the CNAC's leader, Gloria Richardson, blacks formed a defense guard to protect Richardson's home. "For more than a month" after the riot, white activist Paul Cowan wrote later, "at least one gun was always loaded in the Richardson house, and almost every night somebody slept in the living room, between two exposed windows, with a rifle next to his bed."[7]

Initially the imposition of martial law and the presence of armed troops quelled the violence, but white aggression continued throughout July, and so did black resistance. One evening in early July, for example, a SNCC worker reported that "a carload of whites drove down Pine Street, the main thoroughfare of the Negro section, shooting as they went. Some Negroes returned the fire. The evening ended with three whites hospitalized, one man shot in the face, another in the arm, the third near his eye."[8] On July 12, only three days after the National Guard contingent had left the city, the soldiers were ordered to return to stop the renewed fighting. Even before this new outburst, black army veterans had begun to position themselves at streets and fields that divided the Second Ward from the city's white section. Shoot-outs between white invaders and black defenders—who crouched behind cars, peered out of windows, or perched on rooftops—became a common occurrence. Twelve people were injured by gunfire on the night of July 12 alone.[9]

As in Birmingham or Bogalusa, attempts to enforce nonviolent discipline at demonstrations frequently clashed with people's disdain for the idea of nonviolence as a way of life. In a report on its activities in 1963, the CNAC conceded that the organization "was put in the difficult position of maintaining . . . nonviolence and yet continuing to lead a community the large majority of which was not philosophically committed to non-violence." Many blacks, the report continued, "carried guns during demonstrations and around town during periods of critical tension." The CNAC was frank to admit that most of its members viewed nonviolent protest solely as a pragmatic tactic. "The Cambridge movement," the authors wrote, "was non-violent from the beginning not primarily because of philosophical conviction, but because non-violence is practicable, and because it was part of a national movement which was non-violent."[10] While Cambridge contributed to debunking certain myths about the civil rights struggle, black activists thought it wise to nurture the dominant media image of the national movement. Accordingly, the CNAC stressed in a leaflet that the "policy and execution" of demonstrations "has always been, and will continue to be in keeping with our policy of nonviolence."[11]

But in the spring of 1964, when a new wave of civil rights protests swept the city, it became increasingly difficult to uphold this image. Amid continued racial tensions, SNCC activist Cleveland Sellers noted that blacks carried guns "as a matter of course," determined to use them if attacked by whites. During a demonstration against Alabama governor George Wallace, who visited Cambridge during his unsuccessful bid for the Democratic nomination for president, the boundary between defensive and aggressive violence began to blur. When National Guardsmen, who had been encamped in the city since July 1963, dispersed black protestors with tear gas, black men responded with gunfire. "I am certain that a lot of people would have been seriously injured," Sellers remembered, "if a small group of black men had not started shooting at the guardsmen in order to slow them down."[12] During the tense night that followed, a dozen soldiers were injured by gunshots.[13]

When racial tensions finally died down in Cambridge a few weeks later, it was the turn of black activists in Halifax County, North Carolina, to provide armed protection, this time for a massive voter registration campaign. John Salter, who had quit his teaching job at Tougaloo College to work for the Southern Conference Educational Fund (SCEF) as a civil rights organizer, found northeastern North Carolina to be a hotbed of Ku Klux Klan activity. After affiliating with Robert Shelton's United Klans of America, the state's hooded order was stronger than ever, boasting several thousand members.[14] Predictably, when Salter arrived in rural Halifax County in January 1964, his voter registration drive around the town of Enfield provoked an immediate and brutal response. Cross burnings, arson, and armed parades through black neighborhoods became routine, prompting local blacks to guard their communities with guns. "The Negroes in Halifax County are now pretty well armed," Salter wrote in July 1964, "and, in Enfield particularly, are standing night-time guards."[15] Salter himself never left his house without a .38 caliber revolver, which he carried in an old attaché case.[16]

North Carolina governor Terry Sanford and the Justice Department mostly ignored Salter's repeated appeals for protection. The FBI, which had spied on the white activist for years, was well aware of the death threats against him. But, as in the rest of the South, the agents showed little inclination to risk their lives for the safety of a white civil rights organizer, let alone African American citizens.[17] Local police felt even less responsibility to provide security. At times the lawmen seemed indistinguishable from members of the hooded order. Bulletin boards at Halifax County's police station, for instance, featured regular advertisements for local Klan rallies.[18] "Fortunately," Salter later recalled, "we lived in the middle of a heavily armed Black community, with neighbors . . . who were protective, especially when I was away in the field for long periods of time."[19]

Interestingly, these self-defense efforts developed independently of the Monroe movement, which had lost most of its momentum after Robert Williams's escape to Cuban exile. When Salter visited the town in February 1964, he found the local civil rights struggle to be "completely shattered." Local blacks, he noted, continued "to hold Robert Williams in high regard—and I'm certain that they continue to support his self-defense philosophy—but Williams is long gone and far away now and, I daresay, is fading slowly from memory. The Negro community in Monroe is afraid and suspicious and apathetic and disunified [sic]."[20] Monroe blacks seemed unable to pick up where Williams had left off, but the combative marine veteran's style of "armed self-reliance" continued in other parts of North Carolina.

The stories from Halifax County, Cambridge, and St. Augustine underscore that armed resistance to segregationist violence was far from exceptional and raise crucial questions about its benefits and limitations. In terms of its drawbacks, civil rights activists became painfully aware that self-defense could be detrimental to both local and national campaigns. During voter registration drives in rural southern communities, carrying guns frequently served as a pretext for white police officers to arrest black activists. The experience of COFO workers in Moss Point, Mississippi, during Freedom Summer was typical. In early July 1964, a shotgun attack on a civil rights meeting seriously injured a black girl. Shortly thereafter, white policemen arrested a local African American who had pursued the car of the white attackers. Although the man's pistol lay in plain view on the front seat of his car, which was legal according to Mississippi statutes, he was taken into custody for carrying a concealed weapon.[21] Such illegal arrests frequently bordered on the absurd. In January 1964, for instance, Canton's combative civil rights leader C. O. Chinn landed in jail for carrying a "dangerous weapon." Chinn's lawyers noted wryly that the incident was "possibly the only arrest for possession of a pocket knife in the history of the area."[22]

Ludicrous or not, this type of police harassment could have harmful effects on the morale of local freedom movements. While the inspiring C. O. Chinn was in jail, for example, the number of Canton blacks who dared take part in CORE's dangerous voter registration campaign dwindled drastically.[23] SNCC and CORE were dismayed at such incidents and admonished their volunteers to take seriously the risks of armed protection. A SNCC "security handbook" cautioned: "Remove all unnecessary objects from your car which could be construed as weapons (Hammers, files, iron rules, etc.)."[24] And in Canton, as a Mississippi Sovereignty Commission spy reported a few weeks after Chinn's arrest, CORE field organizers lectured people "not to bring any weapons of any type," since "that was what the police department wanted, and that to catch somebody with a pistol or knife would give them an excuse to arrest them."[25]

However, even though Daisy Bates's bodyguards, Birmingham's Civil Rights Guards, or Bogalusa's Deacons chapter faced similar harassment, white attempts to disarm black activists in the 1950s and 1960s remained surprisingly tame when compared with the brutal retributions that armed African Americans had confronted in the past. Prior to the civil rights era, the combined might of white vigilantes, policemen, and state militias tended to crush any open challenge to white supremacy. We can only speculate why no such sweeping actions occurred during the 1960s. Perhaps southern authorities feared that disarming the black population might prompt federal authorities to intervene more forcefully on behalf of African Americans. It is likewise conceivable that white politicians were concerned that such illegal actions might trigger racial warfare in rural southern communities. The fact that blacks had guns and were determined to use them certainly lent credibility to such apprehensions. Regardless of the reasons, these comparably restrained responses could not halt the activities of black defense squads.

Oddly enough, when it came to race and the Second Amendment in the 1960s, law enforcement officers in the North seemed keen to emulate the example of nineteenth-century white supremacists. The paranoid reaction of New York City authorities to Malcolm X was a case in point. Militant rhetoric alone—Malcolm's call for the formation of black defense groups—triggered a police raid of the premises of a Harlem rifle club. Three years later, this time in the midst of actual burning and looting in northern cities, a similar incident occurred in New Jersey. In July 1967, New Jersey state troopers illegally searched the homes of dozens of African American residents in the city of Plainfield, hoping to find a cache of rifles that had been stolen from a local weapons manufacturer. Although there was no legal justification for their actions, white authorities claimed that the volatile situation in New Jersey's cities was reason enough to violate the constitutional rights of black citizens. After all, they explained, African Americans might use the weapons to attack the police.[26]

Such examples of excessive force and overreaction appeared to be primarily a response to the armed assertiveness of certain black nationalists. Unlike their southern peers, Malcolm X or the Black Panthers, at least in their public statements, frequently blurred the boundaries between self-defense and revolutionary aggression. Coupled with almost daily news stories of racial turmoil in America's cities, it was hardly surprising that white authorities became susceptible to persistent rumors of race war. In riot-torn Detroit, for example, white residents feared an imminent black invasion of the city's suburbs, during which it was feared that Black Power militants might attack school buses and shoot children in the street.[27] Northern authorities' attempts to disarm black Americans probably stemmed from similar symptoms of paranoia.

At the same time, these actions reflected a long tradition of white disregard for African Americans' constitutional right to bear arms. Throughout the nineteenth and twentieth centuries, white Americans applied a conspicuous double standard to the Second Amendment.[28] In the 1960s, southern segregationists found it more difficult to deny this right to African Americans, but discrimination persisted across the nation. White people's biased interpretation of the right to bear arms became most visible during the decade's upheavals in urban black communities. In the midst of apocalyptic visions of bloodthirsty armies of black snipers and revolutionary nationalists, numerous journalists and politicians called for stricter gun legislation as a way to disarm "lawless rioters" in American cities.[29]

Most civil rights activists vehemently opposed such plans. They suspected that stricter gun laws would be applied mainly to the black population. In July 1968, CORE's newly elected chairman, Roy Innis, explained on *Meet the Press*: "If I could be guaranteed that all people in this country blacks and whites, would be equally disarmed, and the laws would be equitably enforced, I wouldn't mind. But it would be a utopian dream for me to believe that."[30] Even the NAACP's Roy Wilkins, who had little sympathy for CORE after its espousal of Black Power, voiced suspicion about gun control. When asked on *Meet the Press* whether he would approve of "a massive effort to disarm the Negroes in the ghettos," he replied: "I wouldn't disarm the Negroes and leave them helpless prey to the people who wanted to go in and shoot them up. Every American wants to own a rifle. Why shouldn't the Negroes own rifles?"[31]

The fears that underlay these infractions of constitutional rights were closely intertwined with the second, and more consequential, limitation of armed resistance: the looming prospect of forfeiting legitimacy and financial support. Communicating with a primarily white audience through the national mass media, civil rights leaders clearly understood that widely publicized episodes of armed self-defense would quickly erode the freedom movement's moral power in the eyes of white moderates. The mythical nature that King's teachings had assumed in the eyes of the media and the American public made it difficult to justify the close partnership between CORE and the Deacons or the armed militancy of black farmers in Mississippi. Accordingly, CORE and SNCC went to great lengths to assure their white liberal supporters that the black freedom struggle was devoted to Christian and Gandhian tenets.

After 1966, the artificial binaries that the movement's official rhetoric had created proved to be a tremendous burden for Black Power militants. When contrasted with the Christian symbolism of King's oratory, Black Power's assertive gospel of self-defense probably struck many white moderates as tantamount to heresy. As a result, financial contributions to CORE and SNCC dwindled to a mere trickle. At the same time, the Black Power movement's reinterpretation of revolutionary violence as a justified form of self-defense seemed to confirm such bipolar interpretations. White hostility, government repression, and the eventual decline of the Black Power movement were partly a tragic consequence of these tactical and ideological entanglements.

The benefits of armed resistance were visible primarily in the southern civil rights struggle, where revolutionary violence was seldom discussed and usually dismissed as impractical. Most important, homegrown southern militancy helped numerous local freedom movements survive in the face of racist aggression. Guarding black communities and protecting the lives of black and white activists, armed blacks made sure that nonviolent protestors and their leaders remained safe once they left the picket line. "No one knows what kind of massive racist retaliation would have been directed against grass-roots black people," John Salter later reflected, "had the black community not had a healthy measure of firearms within it."[32] The fact that the number of white attacks against activists sharply declined in Tuscaloosa, Jonesboro, Bogalusa, and other southern locales after black defenders began to return fire strongly suggests that Klansmen hesitated to intimidate the black community if their own lives were at risk.

Armed protection also played a significant role in sustaining the morale of nonviolent protestors. The Ku Klux Klan aimed to erode the confidence and resolve of African Americans through violent terror. In many ways, the actions of black guards neutralized this strategy. Knowing that armed defenders were nearby frequently bolstered the determination of blacks to continue protests despite the omnipresence of menacing whites. "Protected nonviolence," CORE activist Richard Haley said dryly about this phenomenon in Bogalusa, "is apt to be more popular with the participants than unprotected."[33] Jonathan

Weiss, a white lawyer who worked with northern civil rights volunteers in the 1960s, agreed. Writing in the 1970s, he concluded that "those who worked on voter registration in the South almost uniformly report that the possession of guns by Southern blacks gave them the necessary confidence to overcome the threats, harassment, burning crosses and sniper shots to which they were frequently subjected."[34] Although armed resistance reflected a general skepticism toward Gandhian tenets among black defenders, it could help buttress people's commitment to tactical nonviolence.

Another way in which defending black communities made an important, albeit ambiguous, contribution to the black freedom struggle was its role in nurturing and affirming black manhood. Throughout the nineteenth and twentieth centuries, white aggression, in particular sexual aggression, dealt a repeated blow to the self-esteem of African Americans. As late as 1964, black sociologist Nathan Hare concluded, "The fact that the Negro man cannot protect his family presents a special problem to the Negro male psychology."[35] Although the protection efforts of southern defense squads were primarily a pragmatic response to racist terrorism, they provided an opportunity to overcome such feelings of inadequacy. Regardless of whether they were members of the Deacons or individual farmers such as Hartman Turnbow, black defenders tended to regard their armed militancy as a symbol of male assertiveness.

For certain Black Power militants, however, reclaiming black manhood seemed to constitute the major rationale for picking up a gun, an attitude that ultimately proved counterproductive. Unlike their southern peers, who repelled clearly identifiable attackers with real bullets, the US organization or the Black Panthers fired barrages of verbal shots at an enemy that was much more difficult to define and to combat. Ultimately, partly because of these problems, self-defense metamorphosed into a form of discursive insubordination, which, above all, sought to restore black men's self-respect. From the perspective of SCLC activist Andrew Young, such logic "was a dead end," which "provided emotional release and the illusion of manhood without the content."[36] This harsh assessment certainly neglects many positive aspects of Black Power. In particular in the realm of culture, as William Van Deburg has demonstrated, the movement's emphasis on black pride left a vital and constructive legacy of psychological empowerment.[37] But Young's critique does hint at certain negative consequences that the armed symbolism of some Black Power groups caused. In the case of the US organization and the Black Panthers, the initial fixation on armed resistance and manhood clearly reinforced traditional gender inequalities within the movement. Worse, it hampered many of the social and political programs that black nationalists hoped could make a tangible difference in the lives of African Americans.

Few Black Power militants openly acknowledged that affirming manhood alone would do little to bring about black liberation. In 1968, an early critique of the fixation on masculinity appeared to emerge within black nationalist circles. At that year's third national conference on Black Power, the event's organizers instructed delegates to spare everybody "needless loss of critical working time by not engaging in . . . Your passionate let's get guns and undo our castration speech." They insisted that it was much more important to unify the Black Power movement's various factions.[38] But it took several more years until activists began to discuss more critically the sexism that permeated black nationalism. Black feminists in particular scorned the nationalist ideology, arguing that it did not challenge but only reproduced white capitalist models of oppression.[39]

A final benefit of armed resistance, aside from helping local movements survive, bolstering the morale of activists, and affirming black manhood, was that it occasionally became an additional means of coercion in negotiations with white authorities. In Bogalusa, for example, nonviolent demonstrations paralyzed the city and forced the state's segregationist politicians to take seriously black demands. But the prospect of racial warfare between the Ku Klux Klan and the Deacons for Defense and Justice undoubtedly increased the pressure on Louisiana governor McKeithen and the Johnson administration to defuse the local crisis. While less far-reaching, the militant actions of black farmers in Halifax County had a similar effect. When the Ku Klux Klan pledged to hold a large rally in the county in the fall of 1964, John Salter informed Governor Sanford's office in Raleigh that blacks "would have no hesitation about utilizing armed self-defense in the event of Klan violence." It is unclear whether Sanford feared race war, federal intervention, or both when he heard such veiled threats. In any case, according to Salter, the governor promptly dispatched state police officers to Halifax County to protect civil rights activists from the Invisible Empire's wrath.[40]

Incidents of this kind have led some historians to question the efficacy of nonviolent protest. Seeing little distinction between self-defense, race riots, or verbal threats, these scholars argue that violence, not nonviolence, forced social change in the 1960s.[41] Such sweeping claims are problematic because they tend to re-create the very same dichotomies and simplistic interpretations that these historians claim to challenge. First, such interpretations blur the boundaries between armed resistance and aggressive violence. There were important differences between guarding a civil rights meeting, torching white businesses in black ghettos, or pledging to shoot "pig" policemen. If we define violence as behavior that intends to destroy property and aims to harm or kill other persons, armed resistance actually sought to avert such behavior. Charles Sims or Joseph Mallisham strongly objected to the destruction of white property or deliberate attacks on the police. "We had preached nonviolence," Mallisham insisted when looking back at the 1960s. "Now we don't need anybody having 'burn, baby, burn'—that's stupid," he said.[42] Race riots, while being praised by the US organization and other black militants as an expression of collective self-defense, were diametrically opposed to the defensive actions of southern African Americans during the civil rights era.

Similarly, although violence and the fear of violence might have enhanced the bargaining position of civil rights leaders, tactical nonviolence remained the driving force behind social change. The suggestion that peaceful protest lacked transformative power misjudges the tactical shrewdness of black activists. Of course, journalists and historians alike have repeatedly called attention to the "paradox" or "irony" of nonviolence, which they note produced rather than prevented violence.[43] But what many of these critics ignore is that violence was an integral characteristic of nonviolent direct action, a coercive tactic whose application starkly differed from King's abstract references to suffering and reconciliation. As early as 1966, sociologist Jan Howard concluded that the movement's deliberate provocation of violence was "not simply a calculated risk" but "part of an over-all plan."[44]

Occasionally, white America's fear of black violence became an element of these tactical considerations. While they never explicitly stated it, civil rights leaders evidently understood that juxtaposing nonviolence with the menace of black aggression bolstered the appeal of the national movement. News magazines like *Time* and *Newsweek* fostered this dualism by contrasting King's symbolism of love and integration with black nationalist calls for armed resistance and separatism.[45] African American militancy, as sociologist Herbert Haines has argued, significantly bolstered the bargaining position of King and other civil rights leaders. The "radical flank effects" of this constellation enabled nonviolent activists to maintain legitimacy and white support by distancing themselves from the confrontational rhetoric of Malcolm X and others. According to Haines, white support for moderate demands such as desegregation and black voting rights soared in direct proportion to the emergence of more radical alternatives.[46]

In some of his writings and speeches, Martin Luther King astutely exploited white apprehensions about these developments. Sharply distinguishing between "violent" radicalism and the moderating influence of his philosophy, King predicted that the nonviolent movement might soon give way to racial Armageddon if white America continued to ignore black demands. In his widely praised "Letter from Birmingham Jail," King portrayed himself as a mediator between the voices of "complacency" and the forces of "bitterness and hatred." Responding to the criticism of several white ministers who had urged restraint in the Birmingham crisis, King countered that "many streets of the South would be flowing with floods of blood" had nonviolence not emerged.[47] Throughout 1963, King continued to evoke portents of doom. In June, at a press conference in Keuka Park, New York, for example, King foresaw "a season of terror and violence" unless President Kennedy's civil rights program was enacted.[48]

At this point, there is too little evidence to argue that actual, as opposed to rhetorical, black violence aided the nonviolent movement on a widespread basis. One example is certainly the riot that rocked Birmingham during SCLC's protest campaign in 1963, which prompted the Kennedy administration to dispatch additional intermediaries to resolve the crisis. In part, Kennedy's subsequent endorsement of a strong civil rights bill stemmed from concerns that white terrorism might trigger similar upheavals across the region.[49] Black violence in McComb, Mississippi, in late 1964 seems to have brought similar results. On September 20, two bomb attacks against the town's black community triggered black retaliation. According to historian Akinyele Umoja, the prompt arrest and conviction of those Klansmen responsible for the crime resulted partly from Governor Paul Johnson's fear of black rioting in McComb.[50]

But even in Birmingham and McComb, the legitimacy of the nonviolent movement remained a vital counterbalance to perceived threats of violence. Black activists, in the words of a white CORE supporter, were burdened with "the ticklish job of determining just where 'violence'" began.[51] Consequently, if we seek to unravel the complexities of social change in the 1960s, one-sided explanations—one insisting that King's teachings alone transformed American society, the other overemphasizing the long-neglected role of black militancy—will only obscure our understanding of the civil rights era.

When asked about the role of violence and nonviolence in the black freedom movement, Gloria Richardson probably put it best, musing: "I think you have to have some of both. And I think it has to be in balance."[52] Prior to the emergence of Black Power, civil rights leaders succeeded in keeping these two forces in equilibrium, tempering hints of radicalism with vows of allegiance to

Gandhian and Christian principles. Once black militants dismissed even tactical nonviolence, however, this fragile symmetry collapsed. In the southern freedom struggle, shotguns had worked in tandem with the spirit of nonviolent protest. During the Black Power era, the gun, which was no longer offset by this spirit, became a detrimental force that sapped much of the movement's energy and contributed to its eventual demise.

NOTES

Abbreviations

CORE	Congress of Racial Equality
CORE-LSCD	Congress of Racial Equality–Louisiana Sixth Congressional District Files
CORE-SRO	Congress of Racial Equality–Southern Regional Office Files
FBI	Federal Bureau of Investigation
MSSC	Mississippi State Sovereignty Commission Files
NAACP	National Association for the Advancement of Colored People
SCLC	Southern Christian Leadership Conference
SCRLR	Southern Civil Rights Litigation Records for the 1960s
SHSW	State Historical Society of Wisconsin
SNCC	Student Nonviolent Coordinating Committee

Introduction

1. *Tuscaloosa News*, July 9, 1964; Mallisham interview by DeSantis.

2. Harold A. Nelson, "The Defenders," 135; Mallisham interview by DeSantis; Mallisham interview by author, March 22, 2002.

3. This is not meant to suggest that the Black Panther Party was representative of the entire Black Power movement, which was a mélange of different ideologies and agendas. However, many elements of the BPP's concept of armed resistance could also be seen in the programs of other revolutionary nationalists such as the Revolutionary Action Movement, the US organization, or the Republic of New Africa. Similarly, Black Power cannot be reduced to the advocacy of self-defense. Political empowerment, self-determination, antiracism, radical internationalism, to mention just a few themes, were equally important aspects of Black Power programs. Yet these social and political goals were frequently eclipsed by the public advocacy of self-defense. On the various ideological strands of Black Power ideologies, see James Smethurst, *The Black Arts Movement*; Van Deburg, *New Day in Babylon*; and Woodard, *A Nation within a Nation*.

4. Except for Christopher Strain's *Pure Fire*, previous studies tend to concentrate on one particular state. On North Carolina, see Tyson, *Radio Free Dixie*; and Pascoe,

"The Monroe Rifle Club." On Louisiana, see Hill, *The Deacons for Defense*; De Jong, *A Different Day*; and Strain, "'We Walked Like Men.'" On Mississippi, see Umoja, "1964"; Umoja, "'We Will Shoot Back'"; Umoja, "The Ballot and the Bullet"; and Crosby, "'This Nonviolent Stuff Ain't No Good. It'll Get Ya Killed.'" Several of these scholars tend to exaggerate the role of armed resistance, neglecting its complementary character. Lance Hill, for example, considers the Deacons for Defense and Justice "a political movement for self-defense" that posed a "principled challenge to nonviolence." Hill, *The Deacons for Defense*, 54, 58. Christopher Strain also stresses "the centrality of self-defense in the struggle for black equality." Strain, *Pure Fire*, 4. In a similar fashion, Akinyele Umoja portrays nonviolence and armed resistance as opposing rather than complementary forces. See Umoja, "1964," 202; and Umoja, "'We Will Shoot Back,'" 291.

5. Kimmel, *The Gendered Society*, 253. Recently, historian Steve Estes has called attention to the "masculinist rhetoric" that was used by black civil rights activists and segregationists alike. Estes argues that framing their actions as a defense of manhood provided both sides with "a powerful organizing tactic that rested on traditional assumptions about race, gender, and sexuality." Estes, *I Am a Man!* 8.

6. Bederman, *Manliness & Civilization*, 4.

7. Patterson, *Rituals of Blood*, xiii.

8. Hunter and Davis, "Hidden Voices of Black Men," 21.

9. Quoted in Morris, *The Origins of the Civil Rights Movement*, 158.

10. Braden, "Nonviolent Revolution," 7.

11. Muste, "Rifle Squads or the Beloved Community," 8–9.

12. According to Walker, both black and white newspapers frequently chose not to report about violence committed by southern black activists, either out of concern that such reports might jeopardize the moral power of the nonviolent movement or, in the case of white southern reporters, because of the feeling that nonviolent protest already drew enough negative attention to the defenders of white supremacy. Some black newspapers, on the other hand, had to expect economic reprisals and violent threats if they published accounts about black militancy. See Walker, "A Media-Made Movement?" 50–52.

13. Quoted in the *Baltimore Afro-American*, October 29, 1966.

14. *New York Times*, May 21, 1967.

15. Unlike his political heirs, however, Malcolm X eventually came to see the tactical advantages of juxtaposing nonviolent protest and his calls for armed resistance. In a conversation with Martin Luther King's wife, Coretta, during SCLC's voting rights campaign in Selma, Alabama, he acknowledged the importance of nonviolent protest and argued that his militant rhetoric might compel white America to accept King's less radical alternative. See Coretta Scott King, *My Life with Martin Luther King, Jr.*, 256.

16. These findings contradict Timothy Tyson's thesis that the civil rights struggle and what came to be known as Black Power "emerged from the same soil, confronted the same predicaments, and reflected the same quest for African American freedom."

Tyson deserves praise for his compelling analysis of the gendered nature of black militancy and the interrelationship between local, national, and international activism. However, he neglects conspicuous differences between southern advocates of self-defense and Black Power militants, erroneously regarding the exceptional radicalism of Williams as representative of the entire black South. Tyson, *Radio Free Dixie*, 3; see also Tyson, "Robert F. Williams."

Chapter 1. Black Self-Defense and the Emergence of Nonviolent Protest

1. Parks, *Rosa Parks*, 30, 115.

2. Garrow, *Bearing the Cross*, 60–62; Branch, *Parting the Waters*, 165.

3. Martin Luther King Jr., *Stride toward Freedom*, 131.

4. Garrow, *Bearing the Cross*, 62; Abernathy, "The Natural History of a Social Movement," 161.

5. Quoted in Jo Ann Ooiman Robinson, "Diary 6/21/64–6/26/64," entry 6/25/64, box 2, folder 1, Robinson Papers.

6. Rustin, "Montgomery Diary," 8; Raines, *My Soul Is Rested*, 53; "Interview with Bayard Rustin, March 28, 1974," box 58, folder 4, Meier Papers.

7. Franklin, *The Militant South*, 24, 30–31; Cash, *The Mind of the South*, 43.

8. Rotundo, *American Manhood*, 1–9; Franklin, *The Militant South*, 18, 35, 44; Cash, *The Mind of the South*, 73; Wyatt-Brown, *Southern Honor*, 352–53, 369.

9. Gilmore, "Murder, Memory, and the Flight of the Incubus," 73–94; Hall, *Revolt against Chivalry*, xxvi; Hall, "'The Mind That Burns in Each Body,'" 332, 335.

10. Cullen, "'I's a Man Now,'" 77.

11. Litwack, *Been in the Storm So Long*, 428. Across Dixie, African Americans purchased rifles, shotguns, and pistols, considering the right to use them an undeniable privilege of American citizenship. See Litwack, *Been in the Storm So Long*, 428; Fleming, *Documentary History of Reconstruction*, 90; and Vandal, "Black Violence in Post–Civil War Louisiana," 62.

12. I have borrowed the term "discourse of protection" from Griffin, "Black Feminism and Du Bois," 28–40.

13. Schechter, "Unsettled Business," 295.

14. Ida B. Wells, "Southern Horrors: Lynch Law in All Its Phases," in Wells, *On Lynchings*, 23.

15. Quoted in Thornbrough, "T. Thomas Fortune," 22, 23. See also Thornbrough, *T. Thomas Fortune*. John Mitchell of the *Richmond Planet* similarly viewed self-defense as a manly duty. Framed by gun advertisements, his editorials urged African Americans to confront white murderers. "Defend your homes against the midnight assassin [*sic*]," Mitchell urged, "above all protect your women." Quoted in Rabinowitz, *Race Relations in the Urban South*, 234. For a biography of Mitchell, see Alexander, *Race Man*.

16. Du Bois, "Cowardice," *Crisis* 12 (October 1916): 270–71.

17. Du Bois, *The Autobiography of W.E.B. Du Bois*, 286.

18. See Dittmer, *Black Georgia in the Progressive Era*, 126–30.

19. Formwalt, "The Origins of African-American Politics in Southwest Georgia," 211–22; Williamson, *After Slavery*, 260–62; Shapiro, "Afro-American Responses to Race Violence during Reconstruction," 158–70; Escott, *Slavery Remembered*, 157–58.

20. Brundage, "The Darien 'Insurrection' of 1899," 234–53.

21. McMillen, *Dark Journey*, 225–26. For other examples of black resistance to lynch mobs in the late nineteenth and early twentieth century, see Wright, *Racial Violence in Kentucky*, 162, 172; Litwack, *Trouble in Mind*, 423; Ginzburg, *100 Years of Lynching*, 9–10; "Crime," *Crisis* 1 (March 1911): 10; "Crime," *Crisis* 11 (February 1916): 168; "Ghetto," *Crisis* 13 (January 1917): 147; *Chicago Defender*, June 19, 1915.

22. Walter White, *Rope and Faggot*, 189, 191; "Crime," *Crisis* 7 (December 1913): 64.

23. "Crime," *Crisis* 4 (August 1912): 167. For other examples of white retaliation against blacks who resorted to self-defense, see Ginzburg, *100 Years of Lynching*, 9–19, 62–63, 88, 109–10, 139–40, 142, 197.

24. Myrdal, *An American Dilemma*, 559.

25. Ibid., 560; Litwack, *Been in the Storm So Long*, 427–28; McMillen, *Dark Journey*, 226.

26. Ellsworth, *Death in a Promised Land*, 46–66.

27. For a comprehensive study of the riot, see Haynes, *A Night of Violence*.

28. *New York Times*, October 5, 1919.

29. Tuttle, *Race Riot*, 210.

30. Ibid., 239; Haywood, *Black Bolshevik*, 81–82.

31. Rupert Lewis, *Marcus Garvey*, 68; Daniel, "Black Power in the 1920s," 377–78; Woodruff, *American Congo*, 4, 137–39.

32. Cortner, *A Mob Intent on Death*, 15, 184.

33. Schneider, *We Return Fighting*, 301–10. For a detailed account of the Sweet case, see Boyle, *Arc of Justice*.

34. Walter White, "Memorandum to Mr. Seligman," October 22, 1925, group I, series D, box 86, NAACP Papers.

35. Assistant Secretary to Editor of the *Nation*, December 19, 1925, group I, series D, box 86, NAACP Papers.

36. Weinberg, *A Man's Home, A Man's Castle*, 65–68; Secretary to Clarence Darrow, Esq., July 21, 1927, group I, series D, box 87, NAACP Papers.

37. Fairclough, *Race and Democracy*, 26–28; De Jong, *A Different Day*, 58; Litwack, *Trouble in Mind*, 424–25.

38. Kelley, *Hammer and Hoe*, 45; Haywood, *Black Bolshevik*, 401–2, 399; Rosengarten, *All God's Dangers*, 296, 306–13.

39. Kester, *Revolt among the Sharecroppers*, 62.

40. Ibid., 62, 63; "The Elaine Massacre," 9–10.

41. Morris, "A Man Prepared for the Times," 37–47. The literature on civil rights and foreign affairs has been growing extensively in recent years. Some of the most recent studies are Plummer, *Window on Freedom*; Borstelmann, *The Cold War and the Color Line*; and Dudziak, *Cold War Civil Rights*.

42. W. P. Bayles to Walter White, April 20, 1942, group II, series A, box 239, NAACP Papers; Sitkoff, "African American Militancy in the World War II South," 77.

43. *Pittsburgh Courier*, January 24, 1942.

44. *Chicago Defender*, June 12, 1943; Sitkoff, "Racial Militancy and Interracial Violence in the Second World War," 661–81. See also Shapiro, *White Violence and Black Response*, 305; Tyson, "Wars for Democracy," 253–76.

45. Finkle, "The Conservative Aims of Militant Rhetoric," 692–93.

46. *Chicago Defender*, February 2, 1946.

47. McMillen, "Fighting for What We Didn't Have," 95; Lawson, *Black Ballots*, 114; Dittmer, *Local People*, 9.

48. A. Z. Young interview.

49. Matthews interview.

50. Wynn, *The Afro-American and the Second World War*, 112; de Jong, *A Different Day*, 139; Odum, *Race and Rumors of Race*, 96–100.

51. One example of this new militancy is Columbia, Tennessee, where black veterans joined to defend the black neighborhood against an expected white attack in February 1946. See O'Brien, *The Color of the Law*, 7–29; and Beeler, "Race Riot in Columbia, Tennessee," 49–61.

52. DeBenedetti, *The Peace Reform in American History*, 95.

53. On the Social Gospel movement, see Paul Allen Carter, *The Decline and Revival of the Social Gospel*; Ronald C. White Jr., *Liberty and Justice for All*.

54. George M. Houser, "CORE: A Brief History," 1949, box 3, folder 3, Meier-Rudwick Collection.

55. Raines, *My Soul Is Rested*, 27; Houser, "CORE: A Brief History."

56. Meier and Rudwick, "The Boycott Movement against Jim Crow Street Cars in the South," 756–75; Meier and Rudwick, "The Origins of Nonviolent Direct Action in Afro-American Protest," 307–404. On the significant influence of Richard Gregg on nonviolent activism, see Kosek, "Richard Gregg, Mohandas Gandhi, and the Strategy of Nonviolence."

57. Houser, "CORE: A Brief History."

58. Bondurant, *Conquest of Violence*, 8, 16, 23, 25, 34; Shridharani, *War without Violence*, 6.

59. Bondurant, *Conquest of Violence*, 8, 25–28; Mary King, *Mahatma Gandhi and Martin Luther King, Jr.*, 62–66.

60. Mays, *Born to Rebel*, 153–56; Kosek, "Richard Gregg, Mohandas Gandhi, and the Strategy of Nonviolence," 1327–40; Kapur, *Raising up a Prophet*, 2–7, 40, 120.

61. On Randolph and the MOWM, see Pfeffer, *A. Philip Randolph*; and Garfinkel, *When Negroes March*.

62. A. Philip Randolph, "A Reply to My Critics," *Chicago Defender*, June 26, 1943.

63. Kapur, *Raising up a Prophet*, 44, 57. As early as 1924, black sociologist E. Franklin Frazier had warned black leaders in the *Crisis* that love alone would not solve America's race problem. He was convinced that Gandhian protest would provoke "an unprecedented massacre of defenseless black men and women in the name of Law

and Order and there would scarcely be enough Christian sentiment in America to stay the flood of blood." E. Franklin Frazier, "The Negro and Non-Resistance," *Crisis* 27 (March 1924): 213–14; E. Franklin Frazier, "The Negro and Non-Resistance," *Crisis* 28 (June 1924): 59. In the 1930s, even prominent black political scientist and later diplomat Ralph J. Bunche disapproved of Gandhi's approach. See Bunche, "A Critical Analysis of the Tactics and Programs of Minority Groups," 308–20.

64. *Pittsburgh Courier*, May 8, 1943. See also Garfinkel, *When Negroes March*, 137; and Pfeffer, *A. Philip Randolph*, 61.

65. Bayard Rustin, "The Negro and Non-Violence," reprinted from *Fellowship* (October 1942), reel 17, frame 01030, Rustin Papers, microfilm.

66. Marie [Klein] to George Houser, September 15, 1946, series 3, box 6, folder 9, CORE Papers. See also George Houser to Marie Klein, October 16, 1946, series 3, box 6, folder 9, CORE Papers.

67. Farmer, *Lay Bare the Heart*, 109. See also "Interview with James Farmer, Washington, D.C.–October 14, 1970," box 56, folder 6, Meier Papers.

68. *Chicago Defender*, February 2, 1946; R.B., "Terror Hits Again!" *Chi-CORE News*, September 15, 1946, 2, series 3, box 6, folder 9, CORE Papers.

69. Berry Bessler, "Defend Negro Homes!" *Chi-CORE News*, September 15, 1946, 1. See also "CORE-Agenda," *Chi-CORE News*, September 15, 1946, 3.

70. Robert Gemmer to George M. Houser, December 15, 1946, series 3, box 6, folder 9, CORE Papers. See also George M. Houser to Gerald Bullock, January 9, 1946; A. J. Muste to George Houser, May 14, 1946, all in series 3, box 6, folder 9, CORE Papers.

71. George Houser to Marie Klein, October 16, 1946, series 3, box 6, folder 9, CORE Papers.

72. "N.A.C. Meeting-December 31, 1965–Jan. 2, 1966," box 2, folder 5, Meier-Rudwick Collection.

73. Farmer, *Lay Bare the Heart*, 67.

74. Bernice Fisher to George Houser, July 12, 1944, reel 11, frame 00921, CORE Papers, microfilm.

75. "George Houser, Interview–Sept. 6, 1967," box 56, folder 8, Meier Papers.

76. George Houser, "Nonviolently Speaking," June 1945; George Houser, "Memo on a Mass Non-Violent Interracial Movement," 1945, both in series 3, box 6, folder 6, CORE Papers.

77. Farmer, *Lay Bare the Heart*, 94, 111.

78. Farmer, *Freedom When?* 56.

79. Martin Luther King, "Address to MIA Mass Meeting at Holt Street Baptist Church," in Carson, *The Papers of Martin Luther King, Jr.*, 3: 424, 426, 429, 430, 431.

80. Lischer, *The Preacher King*, 142.

81. David L. Lewis, *Martin Luther King*, 35; Hanigan, *Martin Luther King, Jr. and the Foundations of Nonviolence*, 156; Garrow, "The Intellectual Development of Martin Luther King, Jr.," 10; Garrow, *Bearing the Cross*, 41, 43.

82. Raines, *My Soul Is Rested*, 53; "Interview with Bayard Rustin, March 28, 1974"; Fairclough, *To Redeem the Soul of America*, 25.

83. Bayard Rustin, "Report on Montgomery Alabama," published by the War Resisters League, March 21, 1956, reel 17, frame 01140, Rustin Papers, microfilm.

84. Smiley interview, 35; Smiley quoted in Fairclough, *To Redeem the Soul of America*, 25.

85. "Interview with Bayard Rustin"; Jo Ann Ooiman Robinson, "Diary 6/21/64–6/26/64," entry 6/25/64, Robinson Papers.

86. Raines, *My Soul Is Rested*, 53; "Interview with Bayard Rustin"; Smiley interview, 35; Martin Luther King Jr., *Stride toward Freedom*, 134; Coretta Scott King, *My Life with Martin Luther King, Jr.*, 133.

87. Raboteau, *A Fire in the Bones*, 71; Burns, "Overview: The Proving Ground," 23.

88. Parks, *Rosa Parks*, 30, 66–67, 174–75.

89. Jo Ann Gibson Robinson, *The Montgomery Bus Boycott and the Women Who Started It*, 110.

90. Rustin, "Report on Montgomery Alabama."

91. Smiley interview, 35; Rustin, "Montgomery Diary," 8; Abernathy, *And the Walls Came Tumbling Down*, 152; Morris, *The Origins of the Civil Rights Movement*, 158–60.

92. Martin Luther King Jr. to Bayard Rustin, September 20, 1956, reel 3, frame 00054, Rustin Papers, microfilm.

93. Garrow, *Bearing the Cross*, 78; Wilkins, *Standing Fast*, 237.

94. Klarman, "How *Brown* Changed Race Relations," 82, 91. For a history of the Citizens' Councils, see McMillen, *The Citizens' Council*.

95. For a detailed history of the Little Rock movement, see Kirk, *Redefining the Color Line*.

96. Quoted in Summers, *I Dream A World*, 73.

97. Wilkins, *Standing Fast*, 247; Bates, *The Long Shadow of Little Rock*, 94, 96; Beals, *Warriors Don't Cry*, 28–29.

98. Bates, *The Long Shadow of Little Rock*, 111, 162.

99. "Statement by Mrs. L.C. (Daisy) Bates, Arkansas State President National Association for the Advancement of Colored People," August 13, 1959, box 3, folder 5, Bates Papers; Bates, *The Long Shadow of Little Rock*, 168; Clyde Own Jackson to Dwight D. Eisenhower, August 14, 1959; Mrs. L.C. (Daisy) Bates to Dwight D. Eisenhower, August 13, 1959, both in box 2, folder 2, Bates Papers.

100. Tyson, *Radio Free Dixie*, 80–83; Robert F. Williams interview by Mosby, 50.

101. Tyson, *Radio Free Dixie*, 84–89.

102. Manis, *A Fire You Can't Put Out*, 110, 117–18; Eskew, *But for Birmingham*, 141.

103. Shuttlesworth interview, 18.

104. Manis, *A Fire You Can't Put Out*, 169–70.

105. Fairclough, *To Redeem the Soul of America*, 29, 32–33.

106. "Constitution and By-Laws of the Southern Christian Leadership Conference," 5, series 5, box 26, folder 1, CORE Papers.

107. Tyson, *Radio Free Dixie*, 141, 148–49.

108. Quoted in *New York Times*, May 7, 1959.

109. "Telephone Conversation between Mr. Wilkins in New York and Mr. Robert

Williams in Monroe, North Carolina, May 6, 1959 at 11:04 A.M.," group III, series A, box 333, NAACP Papers.

110. Roy Wilkins to Robert F. Williams, May 8, 1959, group III, series A, box 333, NAACP Papers.

111. Quoted in *New York Times*, May 7, 1959.

112. Quoted in "The Robert F. Williams Case," 326.

113. "National Association for the Advancement of Colored People: Board of Directors Meeting, May 11, 1959," group I, series A, box 14, NAACP Papers; *New York Times*, May 12, 1959.

114. "Address of Roy Wilkins . . . at the Freedom Fund Dinner of the Chicago Branch, Morrison Hotel, Chicago, Ill., June 12, 1959, 7:00 P.M.," 10, group III, series A, box 303, NAACP Papers.

115. Warren, *Who Speaks for the Negro?* 148.

116. Cedric Belfrage, *The American Inquisition*, 82; Marable, *Race, Reform, and Rebellion*, 27–28; Berg, *The Ticket to Freedom*, 208–25. See also Berg, *"The Ticket to Freedom": The NAACP and the Struggle for Black Political Integration.*

117. Berg, *The Ticket to Freedom*, 217, 225; Berg, "Schwarze Bürgerrechte und liberaler Antikommunismus," 382–84.

118. *New York Times*, May 18, 1958.

119. Advocating "Williams's position," Mayfield wrote in *Commentary*, "would have exposed the NAACP to widespread criticism from many of the people who now warmly support it." Mayfield, "Challenge to Negro Leadership," 299.

120. Quoted in Levine, "Marcus Garvey and the Politics of Revitalization," 133–34.

121. "Telephone Conversation between Mr. Wilkins in New York and Mr. Robert Williams in Monroe, North Carolina."

122. Roy Wilkins to P. L. Prattis, May 28, 1959, group III, series A, box 333, NAACP Papers.

123. "A Racial Zealot Goes Too Far," *Charlotte Observer*, May 9, 1959, clipping in group III, series A, box 333, NAACP Papers.

124. "Proper Repudiation," *Journal Sunday and Sentinel*, May 10, 1959, clipping in group III, series A, box 333, NAACP Papers.

125. "Curbing Violence," *Newark Evening News*, May 8, 1959, clipping in group III, series A, box 333, NAACP Papers.

126. National Association for the Advancement of Colored People, "The Single Issue in the Robert F. Williams Case," July 1959, group III, series A, box 333, NAACP Papers.

127. *New York Times*, July 18, 1959.

128. "Address by Dr. Martin Luther King, Jr. at the NAACP 50th Annual Convention, New York Coliseum, New York City, Friday, July 17, 1959–8:30 P.M.," group III, series A, box 10, NAACP Papers.

129. Tyson, *Radio Free Dixie*, 164.

130. Current, "Fiftieth Annual Convention," 408–9; "NAACP 50th Annual Convention Resolutions, July 13–19, 1959, New York, New York," 24, group III, series A, box 10, NAACP Papers.

131. Robert F. Williams, "Can Negroes Afford to Be Pacifists?" 5, 6, 7.

132. Wilkins, "The Single Issue in the Robert Williams Case," 8.

133. Martin Luther King Jr., "The Social Organization of Nonviolence," 6.

134. Ling, *Martin Luther King, Jr.*, 58.

135. James R. Robinson to Rev. Martin Luther King Jr., December 22, 1959; James R. Robinson to Rev. Martin Luther King Jr., December 30, 1959, both in series 5, box 34, folder 9, CORE Papers; Martin Luther King Jr. "Give to CORE," *Baltimore Afro-American*, May 23, 1959. See also Morris, *The Origins of the Civil Rights Movement*, 135–36; and Meier and Rudwick, *CORE*, 78.

136. Lillian Smith to George M. Houser, September 24, 1946; Lillian Smith to Marvin Rich, December 1, 1961, both in series 5, box 35, folder 4, CORE Papers; Loveland, *Lillian Smith*, 222–23.

137. James R. Robinson to Dear Friend, July 27, 1959, reel 30, frame 00044, CORE Papers, microfilm.

138. Lillian Smith to James R. Robinson, July 20, 1959, series 5, box 35, folder 4, CORE Papers.

139. Ibid.

140. James R. Robinson to Lillian Smith, July 28, 1959, series 5, box 35, folder 4, CORE Papers.

141. Chafe, *Civilities and Civil Rights*, 99, 114.

142. "Interview with Gordon Carey, December 13, 1963," 1, box 56, folder 3, Meier Papers; Rudwick and Meier, *CORE*, 98, 113, 126.

143. Payne, *I've Got the Light of Freedom*, 67, 85, 93, 101.

144. Student Nonviolent Coordinating Committee, "Report of the Raleigh Conference," series 5, box 26, folder 4, CORE Papers; Sellers, *The River of No Return*, 35; Carson, *In Struggle*, 13, 22.

145. Carson, *In Struggle*, 24.

146. "Statement of Purpose," box 1, folder 14, Zinn Papers.

147. McDew interview, 57, 59, 60.

148. Stoper, *The Student Nonviolent Coordinating Committee*, 27; McDew interview, 60; Cobb interview by Rachal, 29. Writing in 1971, sociologist Allen Matusow also pointed out that most of the students who participated in the sit-ins "accepted King's teachings more out of convenience than conviction and respected his courage more than his philosophy." Matusow, "From Civil Rights to Black Power," 136.

149. *New York Times*, April 28, 1947; Scales, *Cause at Heart*, 27; Anderson, *Bayard Rustin*, 118–19.

150. Jim Peck, "Freedom Ride," *CORE-Lator* 89 (May 1961): 2–3, Scholarship, Education and Defense Fund for Racial Equality Records, box 30, folder 79, SHSW; Garrow, *Bearing the Cross*, 156–61, 167.

151. Stephen D. Pfeiffer to Dear Freedom Riders, May 17, 1961, reel 25, frame 00041, CORE Papers, microfilm.

152. Quoted in Tyson, *Radio Free Dixie*, 266.

153. Robert F. Williams, *Negroes with Guns*, 120.

154. Tyson, *Radio Free Dixie*, 262–86

155. "NAC Meeting, March 23, 1962 Minutes," box 1, folder 1, Meier-Rudwick Collection.

156. Garrow, *Bearing the Cross*, 216.

157. "An Interview with Congressman Andrew J. Young," in Schulke, *Martin Luther King, Jr.*, 66.

158. Transcript of an interview with Andrew Marrisett, in Raines, *My Soul Is Rested*, 148.

159. Fairclough, *To Redeem the Soul of America*, 138.

160. *New York Times*, May 12, 1963.

161. See Walker, "A Media-Made Movement?" 50–52.

162. Branch, *Parting the Waters*, 889; *New York Times*, September 16, 1963.

163. McWorther, *Carry Me Home*, 118; George Lavan, "Armed Birmingham Negroes Conduct Own Safety Patrols," *Militant*, September 23, 1963, 1, 5; Eskew, *But for Birmingham*, 322.

164. King interview. Adam Fairclough similarly argues that King was not as naïve as his religious rhetoric implied. Fairclough, *To Redeem the Soul of America*, 53.

165. Martin Luther King Jr., *Stride toward Freedom*, 81, 96, 97.

166. Southern Christian Leadership Conference, "This is SCLC," part 3, reel 4, frame 00703, SCLC Papers, microfilm.

167. "Manifesto: Institute for Nonviolent Resistance to Segregation, July 22–24, 1959," series 5, box 26, folder 1, CORE Papers.

168. Ed Clayton, ed., "The SCLC Story in Words and Pictures," 1964, part 3, reel 4, frame 00642, SCLC Papers, microfilm.

169. "Seventh Annual Convention: Southern Christian Leadership Conference, Sept. 24–27, 1963, Richmond, Va.," part 3, reel 8, frame 00503, SCLC Papers, microfilm.

170. "Summary of Eighth Annual Convention, Sept. 29–Oct. 1964, Savannah, Georgia," part 3, reel 8, frame 00530, SCLC Papers, microfilm.

171. Martin Luther King Jr., *Why We Can't Wait*, 22, 28.

172. Staunton O. Flanders to Dr. Martin Luther King Jr., April 23, 1963, part 1, reel 5, frame 00019, SCLC Papers, microfilm.

173. G. C. McCallum to Dear Dr. King, May 31, 1963, part 1, reel 6, frame 00465, SCLC Papers, microfilm.

Chapter 2. Gandhi, God, and Guns in Tuscaloosa

1. The following brief account of Rogers's career is based on T. Y. Rogers interview, 2–8; LaPelzia Rogers interview; Martin Luther King Jr. to Rev. T. Y. Rogers, August 31, 1957, in Carson, *The Papers of Martin Luther King, Jr.*, 5: 266–67; Vaughn and Wills, *Reflections on our Pastor*, 118; and Alvin Adams, "Shadow of Montgomery Bus Boycott Falls on Tuscaloosa," *Jet*, September 3, 1964, 8–9.

2. In his study of the 1962 desegregation crisis at the University of Alabama, historian E. Culpepper Clark does not even mention that local African Americans launched a successful nonviolent struggle against discrimination and segregation two years after the standoff. See E. Culpepper Clark, *The Schoolhouse Door*. Only sociolo-

gist Anthony Blasi has examined the city's freedom struggle beyond 1963. See Blasi, *Segregationist Violence and Civil Rights Movements in Tuscaloosa.*

3. E. Culpepper Clark, *The Schoolhouse Door*, xii.

4. Feldman, *Politics, Society, and the Klan in Alabama*, 253, 251–52, 292–93.

5. Mallisham interview by DeSantis; Mallisham interview by author, March 22, 2002; Howard interview; Murphy interview.

6. E. Culpepper Clark, *The Schoolhouse Door*, 57, 71–77.

7. Ibid., 78; "6–29–76 Interview with Robert Glynn"; "June 17, 1976 Interview with Rev. T. W. Linton," both in Blasi Collection; Howard interview; Bolden interview; Gordon interview.

8. Juan Williams, *Thurgood Marshall*, 248–49; E. Culpepper Clark, *The Schoolhouse Door*, 87, 99, 102.

9. Hall interview; Howard interview.

10. Hall interview; "6–25–76 Interview with Joe Mallisham"; "7–8–76 Interview with Ms. Olivia Maniece," both in Blasi Collection; Mallisham interview by author, March 22, 2002; Hughes interview.

11. Linton interview.

12. *Tuscaloosa News*, May 5, 1962; German interview, 1–5; Adams, "Shadow of Montgomery Bus Boycott Falls on Tuscaloosa," 8–9; Rev. Dr. Will L. Herzfeld to Anthony J. Blasi, July 2, 1976, Blasi Collection.

13. "June 17, 1976 Interview with Rev. T. W. Linton," Blasi Collection; Herzfeld interview by Burg, 8–10; Herzfeld interview by DeSantis.

14. Herzfeld interview by Burg, 17–19.

15. Ibid., 23; Mallisham interview by author, March 22, 2002.

16. Mallisham interview by DeSantis; James interview.

17. Margaret Long, "The Imperial Wizard Explains the Klan," *New York Times Magazine*, July 5, 1964, 8; Harold H. Martin and Kenneth Fairly, "'We Got Nothing to Hide,'" *Saturday Evening Post*, January 30, 1965, 29; Wade, *The Fiery Cross*, 313.

18. Wade, *The Fiery Cross*, 305–6, 309, 254.

19. Arnold Forster and Benjamin R. Epstein, "Report on the Ku Klux Klan," published by the Anti-Defamation League of B'nai B'rith, New York, 7, box 255, folder 8, Boone Papers; Mikell, *They Say—Blood on My Hands*, 50; Wade, *The Fiery Cross*, 313, 315; Dan T. Carter, *The Politics of Rage*, 140.

20. Dan T. Carter, *The Politics of Rage*, 130–31.

21. Ibid., 146–51; E. Culpepper Clark, *The Schoolhouse Door*, 225.

22. Linton interview. See also Herzfeld interview by DeSantis; Warrick interview; Maniece interview; Mallisham interview by DeSantis.

23. Herzfeld interview by DeSantis; Herzfeld interview by Burg, 23.

24. Herzfeld interview by DeSantis.

25. T. Y. Rogers interview, 11.

26. Ibid., 10–11; Herzfeld interview by Burg, 22.

27. LaPelzia Rogers interview; Howard interview.

28. Herzfeld interview by DeSantis.

29. T. Y. Rogers interview, 12–13.

30. Ibid., 16; Herzfeld interview by Burg, 25.

31. T. Y. Rogers interview, 17.

32. Ibid., 16; *Tuscaloosa News*, March 5, 1964.

33. Adams, "Shadow of Montgomery Bus Boycott Falls on Tuscaloosa," 9; T. Y. Rogers interview, 17.

34. LeMaistre interview, 8–9; Wallace quoted in Dan T. Carter, *Politics of Rage*, 11.

35. T. Y. Rogers interview, 22.

36. *Tuscaloosa News*, April 16, 17, 1964.

37. James interview; T. Y. Rogers interview, 23, 14–15.

38. T. Y. Rogers interview, 17; *Tuscaloosa News*, April 22, 1964; Rogers quoted in *Tuscaloosa News*, April 22, 1964.

39. *Washington Post*, April 24, 1964; *Tuscaloosa News*, April 22, 23, 1964; T. Y. Rogers interview, 24–26.

40. Quoted in *Tuscaloosa News*, April 24, 1964.

41. *Tuscaloosa News*, April 28, 1964.

42. Warrick interview; Howard interview; Herzfeld interview by Burg, 31.

43. Quoted in *Tuscaloosa News*, May 5, 1964.

44. T. Y. Rogers to Andrew J. Young, May 27, 1964, part 4, reel 4, frame 00171, SCLC Papers, microfilm; Edwina Smith to T. Y. Rogers, [n.d.], part 4, reel 4, frame 00175, SCLC Papers, microfilm; Andrew J. Young to Wiley Branton, June 3, 1964, part 4, reel 3, frame 00435, SCLC Papers, microfilm; *Tuscaloosa News*, May 12, 1964; Maniece interview; Howard interview; Bolden interview; Herzfeld interview by DeSantis.

45. *Tuscaloosa News*, May 19, 20, 1964.

46. T. Y. Rogers interview, 28; LaPelzia Rogers interview.

47. T. Y. Rogers interview, 28.

48. James interview; Adams, "Shadow of Montgomery Bus Boycott Falls on Tuscaloosa," 8; T. Y. Rogers interview, 7; Rogers quoted in *Tuscaloosa News*, April 22, 1964.

49. Bolden interview.

50. T. Y. Rogers interview, 43; *Tuscaloosa News*, June 5, 6, 8, 1964.

51. *New York Times*, June 10, 1964; *Tuscaloosa News*, June 9, 1964; Warrick interview; Bolden interview; Herzfeld interview by DeSantis; "7–8–76 Interview with Ms. Olivia Maniece, Librarian at the VA Hospital," Blasi Collection; Harold A. Nelson, "The Defenders," 129.

52. Quoted in *Tuscaloosa News*, June 9, 1964.

53. The actual course of events that day is not entirely clear. According to newspaper accounts, black students began to throw rocks, bricks, and even furniture at the police. Yet those who participated in the demonstrations denied these accusations in subsequent interviews. They stated that the students only threw back objects that were hurled into the church by police. Others recalled breaking the church's windows only to let in fresh air after the beginning of the tear gas attack. My account of the events is based on *New York Times*, June 10, 1964; *Tuscaloosa News*, June 9, 10, 1964; Warrick interview; Herzfeld interview by DeSantis; Howard interview; Maniece interview; T. Y. Rogers interview, 44; anonymous black teenagers interview, 8, 22, 26–27, 37–39, 61–63, 76–79; and E. G. Williams and anonymous SCLC activist interview.

54. *Tuscaloosa News*, February 20, 2000; Bolden interview.

55. Gordon interview.

56. Adams, "Shadow of Montgomery Bus Boycott Falls on Tuscaloosa," 8; Harold A. Nelson, "The Defenders," 130; Bolden interview; Gordon interview; Mallisham interview by author, March 22, 2002; *Tuscaloosa News*, June 10, 1964.

57. Mallisham interview by author, March 22, 2002.

58. Ibid.; Mallisham quoted in Harold A. Nelson, "The Defenders," 131.

59. Harold A. Nelson, "The Defenders," 130–31; Mallisham interview by author, March 22, 2002; Mallisham interview by DeSantis; Mike Williams, "Smiles and Guns," 127.

60. Mike Williams, "Smiles and Guns," 121–22; Mallisham interview by DeSantis; *Tuscaloosa News*, May 17, 1985.

61. Mallisham interview by author, March 22, 2002.

62. Mike Williams, "Smiles and Guns," 121–22; Mahan, "Alberta Brown Murphy," 106; Gordon interview; "6–25–76 Interview with Joe Mallisham."

63. Harold A. Nelson, "The Defenders," 131–33.

64. Mallisham interview by author, March 22, 2002; Mallisham interview by author, March 19, 2002; Harold A. Nelson, "The Defenders," 146.

65. LaPelzia Rogers interview; *New York Times*, June 13, 1964; Hall interview; Mallisham interview by author, March 22, 2002.

66. *New York Times*, June 11, 1964.

67. Howard interview.

68. Maniece interview; Bolden interview; Mallisham interview by DeSantis; "7–9–76 Interview Martha O'Rourke, Head Librarian, Stillman College," Blasi Collection.

69. Mallisham interview by DeSantis; Herzfeld interview by DeSantis.

70. Mallisham interview by DeSantis; Herzfeld interview by DeSantis; Linton interview; LaPelzia Rogers interview.

71. Mahan, "Alberta Brown Murphy," 104–7; Murphy interview.

72. Mallisham quoted in Mahan, "Alberta Brown Murphy," 108.

73. "6–25–76 Interview with Joe Mallisham"; Mallisham interview by author, March 22, 2002; Harold A. Nelson, "The Defenders," 128–29. Published only three years after the founding of the defense group, Nelson's article used pseudonyms for both Tuscaloosa and Joseph Mallisham to protect black activists against possible repercussions from the white community.

74. Ammerman, "The Civil Rights Movement and the Clergy in a Southern Community," 340; Mallisham interview by DeSantis.

75. "7–2–76 Interview with Professor Jay Murphy of the University of Alabama Law School," Blasi Collection.

76. Jaquith interview, 29.

77. *Tuscaloosa News*, June 12, 22, 26, July 1, 1964.

78. Ibid., June 28, 1964.

79. Ibid., July 1, 1964, 1; "United We Stand," leaflet, box 255, folder 9, Boone Papers.

80. *Tuscaloosa News*, July 5, 6, 8, 1964.

81. Ibid., July 9, 1964.

82. Harold A. Nelson, "The Defenders," 135; Mallisham interview by author, March 22, 2002; Mallisham interview by DeSantis.

83. *Washington Post*, July 11, 1964; Mallisham interview by DeSantis; Mallisham interview by author, March 22, 2002; *Tuscaloosa News*, July 10, 11, 1964.

84. *New York Times*, July 11, 1964; *Tuscaloosa News*, July 12, 23, 1964; Harold A. Nelson, "The Defenders," 135.

85. Unidentified to Eric Kindberry, July 15, 1964, part 4, reel 8, frame 00941, SCLC Papers, microfilm.

86. E. G. Williams and anonymous SCLC activist interview.

87. Anonymous SCLC leaders interview, 12.

88. Mike Williams, "Smiles and Guns," 128; Harold A. Nelson, "The Defenders," 144; Mallisham interview by author, March 22, 2002.

89. Harold A. Nelson, "The Defenders," 138.

90. Ibid., 140; Mallisham interview by author, March 22, 2002.

91. Mueller, "A Voice for Justice," 223–24, 226; "6-28-76 Interview with Buford Boone, Former Publisher of the Tuscaloosa *News*," Blasi Collection.

92. *Tuscaloosa News*, June 9, 1964; the quote is from "Ready for Mob Control?" *Tuscaloosa News*, July 7, 1964.

93. "Lullaby and Good Night," *Tuscaloosa News*, July 8, 1964; "Ready for Mob Control?" *Tuscaloosa News*, July 7, 1964.

94. "The Price of Our Silence," *Tuscaloosa News*, July 9, 1964.

95. *Tuscaloosa News*, July 10, 16, 1964.

96. Ibid., July 25, 1964.

97. Ibid., July 18, 1964; Jones, McEachin, Ormond & Fulton to Larry Worral, September 20, 1968, box 156, folder 1, Boone Papers.

98. Gordon interview; Maniece interview; LaPelzia Rogers interview.

99. James interview; Linton interview.

100. Bolden interview; Hughes interview; Mallisham interview by author, March 22, 2002; Warrick interview; James interview; Hall interview.

101. Adams, "Shadow of Montgomery Bus Boycott Falls on Tuscaloosa," 8; German interview, 5; *Tuscaloosa News*, August 3, 4, 12, 1964.

102. "Mass Meeting Taped by Harvey Burg, August 10, 1964, Tuscaloosa, Alabama," 1964 Civil Rights Movement in Tuscaloosa, Alabama, Collection.

103. "7-8-76 Interview with Ms. Olivia Maniece, Librarian at the VA Hospital," Blasi Collection; *Tuscaloosa News*, August 14, 18, September 12, November 10, 1964.

104. T. Y. Rogers to C. T. Vivian, December 23, 1964, part 2, reel 17, frame 00132, SCLC Papers, microfilm; *Tuscaloosa News*, May 23, 1965; T. Y. Rogers to Barbara H. Suarez, April 21, 1965, part 3, reel 1, frame 00948, SCLC Papers, microfilm.

105. *Tuscaloosa News*, March 13, 1965.

106. *Washington Post*, January 20, 22, 1965.

107. "Editorial Comments," TCHR (Tuscaloosa Committee for Human Rights) Newsletter, February 1965, Alabama Pamphlet Collection, Vertical File.

108. *Tuscaloosa News*, August 15, September 7, 1965.

109. "Tuscaloosa Citizens for Action Committee," 1966, part 4, reel 19, frame 710, SCLC Papers, microfilm; Blasi, *Segregationist Violence and Civil Rights Movements in Tuscaloosa*, 130–32.

110. Mallisham interview by author, March 22, 2002; Garrow, *Bearing the Cross*, 548. Rogers's career as SCLC activist ended abruptly in 1971, when his car slid off a slippery Atlanta road and crashed into a tree. Rogers was killed instantly. *Tuscaloosa News*, March 26, 1971; *New York Times*, March 27, 1971.

111. Mallisham interview by author, March 19, 2002; Mallisham interview by De-Santis; Mike Williams, "Smiles and Guns," 120; *Tuscaloosa News*, May 17, 1985.

112. Howard interview; Davis interview.

113. Harold A. Nelson, "The Defenders," 144; Mike Williams, "Smiles and Guns," 127.

114. Mallisham interview by DeSantis.

Chapter 3. The Deacons for Defense and Justice

1. Mike Lesser to Terry Perlman, November 4, 1963, reel 5, frame 00185, CORE Papers, microfilm.

2. Fairclough, *Race and Democracy*, 340; "The West Feliciana Parish Story," series 1, box 4, folder 1a, CORE-SRO.

3. "The West Feliciana Parish Story"; Warren, *Who Speaks for the Negro?* 9; Bob Adelman, "Birth of a Voter," *Ebony*, February 1964, 88–94.

4. De Jong, *A Different Day*, 183.

5. Mike Lesser to Terry Perlman, November 4, 1963. See also "Interview with Ronnie M. Moore, April 28, 1971," box 56, folder 12, Meier Papers.

6. James Farmer, "Louisiana Story 1963," box 1, folder 7, Holden Papers; *New York Times*, September 1, 1963; "Leon P, [sic] David, September 1, 1963," reel 16, SCRLR, microfilm.

7. "Spiver Gordon," reel 16, SCRLR, microfilm; quoted in Farmer, "Louisiana Story 1963."

8. "Intimidations and Harrassment [sic] against Negroes and CORE Workers Summer 1963 to Summer 1964," 1, box 9, folder 13, CORE-SRO; quoted in Farmer, *Freedom When?* 11.

9. Farmer, *Freedom When?* 11; Farmer, *Lay Bare the Heart*, 252.

10. James Farmer, unpaginated foreword to Bell, CORE *and the Strategy of Nonviolence.*

11. "Bridgeport, Connecticut Area Conference, December 13, 1963," box 56, folder 6, Meier Papers. In a conversation with civil rights scholar August Meier in early January 1964, Farmer explicitly conceded that he no longer considered himself a pacifist. See "Observations on CORE (Jan. 3, 1964)," 2, box 65, folder 6, Meier Papers.

12. "Bridgeport, Connecticut Area Conference, December 13, 1963." Given the fact that even James Farmer abandoned his pacifist convictions during this time, historian Greta de Jong's assertion that CORE intended to change "the social order through nonviolence, love, patience, and appealing to the conscience of white southerners" is

untenable. By 1963, most of CORE's members had already abandoned this ideal. See de Jong, *A Different Day*, 188.

13. *New York Times*, June 28, 29, 1963.

14. Quoted in *New York Times*, June 28, 1963.

15. "Resolution"; "1963 CORE National Convention," both in series 1, box 3, folder 3, CORE Papers.

16. "1963 CORE Convention: Dayton, Ohio, 27–30 July," 4, series 1, box 3, folder 3, CORE Papers.

17. R. Hunter Morey to Fellowship of Reconciliation, May 14, 1963, box 5, folder 9, Morey Papers.

18. Fairclough, *Race and Democracy*, 341; Bell, *CORE and the Strategy of Nonviolence*, 57; Meier and Rudwick, *CORE*, 299; Congress of Racial Equality, "This is CORE," unprocessed accessions, box 1, folder 2, CORE Papers.

19. Marvin Rich, "Memorandum: CORE Contacts," January 1963, 1, reel 47, frame 00890, CORE Papers, microfilm.

20. Farmer, "The New Jacobins and Full Emancipation," 97. In light of Farmer's development, historian Akinyele Umoja's claim that CORE's director was concerned that CORE workers might abandon "nonviolence as a way of life and primary strategy" ignores both the increasing pragmatism that characterized the debate on nonviolence and the fact that Farmer himself had renounced philosophical nonviolence. See Umoja, "1964," 208.

21. Culbert G. Rutenber to James Farmer, March 23, 1962, reel 2, frame 00017, CORE Papers, microfilm.

22. Ibid.

23. Transcript of "The WINS-News Conference," April 21, 1963, 2, reel 5, frame 01026, CORE Papers, microfilm.

24. Adelman, "Birth of a Voter," 96.

25. Farmer, *Freedom When?* 19.

26. "Interview with Ronnie M. Moore, April 28, 1971."

27. Wade, *The Fiery Cross*, 329; "Field Report: East Feliciana Parish Jan. 13–Jan. 26, 1964," box 4, folder 3, CORE-SRO.

28. "Field Report: West Feliciana Parish, Jan. 13–Jan. 26, 1964," 2. A similar assessment can be found in "Field Report: West Feliciana Parish, Jan. 27–Feb. 9, 1964," both in box 1, folder 15, CORE-LSCD.

29. "Clinic on Non-Violence, Plaquemine, Louisiana, February 8, 1964," box 9, folder 10, CORE-SRO.

30. See "Intimidations and Harrassment [*sic*] against Negroes and CORE Workers Summer 1963 to Summer 1964," box 9, folder 13, CORE-SRO.

31. Miriam Feingold, "Field Report: St. Helena, East Feliciana & West Feliciana Parishes, June 28 to July 5, 1964," 1, box 1, folder 12, CORE-LSCD.

32. "Voter Education Project Report: Louisiana Voter Education Project," series 5, box 64, folder 3, CORE Papers.

33. Jim Peck, ed., "Louisiana—Summer, 1964: The Students Report to Their Home Towns," unprocessed accessions, box 1, folder 2, CORE Papers.

34. Ibid.; Redden interview.

35. "Field Report—Intimidation and Harrassment [sic] July 15–30, 1964," box 4, folder 13, CORE-SRO.

36. "Staff Meeting: New Orleans, La., February 14, 1964," notebook number 10, reel 2, frame 422, Miriam Feingold Papers, microfilm.

37. "Louisiana Summer Task Force Staff Meeting, July 15, 1964," 3, box 9, folder 12, CORE-SRO.

38. "Notes on Staff Meeting," Nov. 1963, reel 1, frame 0789, Miriam Feingold Papers, microfilm.

39. Ronnie M. Moore, "Field Report Sept. 1964–Jan. 1965," January 19, 1965, reel 25, frame 00818, CORE Papers, microfilm; "Interview with James Farmer, Washington, D.C.—October 14, 1970," 5.

40. Daniel Mitchell, "Jackson Parish and Jonesboro, Louisiana: A White Paper," box 4, folder 4, CORE–Monroe, Louisiana, Chapter Files; Daniel Mitchell, "A Special Report on Jonesboro, Louisiana with Reference to Voter Registration Activities Involving the Congress of Racial Equality," July 1964, box 10, folder 10, CORE–Jackson Parish, Louisiana, Files.

41. Cathy Patterson and Danny Mitchell, "Field Report, July 15, 1964," series 5, box 64, folder 3, CORE Papers; Ed H. Hollander, "Jonesboro, Swimming Pool Arrests," July 14, 1964, series 5, box 12, folder 7, CORE Papers; Ronnie Moore, "Rights Law Flouted in Rural Louisiana," CORE-Lator (July-August 1964): 3, box 1, Joseph and Nancy Ellin Freedom Summer Collection; "Intimidations and Harrassment [sic] against Negroes and CORE Workers," 7.

42. Mitchell, "A Special Report on Jonesboro," 5.

43. Hamilton Bims, "Deacons for Defense," Ebony, September 1965, 26; New York Times, February 21, 1965; "Deacons of Defense and Justice, Inc.," August 17, 1965, Deacons FBI File 157–2466–41; Hill, The Deacons for Defense, 24.

44. Cathy Patterson, "Field Report," July 15, 1964, reel 20, frame 00706, CORE Papers, microfilm. There are conflicting reports concerning the date of the defense group's formation. One CORE report says the Klan parade took place on July 14; two others state it took place on July 29 or July 30. Moore, "Rights Law Flouted in Rural Louisiana," 3; Mitchell, "Jackson Parish and Jonesboro, Louisiana: A White Paper," 2; "Chronology on Jonesboro," series 5, box 12, folder 7, CORE Papers; letterhead memorandum, "Deacons of Defense and Justice, Inc.," August 17, 1965; Hill, The Deacons for Defense, 45. Although some historians have claimed that Robert F. Williams inspired the formation of the Deacons, the available evidence does not support this conclusion. See Strain, Pure Fire, 72; and Pearson, The Shadow of the Panther, 26–27, 65, 109.

45. Mitchell, "Jackson Parish and Jonesboro, Louisiana: A White Paper," 3; Bims, "Deacons for Defense," 26; letterhead memorandum, "Deacons of Defense and Justice, Inc. Jonesboro, Louisiana," March 25, 1965, Deacons FBI File 157–2466–13.

46. Baltimore Afro-American, March 6, 1965.

47. Quoted in New York Times, February 21, 1965, 52.

48. Ibid.

49. SAC, New Orleans to Director, FBI, January 6, 1965, Deacons FBI File 157–

2446–2; *New York Times*, February 21, 1965; letterhead memorandum, "Deacons for Defense and Justice," August 17, 1965.

50. Letterhead memorandum, "Deacons of Defense and Justice, Inc. Jonesboro, Louisiana," March 25, 1965.

51. Quoted in Mitchell, "Jackson Parish and Jonesboro, Louisiana: A White Paper," 3.

52. "Louisiana—October 1964 through April 1965: Summary of Field Reports," series 1, box 4, folder 2, CORE-SRO.

53. SAC, New Orleans to Director, FBI, January 1, 1965, Deacons FBI File 157–2466–1.

54. James Farmer, "CORE in Bogalusa," series 4, box 1, folder 5, CORE Papers; Steve Miller to Shirley Mesher, February 12, 1965, box 1, folder 8, CORE-LSCD; Fairclough, *Race and Democracy*, 349. On the problem of segregation and discrimination in southern paper mills, see Minchin, *The Color of Work*.

55. Norwood, "Bogalusa Burning," 591–628.

56. Paul Good, "Klantown USA," *Nation*, February 1, 1965, 110; *Baltimore Afro-American*, July 31, 1965; Shirah, "Bogalusa Report," 1.

57. "Fact Sheet on Bogalusa, Louisiana," February 17, 1965, series 5, box 12, folder 7, CORE Papers; Good, "Klantown USA," 110–11; Botnick, "One Man's Stand," 1–2; *New York Times*, January 9, 1965.

58. Quoted in *New York Times*, January 9, 1965, 13.

59. Ibid.

60. A. Z. Young interview; Minchin, *The Color of Work*, 98; "Summer Parish Scouting Report: Washington Parish," box 7, folder 5, CORE-SRO.

61. Hicks interview by Wright, 3; Farmer, "CORE in Bogalusa," 1–2.

62. "Bogalusa, Louisiana, Incident Summary: January 25–February 21, 1965," box 7, folder 5, CORE-SRO.

63. Jenkins interview; Farmer, "CORE in Bogalusa," 2.

64. Quoted in "Bogalusa, Louisiana, Incident Summary: January 25–February 21, 1965."

65. Ibid.; William Yates to E. William Henry, February 22, 1965, box 7, folder 5, CORE-SRO; Jenkins interview; "Fact Sheet on Bogalusa, Louisiana," series 5, box 12, folder 7, CORE Papers; Hicks interview by Wright, 5.

66. Hicks interview by Wright, 5.

67. Jenkins interview; "Fact Sheet on Bogalusa, Louisiana"; "Bogalusa, Louisiana, Incident Summary: January 25–February 21, 1965."

68. Bogalusa Committee for Concern, "The Bogalusa Story," series 5, box 12, folder 7, CORE Papers; "Beaten in Bogalusa. . .," *CORE-Lator* no. 111 (March-April 1965): 1–2, reel 49, frame 00187, CORE Papers, microfilm.

69. Hicks interview by Wright, 5.

70. *Baltimore Afro-American*, July 31, 1965; "Fact Sheet on Bogalusa, Louisiana."

71. *Baltimore Afro-American*, July 3, 1965; Hicks interview by Wright, 11; William Yates to E. William Henry, February 22, 1965; Hill, *The Deacons for Defense*, 98.

72. A. Z. Young interview; Jenkins interview; Nancy Gilmore, "Louisiana Field

Report, January through June 1965," 19, box 4, folder 2, CORE-SRO; Farmer, "CORE in Bogalusa"; Minchin, *The Color of Work*, 94–95, 98.

73. Hicks interview by Feingold; SAC, New Orleans to Director, FBI, March 4, 1965, Deacons FBI File 157–2466–8; SAC, New Orleans to Director, FBI, February 23, 1965, Deacons FBI File 157–2466–3; *Los Angeles Times*, June 13, 1965.

74. Quoted in *Los Angeles Times*, June 13, 1965.

75. Ibid.; New Orleans to Director, February 23, 1965.

76. Memorandum, W. C. Sullivan to F. J. Baumgartner, February 26, 1965, Deacons FBI File 157–2466–5.

77. "Bogalusa, Louisiana, Incident Summary: January 15–February 21."

78. "Statement of Mr. Royan Burris," March 30, 1965, box 1, folder 6, CORE–Bogalusa, Louisiana, Chapter Files; Joel Rubenstein to Richard Haley, March 30, 1965, box 7, folder 5, CORE-SRO; Hugh Robinson, "Bogalusa: Events on May 1, 1965," box 1, folder 8, CORE–Bogalusa, Louisiana, Chapter Files; Charles Currier, "Incident Report," May 15, 1965, box 7, folder 6, CORE-SRO; "WATS Line Report," June 28, 1965, box 4, folder 6, CORE-SRO.

79. Hill, *The Deacons for Defense*, 60–61.

80. "Articles of Incorporation of Deacons of Defense and Justice, Inc.," March 5, 1965, box 5, folder 4, CORE-SRO.

81. "The Deacons—and Their Impact," *National Guardian*, September 4, 1965, 4; letterhead memorandum, "Deacons of Defense and Justice, Inc.," August 17, 1965; "Partial Report of Intimications [*sic*] and Harrassments [*sic*]," box 4, folder 6, CORE-SRO.

82. "Partial Report of Intimications [*sic*] and Harrassments [*sic*]"; "Additions to Bogalusa Intimidations List," box 7, folder 5, CORE-SRO; Botnick, "One Man's Stand," 2; "Summary of Incidents: Bogalusa, Louisiana, January 28–July 1, 1965," box 7, folder 7, CORE-SRO.

83. A. Z. Young interview.

84. "Summary of Incidents in Bogalusa, Louisiana, April 7–9," box 1, folder 6, CORE-SRO; *New York Times*, April 20, 1965; "RE: RANDLE COZELL POUNDS," Original Knights of the Ku Klux Klan FBI File 105–71801–403; "4/7/65 Bogalusa, La.," box 7, folder 6, CORE-SRO.

85. "Summary of Incidents in Bogalusa, Louisiana, April 7–9"; *New York Times*, April 8, 1965; Jeffrey M. Dickeman, "Skeleton in the Closet," *New York Review of Books*, July 5, 2001, 66; "Bogalusa Riflemen Fight Off KKK Attack," *Jet*, April 22, 1965, 5.

86. Quoted in Ralph Blumenfeld and Richard Montague, "Klan and CORE in Gun Battle," *New York Post*, April 8, 1965, 5.

87. *Baltimore Afro-American*, April 17, 1965.

88. *New York Times*, April 9, 1965; "Bogalusa Freedom Struggle," *CORE-Lator* (May-June 1965): 1–2, box 1, Joseph and Nancy Ellin Freedom Struggle Summer Collection; "RE: RANDLE COZELL POUNDS"; "Summary of Incidents: Bogalusa, Louisiana, January 18–July 1, 1965."

89. Farmer, *Lay Bare the Heart*, 285–88.

90. *Baltimore Afro-American*, April 17, 1965; Ed Smith, "Racist Violence Persists in

Alabama, Louisiana," *Militant*, April 19, 1965, 8; Jacobs interview; "Activities in Jonesboro, Louisiana," April 9, 1965, box 5, folder 2, CORE-SRO; "Statement Made by Loretta Estelle on Shooting on April 10, 1965," box 3, folder 4, CORE–Monroe, Louisiana, Chapter Files.

91. "Meeting Memorandum," April 15, 1965, box 1, folder 2, CORE–Bogalusa, Louisiana, Chapter Files.

92. Joel Rubenstein to Ed Hollander, April 16, 1965; "Bogalusa, Thursday April 15, 1965," both in box 7, folder 6, CORE-SRO; "Civil Rights Volunteers Encounter Hostility, 'Warm Friendship' in Bogalusa, LA," press release, box 84, folder 13, Meier Papers.

93. "The Deacons," *Newsweek*, August 2, 1965, 28.

94. Dickeman, "Skeleton in the Closet," 66; Louie Robinson and Charles Brown, "The Negro Feared Most by Whites in Louisiana," *Jet*, July 15, 1965, 18.

95. "The Problem in Focus," *Campus CORE-Lator* 1 (Spring 1965): 25–26, reel 17, frame 0293, CORE Papers, Addendum, microfilm.

96. Honigsberg, *Crossing Border Street*, 33.

97. Quoted in "The Deacons," 28.

98. Shirah, "Bogalusa Report," 1–2; Roy Reed, "The Deacons, Too, Ride by Night," *New York Times Magazine*, August 15, 1965, 20; "The Deacons—and Their Impact," 4–5; Hicks interview by Feingold.

99. Hicks interview by Wright, 16.

100. Quoted in letterhead memorandum, "Deacons for Defense and Justice, Incorporated," June 8, 1966, Deacons FBI File 157–2466–137.

101. Quoted in "Rights Army—The Angry 'Deacons,'" *San Francisco Sunday Chronicle*, July 25, 1965.

102. "The Deacons—and Their Impact," 4.

103. Quoted in *Baltimore Afro-American*, October 23, 1965.

104. Quoted in Reed, "The Deacons, Too, Ride by Night," 11.

105. Reynolds interview, 34.

106. Quoted in letterhead memorandum, "Deacons for Defense and Justice, Incorporated," June 8, 1966.

107. Quoted in Minchin, *The Color of Work*, 92.

108. Hicks interview by Wright, 15.

109. Robinson and Brown, "The Negro Feared Most by Whites in Louisiana," 14–18; "The Deacons," 29; letterhead memorandum, "Deacons for Defense and Justice, also known as 'The Deacons': CHARLES SIMS, Spokesman," June 15, 1965, Deacons FBI File 157–2466–16.

110. "The Bogalusa Deacons," *Militant*, December 27, 1965, 5; "The Deacons—and Their Impact," 5; Honigsberg, *Crossing Border Street*, 51, 52; Reed, "The Deacons, Too, Ride by Night," 22.

111. A. Z. Young interview.

112. Reed, "The Deacons, Too, Ride by Night," 22.

113. Lipsitz, *A Life in the Struggle*, 96.

114. Quoted in Reed, "The Deacons, Too, Ride by Night," 20.

115. *New York Times*, June, 6, 1965; Fred L. Zimmerman, "Race and Violence: More Dixie Negroes Buy Arms to Retaliate against White Attacks," *Wall Street Journal*, July 12, 1965; *Amsterdam News*, July 24, 1965; "The Deacons," 28; letterhead memorandum, "Deacons for Defense and Justice, also known as 'The Deacons': CHARLES SIMS, Spokesman," June 15, 1965; *Baltimore Afro-American*, October 23, 1965.

116. Letterhead memorandum, "Deacons for Defense and Justice: Homer, Louisiana, Chapter," June 24, 1965, Deacons FBI File 157–246–18; Director, FBI to SACs, July 19, 1965, Deacons FBI File 157–2466–20; letterhead memorandum, "Deacons of Defense and Justice, Inc.," August 17, 1965; memorandum, W. C. Sullivan to F. J. Baumgardner, July 15, 1965, Deacons FBI File 157–2466–22.

117. "The Deacons and Their Impact," 5.

118. Quoted in Hunt, "Bogalusa: Town Ruled by Fear," 20.

119. *New York Times*, May 24, 1965; Fairclough, *Race and Democracy*, 365.

120. *New York Times*, June 4, 1965; "Bleeding Louisiana," *Time*, June 11, 1965, 32.

121. *New York Times*, June 10, 1965.

122. Hill interview; *New York Times*, July 9, 1965; Warren Kaplan to Henry Schwarzschild, July 14, 1965, reel 5, SCRLR, microfilm; *Louisiana Weekly*, July 17, 1965.

123. "Statement and Personal Data: Henry Austin," July 27, 1965, 7, reel 5, SCRLR, microfilm.

124. Hill, *The Deacons for Defense*, 143.

125. *New York Times*, July 11, 1965; "Deny Deacons Shot Bogalusa White Youth," *Jet*, July 22, 1965, 5; Warren Kaplan to Henry Schwarzschild, July 14, 1965; Hunt, "Bogalusa: Town Ruled by Fear," 20. According to historian Lance Hill, Austin's membership application was initially rejected. Eventually, however, he was admitted and became an organizer for the Deacons. Hill, *The Deacons for Defense*, 141.

126. Honigsberg, *Crossing Border Street*, 86.

127. "Statement and Personal Data: Henry Austin," July 27, 1965, reel 5, SCRLR, microfilm.

128. Quoted in "'Let Whites Give Something,' Lomax Says in Bogalusa," *Jet*, July 29, 1965, 7.

129. *New York Times*, July 15, 17, September 8, December 13, 29, 1965; "Man in the Middle," *Time*, July 23, 1965, 19. For a more thorough account of the Johnson administration's response to the Bogalusa crisis, see Fairclough, *Race and Democracy*, 370–78.

130. Fairclough, *Race and Democracy*, 377.

131. Lipsitz, *A Life in the Struggle*, 113.

132. Letterhead memorandum, "Deacons of Defense and Justice, Inc.," August 17, 1965; *New York Times*, August 2, 1965; Thomas quoted in *New York Times*, August 30, 1965, 29.

133. Letterhead memorandum, "Deacons of Defense and Justice," November 24, 1965, Deacons FBI File 157–2466–90; letterhead memorandum, "Rally of Deacons for Defense and Justice Sponsored by Congress of Racial Equality," November 22, 1965, Deacons FBI File 157–2466–92; letterhead memorandum, "Deacons of Defense and

Justice, Inc.," November 12, 1965, Deacons FBI File 157–1466–87; SAC, New Orleans to Director, FBI, July 12, 1966, Deacons FBI File 157–2466–156; *New York Times*, April 6, 1966; *Louisiana Weekly*, April 16, 1966.

134. Hill, *The Deacons for Defense*, 216–33.

135. Ibid., 164–83. Hill himself admits that the Deacons chapters in Mississippi "regarded themselves as an autonomous local organization within a loose federation," explaining this with "the independent and democratic nature of most organizations in Southern black communities." Some Mississippi defense organizations such as the one in Natchez deliberately distanced themselves from the Louisiana Deacons. See Hill, *The Deacons for Defense*, 199.

136. Hill, "The Deacons for Defense and Justice," 263.

137. Many members of the Jonesboro group did not even know about the organizing activities of Deacon organizer Thomas, who became increasingly estranged from the parent organization. Rarely if ever informed by Thomas about his activities in the North, many of the Jonesboro Deacons disagreed with his activities and disapproved of his efforts to establish new chapters. See letterhead memorandum, "Deacons of Defense and Justice, Inc.," August 17, 1965; letterhead memorandum, "Deacons of Defense and Justice, Inc.," November 22, 1966, Deacons FBI File 157–2466–176; letterhead memorandum, "Deacons of Defense and Justice, Incorporated," December 23, 1966, Deacons FBI File 157–1466–181.

138. Fairclough, *Race and Democracy*, 345.

139. Memorandum, J. H. Gale to Mr. Belmont, March 15, 1965, Deacons FBI File 157–2466–9.

140. SAC, Los Angeles to Director, FBI, June 15, 1965, Deacons FBI File 157–2466–16; Shana Alexander, "Visit Bogalusa and You Will Look for Me," *Life*, July 2, 1965, 28.

141. "Armed Vigilantes Aren't the Answer," *Los Angeles Times*, June 15, 1965.

142. Zimmerman, "Race and Violence," 1.

143. Unidentified to Rep. Jimmy Morrison, June 23, 1965, Deacons FBI File 157–2466–19.

144. *New York Times*, July 11, 1965, IV, 5; Zimmerman, "Race and Violence," 18.

145. "Miss. KKK Scared Stiff; Say Black Muslims Hide Guns in Graves, Coffins," *Jet*, December 2, 1965, 6–8.

146. *New York Times*, July 14, 1965; "Man in the Middle," *Time*, July 23, 1965, 19; A. Z. Young interview; "The Deacons—and Their Impact," 5.

147. Quoted in *Louisiana Weekly*, July 17, 1965, 11.

148. Rustin quoted in *Los Angeles Times*, June 15, 1965.

149. "The Deacons & The Klan," SCLC *Newsletter* 2 (October–November 1965): 3, part 3, reel 4, frame 00376, SCLC Papers, microfilm.

150. Quoted in Della Rossa, "Organizer of Deacons Explains Purpose," *Militant*, June 28, 1965, 2.

151. Quoted in Bims, "Deacons for Defense," 26.

152. Quoted in Alexander, "Visit Bogalusa and You Will Look for Me," 28.

153. "The Deacons," 29.

154. Carl Hufbauer, "Bogalusa: Negro Community vs. Crown Colony," *Campus CORE-Lator* 1 (Spring 1965): 21, reel 17, frame 0293, CORE Papers, Addendum, microfilm; Dickeman, "Skeleton in the Closet," 66.

155. Mel Acheson to Dear Mother and Dad, July 10, 1965, Acheson Papers.

156. FFM Newsletter, August 15, 1965, 3, Acheson Papers.

157. Meldon Acheson to Dear Mother and Dad, July 22, 1965; Meldon Acheson to Hi, Y'all!, July 30, 1965, both in Acheson Papers; "Concordia Parish (Ferriday): July 16, 1965"; "Concordia (Ferriday) July 21, 1965"; "Concordia Parish (Ferriday) July 24, 1965," all in box 4, folder 7, CORE-SRO; Meldon Acheson to Garry Greenburg, August 17, 1965, Acheson Papers.

158. Meier and Rudwick, *CORE*, 202, 297.

159. Alvin Adams, "CORE Shifts to Politics: Tackles Needy Money Problem," *Jet*, July 22, 1965, 8; "Minutes of 23rd Annual Convention—July 1 through 5, 1965, Durham, North Carolina," 13, box 2, folder 1, Meier-Rudwick Collection.

160. Lonnie X quoted in Adams, "CORE Shifts to Politics: Tackles Needy Money Problem," 8; letterhead memorandum, "Jonesboro, Louisiana," August 14, 1965, Deacons FBI File 157–2466–47.

161. "Brooklyn CORE: National Convention Resolutions," series 4, box 1, folder 4, CORE Papers.

162. Meier and Rudwick, *CORE*, 402.

163. "Convention Decisions, Morning Session, 5 July 1965," series 4, box 1, folder 4, CORE Papers.

164. Blumenfeld and Montague, "Klan and CORE in Gun Battle," 5.

165. Robert Brookins Gore to Mr. Wechsler, April 8, 1965, reel 16, frame 1327, CORE Papers, Addendum, microfilm.

166. "Staff meeting—April 12, 1965," box 4, folder 2, CORE-SRO.

167. Richard Haley, "CORE, Deacons, Relationship," memorandum, reel 19, SCRLR, microfilm.

168. "News Conference–Farmer, McKissick, Wiley–30 June 1965 Durham," series 4, box 1, folder 4, CORE Papers.

169. *Durham Morning Herald*, July 1, 1965; *New York Times*, August 1, 1965; James Farmer, "The CORE of It!" *Amsterdam News*, July 10, 1965.

170. Haley quoted in "Guns, Pickets Down: Talks Begin in Bogalusa Race Crisis," *Jet*, June 24, 1965, 10.

171. Haley interview, 11.

172. Haley, "CORE, Deacons, Relationship."

Chapter 4. Armed Resistance and the Mississippi Movement

1. Tom Scarbrough, "Holmes County," May 14, 1963, 1–4, doc. no. 2–54–2–5–1–1–1, MSSC; Raines, *My Soul Is Rested*, 262; Terkel, *American Dreams*, 196–97; Youth of the Rural Organizing and Cultural Center, *Minds Stayed on Freedom*, 25.

2. Walter Kaufman, "Mississippi Project," August 16, 1964, Kaufman Papers; Tom

Scarbrough, "Holmes County," April 19, 1963, 1–2, doc. no. 2–54–1–79–1–1–1, MSSC; Terkel, *American Dreams*, 193–95; "Now We Confront Us," [n.d.], box 1, folder 12, Zinn Papers; Scarbrough, "Holmes County," May 14, 1963, 3.

3. Terkel, *American Dreams*, 193.

4. Watkins interview, 46.

5. Cobb interview by Dent.

6. Payne, *I've Got the Light of Freedom*, 60.

7. Carson, *In Struggle*, 66.

8. "Chronology of Violence and Intimidation in Mississippi since 1961," 1–12, box 1, folder 12, Zinn Papers.

9. Carson, *In Struggle*, 45–49.

10. McDew interview, 94.

11. Dittmer, *Local People*, 47.

12. Medgar Evers to John A. Morsell, April 10, 1957, group III, series A, box 114, NAACP Papers.

13. Transcript of an interview with Myrlie Evers, in Hampton and Fayer, *Voices of Freedom*, 152.

14. Medgar Evers, "Why I Live in Mississippi," *Ebony*, September 1963, 144; Myrlie Evers, *For Us, the Living*, 92; *Baltimore Afro-American*, June 24, 1967; Payne, *I've Got the Light of Freedom*, 50. According to James H. Meriwether, the Mau Mau insurgency had considerable influence on African Americans and fostered more militant strategies within the civil rights movement. See Meriwether, "African Americans and the Mau Mau Rebellion," 64.

15. Transcript of an interview with Dave Dennis, in Hampton and Fayer, *Voices of Freedom*, 153.

16. John R. Salter to Dear Folks, September 29, 1962, unprocessed accessions, Salter Papers.

17. John R. Salter Jr. to Polly Greenberg, September 27, 1966, box 1, folder 6, Salter Papers.

18. Raines, *My Soul Is Rested*, 271; Salter, *Jackson, Mississippi*, 24; John R. Salter Jr. to Polly Greenberg, September 27, 1966.

19. Henry, *Aaron Henry*, 58–73, 154; Margaret Long, "The Freest Man in Mississippi," *Progressive*, December 1963, 18; Henry interview, 67.

20. Transcript of an interview with Lawrence Guyot, in Raines, *My Soul Is Rested*, 239.

21. The Jackson-area Boycott Movement to Dear Friend, spring 1963, box 1, folder 6, Salter Papers.

22. Salter, *Jackson, Mississippi*, 69; see also Salter and King interview, 52.

23. "Terribly Dangerous," *Newsweek*, June 10, 1963, 29; Moody, *Coming of Age in Mississippi*, 264.

24. Salter and King interview, 51–52.

25. Anne Braden to John R. Salter, February 7, 1963, unprocessed accessions, Salter Papers.

26. Braden, *The Wall Between*, 132–33; Anne Braden to John R. Salter, February 7, 1963.

27. Klibaner, *Conscience of a Troubled South*, 239–40.

28. Rev. G. R. Haughton quoted in *New York Herald Tribune*, June 14, 1963.

29. R.D. to Hi Folks, June 14, 1963, box 1, folder 6, Salter Papers.

30. Salter, *Jackson, Mississippi*, 200.

31. Hodding Carter, "Mississippi Now—Hate and Fear," *New York Times Magazine*, June 23, 1963, 28.

32. Dennis interview by Rogers.

33. Salamon, "The Time Dimension in Policy Evaluation," 131–73.

34. Quoted in ibid., 170.

35. Transcript of an interview with Robert Cooper, in Youth of the Rural Organizing and Cultural Center, *Minds Stayed on Freedom*, 94.

36. Transcript of an interview with Hartman Turnbow, in Raines, *My Soul Is Rested*, 266.

37. Myrlie Evers, *For Us, the Living*, 124.

38. Moody, *Coming of Age in Mississippi*, 129.

39. Transcript of an interview with Jodie "Preacher" Scaffold, in Youth of the Rural Organizing and Cultural Center, *Minds Stayed on Freedom*, 64.

40. Fairly interview, 34.

41. Transcript of an interview with Hartman Turnbow, in Raines, *My Soul Is Rested*, 266.

42. Transcript of an interview with Robert Cooper, in Youth of the Rural Organizing and Cultural Center, *Minds Stayed on Freedom*, 94.

43. Moses, "Commentary," 75.

44. Transcript of an interview with Julian Bond, in Raines, *My Soul Is Rested*, 267.

45. Cobb interview by Dent.

46. McDew interview, 104.

47. Devine interview; Suarez interview by Tanzman.

48. Suarez interview by Dent.

49. Moody, *Coming of Age in Mississippi*, 303.

50. Suarez interview by Dent.

51. C. O. Chinn and Robert Chinn interview.

52. "Report on Canton, Madison County, Mississippi," February 26, 1964, series 5, box 15, folder 2, CORE Papers; Dennis interview by Dent; Suarez interview by Tanzman.

53. Quoted in Moody, *Coming of Age in Mississippi*, 327.

54. Ibid., 329.

55. Watkins interview, 43.

56. "Interview: Charles Jones," in Stoper, *The Student Nonviolent Coordinating Committee*, 176.

57. Stoper, *The Student Nonviolent Coordinating Committee*, 28.

58. Leaflet, reprint of M. W. Newman, "Rugged, Ragged 'Snick': What It Is and What It Does," *Chicago Daily News*, [n.d.], folder 2, Kaufman Papers. Another copy can be found in Zwerling Freedom Summer Collection, box 2.

59. Leaflet, reprint of Ben H. Bagdikian, "Negro Youth's New March on Dixie," *Saturday Evening Post*, [n.d.], reel 1, frame 0745, Belfrage Papers, microfilm.

60. Branch, *Parting the Waters*, 519.

61. Burner, *And Gently He Shall Lead Them*, 3.

62. Thrasher, "Circle of Trust," 224.

63. John Lewis, *Walking with the Wind*, 180.

64. Forman, *The Making of Black Revolutionaries*, 148, 150.

65. Cobb interview by Dent; Dennis interview by Dent.

66. "Staff Meeting Minutes June 9–11, 1964," 12–13, box 2, folder 7, Zinn Papers.

67. Ibid., 13.

68. Mary King, *Freedom Song*, 318.

69. John Lewis, *Walking with the Wind*, 248; Mary King, *Freedom Song*, 324; Wright interview, 47; Forman, *The Making of Black Revolutionaries*, 375.

70. John Lewis, *Walking with the Wind*, 248.

71. Mary King, *Freedom Song*, 314; "Staff Meeting Minutes June 9–11, 1964," 14, 15.

72. Forman, *The Making of Black Revolutionaries*, 375.

73. Carson, *In Struggle*, 111; Rothschild, *A Case of Black and White*, 47.

74. Carmichael, *Ready for Revolution*, 370; O'Reilly, "Racial Matters," 159.

75. Belknap, *Federal Law and the Southern Order*, 111.

76. Clemson interview, 46.

77. Quoted in Mills, *Like a Holy Crusade*, 106.

78. Sugarman, *Stranger at the Gates*, 28; Shaw interview, 13; Zeman interview, 178.

79. Steven Bingham, "Mississippi Letter," 1–2, Bingham Papers.

80. Quoted in Alice Lake, "Last Summer in Mississippi," *Redbook Magazine*, November 1964, 113.

81. "Diary and Notes, 1964, June-Aug," entry June 22, Belfrage Papers, microfilm, frame 0459; Zoya Zeman, handwritten notes on Oxford, Ohio, training session, entry "6–22 noon," box 1, folder 6, Zeman Collection.

82. Wright interview, 47; Quoted in Sellers, *The River of No Return*, 83.

83. Sally Belfrage, *Freedom Summer*, 16.

84. Zoya Zeman, handwritten notes on Oxford, Ohio, training session, entry "6–24," box 1, folder 6, Zeman Collection; Jo Ann Ooiman Robinson, Diary 6/21/64–6/26/64, entry "6/24/64."

85. "I. Orientation at Oxford, Ohio June 14–21; 21–28th," 2, Gould Papers.

86. Belfrage, "Diary and Notes, 1964, June-Aug.," reel 1, frame 0477, Belfrage Papers, microfilm; Sugarman, *Stranger at the Gates*, 25.

87. Sally Belfrage, "Manuscript of *Freedom Summer*," 29, reel 1, frame 0026, Belfrage Papers, microfilm.

88. Quoted in Sutherland, *Letters from Mississippi*, 29.

89. Rothschild, *A Case of Black and White*, 47.

90. Zoya Zeman, handwritten notes on Oxford, Ohio, training session, entry "Lomax," Zeman Collection.

91. Lucia Guest, as told to Carol Illig, "Their Dream Is Not to Be Nervous," *Mademoiselle*, November 1964, 206.

92. Wade, *The Fiery Cross*, 333.

93. Curtis Hayes, "Feb. 1, 1964"; "SNCC Worker Reports Reign of Terror in Mississippi," press release, May 16, 1964, both in unprocessed accessions, King Papers.

94. Memorandum, Erle Johnston to Honorable Herman Glazier, May 28, 1964, box 135, folder 9, Johnson Family Papers. For a history of the Sovereignty Commission, see Katagiri, *The Mississippi State Sovereignty Commission.*

95. O'Reilly, *"Racial Matters,"* 160.

96. Quoted in *New York Times*, June 25, 1964. Contrary to Kennedy's statement, the administration occasionally did order the FBI to serve as a protective agency. When Martin Luther King traveled to Mississippi at the end of July 1964, President Johnson instructed FBI director J. Edgar Hoover to make sure that the civil rights leader remained unharmed. When King arrived in Greenwood, an entourage of FBI agents guarded him wherever he went. See Garrow, *Bearing the Cross*, 341–42; Branch, *Pillar of Fire*, 408–9, 412.

97. *Baltimore Afro-American*, July 4, 1964; "Laws Give U.S. Right to Curb Terror in South," *National Guardian*, July 11, 1964, 3.

98. Belknap, *Federal Law and the Southern Order*, 106.

99. *Jackson (Miss.) Clarion-Ledger*, July 23, 1964.

100. Mars, *Witness in Philadelphia*, 114; Sellers, *The River of No Return*, 88, 90.

101. Sellers, *The River of No Return*, 90.

102. Dennis interview by Dent.

103. "Interview with David J. Dennis, June 30, 1972," 1; Dennis interview by Dent.

104. Walter Kaufman, "Mississippi Project," August 15, 1964, Kaufman Papers; Mike (Michael L. Kenney) to Season's Greetings, December 10, 1964, reel 71, frame 0254, SNCC Papers, microfilm.

105. Eugene Nelson to Dear Parents, July 3, 1964, Nelson Papers.

106. McLaurin interview; Bingham, "Mississippi Letter," 14.

107. Eugene Nelson to Dear Parents, August 2, 1964, Nelson Papers.

108. Youth of the Rural Organizing and Cultural Center, *Minds Stayed on Freedom*, 87, 135.

109. Bingham, "Mississippi Letter," 19; Mary Brumder, "Holmes County, Nov. 21, 1964," box 1, folder 5, Ewen Papers.

110. McLaurin interview; Eugene Nelson to Dear Parents, July 3, 1964.

111. Bruce interview.

112. Von Hoffman, *Mississippi Notebook*, 95.

113. Ibid., 94; Hudson interview, 103; Barber interview; "Harmony Builds Center," *Student Voice*, August 12, 1964, 3.

114. Sutherland, *Letters from Mississippi*, 115.

115. Hudson, *Mississippi Harmony*, 88.

116. Smith interview.

117. Sutherland, *Letters from Mississippi*, 115. Both John Dittmer and Akinyele Umoja have called attention to the significance of armed black resistance in Leake County. See Dittmer, *Local People*, 257; Umoja, "1964," 211–12.

118. Umoja, "1964," 210.

119. Nelson, *Terror in the Night*, 108–9; George Wiley to Melvin S. Cohen, January 27, 1965, box 1, folder 7, Currier Papers; Clark interview.

120. Repr. Charles L. Young Sr. interview.

121. Umoja, "1964," 214–18; Dittmer, *Local People*, 306.

122. Alice Lake to Mr. Burke Marshall, August 21, 1964, Lake Papers.

123. Lake, "Last Summer in Mississippi," 112.

124. William Holdes to Dear Folks, July 28, 1964, Holdes Papers.

125. "WATS Report: Tuesday, July 28, 1964," unprocessed accessions, King Papers.

126. Quoted in McAdam, *Freedom Summer*, 90.

127. "Diary," entry 7/14/64, box 2, folder 1, Robinson Papers; "Mississippi Negroes Near Violence, Says Knox Grad," newspaper clipping, [n.d.], box 1, folder 9, Robinson Papers; Sutherland, *Letters from Mississippi*, 45.

128. WATS Line Digest," July 26, 1964, 2, unprocessed accessions, King Papers.

129. Payne, *I've Got the Light of Freedom*, 266; see also Dittmer, *Local People*, 127.

130. Payne, *I've Got the Light of Freedom*, 233; Lee, *For Freedom's Sake*, 9, 11.

131. Hamer, "To Praise Our Bridges," 324, 325.

132. Sutherland, *Letters from Mississippi*, 44.

133. Mary King, *Freedom Song*, 512.

134. Sugarman, *Stranger at the Gates*, 75.

135. Sutherland, *Letters from Mississippi*, 108.

136. Ibid., 148.

137. Holt, *The Summer That Didn't End*, 241; Sally Belfrage, *Freedom Summer*, 174–75, 176.

138. Sally Belfrage, *Freedom Summer*, 225 (emphasis in the original).

139. "Shocking Notes on Miss. Brutality in Just One 21–Hour Period," *Jet*, July 2, 1964, 6.

140. "Report of Operator #79," box 136, folder 1, Johnson Family Papers.

141. Von Hoffman, *Mississippi Notebook*, 95.

142. Forman, *The Making of Black Revolutionaries*, 375.

143. McAdam, *Freedom Summer*, 32; Carson, *In Struggle*, 123.

144. McDew interview, 130.

145. Hodgson, *America in Our Time*, 212.

146. Joseph Alsop, "Matter of Fact," *Washington Post*, June 17, 1964.

147. Julian Bond to Joseph Alsop, June 30, 1964, reel 13, frame 0320, SNCC Papers, microfilm.

148. WATS Report: Wednesday, July 1, 1964," unprocessed accessions, King Papers; Sales, *From Civil Rights to Black Liberation*, 107.

149. "Statement of John Lewis, July 1, 1964," unprocessed accessions, King Papers.

150. Rustin, "Nonviolence on Trial," 5.

151. Horace Julian Bond to Alfred Hassler, October 18, 1964, reel 13, frame 0517, SNCC Papers, microfilm.

152. Evers interview, 9–26.

153. Charles Evers, *Have No Fear*, 171; "Medgar Evers' Brother Sleeps with Gun in Miss.," *Jet*, July 9, 1964, 4.

154. Joel Bernard to Dear Folks, August 1, 1964, box 1, folder 1, Bernard Papers.

155. Bingham, "Mississippi Letter," 2.

156. Charles Evers, *Have No Fear*, 114.

157. Quoted in Warren, *Who Speaks for the Negro?* 105.

158. "Canton, Mississippi: February 28, 1964," box 135, folder 6, Johnson Family Papers.

159. Robert Churchwell, "'If White Man Shoots at Negro, We Will Shoot Back,'" *Nashville Banner*, February 17, 1964.

160. "Address in Nashville Distorted, Evers Says," NAACP Press Release, February 24, 1964, group III, series A, box 114, NAACP Papers; *New York Times*, March 7, 1964.

161. Crosby, "'God's Appointed Savior,'" 167–69.

162. "Meeting of the Executive Committee, February 14, 1966," group IV, series A, box 12, NAACP Papers; Roy Wilkins to Charles Evers, February 18, 1965, box 7, folder "1965," Wilkins Papers.

163. Charles Evers, *Have No Fear*, 171; "Medgar Evers' Brother Sleeps with Gun in Miss.," 4; "Jackson Mississippi March 6, 1965," box 137, folder 3, Johnson Family Papers; Umoja, "'We Will Shoot Back,'" 277.

164. *New York Times*, August 28, 29, 1965.

165. Quoted in *Baltimore Afro-American*, September 4, 1965.

166. Quoted in Drew Pearson "Washington Merry-Go-Round," *New York Post*, September 1, 1965.

167. Quoted in *Commercial Appeal*, September 1, 1965.

168. *New York Post*, September 2, 1965.

169. Roy Wilkins to Charles Evers, September 3, 1965, box 7, folder "1965," Wilkins Papers.

170. *New York Times*, September 10, 1965; *Baltimore Afro-American*, September 18, 1965; Erle Johnston Jr. to Herman Glazier, September 23, 1965, box 138, folder 2, Johnson Family Papers.

171. Roy Wilkins to Charles Evers, [n.d.], draft, box 7, folder "1965," Wilkins Papers.

172. Roy Wilkins to Charles Evers, June 28, 1967, box 8, folder 8, Wilkins Papers; Roy Wilkins, letter to the editor, *New York Times Magazine*, August 25, 1968, 94. After 1966, Evers's leadership in Mississippi became far more effective, a fact that pleased the NAACP and eased the tensions that his militant statements had provoked. See Crosby, "Common Courtesy," 183–85.

173. "Jackson, Mississippi September 11, 1965," box 138, folder 2, Johnson Family Papers.

174. Berg, "Black Power," 252; "Gloster Current Interview, May 1969," box 56, folder 4, Meier Papers; Johnston, *Mississippi's Defiant Years*, 294.

175. Umoja, "'We Will Shoot Back,'" 277–80; Hill, "The Deacons for Defense and Justice," 306–10.

176. Nix interview, 6–8; Magee interview. Historian Akinyele Umoja erroneously states that "Da Spirit" was formed in Natchez, which is more than two hundred miles west of Hattiesburg. Consequently, his thesis that Natchez served as model for similar Mississippi groups is no longer tenable. See Umoja, "'We Will Shoot Back,'" 285.

177. Nix interview, 17.

178. Daniel J. Wacker, "Mississippi Journal: July 1965," 10, box 1, folder 5, Wacker Papers.

179. Joel Bernard, "Clay County, Miss., August 20, 1965," box 1, folder 2, Bernard Papers.

180. "Executive Committee Meeting, Holly Springs, Mississippi, April 12th thru the 14th," 1965, 9, unprocessed accessions, King Papers.

181. Ibid., 10. In a discussion among Alabama SNCC staff one week later, the activists came to a similar conclusion, which is another indication of the increasing support for armed self-defense. See "Alabama Staff Workshop April 21–23, '65," 10, unprocessed accessions, King Papers.

182. Carson, *In Struggle*, 164; Hodgson, *America in Our Time*, 212.

183. Quoted in *New York Times*, February 22, 1965.

184. Stoper, *The Student Nonviolent Coordinating Committee*, 29.

Chapter 5. Black Power and White Fear

1. Quoted in *New York Times*, June 17, 1966.

2. Quoted in Sellers, *The River of No Return*, 166–67.

3. Paul Good, "A White Look at Black Power," *Nation*, August 6, 1966, 114.

4. James K. Cazales, "Deacons for Defense Play Unannounced Role in March," *Commercial Appeal*, June 25, 1966.

5. Sellers, *The River of No Return*, 111.

6. Carson, *In Struggle*, 2–3; Carmichael, *Ready for Revolution*, 255.

7. "Suggestions for Direction of SNCC," 4–6; "May 11 1966, SNCC Staff Conference," both in box 2, folder 11, SNCC-Arkansas Project Records.

8. "Suggestions for Direction of SNCC," 4.

9. Forman, *The Making of Black Revolutionaries*, 449.

10. *New York Times*, June 6, 1966.

11. Quoted in James H. Meredith, "Big Changes Are Coming," *Saturday Evening Post*, August 13, 1966, 24.

12. *New York Times*, June 7, 1966.

13. Quoted in ibid., 29.

14. *Baltimore Afro-American*, February 12, 1966.

15. Southern Regional Council, Inc., "Press Release," June 13, 1966, box 56, folder 3, Braden Papers.

16. James H. Meredith to Sheriff of Holmes County, March 8, 1966, doc. no. 1–67–4–47–1–1–1, MSSC.

17. Quoted in "'He Shot Me Like . . . a Goddam Rabbit,'" *Newsweek*, June 20, 1966, 30.

18. Quoted in *New York Times*, June 8, 1966.

19. John Oliver Killens, "Negroes Have a Right to Fight Back," *Saturday Evening Post*, July 2, 1966, 10. See also Killens, *Black Man's Burden*, 99.

20. Chester Higgins, "Meredith's Threat to Arm Not Answer, Says Dr. King," *Jet*, June 23, 1966, 17.

21. Ibid., 17.

22. Meredith, "Big Changes Are Coming," 26.

23. Garrow, *Bearing the Cross*, 477; Sellers, *The River of No Return*, 162; King, *Where Do We Go from Here*, 26.

24. Carmichael, *Ready for Revolution*, 497.

25. "Manifesto of the Meredith Mississippi Freedom March," doc. no. 1–67–4–130–1–1–1, MSCC.

26. "The March Meredith Began," *Newsweek*, June 20, 1966, 30; Memorandum, Roy Wilkins to the Delegates of the 57th Annual NAACP Convention, July 5, 1966, group IV, series A, box 81, NAACP Papers.

27. Carmichael, *Ready for Revolution*, 498; Wilkins, *Standing Fast*, 316; Roy Wilkins to the Delegates of the 57th Annual NAACP Convention, July 5, 1966; *New York Times*, June 9, 1966.

28. *New York Times*, June 10, 1966; Cazales, "Deacons for Defense Play Unannounced Role in March," 1; Hampton and Fayer, *Voices of Freedom*, 286; Sellers, *The River of No Return*, 165; Hicks interview, 23.

29. Sellers, *The River of No Return*, 166.

30. *New York Times*, June 14, 1966.

31. Quoted in Dan Styron, "'Black Power' was the Rallying Cry," *Militant*, July 11, 1966, 8.

32. *New York Times*, June 21, 1966; King, *Where Do We Go from Here*, 30; King quoted in *New York Times*, June 22, 1966.

33. "June 20, 1965 [1966] Louise, Mississippi," box 139, folder 1, Johnson Family Papers.

34. "Report Received by Telephone June 23, 1966," box 139, folder 1, Johnson Family Papers.

35. Quoted in Margaret Long, "Black Power in the Black Belt," *Progressive*, October 1966, 21.

36. Ronnie Brown, "Affidavit: State of Mississippi, County of Hinds," June 1966, reel 149, SCRLR, microfilm; Joe Morse, "Meridian Project Report," July 5, 1966, 3, reel 17, frame 0012, CORE Papers, Addendum, microfilm.

37. *New York Times*, June 22, 1966; Barber interview.

38. Nicholas von Hoffman, "Marchers, FBI Differ on Gunfire," *Washington Post*, June 23, 1966.

39. "C. O. Chinn v. State of Mississippi," reel 13, SCRLR, microfilm; "Report Received by Telephone June 23, 1966."

40. *New York Times*, June 24, 1966; Crawford interview.

41. *New York Times*, June 23, 1966.

42. "June 24, 1966," box 139, folder 1, Johnson Family Papers.

43. Quoted in Neil A. Maxwell, "Militancy on the March," *Wall Street Journal*, June 24, 1966.

44. Quoted in *Los Angeles Times*, July 3, 1966.

45. "Minutes of the 23rd Annual Convention of C.O.R.E.," July 1–July 4, 1966, box 2, folder 1, Meier-Rudwick Collection.

46. *New York Times*, July 2, 3, 1966.

47. Richard Haley, "CORE Southern Staff Conference, New Orleans, Louisiana, February 6 and 7, 1966," Curvin Papers.

48. *New York Times*, July 3, 1966; Meier and Rudwick, *CORE*, 399.

49. Quoted in Bell, *CORE and the Strategy of Nonviolence*, 57.

50. Quoted in *New York Times*, June 10, 1966.

51. "Resolutions for the Resolution Committee of the National Convention of CORE, July 1 to July 4 from the Northeast Region," series 4, box 1, folder 4, CORE Papers.

52. "Minutes of the 23rd Annual Convention of C.O.R.E."; "Minutes of Western Regional Convention of September 3 and 4, 1966," box 2, folder 12, CORE Papers—Western Regional Office Files.

53. Bill Bradley, "Our Southern Projects 'A Review,'" Gartner Papers.

54. Quoted in *New York Times*, June 12, 1966.

55. Quoted in "At the Breaking Point," *Time*, July 15, 1966, 15.

56. Loveland, *Lillian Smith*, 223, 237–38.

57. Quoted in George B. Leonard, "Not Black Power, But Human Power," *Look*, September 1966, 42. See also *New York Times*, July 6, 1966.

58. "The New Racism," *Time*, July 1, 1966, 9–11; "Black Power: Road to Disaster," *Newsweek*, August 22, 1966, 32–36.

59. Good, "The Meredith March," 3.

60. Lester, *Look Out, Whitey!* 101.

61. Transcript of an interview with Floyd McKissick, in Hampton and Fayer, *Voices of Freedom*, 292.

62. Quoted in Good, "A White Look at Black Power," 114.

63. Wilkins, *Standing Fast*, 318.

64. "Keynote Address of ROY WILKINS, Executive Director National Association for the Advancement of Colored People before Its Fifty-Seventh Annual Convention First Methodist Church, Los Angeles, California, July 5, 1966," group IV, series A, box 3, NAACP Papers. See also *New York Times*, July 6, 1966.

65. Martin Luther King Jr., *Where Do We Go from Here*, 33, 36, 38, 40; Ling, *Martin Luther King, Jr.*, 248–49, 252–53; Kirk, *Martin Luther King, Jr.*, 150.

66. Martin Luther King Jr., *Where Do We Go From Here*, 54, 52.

67. Garrow, *Bearing the Cross*, 490.

68. "Excerpts from the Text of an Address by Martin Luther King Jr.: Southern Christian Leadership Conference Tenth Annual Convention, Jackson, Mississippi, August 11, 1966," part 3, reel 9, frame 00712, SCLC Papers, microfilm.

69. Martin Luther King, "It Is Not Enough to Condemn Black Power," advertisement, *New York Times*, July 26, 1966.

70. Berg, "Black Power," 239.

71. Roy Wilkins to Dear Friend, October 21, 1966, box 86, folder 9, Meier Papers. Another copy can be found in Holden Papers, box 1, folder 3.

72. Roy Wilkins, "Separatism in 'Black Power' Seen by Wilkins," *New York Times*, October 31, 1966.

73. Wilkins, *Standing Fast*, 319.

74. Berg, "Black Power," 245.

75. Between 1966 and 1968, the NAACP's income rose from $597,425 to $1,904,512. SCLC's income increased by a more modest 10 percent. See Haines, *Black Radicals and the Civil Rights Mainstream*, 84, table 8. By 1968, however, the NAACP supported

Black Power and adopted many of the positions that its leaders had denounced in 1966. It defined Black Power as the control of the black community's "economic, educational, and political institutions," an interpretation that clearly echoed the positions that SNCC and CORE had adopted shortly after the Meredith March. See Berg, "Black Power," 241.

76. Quoted in *Washington Post*, June 17, 1963.

77. "Wilkins vs. 'Black Power,'" *Rocky Mountain News*, July 9, 1966.

78. Michael G. Bradley to Dr. Martin Luther King, received August 22, 1966, part 1, reel 16, frame 00812, SCLC papers, microfilm.

79. Mary Budesa to Martin Luther King Jr., July 27, 1966, part 1, reel 16, frame 00629, SCLC Papers, microfilm.

80. *Meet the Press*, Sunday, August 21, 1966, 10, 11.

81. R. J. Bob Baldun to My Dear Dr. King, June 11, 1966, part 1, reel 15, frame 00533, SCLC Papers, microfilm.

82. *Meet the Press*, Sunday, August 21, 1966, 21.

83. Ibid., 21.

84. Mrs. C. Temple to Dear Sirs, August 22, 1966, box 55, folder "civil rights," Spivak Papers.

85. Braden, "Not Violence, but Political Action," 3.

86. Abbie Hoffman, "SNCC: The Desecration of a Delayed Dream," *Village Voice*, December 15, 1966, 6.

87. Carmichael, *Ready for Revolution*, 540.

88. Joe W. Walker to Harry Belafonte, [n.d.], SNCC Papers, reel 2, frame 0217, microfilm.

89. Handwritten notes on fund-raising letter by Stokely Carmichael to Dear Friend, [n.d.], reel 2, frame 0128, 0125, SNCC Papers, microfilm.

90. "CORE Offers to Pay 25 Cents on the Dollar for $200,000 It Owes," *Wall Street Journal*, November 4, 1966; "Fund Appeal by CORE Concedes 'Black Power' Alienates Some Whites," *Wall Street Journal*, November 8, 1966.

91. Martin Luther King, "Nonviolence: The Only Road to Freedom," *Ebony*, October 1966, 30.

92. A. L. Hopkins, "Investigation of a Report That a Group of Negro Males Have Organized a Unit of 'Black Panthers' in Port Gibson, Mississippi," July 11, 1966, box 139, folder 2, Johnson Family Papers; L. E. Cole, "Boycott and Civil Rights Activities in Area of Fayette and Port Gibson, Mississippi," September 30, 1966, box 139, folder 4, Johnson Family Papers; L. E. Cole, "Port Gibson, Mississippi, Claiborne County," December 30, 1966, box 139, folder 7, Johnson Family Papers.

93. Umoja, "'We Will Shoot Back,'" 271.

94. Letterhead memorandum, "Deacons of Defense and Justice, Inc.," November 27, 1967, Deacons FBI File 157–2466–250; L. E. Cole Jr., "Boycott and Civil Rights Activity, Port Gibson, Mississippi and Fayette, Mississippi," September 27, 1966, doc. no. 2–51–0–51–1–1–1, MSSC.

95. A. L. Hopkins, "General Investigation in Several Delta Counties," January 27, 1967, box 139, folder 8, Johnson Family Papers.

96. Crosby, "Common Courtesy," 233.

97. Evers quoted in *New York Times*, October 12, 1967.

98. Letterhead memorandum, "Deacons for Defense and Justice, Inc.," November 27, 1967, Deacons FBI File 157–2466–250.

99. *New York Times*, September 15, 1966.

100. Fairclough, *Race and Democracy*, 374; Honigsberg, *Crossing Border Street*, 24, 33, 43–44.

101. Honigsberg, *Crossing Border Street*, 52.

102. *New York Times*, July 24, 25, 1967.

103. Lynch quoted in *New Orleans Times-Picayune*, July 25, 1967.

104. *New York Times*, August 11, 14, 18, 1967.

105. Honigsberg, *Crossing Border Street*, 139.

106. *New York Times*, August 19, 21, 1967.

107. Letterhead memorandum, "Deacons of Defense and Justice, Inc.," November 27, 1967; memorandum, W. C. Sullivan to R. W. Smith, March 26, 1968, Deacons FBI File 157–2466–266. In early 1970, the FBI terminated its investigation of the group. SAC, New Orleans to Director, FBI, February 17, 1970, Deacons FBI File 157–2466–279.

108. Crosby, "Common Courtesy," 405.

109. Hicks interview by Wright, 12.

Chapter 6. Black Manhood and the End of Nonviolence

1. Transcript of an interview with Charles Sims, in Raines, *My Soul Is Rested*, 423.

2. Charles Evers, *Evers*, 145.

3. P. L. Prattis, "Non-Violence," *Pittsburgh Courier*, November 30, 1957.

4. P. L. Prattis, "Non-Violence II," *Pittsburgh Courier*, December 7, 1957.

5. P. L. Prattis, "Non-Violence IV," *Pittsburgh Courier*, December 21, 1957; P. L. Prattis, "Non-Violence V," *Pittsburgh Courier*, December 28, 1957.

6. Charles X, "Law and Buckshot," *Baltimore Afro-American*, May 30, 1959.

7. "Freedom Riders Go beyond the New Frontier," 2.

8. McDonald interview, 21.

9. Keith Younger, "Violence vs Nonviolence," *Baltimore Afro-American*, June 1, 1963.

10. Mr. Revresbo, "Eye for an Eye," *Baltimore Afro-American*, August 24, 1963.

11. *New York Times*, September 21, 1963; *Baltimore Afro-American*, September 18, 1963.

12. Edgar Leslie to Dear Friends, September 19, 1963, box 1, folder 4, CORE–Western Regional Office Files.

13. Malcolm's *Autobiography of Malcolm X* remains one of the most impressive accounts of his life. Good scholarly studies on Malcolm X include Breitman, *The Last Year of Malcolm X*; Goldman, *The Death and Life of Malcolm X*; Perry, *Malcolm*; and Wolfenstein, *The Victims of Democracy*. On the NOI, see Clegg, *An Original Man* and Lincoln, *The Black Muslims in America*.

14. "Malcolm X Talks with Kenneth B. Clark," in Clarke, *Malcolm X*, 176.

15. Quoted in *New York Times*, June 5, 1963, 29.

16. "Message to the Grass Roots," in Breitman, *Malcolm X Speaks*, 9, 12.

17. *New York Times*, June 17, 1963; Lincoln, *The Black Muslims in America*, 4, 20, 154, 186, 205; Clegg, *An Original Man*, 122; Strain, "Civil Rights & Self-Defense," 65.

18. Malcolm X, *The Autobiography of Malcolm X*, 416. On the Organization of Afro-American Unity, see Sales, *From Civil Rights to Black Liberation*.

19. Quoted in *New York Times*, March 13, 1964.

20. *Amsterdam News*, March 28, 1964, 35; Gertrude Samuels, "Feud within the Black Muslims," *New York Times Magazine*, March 22, 1964, 104; *Baltimore Afro-American*, March 21, 1964.

21. Quoted in *Amsterdam News*, July 4, 1964.

22. Quoted in *New York Times*, May 11, 1963.

23. "With Mrs. Fannie Lou Hamer," in Breitman, *Malcolm X Speaks*, 107.

24. Quoted in Perry, *Malcolm*, 282.

25. "The Founding Rally of the OAAU," in Malcolm X, *By Any Means Necessary*, 53. The OAAU's membership card, for example, stated only one declaration of purpose: "We assert and affirm the right of self-defense, which is one of the most basic human rights known to mankind." Quoted in Goldman, *The Death and Life of Malcolm X*, 187.

26. Perry, "Malcolm X and the Politics of Masculinity," 22.

27. Estes, "'I Am A Man,'" 93–94, 103. The banner heading can be seen in a picture reproduced in Goldman, *The Death and Life of Malcolm X*.

28. Clegg, *An Original Man*, 101, 122; Estes, *I Am a Man!* 91.

29. Griffin, "Black Feminists and Du Bois," 35; Griffin, "'Ironies of the Saint,'" 214–17.

30. "To Arms with Malcolm X," *New York Times*, March 14, 1964.

31. "The Pied Piper of Harlem," *Christian Century*, April 1, 1964, 422.

32. "Brother Malcolm: His Theme Now Is Violence," *U.S. News & World Report*, March 23, 1964, 19.

33. *New York Times*, March 16, 1964.

34. *Amsterdam News*, May 9, 1964.

35. *Baltimore Afro-American*, May 23, 1964.

36. Quoted in "Clear Harlem Rifle Club of Link to Any Hate Group," *Jet*, June 4, 1964, 52.

37. "Whatever Is Necessary: The Last Television Interview, with Pierre Berton," in Gallen, *Malcolm X As They Knew Him*, 184.

38. *New York Times*, December 21, 1964; "Malcolm X: Power in Defense of Freedom Is Greater than Power in Behalf of Tyranny," *Militant*, January 25, 1965, 4; *New York Times*, February 22, 1965; Goldman, "Malcolm X: Witness for the Prosecution," 318.

39. See Theoharis and Woodard, *Freedom North*.

40. Zannes, *Checkmate in Cleveland*, 8; "An Open Letter to the Power Structure," [n.d.], box 1, folder 3, Gordon Papers.

41. Lewis G. Robinson, *The Making of a Man*, 2–57.

42. "The Freedom Fighters Speak" [n.d], box 1, folder 4, Gordon Papers.

43. Moore, "The School Desegregation Crisis of Cleveland, Ohio," 137–47.

44. *Cleveland Press*, January 30, 1964.

45. Ibid., January 31, 1964.

46. Lewis G. Robinson, *The Making of a Man*, 61.

47. Larry Still, "Talk Is of a Revolution—Complete with Mixed Blood," *Jet*, November 28, 1963, 14–19; "Resolutions Passed at the Northern Grass Roots Leadership Conference, Detroit, Michigan, November 9–10, 1963," box 1, folder 4, Gordon Papers.

48. "Interview with Mr. Arthur Evans, March 13, 1971," 6, box 56, folder 5, Meier Papers.

49. Lewis G. Robinson, *The Making of a Man*, 76.

50. "Ruth and Antoine Perot, Jr., Interview, April 17, 1972," 7, box 57, folder 1, Meier Papers.

51. Robinson interview, 19–20.

52. Lewis G. Robinson, *The Making of a Man*, 76–77.

53. *Baltimore Afro-American*, April 18, 1964; "The Ballot or the Bullet," in Breitman, *Malcolm X Speaks*, 30.

54. Lewis G. Robinson, *The Making of a Man*, 78.

55. Quoted in *Cleveland Press*, April 6, 1964.

56. "'Rights' Rifle Club Asking for Trouble," *Cleveland Press*, April 6, 1964.

57. *Cleveland Press*, April 7, 1964; *Washington Post*, April 8, 1964; *Amsterdam News*, April 11, 1964.

58. Lewis G. Robinson, *The Making of a Man*, 98.

59. *Cleveland Press*, April 10, 1964.

60. Ibid., April 13, 1964.

61. Lewis G. Robinson, *The Making of a Man*, 79; "Interview with Mr. Arthur Evans, March 13, 1971," 6; "Ruth and Antoine Perot, Jr., Interview, April 17, 1972," 8; "David Cohen Interview, Dec. 19, 1970," 2, all in box 56, folder 3, Meier Papers; "Interview with Bernard Mandel, April 25, 1970," 11, box 56, folder 12, Meier Papers.

62. Lewis G. Robinson, *The Making of a Man*, 61.

63. Ibid., 121.

64. Ibid., 122–30.

65. Robinson interview, 8.

66. Lewis G. Robinson, *The Making of a Man*, 112.

67. Robinson interview, 8.

68. Watts, "Malcolm X," 3.

69. Quoted in "Form Rifle Clubs, Militant Detroiter Urges," *Jet*, July 16, 1964, 7; "'Have Guns and Will Travel,'" *Baltimore Afro-American*, July 11, 1964, 13.

70. Dealia Mathis, letter to the editor, *Ebony*, November 1964, 16.

71. Van Deburg, *New Day in Babylon*, 2.

72. Coretta Scott King, *My Life with Martin Luther King, Jr.*, 256.

73. Jones, "What Does Nonviolence Mean?" 15.

74. Bond, "Nonviolence," 162.

75. Sykes, "Self-Defense," 12.

76. L. Y. Lemon, letter to the editor, *Ebony*, November 1965, 13.

77. Braden, "New Light on Monroe, N.C.," 2.

78. Robert F. Williams, "USA: The Potential of a Minority Revolution," *Crusader* 5 (May-June 1964): 6.

79. *New York Times*, July 28, 1964.

80. Jane McManus, "An Exile Warns of Race 'Explosion' in the U.S.," *National Guardian*, September 12, 1964, 6.

81. "Trigger of Hate," *Time*, August 20, 1965, 16; Conot, *Rivers of Blood*, 219.

82. *New York Times*, August 14, 1965; Horne, *Fire This Time*, 3.

83. Scot Brown, *Fighting for US*, 32.

84. Feagin and Hahn, *Ghetto Revolts*, 44.

85. Russell Sacket, "A War on Whitey," *Life*, June 10, 1966, 100.

86. Ibid., 101; *New York Times*, May 17, 1967.

87. Philip A. McCombs, "Who Is Behind the Race Riots?" *National Review*, September 20, 1966, 934–35.

88. Scot Brown, *Fighting for US*, 29, 38–39.

89. *New York Times*, March 27, 1966.

90. Fanon, *The Wretched of the Earth*, 73.

91. Scot Brown, *Fighting for US*, 40, 32, 120.

92. Carmichael and Hamilton, *Black Power*, 34, 37, 52.

93. "What We Want," October 1966, in Foner, *The Black Panthers Speak*, 2–4.

94. Newton, *Revolutionary Suicide*, 111, 120; Seale, *Seize the Time*, 25; Robert L. Allen, "Panthers Assert Right to Armed Self-Defense," *National Guardian*, January 6, 1968, 6; Seale interview, 9.

95. Seale, *A Lonely Rage*, 130; Newton, *Revolutionary Suicide*, 111–12.

96. Sol Stern, "The Call of the Black Panthers," *New York Times Magazine*, August 6, 1967, 10–11; *New York Times*, May 3, 1967; Seale, *Seize the Time*, 153–56.

97. Seale, *Seize the Time*, 157.

98. "Executive Mandate No. 1: May 2, 1967," in Newton, *To Die for the People*, 7, 8.

99. Newton, *Revolutionary Suicide*, 120–27, 146; Seale, *Seize the Time*, 85–101; "Reagan Signs Curb on Loaded Weapons," *New York Times*, July 19, 1967.

100. Huey P. Newton, "The Correct Handling of a Revolution: July 20, 1967," in Newton, *To Die for the People*, 15–16.

101. Newton, *Revolutionary Suicide*, 122.

102. "The Spirit of Lawlessness," *New York Times*, 1967, May 7.

103. Seale, *Seize the Time*, 71.

104. Quoted in Allen, "Panthers Assert Right to Armed Self-Defense," 6.

105. "Executive Mandate No. 3: March 1, 1968," in Newton, *To Die for the People*, 12.

106. Newton, *Revolutionary Suicide*, 111.

107. It is important to emphasize that the BPP's ideology evolved over several stages, beginning with a black nationalist analysis that was based on racial solidarity but incorporated elements of Marxist class analysis. From 1968 to 1970, the organization advocated a fusion of Marxist socialism and revolutionary nationalism that called for class alliances. After 1970, the BPP sought to establish global socialism through revolutionary intercommunalism, which would overthrow U.S. imperialism and capitalism through alliances among revolutionaries around the world. See Hayes and Kiene, "'All Power to the People,'" 157–76.

108. Sales, *From Civil Rights to Black Liberation*, 129–30; Anne Braden, "Nationalist," [n.d.], box 1, folder 9, Braden Papers.

109. When asked how he felt about Black Power in the 1960s, Mallisham was highly critical of the militant posture of the new militants and condemned what he termed a "destructive" program. Mallisham interview by author, March 19, 2002.

110. Quoted in Garrow, *Bearing the Cross*, 566.

111. Quoted in *New York Times*, May 21, 1967; "From 'In Defense of Self-Defense' II: July 3, 1967," in Newton, *To Die for the People*, 90.

112. Seale, *A Lonely Rage*, 131.

113. Quoted in Ronald Stevenson, "Why They Joined the Panthers," *New York Daily World*, July 19, 1968.

114. "Interview with Huey Newton," in Meier, Rudwick, and Brodwick, *Black Protest Thought in the Twentieth Century*, 508.

115. Cleaver, *Soul on Ice*, 26.

116. Ibid., 101–6.

117. Harper, *Are We Not Men?* 50.

118. In a letter to his lawyer, Beverly Axelrod, Cleaver described the power struggle among prisoners, who labeled any sign of weakness as evidence of effeminacy. His admission of having had sex with fellow prisoners due to lack of access to women further indicates how the traumatic experience of imprisonment influenced Cleaver's obsession with regaining his manhood after his release. For the complete text of the letter, see Finzsch, "'Picking up the Gun,'" 242 n. 58. On the problem of homophobia in the BPP, see Estes, *I am a Man!* 162–63.

119. Cleaver, *Soul on Ice*, 189.

120. "Playboy Interview: Eldridge Cleaver," *Playboy*, December 1968, 92.

121. Huey Newton later stated that Cleaver's preoccupation with manhood alienated the BPP from the black community and contributed to the difficulties that the party faced in the early 1970s. See Newton, *Revolutionary Suicide*, 330–31.

122. Doss, "Imaging the Panthers," 491.

123. Newton, *Revolutionary Suicide*, 133.

124. Ogbar, *Black Power*, 102; Doss, "Imaging the Panthers," 493; LeBlanc-Ernest, "'The Most Qualified Person to Handle the Job,'" 307; Matthews, "'No One Ever Asks What a Man's Place in the Revolution Is,'" 269, 278; Finzsch, "'Picking up the Gun,'" 239.

125. Scot Brown, *Fighting for US*, 56.

126. LeBlanc-Ernest, "'The Most Qualified Person to Handle the Job,'" 309–23; Matthews, "'No One Ever Asks What a Man's Place in the Revolution Is,'" 273, 293.

127. Transcript of an interview with Sonia Sanchez, in Hampton and Fayer, *Voices of Freedom*, 255.

128. Wallace, *Black Macho and the Myth of the Superwoman*, 37.

129. Richardson (Dandridge) interview, 53.

130. Speech by Stokely Carmichael at Tougaloo College, Jackson, Mississippi, April 11, 1967, tape recording, box 183, tape 22, Johnson Family Papers.

131. Quoted in "Stokely Carmichael," May 16, 1967, 2, FBI Deacons File 157-2466-232.

132. Price, *Civil Rights*, 2: 5, 20, 44.

133. "Executive Mandate No. 2: June 29, 1967," in Newton, *To Die for the People*, 9.

134. Quoted in Jack A. Smith, "'Guns are the Only Way . . .,'" *National Guardian*, August 12, 1967, 6. See also *New York Times*, August 3, 1967.

135. "Statement Made by SNCC Chairman H. Rap Brown Minutes before He was Arrested in Washington, D.C. Airport, July 26, 1967," box 2, folder 18, Clark Collection.

136. *New York Times*, July 25, 1967; "Black Militants Talk of Guns and Guerillas," *U.S. News & World Report*, August 7, 1967, 32.

137. Peter Levy has shown that, during what white authorities castigated as a riot, only one building burned to the ground, and that no looting or clashes between blacks and white police officers occurred. See Levy, *Civil War on Race Street*, 141–44.

138. *Meet the Press*, August 13, 1967, 3.

139. Quoted in *New York Times*, July 10, 1967.

140. McKnight, *The Last Crusade*, 21–22.

141. Quoted in *New York Times*, May 4, 1967.

142. H. Rap Brown, *Die Nigger Die!* 37, 114.

143. Quoted in *New York Times*, April 5, 1968, 26.

144. "Black Catholic Clergy Caucus Position Paper," April 16–18, 1968, 2, box 27, folder 17, Scholarship, Education and Defense Fund for Racial Equality Records.

145. *New York Times*, August 1, 1967; Price, *Civil Rights*, 2: 230–31.

146. Kenneth Marshal, "National Convention–CORE–Oakland, California, July 1–July 5, 1967," 1–2, 7, box 2, folder 2, Meier-Rudwick Collection; Allen, *Black Awakening in Capitalist America*, 130–32; *New York Times*, July 6, 1967; David Feingold to Valerie Jorrin, Supervisor CORE Unit, [n.d.], folder 1, David Feingold Papers.

147. McKissick interview, 18.

148. Congress of Racial Equality, "A Brief History of the Congress of Racial Equality," February 1969, box 3, folder 3, Meier-Rudwick Collection.

149. "Carmichael's News Conference—Inciting to Violence?" *U.S. News & World Report*, April 22, 1968, 49–50.

150. Robert Carl Cohen, "The Negro Che Guevara: Will He Turn the U.S.A. into Another Viet Nam?" 19–21, 27, box 5, folder 3, Cohen Papers.

151. *New York Times*, August 24, 30, 1967.

152. Ibid., April 1, 1968; "Now We Have a Nation: The Republic of New Africa," 12, Third National Black Power Conference Records.

153. Van Deburg, *New Day in Babylon*, 147.

154. Cohen, *Black Crusader*, 333.

155. Robert F. Williams interview by Cohen, July 20, 1968, 22.

156. Robert F. Williams interview by Cohen, ca. 1968.

157. "His Best Credentials: On the Air with Joe Rainey," in Gallen, *Malcolm X As They Knew Him*, 164–65.

158. Cruse, *The Crisis of the Negro Intellectual*, 382, 390.

159. Austin, "The Role of Violence in the Creation, Sustenance, and Destruction of the Black Panther Party," 323; Churchill, "'To Disrupt, Discredit, and Destroy,'" 78–117; O'Reilly, "*Racial Matters*," 293–324.

160. *New York Times*, August 8, 1967.

161. Quoted in *New York Times*, May 19, 1968.

162. Umoja, "Repression Breeds Resistance," 3–19.

163. Newton, *Revolutionary Suicide*, 149–50.

164. Van Deburg, *New Day in Babylon*, 160.

165. Newton, *Revolutionary Suicide*, 329.

166. "On the Defection of Eldridge Cleaver from the Black Panther Party and the Defection of the Black Panther Party from the Black Community: April 17, 1971," in Newton, *To Die for the People*, 48–49.

167. Seale interview, 1; Courtwright, "Rhetoric of the Gun," 249–67.

Conclusion

1. Reynolds interview, 32.

2. Garrow, *Bearing the Cross*, 316–17; Colburn, *Racial Change and Community Crisis*, 50–55; Kallal, "St. Augustine and the Ku Klux Klan," 136–37.

3. Quoted in Hartley, "A Long Hot Summer," 21.

4. Garrow, *Bearing the Cross*, 317–34; Colburn, *Racial Change and Community Crisis*, 84–89, 212.

5. Levy, *Civil War on Race Street*, 10–59.

6. *New York Times*, June 12, 1963.

7. Paul Cowan, unpublished manuscript, 14, box 1, folder 2, Cowan Papers. See also "Gloria Richardson," *Newsweek*, August 5, 1963, 26.

8. Student Nonviolent Coordinating Committee, "Martial Law Declared Again after Shooting in Cambridge," July 12, 1963, box 1, folder 16, Zinn Papers.

9. Levy, *Civil War on Race Street*, 83–86; Szabo, "An Interview with Gloria Richardson Dandridge," 354; *Baltimore Afro-American*, July 20, 1963.

10. Cambridge Nonviolent Action Committee, "The Negro Ward of Cambridge, Maryland: A Study in Social Change," September 1963, 56, folder 1, Cambridge Nonviolent Action Committee Papers. See also Levy, *Civil War on Race Street*, 99.

11. Cambridge Nonviolent Action Committee, "Cambridge, Maryland: Background Information," box 1, folder 6, Zinn Papers.

12. Sellers, *The River of No Return*, 68, 74. See also Carmichael, *Ready for Revolution*, 339.

13. "Gloria Richardson: Lady General of Civil Rights," *Ebony*, July 1964, 24.

14. Wade, *The Fiery Cross*, 315.

15. John R. Salter Jr. to Francis Mitchell and Mandy Samstein, October 6, 1964, box 1, folder 33, Salter Papers; John R. Salter Jr. to Dear Folks, July 6, 1964, box 1, folder 6, Salter Papers.

16. Salter, *Jackson, Mississippi*, 240.

17. John R. Salter to Governor Terry Sanford, [n.d.], telegram, box 1, folder 22, Salter Papers; *Baltimore Afro-American*, August 15, 1964; "6/14/65," 27–30, John R. Salter, Jr. FBI File 44–29407, unprocessed accessions, Salter Papers.

18. John R. Salter Jr. to Francis Mitchell and Mandy Samstein, October 6, 1964.

19. Salter, "Civil Rights and Self-Defense," 24.

20. John R. Salter, Jr., "Memo to Jim Dombrowski and Carl Braden RE Monroe, N.C.," February 19, 1964, box 56, folder 5, Braden Papers.

21. "Chronology of Events—Moss Point Shooting 6 July, 10:10 P.M.," reel 39, frame 0263, SNCC Papers, microfilm; Mary King, "Report: July 6–7, 1964," unprocessed accessions, King Papers.

22. "C. O. Chinn, Sr.," reel 13, SCRLR, microfilm.

23. Andy Hopkins to Erle Johnston Jr., April 13, 1964, box 135, folder 8, Johnson Family Papers.

24. "Security Handbook," box 1, folder 5, Clark Collection.

25. "Canton, Mississippi: February 26, 1964," box 135, folder 6, Johnson Family Papers.

26. *New York Times*, July 19, 20, 22, 23, 1967.

27. Rosenthal, "Where Rumor Raged," 212.

28. Already in the aftermath of the Civil War, southern white authorities had attempted to restrict black access to firearms through state legislation. For example, the so-called Black Codes that southern state legislatures passed after the war not only restricted the rights of black plantation workers but also limited their ability to defend themselves. Some legal scholars have suggested that former Confederate states attempted to continue this practice after the repeal of the Black Codes in 1867 by passing concealed weapons laws. Fleming, *A Documentary History of Reconstruction*, 279–80, 289–90, 271–72; Cottrol and Diamond, "'Never Intended to Be Applied to the White Population,'" 1307–35; DeConde, *Gun Violence in America*, 72; Cramer, *For the Defense of Themselves and the State*, 138.

29. DeConde, *Gun Violence in America*, 177; *New York Times*, July 2, 19, August 2, 1967.

30. *Meet the Press*, July 14, 1968, 6. In this spirit, CORE collaborated with the National Rifle Association (NRA) in the 1980s to liberalize the handgun laws in the state of New York, promoting it as a crime-prevention strategy. See "Congress of Racial Equality (CORE)," 70.

31. *Meet the Press*, July 16, 1967, 9. Hitherto, legal historians have largely ignored such allusions to the racial dimension of the Second Amendment. Armed self-defense in the black freedom struggle of the 1960s could open up avenues for fresh research perspectives in this field. Legal historian Robert Cottrol and his colleague Raymond Diamond have long lamented the fact that legal scholars have neglected the racial dimension of the Second Amendment. Except for Stephen Halbrook, few historians have heeded their pleas for a more inclusive research agenda. See Cottrol and Diamond, "The Second Amendment: Toward an Afro-American Reconsideration"; Halbrook, *Freedmen, the Fourteenth Amendment, and the Right to Bear Arms.*

32. Salter and Kates, "The Necessity of Access to Firearms by Dissenters and Minorities," 192.

33. Quoted in *New York Times*, June 6, 1965.

34. Weiss, "A Reply to Advocates of Gun-Control Law," 583.

35. Hare, "The Frustrated Masculinity of the Negro Male," 7.

36. Young, *An Easy Burden*, 404.

37. Van Deburg, *New Day in Babylon*, 9–10.

38. "The 3rd National Conference on Black Power—1968, Philadelphia, Penna., August 29–September 1," Third National Black Power Conference Records.

39. Van Deburg, *New Day in Babylon*, 297–98.

40. Salter, "Civil Rights and Self-Defense," 25.

41. For example, Jenny Walker contends that "it was the constant threat and occasional outbreaks of black violence—rather than the nonviolent marches themselves—that actually convinced civic leaders to negotiate and ultimately yield to the demonstrators' demands." Walker, "A Media-Made Movement?" 59. Lance Hill ventures even further, conceptualizing race riots as "acts of defensive violence" that protected "the black community from police or white terrorist violence." Coupled with the self-defense program of the Louisiana Deacons, writes Hill, these various forms of "black collective force did not simply *enhance* the bargaining power of moderates" but became "the very *source* of their power." Hill, *The Deacons for Defense*, 260, 262. Like Hill, Christopher Strain interprets the Watts riot of 1965 as a form of "collective self-defense." Strain, *Pure Fire*, 127.

42. Mallisham interview by author, March 19, 2002.

43. "Man of the Year," *Time*, January 3, 1964, 13; Frank Meyer, "The Violence of Nonviolence," *National Review*, April 20, 1965, 327; Colaiaco, "Martin Luther King, Jr. and the Paradox of Nonviolent Direct Action," 17; Perry, *Malcolm*, 346; Tyson, *Radio Free Dixie*, 103.

44. Howard, "The Provocation of Violence," 95. See also Garrow, *Protest at Selma*, 2.

45. Lentz, *Symbols, the News Magazines, and Martin Luther King*, 39, 129.

46. Haines, *Black Radicals and the Civil Rights Mainstream*, 2–10, 75, 167; Haines, "Black Radicalization and the Funding of Civil Rights," 31.

47. Martin Luther King Jr., "Letter from Birmingham Jail," 14.

48. Quoted in *New York Times*, June 17, 1963. See also *New York Times*, November 7, 1963; *San Francisco Chronicle*, September 16, 1963; "Dr. King, Others Forecast Violence in Rights Struggle," *Jet*, November 21, 1963, 6.

49. Garrow, *Bearing the Cross*, 260.

50. The arrest and convictions of the nine white men was largely symbolic, however, since all defendants received probationary sentences. Umoja, "1964," 219–20.

51. Jerome Wyckoff to James Farmer, July 15, 1963, reel 29, frame 00420, CORE Papers, microfilm.

52. Szabo, "An Interview with Gloria Richardson Dandridge," 358.

BIBLIOGRAPHY

Archival Collections

1964 Civil Rights Movement in Tuscaloosa, Alabama, Collection. Oral History Research Office, Columbia University, New York.

Acheson, Meldon. Papers. State Historical Society of Wisconsin, Madison.

Alabama Pamphlet Collection, Vertical File. W. S. Hoole Special Collections Library, University of Alabama, Tuscaloosa.

Bates, Daisy. Papers. State Historical Society of Wisconsin, Madison.

Belfrage, Sally. Papers. Microfilm. State Historical Society of Wisconsin, Madison.

Bernard, Jacqueline. Papers. State Historical Society of Wisconsin, Madison.

Bingham, Steven. Papers. State Historical Society of Wisconsin, Madison.

Blasi, Anthony J. Collection. W. S. Hoole Special Collections Library, University of Alabama, Tuscaloosa.

Boone, Buford. Papers. W. S. Hoole Special Collections Library, University of Alabama, Tuscaloosa.

Braden, Carl and Anne. Papers. State Historical Society of Wisconsin, Madison.

Cambridge Nonviolent Action Committee Papers. State Historical Society of Wisconsin, Madison.

Clark, Catherine. Collection. Schomburg Center for Research in Black Culture, New York Public Library.

Cohen, Robert Carl. Papers. State Historical Society of Wisconsin, Madison.

Congress of Racial Equality Papers. State Historical Society of Wisconsin, Madison.

——, 1941–67. Microfilm. Sanford, N.C., Microfilming Corporation of America, 1980.

——, Addendum, 1944–68. Microfilm. Sanford, N.C., Microfilming Corporation of America, 1980.

——, Bogalusa, Louisiana, Chapter Files. State Historical Society of Wisconsin, Madison.

——, Jackson Parish Files. State Historical Society of Wisconsin, Madison.

——, Louisiana Sixth Congressional District Files. State Historical Society of Wisconsin, Madison.

——, Monroe, Louisiana, Chapter Files. State Historical Society of Wisconsin, Madison.

————, Southern Regional Office Files. State Historical Society of Wisconsin, Madison.

————, Western Regional Office Files. State Historical Society of Wisconsin, Madison.

Cowan, Paul. Papers. State Historical Society of Wisconsin, Madison.

Currier, Charles G. L. Papers. State Historical Society of Wisconsin, Madison.

Curvin, Robert. Papers. State Historical Society of Wisconsin, Madison.

Deacons of Defense and Justice, Inc. Federal Bureau of Investigation File. Federal Bureau of Investigation, Washington, D.C.

Ellin, Joseph and Nancy. Freedom Summer Collection. McCain Library and Archives, University of Southern Mississippi, Hattiesburg.

Ewen, Stewart. Papers. State Historical Society of Wisconsin, Madison.

Feingold, David. Papers. State Historical Society of Wisconsin, Madison.

Feingold, Miriam. Papers. State Historical Society of Wisconsin, Madison.

Gartner, Allan. Papers. State Historical Society of Wisconsin, Madison.

Gordon, Bonnie. Papers. State Historical Society of Wisconsin, Madison.

Gould, Richard. Papers. State Historical Society of Wisconsin, Madison.

Holden, Anna. Papers. State Historical Society of Wisconsin, Madison.

Holdes, William. Papers. State Historical Society of Wisconsin, Madison.

Johnson Family Papers. McCain Library and Archives, University of Southern Mississippi, Hattiesburg.

Kaufman, Walter. Papers. State Historical Society of Wisconsin, Madison.

King, Mary E. Papers. State Historical Society of Wisconsin, Madison.

Lake, Ellen. Papers. State Historical Society of Wisconsin, Madison.

Meier, August. Papers. Schomburg Center for Research in Black Culture, New York Public Library, New York.

Meier-Rudwick Collection of CORE Records. State Historical Society of Wisconsin, Madison.

Mississippi State Sovereignty Commission Files. Mississippi State Archives, Jackson.

Morey, R. Hunter. Papers. State Historical Society of Wisconsin, Madison.

National Association for the Advancement of Colored People (NAACP) Papers. Library of Congress, Manuscript Division, Washington, D.C.

Nelson, Eugene. Papers. State Historical Society of Wisconsin, Madison.

Original Knights of the Ku Klux Klan. Federal Bureau of Investigation File. Federal Bureau of Investigation, Washington, D.C.

Robinson, Jo Ann Ooiman. Papers. State Historical Society of Wisconsin, Madison.

Rustin, Bayard. Papers. Microfilm. Frederick, Md.: University Publications of America, 1988.

Salter, John R., Jr. Papers. State Historical Society of Wisconsin, Madison.

Scholarship, Education and Defense Fund for Racial Equality Records. State Historical Society of Wisconsin, Madison.

Smith, Donald. Papers. State Historical Society of Wisconsin, Madison.

Southern Christian Leadership Conference (SCLC) Papers. Microfilm. Bethesda, Md.: University Publications of America, 1995.

Southern Civil Rights Litigation Records for the 1960s. Microfilm. Middletown, Conn.: Wesleyan University, 1980.

Spivak, Lawrence E. Papers. Library of Congress, Manuscript Division, Washington, D.C.

Student Nonviolent Coordinating Committee Papers. Microfilm. Library of Congress, Manuscript Division, Washington, D.C.

Student Nonviolent Coordinating Committee—Arkansas Project Records. State Historical Society of Wisconsin, Madison.

Third National Black Power Conference Records. State Historical Society of Wisconsin, Madison.

Wacker, Daniel J. Papers. State Historical Society of Wisconsin, Madison.

Wilkins, Roy. Papers. Library of Congress, Manuscript Division, Washington, D.C.

Zeman, Zoya. Freedom Summer Collection. McCain Library and Archives, University of Southern Mississippi, Hattiesburg.

Zinn, Howard. Papers. State Historical Society of Wisconsin, Madison.

Zwerling, Matthew. Freedom Summer Collection. McCain Library and Archives, University of Southern Mississippi, Hattiesburg.

Interviews

Anonymous black teenagers. Interview by Harvey Burg. Transcript. Summer 1964. Tuscaloosa. 1964 Civil Rights Movement in Tuscaloosa, Alabama, Collection, Oral History Research Office, Columbia University, New York.

Anonymous SCLC leaders. Interview by Harvey Burg. Transcript. Summer 1964. Tuscaloosa. 1964 Civil Rights Movement in Tuscaloosa, Alabama, Collection, Oral History Research Office, Columbia University, New York.

Barber, Rims. Interview by Kim Lacy Rogers and Owen Brooks. Tape recording. August 30, 1995. N.p. Delta Oral History Project, L. Zenobia Coleman Library, Tougaloo College, Tougaloo, Miss.

Bolden, Ruth. Interview by Alan DeSantis. Tape recording. June 16, 1987. Tuscaloosa. Alan DeSantis Collection, W. S. Hoole Special Collections Library, University of Alabama, Tuscaloosa.

Bruce, Walter. Interview by Harriet Tanzman. Tape recording. October 8, 1999. Durant, Miss. Civil Rights Documentation Project, L. Zenobia Coleman Library, Tougaloo College, Tougaloo, Miss.

Burris, Royan. Interview by Miriam Feingold. Tape recording. Ca. July 1966. Bogalusa, La. Miriam Feingold Papers, State Historical Society of Wisconsin, Madison.

Chinn, C. O., and Robert Chinn. Interview by Owen Brooks and Kim Lacy Rogers. Tape recording. January 28, 1996. Canton, Miss. Delta Oral History Project, L. Zenobia Coleman Library, Tougaloo College, Tougaloo, Miss.

Clark, Obie. Interview by Don Williams. Tape recording. March 13, 1999. N.p. Civil Rights Documentation Project, L. Zenobia Coleman Library, Tougaloo College, Tougaloo, Miss.

Clemson, Barry. Telephone interview by John Rachal. Transcript. November 14, 1995. Mississippi Oral History Program, McCain Library and Archives, University of Southern Mississippi, Hattiesburg.

Cobb, Charles. Interview by Tom Dent. Tape recording. February 11, 1983. Washington, D.C. Tom Dent Collection, L. Zenobia Coleman Library, Tougaloo College, Tougaloo, Miss.

———. Telephone interview by John Rachal. Transcript. October 21, 1996. Mississippi Oral History Program, McCain Library and Archives, University of Southern Mississippi, Hattiesburg.

Collins, Virginia. Interview by Glenda Stevens. Transcript. August 31, 1979. New Orleans. Kim Lacy Rogers–Glenda Stevens Collection, Amistad Research Center, Tulane University, New Orleans.

Crawford, Homer. Interview by Kim Lacy Rogers and Owen Brooks. Tape recording. February 10, 1996. N.p. Delta Oral History Project, L. Zenobia Coleman Library, Tougaloo College, Tougaloo, Miss.

Davis, Rev. Frank. Interview by Alan DeSantis. Tape recording. August 12, 1987. Tuscaloosa. Alan DeSantis Collection, W. S. Hoole Special Collections Library, University of Alabama, Tuscaloosa.

Dennis, Dave. Interview by Tom Dent. Tape recording. October 8, 1983. Lafayette, La. Tom Dent Collection, L. Zenobia Coleman Library, Tougaloo College, Tougaloo, Miss.

———. Interview by Kim Lacy Rogers. Tape recording. December 4, 1995. Jackson, Miss. Delta Oral History Project, L. Zenobia Coleman Library, Tougaloo College, Tougaloo, Miss.

Devine, Annie. Interview by Tom Dent. Tape recording. September 17, 1974. Milestone, Miss. Tom Dent Collection, L. Zenobia Coleman Library, Tougaloo College, Tougaloo, Miss.

Evers, Charles. Interview by Dr. Robert Smith. Transcript. December 3, 1971. Fayette, Miss. Mississippi Oral History Program, McCain Library and Archives, University of Southern Mississippi, Hattiesburg.

Fairly, J. C. Interview by Mike Garvey. Transcript. January 31, 1972. Hattiesburg, Miss. Mississippi Oral History Program, McCain Library and Archives, University of Southern Mississippi, Hattiesburg.

German, Millie. Interview by Harvey Burg. Transcript. Summer 1964. Tuscaloosa. 1964 Civil Rights Movement in Tuscaloosa, Alabama, Collection, Oral History Research Office, Columbia University, New York.

Gordon, Rev. David. Interview by Alan DeSantis. Tape recording. July 28, 1987. Tuscaloosa. Alan DeSantis Collection, W. S. Hoole Special Collections Library, University of Alabama, Tuscaloosa.

Haley, Richard. Interview by Robert Wright. Transcript. August 12, 1969. New Orleans. Ralph J. Bunche Oral History Collection, Moorland-Spingarn Research Center, Howard University, Washington, D.C.

Hall, L. V. Interview by Alan DeSantis. Tape recording. June 23, 1987. Tuscaloosa. Alan DeSantis Collection, W. S. Hoole Special Collections Library, University of Alabama, Tuscaloosa.

Henry, Dr. Aaron. Interview by Neil McMillen and George Burson. Transcript. May

1, 1972. Clarksdale, Miss. Mississippi Oral History Program, McCain Library and Archives, University of Southern Mississippi, Hattiesburg.

Herzfeld, Willie. Interview by Harvey Burg. Transcript. Summer 1964. Tuscaloosa. 1964 Civil Rights Movement in Tuscaloosa, Alabama, Collection, Oral History Research Office, Columbia University, New York.

———. Telephone interview by Alan DeSantis. Tape recording. August 12, 1987. Alan DeSantis Collection, W. S. Hoole Special Collections Library, University of Alabama, Tuscaloosa.

Hicks, Robert. Interview by Miriam Feingold. Tape recording. Ca. July 1966. Bogalusa, La. Miriam Feingold Papers, State Historical Society of Wisconsin, Madison.

———. Interview by Robert Wright. Transcript. August 10, 1969. Bogalusa, La. Ralph J. Bunche Oral History Collection, Moorland-Spingarn Research Center, Howard University, Washington, D.C.

Hill, Hattie Mae. Interview by Miriam Feingold. Tape recording. Ca. July 1966. Bogalusa, La. Miriam Feingold Papers, State Historical Society of Wisconsin, Madison.

Howard, Nathaniel, Jr. Interview by Alan DeSantis. Tape recording. June 29, 1987. Tuscaloosa. Alan DeSantis Collection, W. S. Hoole Special Collections Library, University of Alabama, Tuscaloosa.

Hudson, Ms. Winson. Telephone interview by John Rachal. Transcript. August 31, 1995. Mississippi Oral History Program, McCain Library and Archives, University of Southern Mississippi, Hattiesburg.

Hughes, McDonald. Interview by Alan DeSantis. Tape recording. June 22, 1987. Tuscaloosa. Alan DeSantis Collection, W. S. Hoole Special Collections Library, University of Alabama, Tuscaloosa.

Jacobs, Elmo. Interview by Miriam Feingold. Tape recording. Ca. July 1966. Jonesboro, La. Miriam Feingold Papers, State Historical Society of Wisconsin, Madison.

James, Rev. E. J. Interview by Alan DeSantis. Tape recording. July 23, 1987. Northport, Ala. Alan DeSantis Collection, W. S. Hoole Special Collections Library, University of Alabama, Tuscaloosa.

Jaquith, James. Interview by Harvey Burg. Transcript. Summer 1964. Tuscaloosa. 1964 Civil Rights Movement in Tuscaloosa, Alabama, Collection, Oral History Research Office, Columbia University, New York.

Jenkins, Gayle. Interview by Miriam Feingold. Tape recording. Ca. July 1966. Bogalusa, La. Miriam Feingold Papers, State Historical Society of Wisconsin, Madison.

King, Martin Luther, Jr. Interview by Donald H. Smith. Tape recording. November 29, 1963. Atlanta, Ga. Donald Smith Papers, State Historical Society of Wisconsin, Madison.

LeMaistre, George. Interview by Harvey Burg. Transcript. August 1964. Tuscaloosa. 1964 Civil Rights Movement in Tuscaloosa, Alabama, Collection, Oral History Research Office, Columbia University, New York.

Linton, Rev. T. W. Interview by Alan DeSantis. Tape recording. July 22, 1987. Tuscaloosa. Alan DeSantis Collection, W. S. Hoole Special Collections Library, University of Alabama, Tuscaloosa.

Love, Robert. Interview by Kim Lacy Rogers and Owen Brooks. Tape recording. September 27, 1995. Indianola, Miss. Delta Oral History Project, L. Zenobia Coleman Library, Tougaloo College, Tougaloo, Miss.

Magee, Clarence E. Interview by Charles Bolton. Transcript. September 22, 1997. Hattiesburg, Miss. Mississippi Oral History Program, McCain Library and Archives, University of Southern Mississippi, Hattiesburg.

Mallisham, Joseph. Interview by Alan DeSantis. Tape recording. July 22, 1987. Tuscaloosa. Alan DeSantis Collection, W. S. Hoole Special Collections Library, University of Alabama, Tuscaloosa.

———. Interview by author. Tape recording. March 19, 2002. Tuscaloosa, Ala.

———. Interview by author. Tape recording. March 22, 2002. Tuscaloosa, Ala.

Maniece, Olivia. Interview by Alan DeSantis. Tape recording. June 24, 1987. Tuscaloosa. Alan DeSantis Collection, W. S. Hoole Special Collections Library, University of Alabama, Tuscaloosa.

Matthews, David. Interview by Kim Lacy Rogers and Owen Brooks. Tape recording. October 27, 1995. Indianola, Miss. Delta Oral History Project, L. Zenobia Coleman Library, Tougaloo College, Tougaloo, Miss.

McDew, Charles. Interview by Katherine M. Shannon. Transcript. August 24, 1967. Washington, D.C. Ralph J. Bunche Oral History Collection, Moorland-Spingarn Research Center, Howard University, Washington, D.C.

McDonald, Jimmy. Interview by James Mosby. Transcript. November 5, 1969. New York City. Ralph J. Bunche Oral History Collection, Moorland-Spingarn Research Center, Howard University, Washington, D.C.

McKissick, Floyd. Interview by Robert Wright. Transcript. October 16, 1968. Durham, N.C. Ralph J. Bunche Oral History Collection, Moorland-Spingarn Research Center, Howard University, Washington, D.C.

McLaurin, Griffin. Interview by Harriet Tanzman. Tape recording. March 6, 2000. Milestone, Miss. Civil Rights Documentation Project, L. Zenobia Coleman Library, Tougaloo College, Tougaloo, Miss.

Murphy, Alberta. Interview by Alan DeSantis. Tape recording. August 4, 1987. Tuscaloosa. Alan DeSantis Collection, W. S. Hoole Special Collections Library, University of Alabama, Tuscaloosa.

Nix, James. Interview by Sarah Rowe. Transcript. March 7, 1993. Hattiesburg, Miss. Transcript. Mississippi Oral History Program, McCain Library and Archives, University of Southern Mississippi, Hattiesburg.

Redden, Meg (formerly Peggy Ewan). Telephone interview by Greta de Jong. Tape recording. December 8, 1996. T. Harry Williams Center for Oral History, Louisiana State University, Baton Rouge.

Reynolds, Isaac. Interview by James Mosby. Transcript. May 27, 1970. New Orleans. Ralph J. Bunche Oral History Collection, Moorland-Spingarn Research Center, Howard University, Washington, D.C.

Richardson (Dandridge), Gloria. Interview by John Britton. Transcript. October 11, 1967. New York City. Ralph J. Bunche Oral History Collection, Moorland-Spingarn Research Center, Howard University, Washington, D.C.

Robinson, Lewis. Interview by John Britton. Transcript. November 15, 1967. Cleveland, Ohio. Ralph J. Bunche Oral History Collection, Moorland-Spingarn Research Center, Howard University, Washington, D.C.

Rogers, LaPelzia. Telephone interview by Alan DeSantis. Tape recording. August 19, 1987. Alan DeSantis Collection, W. S. Hoole Special Collections Library, University of Alabama, Tuscaloosa.

Rogers, T. Y. Interview by Harvey Burg. Transcript. Summer 1964. Tuscaloosa. 1964 Civil Rights Movement in Tuscaloosa, Alabama, Collection, Oral History Research Office, Columbia University, New York.

Salter, John R., and Rev. Edwin King. Interview by John Jones. Transcript. January 6, 1981. N.p. John R. Salter Jr. Papers, State Historical Society of Wisconsin, Madison.

Seale, Bobby. Interview by Robert Wright. Transcript. November 14, 1968. Berkeley, Calif. Ralph J. Bunche Oral History Collection, Moorland-Spingarn Research Center, Howard University, Washington, D.C.

Shaw, Terri. Interview by Stephanie Scull Millet. Transcript. June 7, 1999. N.p. Mississippi Oral History Program, McCain Library and Archives, University of Southern Mississippi, Hattiesburg.

Shuttlesworth, Rev. Fred. Interview by James Mosby. Transcript. September 1968. Cincinnati, Ohio. Transcript. Ralph J. Bunche Oral History Collection, Moorland-Spingarn Research Center, Howard University, Washington, D.C.

Smiley, Glenn E. Interview by Katherine Shannon. Transcript. September 12, 1967. Nyack, N.Y. Ralph J. Bunche Oral History Collection, Moorland-Spingarn Research Center, Howard University, Washington, D.C.

Smith, Jerome. Interview by Tom Dent. Tape recording. September 25, 1983. New Orleans. Tom Dent Collection, L. Zenobia Coleman Library, Tougaloo College, Tougaloo, Miss.

Suarez, Matthew. Interview by Tom Dent. Tape recording. July 31, 1977. New Orleans. Tom Dent Collection, L. Zenobia Coleman Library, Tougaloo College, Tougaloo, Miss.

———. Interview by Harriet Tanzman. Tape recording. March 26, 2000. New Orleans. Civil Rights Documentation Project, L. Zenobia Coleman Library, Tougaloo College, Tougaloo, Miss.

Warrick, Odessa. Interview by Alan DeSantis. Tape recording. July 6, 1987. Tuscaloosa. Alan DeSantis Collection, W. S. Hoole Special Collections Library, University of Alabama, Tuscaloosa.

Watkins, Hollis. Telephone interview by John Rachal. Transcript. October 23, 1995. Mississippi Oral History Program, McCain Library and Archives, University of Southern Mississippi, Hattiesburg.

Williams, E. G., and anonymous SCLC activist. Interview by Marsha Tompkins. Tape recording. June 29, 1964. Tuscaloosa. In possession of author.

Williams, Robert F. Interview by Robert Carl Cohen. Transcript. July 20, 1968. Dar Es Salaam, Tanzania. Box 1, folder 4, Robert Carl Cohen Papers, State Historical Society of Wisconsin, Madison.

———. Interview by Robert Carl Cohen. Transcript. Ca. 1968. Dar Es Salaam, Tanzania. Box 1, folder 12, Robert Carl Cohen Papers, State Historical Society of Wisconsin, Madison.

———. Interview by James Mosby. Transcript. July 22, 1970. Detroit, Mich. Ralph J. Bunche Oral History Collection, Moorland-Spingarn Research Center, Howard University, Washington, D.C.

Wright, Robert E. Interview by John Britton. Transcript. July 22, 1968. Washington, D.C. Ralph J. Bunche Oral History Collection, Moorland-Spingarn Research Center, Howard University, Washington, D.C.

Young, A. Z. Interview by Miriam Feingold. Tape recording. Ca. July 1966. Bogalusa, La. Miriam Feingold Papers, State Historical Society of Wisconsin, Madison.

Young, Repr. Charles L., Sr. Interview by Don Williams. Tape recording. November 14, 1998. Jackson, Miss. Civil Rights Documentation Project, L. Zenobia Coleman Library, Tougaloo College, Tougaloo, Miss.

Zeman, Zoya. Telephone interview by John Rachal. Transcript. April 18, 1996. Mississippi Oral History Program, McCain Library and Archives, University of Southern Mississippi, Hattiesburg.

Newspapers and Periodicals

Afro-American (Baltimore), 1959, 1963–64, 1966

Amsterdam News (New York City), 1964–65

Chicago Defender, 1915, 1943, 1946

Christian Century, 1964

Clarion-Ledger (Jackson, Miss.), 1964

Cleveland Press, 1964

Commercial Appeal (Memphis, Tenn.), 1965–66

Crusader, 1964

Daily World (New York City), 1968

Durham Morning Herald (Durham, N.C.), 1965

Ebony, 1963–66

Jet, 1963–66

Life, 1965

Los Angeles Times, 1965–66

Louisiana Weekly, 1965

Mademoiselle, 1964

Militant (New York City), 1963, 1965

Nashville Banner, 1964

Nation, 1965–66

National Guardian, 1964–65, 1967–68

National Review, 1965–66

Newsweek, 1963, 1965–66

New York Herald Tribune, 1963

New York Post, 1965

New York Review of Books, 2001

New York Times, 1919, 1947, 1958–59, 1963–68, 1971

New York Times Magazine, 1963–65, 1967–68
Pittsburgh Courier, 1942–43, 1957
Playboy, 1968
Rocky Mountain News (Denver), 1966
San Francisco Chronicle, 1963
San Francisco Sunday Chronicle, 1965
Saturday Evening Post, 1965–66
Student Voice, 1964
Time, 1964–66
Times-Picayune (New Orleans), 1967
Tuscaloosa News, 1962, 1964–65, 1971, 1985, 2000
U.S. News & World Report, 1964, 1967
Village Voice, 1966
Wall Street Journal, 1965–66
Washington Post, 1963–64, 1966

Books, Articles, Dissertations, and Theses

Abernathy, Ralph David. *And the Walls Came Tumbling Down*. New York: Harper and Row, 1989.

———. "The Natural History of a Social Movement: The Montgomery Improvement Association." In *The Walking City: The Montgomery Bus Boycott, 1955–1956*, edited by David Garrow, 99–172. Brooklyn, N.Y.: Carlson, 1989.

Albert, Peter J., and Ronald Hoffman, eds. *We Shall Overcome: Martin Luther King, Jr. and the Black Freedom Struggle*. New York: Pantheon, 1990.

Alexander, Ann Field. *Race Man: The Rise and Fall of the 'Fighting Editor' John Mitchell, Jr.* Charlottesville: University of Virginia Press, 2002.

Allen, Robert L. *Black Awakening in Capitalist America*. New York: Doubleday, 1969.

Ammerman, Nancy T. "The Civil Rights Movement and the Clergy in a Southern Community." *Sociological Analysis* 41, no. 4 (Winter 1980): 339–50.

Anderson, Jervis. *Bayard Rustin: Troubles I've Seen*. Berkeley and Los Angeles: University of California Press, 1998.

Austin, Curtis Jerome. "The Role of Violence in the Creation, Sustenance, and Destruction of the Black Panther Party, 1966–1972." Ph.D. diss., Mississippi State University, 1998.

Bates, Daisy. *The Long Shadow of Little Rock: A Memoir*. New York: David McKay, 1962.

Beals, Melba Pattillo. *Warriors Don't Cry*. Abridged ed. New York: Simon Pulse, 2002.

Bederman, Gail. *Manliness & Civilization: A Cultural History of Gender and Race in the United States, 1880–1917*. Chicago: University of Chicago Press, 1995.

Beeler, Dorothy. "Race Riot in Columbia, Tennessee: February 25–27, 1946." *Tennessee Historical Quarterly* 39, no. 1 (Spring 1980): 49–61.

Belfrage, Cedric. *The American Inquisition: 1945–1960*. New York: Thunder's Mouth Press, 1989.

Belfrage, Sally. *Freedom Summer*. New York: Viking Press, 1965.

Belknap, Michael R. *Federal Law and the Southern Order: Racial Violence and Constitutional Conflict in the Post-Brown South.* 2nd ed. Athens: University of Georgia Press, 1995.

Bell, Inge Powell. CORE *and the Strategy of Nonviolence.* New York: Random House, 1968.

Berg, Manfred. "Black Power: The National Association for the Advancement of Colored People and the Resurgence of Black Nationalism during the 1960s." In *The American Nation—National Identity—Nationalism,* edited by Knud Krakau, 235–62. New Brunswick, N.J.: Transaction, 1997.

——. "Schwarze Bürgerrechte und liberaler Antikommunismus: Die NAACP in der McCarthy Ära." *Vierteljahreshefte für Zeitgeschichte* 51, no. 3 (July 2003): 363–84.

——. *The Ticket to Freedom: Die* NAACP *und das Wahlrecht der Afro-Amerikaner.* Frankfurt, Germany: Campus, 2000.

——. *"The Ticket to Freedom": The* NAACP *and the Struggle for Black Political Integration.* Gainesville: University Press of Florida, 2005.

Blasi, Anthony J. *Segregationist Violence and Civil Rights Movements in Tuscaloosa.* Washington, D.C.: University Press of America, 1980.

Bond, Julian. "Nonviolence: An Interpretation." *Freedomways* 3, no. 2 (Spring 1963): 159–62.

Bondurant, Joan V. *Conquest of Violence: The Gandhian Philosophy of Conflict.* Princeton, N.J.: Princeton University Press, 1988.

Borstelmann, Thomas. *The Cold War and the Color Line: American Race Relations in the Global Arena.* Cambridge: Harvard University Press, 2001.

Botnick, A. I. "One Man's Stand." ADL *Bulletin* 22, no. 5 (May 1965): 1–2.

Boyle, Kevin. *Arc of Justice: A Saga of Race, Civil Rights, and Murder in the Jazz Age.* New York: Henry Holt, 2004.

Braden, Anne. "New Light on Monroe, N.C." *Southern Patriot* 21, no. 2 (February 1963): 2.

——. "Nonviolent Revolution: An Idea That Wasn't Tried." *Southern Patriot* 25, no. 2 (February 1967): 7.

——. "Not Violence, but Political Action." *Southern Patriot* 25, no. 1 (January 1967): 3.

——. *The Wall Between.* New York: Monthly Review Press, 1958.

Branch, Taylor. *Parting the Waters: America in the King Years, 1954–63.* New York: Simon and Schuster, 1988.

——. *Pillar of Fire: America in the King Years, 1963–65.* New York: Simon and Schuster, 1998.

Breitman, George. *The Last Year of Malcolm X: The Evolution of a Revolutionary.* New York: Schocken Books, 1968.

——, ed. *Malcolm X Speaks: Selected Speeches and Statements.* New York: Pathfinder, 1989.

Brown, H. Rap. *Die Nigger Die!* New York: Dial Press, 1969.

Brown, Richard Maxwell. *No Duty to Retreat: Violence and Values in American History and Society.* New York: Oxford University Press, 1991.

———. *Strain of Violence: Historical Studies of American Violence and Vigilantism.* New York: Oxford University Press, 1975.

Brown, Scot. *Fighting for US: Maulena Karenga, the US Organization, and Black Cultural Nationalism.* New York: New York University Press, 2003.

Brundage, W. Fitzhugh. "The Darien 'Insurrection' of 1899: Black Protest during the Nadir of Race Relations." *Georgia Historical Quarterly* 74, no. 2 (Summer 1990): 234–53.

Bunche, Ralph J. "A Critical Analysis of the Tactics and Programs of Minority Groups." *Journal of Negro Education* 4, no. 3 (July 1935): 308–20.

Burner, Eric. *And Gently He Shall Lead Them: Robert Parris Moses and Civil Rights in Mississippi.* New York: New York University Press, 1994.

Burns, Stewart. "Overview: the Proving Ground." In *Daybreak of Freedom: The Montgomery Bus Boycott*, edited by Stewart Burns, 1–37. Chapel Hill: University of North Carolina Press, 1997.

Carmichael, Stokely, with Ekwueme Michael Thelwell. *Ready for Revolution: The Life and Struggle of Stokely Carmichael (Kwame Ture).* New York: Scribner, 2003.

Carmichael, Stokely (Kwame Ture), and Charles V. Hamilton. *Black Power: The Politics of Black Liberation in America.* 1967. Reprint, New York: Vintage, 1992.

Carson, Clayborne. *In Struggle: SNCC and the Black Awakening of the 1960s.* New ed. Cambridge: Harvard University Press, 1995.

———, ed. *The Papers of Martin Luther King, Jr.* 5 vols. Berkeley and Los Angeles: University of California Press, 1992–2005.

Carter, Dan T. *The Politics of Rage: George Wallace, the Origins of the New Conservatism, and the Transformation of American Politics.* Baton Rouge: Louisiana State University Press, 1995.

Carter, Paul Allen. *The Decline and Revival of the Social Gospel: Social and Political Liberalism in American Protestant Churches, 1920–1940.* Ithaca, N.Y.: Cornell University Press, 1954.

Cash, W. J. *The Mind of the South.* New York: Knopf, 1941.

Chafe, William H. *Civilities and Civil Rights: Greensboro, North Carolina, and the Black Struggle for Freedom.* New York: Oxford University Press, 1981.

Churchill, Ward. "'To Disrupt, Discredit, and Destroy': The FBI's Secret War against the Black Panther Party." In *Liberation, Imagination, and the Black Panther Party: A New Look at the Panthers and their Legacy*, edited by Kathleen Cleaver and George Katsiaficas, 78–117. New York: Routledge, 2001.

Clark, E. Culpepper. *The Schoolhouse Door: Segregation's Last Stand at the University of Alabama.* New York: Oxford University Press, 1993.

Clark, Septima, with Cynthia Stokes Brown. *Ready from Within: Septima Clark and the Civil Rights Movement.* Navarro, Calif.: Wild Trees Press, 1986.

Clarke, John Henrik, ed. *Malcolm X: The Man and His Times.* New York: Macmillan, 1969.

Cleaver, Eldridge. *Soul on Ice.* 1968. Reprint, New York: Dell, 1992.

Clegg, Claude Andrew, III. *An Original Man: The Life and Times of Elijah Muhammad.* New York: St. Martin's Press, 1997.

Cohen, Robert Carl. *Black Crusader: A Biography of Robert Franklin Williams*. Secaucus, N.J.: Lyle Stuart, 1972.

Colaiaco, James A. "Martin Luther King, Jr. and the Paradox of Nonviolent Direct Action." *Phylon* 47, no. 1 (Spring 1986): 16–28.

Colburn, David R. *Racial Change and Community Crisis: St. Augustine, Florida, 1877–1980*. New York: Columbia University Press, 1985.

"Congress of Racial Equality (CORE)." In *Encyclopedia of Gun Control and Gun Rights*, edited by Glenn H. Utter, 69–70. Phoenix, Ariz.: Oryx Press, 2000.

Conot, Robert L. *Rivers of Blood, Years of Darkness: The Unforgettable Classic Account of the Watts Riot*. New York: William Morrow, 1968.

Cortner, Richard C. *A Mob Intent on Death: The NAACP and the Arkansas Riot Cases*. Middletown, Conn.: Wesleyan University Press, 1988.

Cottrol, Robert J., and Raymond T. Diamond. "'Never Intended to Be Applied to the White Population': Firearms, Regulation, and Racial Disparity—The Redeemed South's Legacy to National Jurisprudence." *Chicago-Kent Law Review* 70, no. 3 (1995): 1307–35.

———. "The Second Amendment: Toward an Afro-American Reconsideration." *Georgetown Law Journal* 80 (1991): 309–61.

Courtwright, John A. "Rhetoric of the Gun: An Analysis of the Rhetorical Modifications of the Black Panther Party." *Journal of Black Studies* 4, no. 3 (March 1974): 249–67.

Cramer, Clayton E. *For the Defense of Themselves and the State: The Original Intent and Judicial Interpretation of the Right to Keep and Bear Arms*. Westport, Conn.: Praeger, 1994.

Crosby, Emilye J. "Common Courtesy: The Civil Rights Movement in Claiborne County, Mississippi." Ph.D. diss., Indiana University, 1995.

———. "'God's Appointed Savior': Charles Evers's Use of Local Movements for National Stature." In *Groundwork: Local Black Freedom Movements in America*, edited by Jeanne Theoharis and Komozi Woodard, 165–92. New York: New York University Press, 2005.

———. "'This Nonviolent Stuff Ain't No Good. It'll Get Ya Killed': Teaching about Self-Defense in the African American Freedom Struggle." In *Teaching the American Civil Rights Movement: Freedom's Bittersweet Song*, edited by Julie Buckner Armstrong, Susan Edwards, Houston Roberson, and Rhonda Williams, 159–73. New York: Routledge, 2002.

Cruse, Harold. *The Crisis of the Negro Intellectual*. New York: William Morrow, 1967.

Cullen, Jim. "'I's a Man Now': Gender and African American Men." In *Divided Houses: Gender and the Civil War*, edited by Catherine Clinton and Nina Silber, 76–91. New York: Oxford University Press, 1992.

Current, Gloster B. "Fiftieth Annual Convention—A Jubilee for Civil Rights." *Crisis* 66, no. 7 (August-September 1959): 400–410.

Daniel, Pete. "Black Power in the 1920s: The Case of Tuskegee Veterans Hospital." *Journal of Southern History* 36, no. 3 (August 1970): 368–88.

DeBenedetti, Charles. *The Peace Reform in American History*. Bloomington: Indiana University Press, 1980.

DeConde, Alexander. *Gun Violence in America: The Struggle for Control*. Boston: Northeastern University Press, 2001.

De Jong, Greta. *A Different Day: African American Struggles for Justice in Rural Louisiana, 1900–1970*. Chapel Hill: University of North Carolina Press, 2002.

Dittmer, John. *Black Georgia in the Progressive Era, 1900–1920*. Urbana: University of Illinois Press, 1977.

———. *Local People: The Struggle for Civil Rights in Mississippi*. Urbana: University of Illinois Press, 1994.

Doss, Erika. "Imaging the Panthers: Representing Black Power and Masculinity, 1960s-1990s." *Prospects* 23 (1998): 483–516.

Du Bois, W.E.B. *The Autobiography of W.E.B. Du Bois*. New York: International, 1968.

Dudziak, Mary L. *Cold War Civil Rights: Race and the Image of American Democracy*. Princeton, N.J.: Princeton University Press, 2000.

"The Elaine Massacre . . ." *Southern Exposure* 1, no. 3–4 (1974): 9–10.

Ellsworth, Scott. *Death in a Promised Land: The Tulsa Race Riot of 1921*. Baton Rouge: Louisiana University Press, 1982.

Escott, Paul D. *Slavery Remembered: A Record of Twentieth-Century Slave Narratives*. Chapel Hill: University of North Carolina Press, 1979.

Eskew, Glenn T. *But for Birmingham: The Local and National Movements in the Civil Rights Struggle*. Chapel Hill: University of North Carolina Press, 1997.

Estes, Steve. *I Am a Man!: Race, Manhood, and the Civil Rights Movement*. Chapel Hill: University of North Carolina Press, 2005.

———. "'I Am a Man': Race, Manhood, and the Struggle for Civil Rights." Ph.D. diss., University of North Carolina at Chapel Hill, 2001.

Evers, Charles, and Andrew Szanton. *Have No Fear: The Charles Evers Story*. New York: John Wiley and Sons, 1997.

———. *Evers*. New York: World, 1971.

Evers, Myrlie, with William Peters. *For Us, the Living*. Garden City, N.Y.: Doubleday, 1967.

Fairclough, Adam. "Martin Luther King, Jr. and the Quest for Nonviolent Social Change." *Phylon* 47, no. 1 (Spring 1986): 1–15.

———. *Race and Democracy: The Civil Rights Movement in Louisiana, 1915–1972*. Athens: University of Georgia Press, 1995.

———. *To Redeem the Soul of America: The Southern Christian Leadership Conference and Martin Luther King, Jr.* Athens: University of Georgia Press, 1987.

Fanon, Frantz. *The Wretched of the Earth*. New York: Grove Press, 1963.

Farmer, James. *Freedom When?* New York: Random House, 1965.

———. *Lay Bare the Heart: An Autobiography of the Civil Rights Movement*. New York: Arbor House, 1985.

———. "The New Jacobins and Full Emancipation." In *100 Years of Emancipation*, edited by Robert A. Goldwin, 95–102. Chicago: Rand McNally, 1964.

Feagin, Joe R. and Harlan Hahn. *Ghetto Revolts: The Politics of Violence in American Cities*. New York: Macmillan, 1973.

Feldman, Glenn. *Politics, Society, and the Klan in Alabama, 1915–1949*. Tuscaloosa: University of Alabama Press, 1999.

Finkle, Lee. "The Conservative Aims of Militant Rhetoric: Black Protest during World War II." *Journal of American History* 60, no. 3 (December 1973): 692–713.

Finzsch, Norbert. "'Picking up the Gun': Die Black Panther Party zwischen gewaltsamer Revolution und sozialer Reform, 1966–1984." *Amerikastudien* 44, no. 2 (1999): 223–45.

Fleming, Walter L., ed. *Documentary History of Reconstruction: Political, Military, Social, Religious, Educational and Industrial 1865 to the Present.* Vol. 1. 1906. Reprint, Gloucester, Mass.: Peter Smith, 1960.

Foner, Philip S., ed. *The Black Panthers Speak.* Philadelphia: Lippincott, 1970.

Forman, James. *The Making of Black Revolutionaries.* New York: Macmillan, 1972.

Formwalt, Lee W. "The Origins of African-American Politics in Southwest Georgia: A Case Study of Black Political Organization during Presidential Reconstruction, 1865–1867." *Journal of Negro History* 77, no. 4 (Fall 1992): 211–22.

Franklin, John Hope. *The Militant South, 1800–1861.* Cambridge: Harvard University Press, 1956.

"Freedom Riders Go beyond the New Frontier." *Liberator* 1, no. 6 (June 1961): 1–2.

Gallen, David, ed. *Malcolm X As They Knew Him.* New York: Carroll and Graf, 1992.

Garfinkel, Herbert. *When Negroes March: The March on Washington Movement in the Organizational Politics for FEPC.* 1959. Reprint, New York: Atheneum, 1969.

Garrow, David J. *Bearing the Cross: Martin Luther King, Jr. and the Southern Christian Leadership Conference.* New York: Random House, 1986.

———. "The Intellectual Development of Martin Luther King, Jr.: Influences and Commentaries." *Union Seminary Quarterly Review* 15, no. 4 (1986): 5–20.

———. *Protest at Selma: Martin Luther King, Jr. and the Voting Rights Act of 1965.* New Haven: Yale University Press, 1978.

Gilmore, Glenda E. "Murder, Memory, and the Flight of the Incubus." In *Democracy Betrayed,* edited by Timothy B. Tyson and David Cecelsky, 73–94. Chapel Hill: University of North Carolina Press, 1998.

Ginzburg, Ralph. *100 Years of Lynching.* Baltimore: Black Classic Press, 1962.

Goldman, Peter. *The Death and Life of Malcolm X.* New York: Harper and Row, 1973.

———. "Malcolm X: Witness for the Prosecution." In *Black Leaders of the Twentieth Century,* edited by John Hope Franklin and August Meier, 305–30. Urbana: University of Illinois Press, 1982.

Good, Paul. "The Meredith March." *New South* 21, no. 3 (Summer 1966): 2–16.

Griffin, Farah Jasmine. "Black Feminism and Du Bois: Respectability, Protection, and Beyond." *Annals of the American Academy of Political and Social Science* 568 (March 2000): 28–40.

———. "'Ironies of the Saint': Malcolm X, Black Women, and the Price of Protection." In *Sisters in the Struggle: African American Women in the Civil Rights–Black Power Movement,* edited by Bettye Collier-Thomas and V. P. Franklin, 214–29. New York: New York University Press, 2001.

Haines, Herbert. "Black Radicalization and the Funding of Civil Rights: 1957–1970." *Social Problems* 32, no. 1 (October 1984): 31–43.

———. *Black Radicals and the Civil Rights Mainstream, 1954–1970.* Knoxville: University of Tennessee Press, 1988.

Halbrook, Stephen P. *Freedmen, the Fourteenth Amendment, and the Right to Bear Arms, 1866–1876*. Westport, Conn.: Praeger, 1998.

Hall, Jacqueline Dowd. "'The Mind That Burns in Each Body': Women, Rape, and Racial Violence." In *Powers of Desire: The Politics of Sexuality*, edited by Ann Snitow, Christine Stansell, and Sharon Thompson, 328–49. New York: Monthly Review Press, 1983.

———. *Revolt against Chivalry: Jesse Daniel Ames and the Women's Campaign against Lynching*. Rev. ed. New York: Columbia University Press, 1993.

Hamer, Fannie Lou. "To Praise Our Bridges." In *Mississippi Writers: Reflections of Childhood and Youth*. Vol. 2, edited by Dorothy Abbot, 321–30. Jackson: University Press of Mississippi, 1986.

Hampton, Henry, and Steve Fayer, eds. *Voices of Freedom: An Oral History of the Civil Rights Movement from the 1950s through the 1980s*. New York: Bantam Books, 1990.

Hanigan, James P. *Martin Luther King, Jr. and the Foundations of Nonviolence*. Lanham, Md.: University Press of America, 1984.

Hare, Nathan. "The Frustrated Masculinity of the Negro Male." *Negro Digest* 13, no. 10 (August 1964): 5–9.

Harper, Philip Brian. *Are We Not Men? Masculine Anxiety and the Problem of African-American Identity*. New York: Oxford University Press, 1996.

Hartley, Robert W. "A Long Hot Summer: The St. Augustine Racial Disorders of 1964." In *St. Augustine, Florida, 1963–1964: Mass Protest and Racial Violence*, edited by David J. Garrow, 3–92. Brooklyn, N.Y.: Carlson, 1989.

Hayes, Floyd W., III, and Francis A. Kiene, III. "'All Power to the People': The Political Thought of Huey P. Newton and the Black Panther Party." In *The Black Panther Party [Reconsidered]*, edited by Charles Jones, 157–76. Baltimore: Black Classic Press, 1998.

Haynes, Robert V. *A Night of Violence: The Houston Riot of 1917*. Baton Rouge: Louisiana State University Press, 1976.

Haywood, Harry. *Black Bolshevik: Autobiography of an Afro-American Communist*. Chicago: Liberator Press, 1978.

Henry, Aaron, with Constance Curry. *Aaron Henry: The Fire Ever Burning*. Jackson: University Press of Mississippi, 2000.

Hill, Lance E. *The Deacons for Defense: Armed Resistance and the Civil Rights Movement*. Chapel Hill: University of North Carolina Press, 2004.

———. "The Deacons for Defense and Justice: Armed Self-Defense and the Civil Rights Movement." Ph.D. diss., Tulane University, 1997.

Hodgson, Godfrey. *America in Our Time*. Garden City, N.Y.: Doubleday, 1976.

Holt, Len. *The Summer That Didn't End: The Story of the Mississippi Civil Rights Project of 1964*. 1965. Reprint, New York: Da Capo Press, 1992.

Honigsberg, Peter Jan. *Crossing Border Street: A Civil Rights Memoir*. Berkeley and Los Angeles: University of California Press, 2000.

Horne, Gerald. *Fire This Time: The Watts Uprising and the 1960s*. New York: Da Capo Press, 1997.

Howard, Jan. "The Provocation of Violence: A Civil Rights Tactic?" *Dissent* 13 (January-February 1966): 94–99.

Hudson, Winson, with Constance Curry. *Mississippi Harmony: Memoirs of a Freedom Fighter*. New York: Palgrave Macmillan, 2002.

Hunter, Andrea G., and James Earl Davis. "Hidden Voices of Black Men: The Meaning, Structure, and Complexity of Manhood." *Journal of Black Studies* 25, no. 1 (September 1994): 20–40.

Johnston, Erle. *Mississippi's Defiant Years, 1953–1973: An Interpretive Documentary with Personal Experiences*. Forest, Miss.: Lake Harbor, 1990.

Jones, LeRoi. "What Does Nonviolence Mean?" *Negro Digest* 13, no. 12 (October 1964): 4–18.

Kallal, Edward W., Jr. "St. Augustine and the Ku Klux Klan: 1963 and 1964." In *St. Augustine, Florida, 1963–1964: Mass Protest and Racial Violence*, edited by David J. Garrow, 93–176. Brooklyn, N.Y.: Carlson, 1989.

Kapur, Sudarshan. *Raising up a Prophet: The African American Encounter with Gandhi*. Boston: Beacon Press, 1992.

Katagiri, Yahuhiro. *The Mississippi State Sovereignty Commission: Civil Rights and States' Rights*. Jackson: University Press of Mississippi, 2001.

Kelley, Robin D. G. *Hammer and Hoe: Alabama Communists during the Great Depression*. Chapel Hill: University of North Carolina Press, 1990.

Kester, Howard. *Revolt among the Sharecroppers*. Knoxville: University of Tennessee Press, 1997.

Killens, John Oliver. *Black Man's Burden*. New York: Trident Press, 1965.

Kimmel, Michael S. *The Gendered Society*. New York: Oxford University Press, 2000.

King, Coretta Scott. *My Life with Martin Luther King, Jr.* New York: Holt, Rinehart, and Winston, 1969.

King, Martin Luther, Jr. "Letter from Birmingham Jail." *Liberation* 8, no. 4 (June 1963): 10–23.

———. "The Social Organization of Nonviolence." *Liberation* 4, no. 7 (October 1959): 5–6.

———. *Stride toward Freedom: The Montgomery Story*. London: Victor Gollacz LTD, 1959.

———. *Where Do We Go from Here: Chaos or Community?* New York: Harper and Row, 1967.

———. *Why We Can't Wait*. New York: Harper and Row, 1964.

King, Mary. *Freedom Song: A Personal Story of the 1960s Civil Rights Movement*. New York: Morrow, 1987.

———. *Mahatma Gandhi and Martin Luther King, Jr.: The Power of Nonviolent Action*. Paris: UNESCO, 1999.

Kirk, John A. *Martin Luther King, Jr.* Harlow, Great Britain: Pearson, 2005.

———. *Redefining the Color Line: Black Activism in Little Rock, Arkansas, 1940–1970*. Gainesville: University Press of Florida, 2002.

Klarman, Michael J. "How Brown Changed Race Relations: The Backlash Thesis." *Journal of American History* 81, no. 1 (June 1994): 81–118.

Klibaner, Irwin. *Conscience of a Troubled South: The Southern Conference Educational Fund, 1946–1966*. Brooklyn, N.Y.: Carlson, 1989.

Kosek, Joseph Kip. "Richard Gregg, Mohandas Gandhi, and the Strategy of Nonviolence." *Journal of American History* 91, no. 4 (March 2005): 1318–48.

Lawson, Steven. *Black Ballots: Voting Rights in the South, 1944–1969*. New York: Columbia University Press, 1976.

LeBlanc-Ernest, Angely D. "'The Most Qualified Person to Handle the Job': Black Panther Party Women, 1966–1982." In *The Black Panther Party [Reconsidered]*, edited by Charles Jones, 305–34. Baltimore: Black Classic Press, 1998.

Lee, Chana Kai. *For Freedom's Sake: The Life of Fannie Lou Hamer*. Urbana: University of Illinois Press, 1999.

Lentz, Richard. *Symbols, the News Magazines, and Martin Luther King*. Baton Rouge: Louisiana State University Press, 1990.

Lester, Julius. *Look Out Whitey! Black Power's Gon' Get Your Mama!* New York: Dial Press, 1968.

Levine, L. W. "Marcus Garvey and the Politics of Revitalization." In *Black Leaders of the Twentieth Century*, edited by John Hope Franklin and August Meier, 105–37. Urbana: University of Illinois Press, 1982.

Levy, Peter B. *Civil War on Race Street: The Civil Rights Movement in Cambridge, Maryland*. Gainesville: University Press of Florida, 2003.

Lewis, David L. *Martin Luther King: A Critical Biography*. New York: Praeger, 1970.

Lewis, John, with Michael D'Orso. *Walking with the Wind: A Memoir of the Movement*. New York: Simon and Schuster, 1998.

Lewis, Rupert. *Marcus Garvey: Anti-Colonial Champion*. Trenton, N.Y.: Africa World Press, 1988.

"Life in Mississippi: An Interview with Fannie Lou Hamer." *Freedomways* 5, no. 2 (Spring 1965): 231–42.

Lincoln, C. Eric. *The Black Muslims in America*. Boston: Beacon Press, 1961.

Ling, Peter J. *Martin Luther King, Jr.* New York: Routledge, 2002.

Lipsitz, George. *A Life in the Struggle: Ivory Perry and the Culture of Opposition*. Philadelphia: Temple University Press, 1988.

Lischer, Richard. *The Preacher King: Martin Luther King, Jr. and the World That Moved America*. New York: Oxford University Press, 1995.

Litwack, Leon F. *Been in the Storm So Long: The Aftermath of Slavery*. New York: Knopf, 1979.

———. *Trouble in Mind: Black Southerners in the Age of Jim Crow*. New York: Knopf, 1999.

Lockwood, Lee. *Conversation with Eldridge Cleaver: Algiers*. London: Jonathan Cape, 1971.

Lomax, Louis. *To Kill a Black Man*. Los Angeles: Holloway House, 1968.

Loveland, Anne C. *Lillian Smith, A Southerner Confronting the South: A Biography*. Baton Rouge: Louisiana State University Press, 1986.

Mahan, Joyce. "Alberta Brown Murphy." In *A Collection of Biographies of Women Who Made a Difference in Alabama*, edited by Miriam Abigail Toffel, 103–9. Birmingham, Ala.: League of Women Voters of Alabama, 1995.

Malcolm X. *By Any Means Necessary*. 2nd ed. New York: Pathfinder, 1992.

———. *February 1965: The Final Speeches*. New York: Pathfinder, 1992.

Malcolm X, with the assistance of Alex Haley. *The Autobiography of Malcolm X*. New York: Grove Press, 1965.

Manis, Andrew M. *A Fire You Can't Put Out: The Civil Rights Life of Birmingham's Reverend Fred Shuttlesworth*. Tuscaloosa: University of Alabama Press, 1999.

Marable, Manning. *Race, Reform, and Rebellion: The Second Reconstruction in Black America, 1945–1990*. 2nd ed. Jackson: University Press of Mississippi, 1991.

Mars, Florence. *Witness in Philadelphia*. Baton Rouge: Louisiana State University Press, 1977.

Matthews, Tracye. "'No One Ever Asks What a Man's Place in the Revolution Is': The Politics of Gender in the Black Panther Party, 1966–1971." In *The Black Panther Party [Reconsidered]*, edited by Charles Jones, 267–304. Baltimore: Black Classic Press, 1998.

Matusow, Allen J. "From Civil Rights to Black Power: The Case of SNCC, 1960–1966." In *Conflict and Competition: Studies in the Recent Black Protest Movement*, edited by John H. Bracey, August Meier, and Elliot Rudwick, 135–53. Belmont, Calif.: Wadsworth, 1971.

Mayfield, Julian. "Challenge to Negro Leadership: The Case of Robert F. Williams." *Commentary* 31, no. 4 (April 1961): 297–305.

Mays, E. Benjamin. *Born to Rebel*. New York: Charles Scribner's Sons, 1971.

McAdam, Doug. *Freedom Summer*. New York: Oxford University Press, 1988.

McKnight, Gerald D. *The Last Crusade: Martin Luther King, Jr., the FBI, and the Poor People's Campaign*. Boulder, Colo.: Westview Press, 1998.

McMillen, Neil R. *The Citizens' Council: Organized Resistance to the Second Reconstruction, 1954–64*. Urbana: University of Illinois Press, 1971.

———. *Dark Journey: Black Mississippians in the Age of Jim Crow*. Urbana: University of Illinois Press, 1990.

———. "Fighting for What We Didn't Have: How Mississippi's Black Veterans Remember World War II." In *Remaking Dixie: The Impact of World War II on the American South*, edited by Neil R. McMillen, 93–110. Jackson: University Press of Mississippi, 1997.

McWorther, Diane. *Carry Me Home: Birmingham, Alabama, the Climactic Battle of the Civil Rights Revolution*. New York: Simon and Schuster, 2001.

Meet the Press. August 21, 1966, vol. 10, no. 34, 1–31. Washington, D.C.: Merkle Press, 1966.

———. July 16, 1967, vol. 11, no. 29, 1–9. Washington, D.C.: Merkle Press, 1967.

———. August 13, 1967, vol. 11, no. 33, 1–9. Washington, D.C.: Merkle Press, 1967.

———. July 14, 1968, vol. 12, no. 28, 1–9. Washington, D.C.: Merkle Press, 1968.

Meier, August. "New Currents in the Civil Rights Movement." *New Politics* 2, no. 3 (Summer 1963): 7–32.

———. "The Origins of Nonviolent Direct Action in Afro-American Protest: A Note on Historical Discontinuities." In *Along the Color Line: Explorations in the Black Experience*, edited by August Meier and Elliot Rudwick, 307–404. Urbana: University of Illinois Press, 1976.

———. *A White Scholar and the Black Community, 1945–1965*. Amherst: University of Massachusetts Press, 1992.

Meier, August, and Elliot Rudwick. CORE: *A Study in the Civil Rights Movement, 1942–1968*. Urbana: University of Illinois Press, 1975.

———. "The Boycott Movement against Jim Crow Street Cars in the South, 1900–1906." *Journal of American History* 55, no. 4 (March 1969): 756–75.

Meier, August, Elliott Rudwick, and Francis L. Brodwick, eds. *Black Protest Thought in the Twentieth Century*. 2nd ed. Indianapolis: Bobbs-Merrill, 1971.

Meriwether, James H. "African Americans and the Mau Mau Rebellion: Militancy, Violence, and the Struggle for Freedom." *Journal of American Ethnic History* 17, no. 4 (Summer 1998): 63–83.

Mikell, Robert M. *They Say—Blood on My Hands: The Story of Robert M. Shelton, Imperial Wizard of the United Klans of America*. Huntsville, Ala.: Publishers Enterprise, 1966.

Mills, Nicolaus. *Like a Holy Crusade: Mississippi 1964—The Turning of the Civil Rights Movement in America*. Chicago: Ivan R. Dee, 1992.

Minchin, Timothy J. *The Color of Work: The Struggle for Civil Rights in the Southern Paper Industry, 1945–1980*. Chapel Hill: University of North Carolina Press, 2001.

Moody, Anne. *Coming of Age in Mississippi*. New York: Dial Press, 1968.

Moore, Leonard Nathaniel. "The School Desegregation Crisis of Cleveland, Ohio, 1963–1964: The Catalyst for Black Political Power in a Northern City." *Journal of Urban History* 28, no. 2 (January 2002): 135–57.

Morris, Aldon D. "A Man Prepared for the Times: A Sociological Analysis of the Leadership of Martin Luther King, Jr." In *We Shall Overcome: Martin Luther King*, edited by Peter J. Albert and Ronald Hoffman, 25–58. New York: Pantheon, 1990.

———. *The Origins of the Civil Rights Movement: Black Communities Organizing for Change*. New York: Free Press, 1984.

Moses, Robert Parris. "Commentary." In *We Shall Overcome: Martin Luther King*, edited by Peter J. Albert and Ronald Hoffman, 69–76. New York: Pantheon, 1990.

Mueller, Charles Wendell. "A Voice for Justice: The Tuscaloosa *News* Views the Autherine Lucy Incident." Master's thesis, University of Missouri, 1958.

Murray, Pauli. *Song in a Weary Throat: An American Pilgrimage*. New York: Harper and Row, 1987.

Muste, A. J. "Rifle Squads or the Beloved Community." *Liberation* 9, no. 3 (May 1964): 7–11.

Myrdal, Gunnar. *An American Dilemma: The Negro Problem and Modern Democracy*. 1944. Reprint, New York: Harper and Row, 1962.

Nelson, Harold A. "The Defenders: A Case Study of an Informal Police Organization." *Social Problems* 15, no. 2 (Fall 1967): 127–47.

Nelson, Jack. *Terror in the Night: The Klan's Campaign against the Jews*. New York: Simon and Schuster, 1993.

Newton, Huey P. *Revolutionary Suicide*. New York: Harcourt Brace Jovanovich, 1973.

———. *To Die for the People: The Writings of Huey P. Newton*. New York: Random House, 1972.

Norwood, Stephen H. "Bogalusa Burning: The War against Biracial Unionism in the Deep South, 1919." *Journal of Southern History* 63, no. 3 (August 1997): 591–628.

O'Brien, Gail Williams. *The Color of the Law: Race, Violence, and Justice in the Post–World War II South.* Chapel Hill: University of North Carolina Press, 1999.

Odum, Howard W. *Race and Rumors of Race: Challenge to American Crisis.* Chapel Hill: University of North Carolina Press, 1943.

Ogbar, Jeffrey O. G. *Black Power: Radical Politics and African American Identity.* Baltimore: Johns Hopkins University Press, 2004.

O'Reilly, Kenneth. *"Racial Matters": The FBI's Secret File on Black America, 1960–1972.* New York: Free Press, 1989.

Parks, Rosa, with Jim Haskins. *Rosa Parks: My Story.* New York: Penguin, 1992.

Pascoe, Craig S. "The Monroe Rifle Club: Finding Justice in an 'Ungodly and Social Jungle Called Dixie.'" In *Lethal Imagination: Violence and Brutality in American History,* edited by Michael A. Bellesiles, 393–424. New York: New York University Press, 1999.

Patterson, Orlando. *Rituals of Blood: Consequences of Slavery in Two American Centuries.* Washington, D.C.: Civitas Counterpoint, 1998.

Payne, Charles. *I've Got the Light of Freedom: The Organizing Tradition and the Mississippi Freedom Struggle.* Berkeley and Los Angeles: University of California Press, 1995.

Pearson, Hugh. *The Shadow of the Panther: Huey Newton and the Price of Black Power in America.* Reading, Mass.: Addison-Wesley, 1994.

Peck, Jim. "Freedom Ride." *CORE-Lator* 89 (May 1961): 2–3, Scholarship, Education, and Defense Fund for Racial Equality records, box 30, folder 79, SHSW.

Perry, Bruce. *Malcolm: The Life of a Man Who Changed Black America.* New York: Station Hill, 1991.

———. "Malcolm X and the Politics of Masculinity." *Psychohistory Review* 13, no. 2–3 (Winter 1985): 18–25.

Pfeffer, Paula F. *A. Philip Randolph, Pioneer of the Civil Rights Movement.* Baton Rouge: Louisiana State University Press, 1990.

Plummer, Brenda Gayle, ed. *Window on Freedom: Race, Civil Rights, and Foreign Affairs, 1945–1988.* Chapel Hill: University of North Carolina Press, 2002.

Powledge, Fred. *Free At Last? The Civil Rights Movement and the People Who Made It.* Boston: Little, Brown, 1991.

Price, Steven D. *Civil Rights.* Volume 2, *1967–1968.* New York: Facts on File, 1973.

Rabinowitz, Howard N. *Race Relations in the Urban South, 1865–1890.* New York: Oxford University Press, 1978.

Raboteau, Albert J. *A Fire in the Bones: Reflections on African-American History.* Boston: Beacon Press, 1995.

Raines, Howell, ed. *My Soul Is Rested: Movement Days in the Deep South Remembered.* New York: G. P. Putnam's Sons, 1977.

Ransby, Barbara. *Ella Baker and the Black Freedom Movement: A Radical Democratic Vision.* Chapel Hill: University of North Carolina Press, 2003.

"The Robert F. Williams Case." *Crisis* 66, no. 6 (June-July 1959): 325–29.

Robinson, Jo Ann Gibson, with David J. Garrow. *The Montgomery Bus Boycott and the Women Who Started It*. Knoxville: University of Tennessee Press, 1987.

Robinson, Lewis G. *The Making of a Man: An Autobiography*. Cleveland: Green and Sons, 1970.

Rosengarten, Theodore. *All God's Dangers: The Life of Nate Shaw*. New York: Knopf, 1975.

Rosenthal, Marilyn. "Where Rumor Raged." In *Ghetto Revolts*, edited by Peter H. Rossi, 209–33. 2nd ed. New Brunswick, N.J.: Transaction Books, 1973.

Rothschild, Mary Aickin. *A Case of Black and White: Northern Volunteers and the Southern Freedom Summers, 1964–1965*. Westport, Conn.: Greenwood Press, 1982.

Rotundo, Anthony. *American Manhood: Transformations in Masculinity from the Revolution to the Modern Era*. New York: Basic Books, 1993.

Rustin, Bayard. "Montgomery Diary." *Liberation* 1, no. 2 (April 1956): 7–10.

———. "Nonviolence on Trial." *Fellowship* 31 (July 1964): 5–10.

Salamon, Lester M. "The Time Dimension in Policy Evaluation: The Case of the New Deal Land-Reform Experiments." *Public Policy* 27, no. 2 (Spring 1979): 129–83.

Sales, William W., Jr. *From Civil Rights to Black Liberation: Malcolm X and the Organization of Afro-American Unity*. Boston: South End Press, 1994.

Salter, John R. "Civil Rights and Self-Defense." *Against the Current* 3, no. 3 (July-August 1988): 23–25.

———. *Jackson, Mississippi: An American Chronicle of Struggle and Schism*. Hicksville, N.Y.: Exposition Press, 1979.

Salter, John R., and Don B. Kates Jr. "The Necessity of Access to Firearms by Dissenters and Minorities Whom Government Is Unwilling or Unable to Protect." In *Restricting Handguns: The Liberal Skeptics Speak Out*, edited by Donald B. Kates, Jr., 185–93. Croton-on-Hudson, N.Y.: North River Press, 1979.

Scales, Junius Irving, and Richard Nickson. *Cause at Heart: A Former Communist Remembers*. Athens: University of Georgia Press, 1987.

Schechter, Patricia A. "Unsettled Business: Ida B. Wells against Lynching, or, How Lynching Got Its Gender." In *Under the Sentence of Death: Lynching in the South*, edited by Fitzhugh W. Brundage, 292–317. Chapel Hill: University of North Carolina Press, 1997.

Schneider, Mark Robert. *We Return Fighting: The Civil Rights Movement in the Jazz Age*. Boston: Northeastern University Press, 2002.

Schulke, Flip, ed. *Martin Luther King, Jr.: A Documentary*. New York: Norton, 1976.

Seale, Bobby. *A Lonely Rage: The Autobiography of Bobby Seale*. New York: New York Times Books, 1978.

———. *Seize the Time: The Story of the Black Panther Party and Huey P. Newton*. New York: Vintage, 1970.

Sellers, Cleveland. *The River of No Return: The Autobiography of a Black Militant and the Life and Death of SNCC*. Jackson: University Press of Mississippi, 1973.

Shapiro, Herbert. "Afro-American Responses to Race Violence during Reconstruction." *Science and Society* 36, no. 2 (1972): 158–70.

———. *White Violence and Black Response: From Reconstruction to Montgomery*. Amherst: University of Massachusetts Press, 1988.

Shirah, Liz. "Bogalusa Report." *Southern Patriot* 23, no. 5 (May 1965): 1–4.

Shridharani, Krishnalal. *War without Violence: A Study of Gandhi's Method and Its Accomplishments*. 1939. Reprint, New York: Garland, 1972.

Sitkoff, Harvard. "African American Militancy in the World War II South: Another Perspective." In *Remaking Dixie: The Impact of World War II on the American South*, edited by Neil R. McMillen, 70–92. Jackson: University Press of Mississippi, 1997.

———. "Racial Militancy and Interracial Violence in the Second World War." *Journal of American History* 58, no. 3 (December 1971): 661–81.

Smethurst, James Edward. *The Black Arts Movement: Literary Nationalism in the 1960s and 1970s*. Chapel Hill: University of North Carolina Press, 2005.

Solomon, Mark. *The Cry Was Unity: Communists and African Americans, 1917–1936*. Jackson: University Press of Mississippi, 1998.

Stoper, Emily. *The Student Nonviolent Coordinating Committee: The Growth of Radicalism in a Civil Rights Organization*. Brooklyn, N.Y.: Carlson, 1989.

Strain, Christopher B. "Civil Rights and Self-Defense: The Fiction of Nonviolence, 1955–1968." Ph.D. diss., University of California, Berkeley, 2000.

———. *Pure Fire: Self-Defense as Activism in the Civil Rights Era*. Athens: University of Georgia Press, 2005.

———. "'We Walked Like Men': The Deacons for Defense and Justice." *Louisiana History* 38, no. 1 (Winter 1997): 43–62.

Sugarman, Tracy. *Stranger at the Gates: A Summer in Mississippi*. New York: Hill and Wang, 1966.

Summers, Barbara, ed. *I Dream a World: Portraits of Black Women Who Changed America*. New York: Steward, Tabori, and Chang, 1989.

Sutherland, Elizabeth, ed. *Letters from Mississippi*. New York: McGraw-Hill, 1965.

Sykes, Ossie. "Self-Defense: A Right and a Necessity." *Liberator* 5, no. 9 (September 1965): 10–13.

Szabo, Peter S. "An Interview with Gloria Richardson Dandridge." *Maryland Historical Magazine* 89, no. 3 (Fall 1994): 347–58.

Terkel, Studs. *American Dreams: Lost and Found*. New York: Pantheon Books, 1980.

Theoharis, Jeanne F., and Komozi Woodard, eds. *Freedom North: Black Freedom Struggles outside the South*. New York: Palgrave Macmillan, 2003.

Thornbrough, Emma Lou. "T. Thomas Fortune: Militant Editor in the Age of Accommodation." In *Black Leaders of the Twentieth Century*, edited by John Hope Franklin and August Meier, 19–37. Urbana: University of Illinois Press, 1982.

———. *T. Thomas Fortune: Militant Journalist*. Chicago: University of Chicago Press, 1992.

Thrasher, Sue. "Circle of Trust." In *Deep in Our Hearts: Nine White Women in the Freedom Movement*, edited by Constance Curry, Joan C. Browning, and Dorothy Dawson Burlage, 207–51. Athens: University of Georgia Press, 2000.

Tuttle, William M., Jr. *Race Riot: Chicago in the Red Summer of 1919*. New York: Atheneum, 1972.

Tyson, Timothy. *Radio Free Dixie: Robert F. Williams and the Roots of Black Power.* Chapel Hill: University of North Carolina Press, 1999.

———. "Robert F. Williams, 'Black Power,' and the Roots of the African American Freedom Struggle." *Journal of American History* 85, no. 2 (September 1998): 540–70.

———. "Wars for Democracy: African American Militancy and Interracial Violence in North Carolina during World War II." In *Democracy Betrayed: The Wilmington Race Riot of 1898 and Its Legacy,* edited by Timothy B. Tyson and David Cecelsky, 253–76. Chapel Hill: University of North Carolina Press, 1998.

Umoja, Akinyele O. "1964: The Beginning of the End of Nonviolence in the Mississippi Freedom Movement." *Radical History Review* 85 (Winter 2003): 201–26.

———. "The Ballot and the Bullet: A Comparative Analysis of Armed Resistance in the Civil Rights Movement." *Journal of Black Studies* 29, no. 4 (March 1999): 558–78.

———. "Repression Breeds Resistance: The Black Liberation Army and the Radical Legacy of the Black Panther Party." In *Liberation, Imagination, and the Black Panther Party: A New Look at the Panthers and Their Legacy,* edited by Kathleen Cleaver and George Katsiaficas, 3–19. New York: Routledge, 2001.

———. "'We Will Shoot Back': The Natchez Model and Paramilitary Organization in the Mississippi Freedom Movement." *Journal of Black Studies* 32, no. 3 (January 2002): 271–94.

Vandal, Gilles. "Black Violence in Post–Civil War Louisiana." *Journal of Interdisciplinary History* 25, no. 1 (Summer 1994): 45–64.

Van Deburg, William L. *New Day in Babylon: The Black Power Movement and American Culture, 1965–1975.* Chicago: University of Chicago Press, 1992.

Vaughn, Wally G., and Richard W. Wills, eds. *Reflections on Our Pastor: Dr. Martin Luther King, Jr. at Dexter Avenue Baptist Church, 1954–1960.* Dover, Mass.: Majority Press, 1999.

Vincent, Theodore G. *Black Power and the Garvey Movement.* Berkeley, Calif.: Ramparts Press, 1971.

Von Eschen, Donald, Jerome Kirk, and Maurice Pinard. "The Disintegration of the Negro Non-Violent Movement." In *Conflict and Competition: Studies in the Recent Black Protest Movement,* edited by John H. Bracey Jr., August Meier, and Elliot Rudwick, 113–34. Belmont, Calif.: Wadsworth, 1971.

Von Hoffman, Nicholas. *Mississippi Notebook.* New York: David White, 1964.

Wade, Wynn Craig. *The Fiery Cross: The Ku Klux Klan in America.* New York: Oxford University Press, 1987.

Walker, Jenny. "A Media-Made Movement? Black Violence and Nonviolence in the Historiography of the Civil Rights Movement." In *Media, Culture, and the Modern African American Freedom Struggle,* edited by Brian Ward, 41–66. Gainesville: University Press of Florida, 2001.

Wallace, Michelle. *Black Macho and the Myth of the Superwoman.* New York: Dial Press, 1978.

Warren, Robert Penn. *Who Speaks for the Negro?* New York: Random House, 1965.

Watts, Daniel H. "Malcolm X: Self-Defense vs. Submission." *Liberator* 4, no. 4 (April 1964): 3.

Weinberg, Kenneth G. *A Man's Home, A Man's Castle*. New York: McCall, 1971.

Weiss, Jonathan A. "A Reply to Advocates of Gun-Control Law." *Journal of Urban Law* 52, no. 3 (Winter 1974): 578–89.

Wells, Ida B. *On Lynchings*. New York: Arno Press, 1969.

Wells, Ida B., with Alfred M. Duster. *Crusade for Justice: The Autobiography of Ida B. Wells*. Chicago: University of Chicago Press, 1970.

White, Ronald C., Jr. *Liberty and Justice for All: Racial Reform and the Social Gospel, 1877–1925*. New York: Harper and Row, 1990.

White, Walter. *Rope and Faggot: A Biography of Judge Lynch*. New York: Knopf, 1929.

Wilkins, Roy. "The Single Issue in the Robert Williams Case." *Liberation* 4, no. 7 (October 1959): 7–8.

Wilkins, Roy, with Tom Mathews. *Standing Fast: The Autobiography of Roy Wilkins*. 1982. Reprint, New York: Da Capo Press, 1994.

Williams, Juan. *Thurgood Marshall: American Revolutionary*. New York: Random House, 1998.

Williams, Mike. "Smiles and Guns: The Fragile Sensitivity of Race Relations in the South." Honors thesis, Amherst College, 1978.

Williams, Robert F. "Can Negroes Afford to Be Pacifists?" *Liberation* 4, no. 6 (September 1959): 4–7.

———. *Negroes with Guns*. 1962. Reprint, Chicago: Third World Press, 1973.

Williamson, Joel. *After Slavery: The Negro in South Carolina during Reconstruction, 1861–1877*. Chapel Hill: University of North Carolina Press, 1965.

Wolfenstein, Eugene. *The Victims of Democracy: Malcolm X and the Black Revolution*. Berkeley and Los Angeles: University of California Press, 1981.

Woodard, Komozi. *A Nation within a Nation: Amiri Baraka (LeRoi Jones) and Black Power Politics*. Chapel Hill: University of North Carolina Press, 1999.

Woodruff, Nan Elizabeth. *American Congo: The African American Freedom Struggle in the Delta*. Cambridge: Harvard University Press, 2003.

Wright, George C. *Racial Violence in Kentucky, 1865–1940*. Baton Rouge: Louisiana State University Press, 1990.

Wyatt-Brown, Bertram. *Southern Honor: Ethics and Behavior in the Old South*. New York: Oxford University Press, 1982.

Wynn, Neil A. *The Afro-American and the Second World War*. 2nd ed. New York: Holmes and Meier, 1993.

Young, Andrew. *An Easy Burden: The Civil Rights Movement and the Transformation of America*. New York: HarperCollins, 1996.

Youth of the Rural Organizing and Cultural Center. *Minds Stayed on Freedom: The Civil Rights Struggle in the Rural South, an Oral History*. Boulder, Colo.: Westview Press, 1991.

Zannes, Estelle. *Checkmate in Cleveland: The Rhetoric of Confrontation During the Stokes Years*. Cleveland: Press of Case Western Reserve University, 1972.

INDEX

Simon Wendt teaches American
history at the University of Heidelberg.

New Perspectives on the History of the South   Edited by John David Smith